Public Administration
in the
United States

Public Administration in the United States

David Schuman
University of Massachusetts

Dick W. Olufs III
Pacific Lutheran University

D.C. HEATH AND COMPANY
Lexington, Massachusetts   Toronto

Photo credits:
p. 1, National Archives; p. 23, reprinted by special permission from HOLIDAY, Thomas Hollyman/Photo Researchers, Inc.; p. 63, Frank Siteman/The Picture Cube; p. 93, J. Berndt/Stock, Boston; p. 117, Sarah Putnam/The Picture Cube; p. 141, Paul Conklin/Monkmeyer Press Photo Service; p. 169, Art Stein/Photo Researchers, Inc.; p. 195, Ellis Herwig/Stock, Boston; p. 225, Mark Antman/The Image Works; p. 261, AP/Wide World Photos; p. 289, Guy Gillette/Photo Researchers, Inc.; p. 321, Joel Gordon; p. 361, Frank Siteman/The Picture Cube; p. 389, Clif Garboden/Stock, Boston; p. 415, David Wells/The Image Works.

Copyright © 1988 by D. C. Heath and Company.

All rights reserved. No part of this publication may be reproduced or transmitted in any form or by any means, electronic or mechanical, including photocopy, recording, or any information storage or retrieval system, without permission in writing from the publisher.

Published simultaneously in Canada.

Printed in the United States of America.

International Standard Book Number: 0-669-11267-4

Library of Congress Catalog Card Number: 87-80887

Preface

Textbooks in public administration have, through the years, tried to fill a variety of valid needs. There have been grand defenses of public organizations and equally grand critiques. Authors have written books for managers and for theoreticians. Some books have emphasized historical analysis, others have been heavily speculative. Each book offered its own definition of public administration and entered the continuing dialogue of the discipline.

We sought to write a public administration textbook that will take us and our students out of the 1980s and toward the turn of the century. Two major themes in the book make it, we believe, more current, interesting, and usable than other books. The first theme has to do with the difference between politics and administration. We show readers that there is an irreducible tension between the two. This shows up in the definition of *public administration*. The word *public* implies the idea of participation in politics, whereas *administration* suggests an organization involved in an almost wholly internal decision-making process. We try to show that there are special pressures on those who work in the public service, along with the normal pressures of making an organization run smoothly and efficiently. These pressures have important implications for citizens as well. We argue that much of what we think of as political has become the concern of large organizations. The second theme is that, since the early 1980s, state and local governments have become more and more important. In most books, it is clear that the state and local material has merely been added to a book that is focused on the national government. But, as the Reagan administration has cut back many aspects of federal involvement, these other governments and administrations have become increasingly important. We maintain a steady focus on such issues.

Our book is not an encyclopedia of public administration. We discuss the major issues of the field, new technologies, recent political developments, and the latest research. We provide many current examples, numbers, and trends. We spend time on how agencies are managed, so that readers can see how the larger questions of public administration are connected to the roles of individuals. We want to have the student appreciate both the theoretical and the practical parts of public administration. Our most important aim, however, is to present the material in a way that gets students to *think* about public administration. We point to the tensions surrounding our major themes and pose questions in ways students have not encountered before.

Rather than simply provide information, we have sought to make a dynamic teaching tool. In order to do so, we use several pedagogical features in the book. The first is the writing itself. We wanted a book that was more than simply very readable. The style we use is deliberately engaging and provocative, and although many readers will agree with us on most issues, we anticipate a good deal of thoughtful disagreement and discussion. A second feature is the use of several brief boxed cases and examples in each chapter. These help keep the textual material within reasonable bounds while still giving the student a sense of the richness and complexity of public administration. For example, we take a look at the Federal Reserve, the PATCO strike, an actual arbitration case, the Senior Executive Service, and several sample budgets. Other boxes focus on state and local governments, and at least one per chapter prompts students to look at circumstances where they live. Again, our purpose is to encourage students to react thoughtfully to the material. We also use numerous graphs and tables to illustrate and reinforce major concepts in public administration.

We have written the book so that the chapters can be assigned in any order without loss of coherence. We hope it will be as flexible as the instructor needs it to be. The book is divided, roughly, into four parts. The first two chapters stand together as a strong introduction to the study of public administration. They provide a sense of the field, as well as the American context.

Chapters 3, 4, and 5 concentrate on organization theory. We provide an overview of historical development in Chapter 3 and modern theories in Chapter 4. Chapter 5 is concerned with organization psychology.

In Chapters 6 through 10, we look at different aspects of personnel. Chapter 6 is about the civil service, Chapter 7 deals with administrative leadership, and Chapter 8 covers personnel administration. In Chapter 9, we discuss the managing of public agencies. Finally, Chapter 10 examines labor-management relations.

In Chapters 11 through 14, we discuss money and financial decision making of various types. Budgeting is the topic of Chapter 11 and fiscal administration, of Chapter 12. Chapters 13 and 14 deal with decision making and policy evaluation.

In the last chapter, "Public Administration in Post-Property America," we review what we have done and speculate.

We have tried, then, to make this a special book in a variety of ways. We hope that the people who use the book will find it an interesting, solid, and provocative introduction to the field of public administration. We hope that if you have comments or suggestions about how the next edition could be better, you will write to us.

Generally, there are good stories about the writing of a book. There is the genesis of the idea, the finding of a publisher, the interplay of the world and the writing, the production process, and so on. By far the nicest part of the writing of this book was that it was coauthored. That we live three thousand miles apart is a burden. Every day questions went unanswered, but we still had huge phone bills and spent more than our share of time at the post office. In the end, we agreed that whatever the merits of the book (and in truth, we both like it), this is an undeniable fact: the final product is certainly much better than either of us could have done alone.

Of course, there were many others involved. For their helpful suggestions, we would like to thank our manuscript reviewers, including Larry Elowitz, Georgia College; Andy Felts, East Tennessee State University; Dennis Hale, Boston College; Ernie Miller, University of Washington; and William West, Texas A&M University. And, for his superbly professional advice on the manuscript, Peter Koehn of the University of Montana has earned our admiration and gratitude. We would also like to thank the people at D. C. Heath who helped put the book together: our editor, Linda Halvorson; production editor, Karen Potischman; and designer, Henry Rachlin. Special thanks to Larry Spence.

Ben has entered the age of understanding and is kind to me when I write. He is genuinely interested in what it's about and when he can see it. Barbara was very involved in the process of the book. She counseled me about right and wrong and what to do in some very strange situations. She took care of me, got me well, and insisted that I stay healthy. Lucky me.

Fran and three sons know about the work and aspirations, and helped every bit of the way. They know that a book should not cancel trips to the zoo.

David Schuman
Dick Olufs

Contents

1

What Is Public Administration? *1*

The Study of Public Administration *6*
Defining Public Administration *13*

2

Politics and Administration: The Context *23*

Liberalism *24*
The Constitution *28*
Political Relationships *40*
Waves and Fads: The Constantly Changing
   Options *51*

3

Organization Theory *63*

Public/Administration *64*
Max Weber (Administration) *67*
Max Weber (Politics) *71*
Frederick Winslow Taylor *71*
Early Principles *77*
The Hawthorne Studies *81*
Human Relations and Authority *84*
Mary Parker Follett: A Public Emphasis *87*

4

Modern Organization Theories *93*

Organization Theory *95*
Reconceptualizing Organizations *101*
Recent Organization Theory *108*
The Larger Questions *111*

5

Organization Psychology *117*

Major Themes in Organization Psychology *119*
Rearranging Organizations *129*
Organization Psychology and Public
    Administration *133*

6

The Civil Service *141*

The Federalists and Andrew Jackson *143*
Reform *147*
People in the Public Service *151*
The Personnel Question *164*

7

Administrative Leadership *169*

Elements of Leadership *171*
Administrative Leadership and Democratic
    Government *175*
Research on Leadership *177*
Leadership in Public Administration *184*
Possibilities for Leadership *185*

8

Personnel Administration *195*

Structure, Functions, and Goals *196*
Managers and Personnel Administration *199*
The Nuts and Bolts of Personnel
  Administration *202*
Equal Employment Opportunity and Affirmative
  Action (EEO/AA) *216*
Other, Occasional Policy Responsibilities *219*
Cheating on the Nuts and Bolts *221*

9

Managing Public Agencies *225*

What Do Managers Do? *227*
What Is Public about Public
  Management? *234*
Management Systems *237*
Supervision and Motivation *240*
Motivation Theory and Practice *243*
Cutback Management *246*
Productivity *252*
What Is the Difference Between Good and Poor
  Management? *255*

10

Labor-Management Relations *261*

Conflict in the Workplace *264*
The Legal Framework of Collective Bargaining *265*
The Practice of Collective Bargaining *275*
The Future of Collective Bargaining in the
  Public Sector *286*

11

Public Budgeting 289

Thinking about Budgeting 290
The Evolution of Budgets 292
Budget Behavior 306
Congressional Budgeting 308
Big Money 312
Economic Theories 312
Budget Making in Two Contexts 316

12

Fiscal Administration 321

Revenues: The Other Half of the Budget 322
Predicting Revenues 338
The Political Economy of Tax Revenues 342
After the Budget Passes 349
Government Accounting and Auditing 354

13

Decision Making 361

Theories of Decision Making 366
Administrative Law and Decision Making 375
Making Decisions about Programs 382
The State of Government Decision Making 385

14
Policy Evaluation *389*

Public Policy *390*
Implementation *393*
Early Evaluations *395*
The Experimental Method *396*
Evaluation Problems *402*
Some Reasons Why Things Don't Work *407*
The Tool of Evaluation *408*

15
Public Administration in Post-Prosperity America *415*

Ethics *416*
Silent Tensions *419*
Democracy and Public Administration *427*

Index *433*

CHAPTER ONE

What Is Public Administration?

> "The true test of good government is its aptitude and tendency to produce good administration."
>
> — *Alexander Hamilton*

Before we begin our exploration of the field of public administration, let's first look at the dictionary definition of the terms *public, administer,* and *administration* to get a feeling for the different levels of meaning of these terms.

pub·lic, *a.* [L. *publics*, from *populus*, people.]
  1. of, belonging to, concerning, or pertaining to the people of a nation, state, or community as a whole, as: the *public welfare,*
  2. open to common use, as: a *public* road,
  3. acting in an official capacity on behalf of the people as a whole, as: a *public* prosecutor,
  4. known by, or open to the knowledge of, all or most people, as: he will make this information *public.*

ad·min·is·ter, *v.t.* [*administren*; Fr. *administrer*; L. *administrare*; and *ministrare*, to serve.]
  1. to have a charge of as chief agent in managing,
  2. to dispense,
  3. to give or furnish.

ad·min·is·tra·tion, *n.*
  1. the act of administering,
  2. the management of governmental or institutional affairs,
  3. [often A] the executive officials of a government or institution and their policy,
  4. the power, office, or commission of an administrator.

There are many levels of government — local, county, state, and special district governments, as well as the national government of the United States. Together these various governments hire more people than any other employer in the United States. These people, in one way or another, are members of the public administration of our country, from the people in the Postal Service to those at the Internal Revenue Service (IRS), as well as the people who take care of our national parks and guard our prisons.

Our task in this chapter is to begin to define the term *public administration*. A simple and revealing way is to look up the words in a dictionary. Our definitions come from *Webster's New Universal Unabridged Dictionary*, second edition. Although it is simple to see what *public* and *administration* mean, it is no easy matter to then put these two words together and understand what *public administration* means. Indeed, *public* and *administration* seem at times to be mutually exclusive terms. The task of definition may well be a formidable one.

We traced the words to their sources and found some revealing information. The word "public" actually comes from *populus*, the Latin word for "people," which referred collectively to the state's citizens.[1] The notion of the public, then, pertains to the people of a nation as a whole. It has the unmistakable connotation of being open, of being held — or beheld — in common. The root of public is plural; it is people.

The root of administration is curious. It reaches back to the name of the Cretan king *Minos*. Minos was the son of Zeus and Europa and was so renowned for his just rule that he was made supreme judge in the underworld. He also made one big mistake. Minos was given a sacrificial bull by Poseidon, but he kept the bull for himself. Poseidon, in his rage, instilled a passion for the bull in Minos' wife — and their next born was the Minotaur. Even then administration had its bad days.

Words that come from this root word include "minor," "minus," "minister," and, of course, "administration." In current usage, the definitions of administration revolve around management, power, office, and policy. Buried in the word "administration" are also meanings like "small points, trifling details, to break into little pieces." Such words do not bring to mind the same kind of images of openness that "public" does. "Administration," then, seems to ask us to turn inward, as "public" urges us to turn outward.

We can put the thought together this way. Public, especially when we think of our government, of we, the people, suggests the idea of politics. By *politics*, we mean an individual participating in the deliberation and decision-making process of governing. Included in that participation is the activity of being seen and heard by other citizens. In appropriate instances, voting would be a part of that activity.

Administration, on the other hand, brings to mind the efficient delivery of services from the government to the people. It implies an internal decision-making process that is concerned, in many ways, with the internal dynamics of the organization. Although general direction may be given by an outside source (the Congress may pass a law with general instructions to a particular part of the federal bureaucracy), it is easy to understand that the dynamics of administration are anything but public. For example although the Congress appropriated money for Head Start, the program itself was put together and run by administrators. As we will see, there are theories which suggest that organizations work best if their decision-making processes are shut off from the outside world.

Given what has been said, when we use the phrase "public administration," we are using words that clash. One word has to do with people and openness; the other has to do with turning inward and being concerned with organizational needs.

There are ways in which we can bypass the apparent contradiction in terms; we could, for example, talk about public administration as the art of serving the public. However, to ignore the contradiction is to ignore a tension that has become a common theme in our times. The tension can be thought of this way: An individual goes into the public service in order to do good for his or her country. "To serve," in the administrative sense. Yet, there are many demands that make that service very difficult. The administrator must heed the demands of the public and of his or her organization, and these demands are not necessarily the same. This tension between public and administration, or politics and administration, is a central focus of this book.

To know about public administration requires knowing how to see public and administration, but we also need to know where to look. We mentioned there are many governments in the United States — 80,000 is the common estimate — and an adequate treatment of public administration has to convey that variety. A second theme of this book is that state and local governments are becoming more important than they have been for a generation or so. For more than a decade, citizens and elected officials have been talking about limits and doing less through large governments. New ideas and new ways to cope with the resultant increase of demands on state and local governments have had to come more from these subnational jurisdictions. The reason, of course, is that the national government cannot afford to do as many new things as before. This is an era of postprosperity. We are not poor, but our available wealth does not cover enough of our needs, and citizens and elected officials are reluctant to raise taxes. The postprosperity era will likely last for at least another decade, if not much longer. Because of limited national support for new policies and programs administered by Washington, state and local governments will continue to increase in importance. We will address this theme in the chapters of this book.

FIGURE 1.1 What Does Public Administration Look Like?

A. A hierarchy

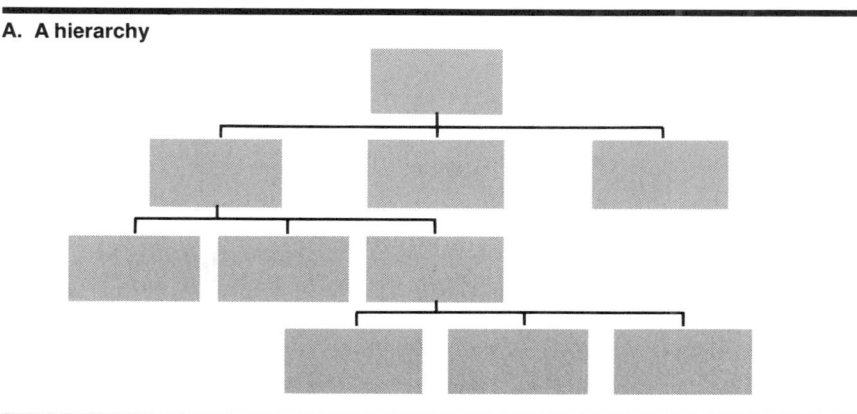

B. Places and things

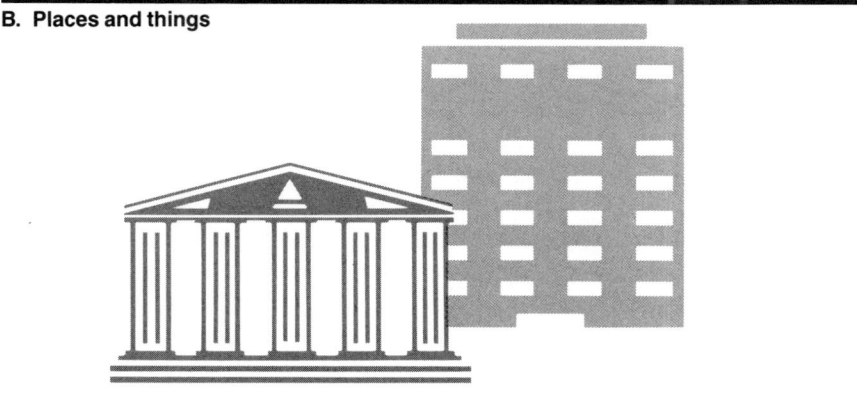

C. People working

The Study of Public Administration

Public administration is both an academic discipline and a professional activity. In this book we will adopt the convention of capitalizing Public Administration when referring to the academic discipline and using the lowercase public administration to refer to professional activities.[2] In practice, the two are quite different.

Academics believe their theoretical knowledge is an important contribution to public administration. It is their contention that because they have some distance from the everyday working of public organizations, they have much-needed perspective in the broader meaning of how things work. There is also an implicit claim that unless knowledge is collected according to the canons of social science research, it is not quite reliable.

The millions of civil servants also believe they know something about public organizations and have something to contribute because they do administration every day. Moreover, many of these people have extensive background in the academic study of Public Administration.

The two perspectives are generally different, and the differences can be striking. They are played out in schools of Public Administration (or public affairs), in professional organizations, and in books which define the field. Some of the tension comes out in the editorial concerns of the major journal in the field, *Public Administration Review*, described in Box 1.1.

Another difficulty in studying public administration is a broad-based one and revolves around everything from epistemology (how we know what we know) to work style. Put in its most traditional form, the question is this: Is public administration an art or a science?[3]

If public administration is an art, then the study of administration takes on a particular set of questions, asked in a particular way. If public administration is a science, then an opposite set of assumptions is made about human beings, how knowledge is obtained (Public Administration becomes much more important), what questions get asked, and the way in which they are asked. Because this tension goes to the very heart of how we know what we know and why we act the way we act, there is little overlap in approaches.

What follows are several ways to begin to study Public Administration. Each element will tell us something of what we need to know.

Organization Theory

One way to understand public administration is to study how organizations are designed, that is, organization theory. Although it is impossible to understand public administration without knowing organization theory (the subject of Chapters 3 and 4), it is wrong to believe that by knowing organization theory one would know public administration.

> **BOX 1.1** *Public Administration Review* and Public Administration*
>
> *Public Administration Review* (*PAR*), published by the American Society for Public Administration (ASPA), is the principal journal in the field for both practitioners and academicians. Its editors face the perennial challenge of balancing the interests and approaches of practitioners and academicians.
>
> ASPA's membership is about 80 percent practitioners and 20 percent academicians, yet the authorship of *PAR* features is almost 80 percent academics, about 20 percent practitioners, and a few percent of collaborative articles. Many of the academics have held government positions in their careers, so the figures are not quite as stark as they appear. Yet the division remains, and the editor of *PAR* acknowledges a continuing search for "balance" and "reasonableness."
>
> He writes,
>
>> More high-quality research and writing are needed in public administration. That is not an issue which should divide academicians from practitioners, and for most ASPA members and other *PAR* subscribers it does not. But a little name calling between practitioners and academicians has occurred throughout ASPA's history, and it requires persistent editorial attention in *PAR* to keep the focus on the real problem: a need for high-quality work.
>
> *This draws heavily on Chester A. Newland, "*PAR*: A Professional Journal for Practitioners and Academicians," in *PS* (A journal of the American Political Science Association) XIX (Winter 1986) no. 1, pp. 90–92.

It is tempting to believe that all large organizations operate in the same way and that the aim of one is the aim of all the rest. It is tempting because that is often the case. When one reads about how those in business administration are always trying to be more efficient and effective, and then reads that officials in the Pentagon or a school district are applying the same ideas, it is easy to believe that some kind of organizational imperative is in operation.

We will demonstrate that there are important differences between the concepts of public administration and business administration. Some of the differences are discussed in Box 1.2. If we lose that difference — if we lose the public — we will have a fundamentally different kind of governing structure. The changes would reach to the core of our society.

BOX 1.2 Public Administration and Business Administration*

> Public and private management are
> fundamentally alike in all unimportant aspects.
> — *Wallace Sayre*

A simple way to compare business and public administration is to ask the opinions of people who have done both. An impressive literature shows a strong consensus: public management is different from, and harder than, business management.

There are many lists which attempt a detailed comparison of the two fields. Most include the following elements:

1. In the public sector managers have relatively short time horizons. The budget process and political pressures are chiefly responsible for the short-term focus.
2. Leadership does not last long in the public service. Appointees who occupy the highest positions average 18 months in office.
3. Performance measures are often vague or arbitrary in the public service. There is no inherent standard for measuring rate of return or overall effect of most public services.
4. Public managers have less discretion over personnel decisions. Hiring, firing, promotions, salary, and discipline issues are constrained by legislation, conflicts between appointive and career positions, and legal concerns over the way the state treats individuals.
5. Public programs must often pursue the values of equity, fairness, and negotiated consensus, rather than narrowly pursue efficiency and competitive performance.
6. Government officials operate under more and more open scrutiny from the public, which expects that public officials act with more fairness, responsibility, accountability, and honesty. The mass media pay closer attention to the operations and decisions of public agencies.
7. Public managers usually have less authority over the enterprise and over all who may influence a policy area. They must resort to persuasion and build political coalitions in order to enact policies.

> 8. Public officials are more often subject to scrutiny and direction by outside institutions such as courts and legislatures.
>
> *This relies heavily on Graham T. Allison, Jr., "Public and Private Management: Are They Fundamentally Alike in All Unimportant Respects?", in James L. Perry and Kenneth L. Kraemer, *Public Management: Public and Private Perspectives* (Palo Alto: Mayfield Publishing Company, 1983), pp. 72–92.

Public Service

Another way to study public administration is to think in terms of public service. In Chapter 6 we look at who goes into public service and what the life of a public servant is like. A career in public service has many benefits, and those in the field are often highly respected professionals.

We should know something about those who work in public administration, but to know that educated white males hold a preponderant number of top positions in the federal government does not tell us much about the federal government. Although we can infer something about an organization by knowing who works in it, knowing only about the people cannot tell us about the dynamics that underlie a complex social organization.

As you will see, there are ways in which the people in the field are faced with problems that are truly difficult and ongoing. For example, the National Aeronautics and Space Administration (NASA) was apparently under remarkable cross-pressures in the space shuttle program. Administrators felt pressure to send up space shuttles on a regular basis in order to keep funding; they were also under pressure from the military, from private industry, from research scientists, and from the public (to do spectacular things that were understandable to the layperson), and, of course, there was internal organizational pressure for safety. The pressures, we found out, were too great. A hurried launch on a cold morning resulted in a destroyed shuttle and the death of all on board. What is important to remember is that, in many ways, we owe much to those who work in our public organizations.

Politics

Another way to understand public administration is to study politics. In the United States there have been two major results of this approach. Woodrow Wilson, while still an academic, wrote an essay about public administration and politics.[4] Most people who read the essay hear him dividing the two. In Wilson's view, there was to be politics, which was generally elective politics, and there was to be administration, which was to be a "clean" and separate operation set up to carry out the orders of those elected to make decisions.

As we shall see, it has never worked in that neat kind of way. Even in mundane matters of school bus route selection, problems arise. Although elected officials set policies and control the administration of school districts (the politics part), professionals in such areas as transportation are assigned to find the most efficient means to carry out their tasks (the administration part). But when the transportation office decides that the most efficient use of buses requires that all children in a certain area be assigned to afternoon kindergarten, the phone starts ringing. Pressure is exerted on the transportation people, the school principal, and the school superintendent. In many cases decisions are modified under such pressure. The way politics affects the everyday conduct of organizations is discussed in Chapters 7–10.

Another understanding of politics and public administration is the notion that administration has become "politicized." In this view, those in politics impose their priorities on those in administration. To use the example of NASA again, the political pressure to perform overwhelmed the administrative decision-making structure so that the kind of clean process envisioned by Wilson was constantly cluttered by "political" influence. There is, as we shall see, an impressive literature which makes this argument.

Recently it has become clear that there needs to be another understanding of the relationship of politics and public administration. We believe a compelling argument can be made that the space of politics is being taken over by administration. The most dramatic example of this is the budgetary process. The budget is at heart a political document, because elected members of the Congress, who are politicians, must pass what is to be taxed, what is to be spent, and how it is to be spent. The reasons for their decisions are political at heart.

In 1986, the Balanced Budget and Emergency Deficit Control Act of 1985 (commonly called the Gramm-Rudman-Hollings Balanced Budget Act, or just "Gramm-Rudman") took effect. The bill legislated that, if spending went over a certain amount, cuts would be made. However, the cuts would not be made by Congress, but by a semi-independent agency. (The Supreme Court ruled that the original automatic mechanism was unconstitutional, but the Congress restored most of the procedure in a way acceptable to the court.) And, the cuts would be made according to a formula, not an analysis of where they were most needed. The purpose of the law was to take the politics out of the process altogether and replace it with administrative procedure. Gramm-Rudman and other budget concerns are further discussed in Chapters 11 and 12.

Policy

The study of policy has become a popular way to understand our public administration. Since the end of the 1960s, the study of public policy has assumed a central role in the story of public administration. Basically, the study of policy is divided into three areas. First, there are those who study the formulation and making of a policy. How, for example, did the policy of airline deregulation come about in the early 1980s? What were the pressures to have such a policy, who was involved, what was the political procedure, and what were the stakes?[5]

Second, there are policy implementation studies. In these, people study how administration takes a law and makes it into a workable program. We learn about the real world of problems of taking vague legislative goals and making them into everyday actions. For example, when Congress passes a law permitting blind people who are also poor to receive benefits, the administrative agency in charge of the program must make several decisions. One is to determine who is blind.[6] We might say those people who cannot see with the aid of corrective lenses well enough to work are blind. A standard of blindness is needed, say, 20/200, in the better eye. What if someone had 20/100 tunnel vision in one eye? We need a standard for degrees of the field of vision above 20/200 in the better eye. And so on. Which of these people are poor? Do we count all income? Even sources that go to cover other disabilities or special equipment? How about educational scholarships? Are special considerations given to children? Does the number of siblings or disabled siblings make a difference? What if the blind person owns a home? Such decisions coalesce into sets of rules that guide agencies in the implementation of a program.

Finally, there is policy evaluation. In these studies, people try to judge the effectiveness of everyday actions of government. Evaluation studies can have powerful effects on what is being evaluated, and so this aspect of policy studies is the least well defined. There are arguments about what to study and how to study it. We will talk more about policy evaluation in Chapters 13 and 14.

The Context and the Dynamic

There are two less obvious ways of trying to learn about public administration. First, one can learn about the cultural, social, political, and economic context of a particular administrative system. Certainly it is necessary to understand the context in order to know underlying biases and to see more clearly why some sets of actions seem so normal. For example, when civil rights legislation was taking effect in the 1960s, we found that the Attorney General of the United States and law enforcement officers in small Southern towns had different ideas about the meaning of the law. This is not to suggest that one administrator is superior to another. It

FIGURE 1.2 Changing American Values: From Individual America to Organizational America

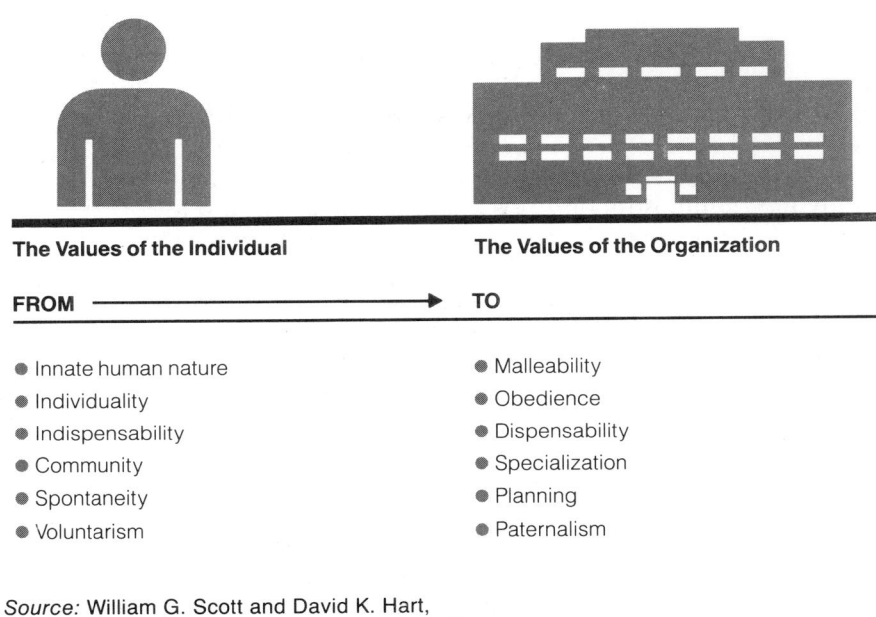

The Values of the Individual	The Values of the Organization
FROM ⟶	TO
• Innate human nature	• Malleability
• Individuality	• Obedience
• Indispensability	• Dispensability
• Community	• Specialization
• Spontaneity	• Planning
• Voluntarism	• Paternalism

Source: William G. Scott and David K. Hart, *Organizational America* (Boston: Houghton Mifflin Company, 1980), p. 54.

---

simply means that even in the same country there may be different sets of cultural, social, political, and economic truths. In order to understand fully how any particular public administration works, it is necessary to know about the context. This will be the subject of Chapter 2.

By *dynamics*, we mean the underlying principles and values of an organization. There is a whole series of tendencies that are part of a large, bureaucratic organization. These tendencies are not openly articulated and become visible only when compared to principles and values that operate outside of large bureaucratic organizations. Figure 1.2 offers this comparison. What has become increasingly clear is that as organizations have become larger and more powerful, the demands of organizations have gradually seeped into other parts of our society.

If we know all of the above areas, organization theory, public service, politics, policy, the context, and the dynamic, will we then know about public administration? By studying and learning all we can about these organizations and their surroundings, will we be able to somehow overcome the contradictions we have seen that belong to the words "public" and "administration"?

In truth, the contradictions will still be there. The knowledge people seek of public administration — the models and explanations which enable us to act in ways that meet human needs — is complex.[7] We propose that to study public administration is only part of what is necessary to truly know about it. It is our feeling that one must also think about what it all means. It is important to put together what we know with what we believe and begin to get a list of priorities of what we would like to have happen.

Defining Public Administration

So far we have discussed various parts of public administration, but we have not provided precise definitions. There is no specific agreement among those people who set out to define public administration. As we shall see, each person does something just a little different with the definition. We can learn a great deal about the breadth of the field of public administration by reviewing just some of these definitions.

We will begin with an early definition: "Whenever people associate for common purposes, the problem of administration presents itself. . . . When a government is organized for the effectuation of community business, we have what has come to be called 'public administration.'"[8]

This is a particularly helpful definition because we can get an idea of what some of our prejudices are. We see two clear thoughts. First, there is the notion that administration is a natural consequence of life. The problem simply "presents itself." That may well be true for us in the United States who are a part of a tradition that thinks like that. But not all people who associate for common purposes see the problem of administration. The native Americans did not see the need for what we know as administration. Many prominent American reformers of the nineteenth century searched for social institutions that would do without administration entirely.[9]

The second bias is just as clear. When we do organize, it is to do "business." In our culture, the word business is far from a neutral term. To do business we act in certain very purposive ways. It is, to recall our earlier discussion, to emphasize administration and ignore public. In this particular definition, we get a straightforward picture: people get together for common purposes; the need for administration is immediately felt; the problem is put in business terms and public administration then takes care of business.

Leonard White, one of the great names in the field, uses this definition: "Public administration consists of all those operations having for their purpose the fulfillment or enforcement of public policy . . . a system

BOX 1.3   Public Administration: What Does It Mean?

Knowing the various parts of public administration is not enough. We need to know where it fits, what we believe, and what we would like to happen. The experience of developing nations seeking to apply American ideas and techniques in public administration illustrates this point.

Saudi Arabia, for example, sends many of its young administrators to the United States to pursue Master of Public Administration degrees. The students are well supported during their studies, and they may return to their former jobs (with greater chances for advancement) once their degrees are completed. It is not at all clear, however, that American administrative ideas are suited to Saudi Arabia, which is an Islamic republic headed by a royal family. Various relations of the family hold the key administrative positions, both out of personal favoritism (a traditional value among most of the tribes that formed the Kingdom of Saudi Arabia in 1932) and a need to encourage a stable state. Yet, Saudi students are exposed to many forbidden and dangerous ideas in the United States. Pork, pornography, alcohol, and drugs are outlawed in their kingdom, and all are readily available in the United States. This freedom from constraints spills over into American administrative ideas as well. Traditionalism, personalism, and nepotism are actively shunned in the United States, and in their place are substituted analysis, efficiency, and merit. Saudi officials want to develop their nation. They want efficient administration. But it is not at all clear that they can acquire these from the United States without also importing a host of other, unwelcome ideas.

Nigeria is in a similar situation, sending many students to study administration in the United States. Its leaders are used to borrowing ideas; in the 1970s Nigeria adopted a constitution modeled after that of the United States. Yet strong ethnic and religious divisions and crushing poverty contributed to a military coup before the decade was through.

Nigeria kept the administrative norms and practices of its former colonial masters, the British, yet is saddled with the administrative difficulties faced by most developing nations: poverty, inequalities of wealth, uneven development, and dependent status in the world political economy.

Nigerian students may learn useful ideas in the United States, but the process of development is long and slow. One of the key issues faced by this administrative class of the future is how to adapt foreign ideas to their own context.

of public administration is the composite of all laws, regulations, practices, relationships, codes, and customs that prevail at any time in any jurisdiction for the fulfillment or execution of public policy."[10]

This definition serves as an interesting warning. White, in a narrow manner, concentrates our attention on things which are legal, or those things which come from public sources. In other words, the *public* in public administration is defined in a relatively narrow way. Only governmental bodies can do those things brought up by White: pass laws, regulations, codes, and so on. But, by the very narrowness of the definition, we must anticipate problems. Any administration must deal with many different publics. For example, the people who run our public lands must try to satisfy environmentalists, loggers, livestock grazers, and those who want to mine minerals in those lands. To understand public administration, it is necessary to go far beyond governmental bodies.

Although public administration does, of course, have its central focus on what the government does, there are other administrations which influence each of us a great deal. For example, the administrations of the huge oil companies (Exxon, Texaco, and the like) have a much greater impact on the public than many of the agencies of government. The amount these oil companies decide to pay for crude oil has consequences on interest rates, international banking, whole industries, localized economies, and eventually the world economy. If we include having an impact on the public as part of our definition of public administration, it is important, at some point, to decide if private business is a part of our public administration. As illustrated in Box 1.4, we have sometimes tried to do that, and the results can be confusing.

Let us continue with an idea of one of the founders of our modern public administration thought. Paul Appleby writes: "The need is for the administrative mind that can hold fast to the public interest and bind conflicting special interests to it by skillful contrivance, based on knowledge but exceeding mere expertise."[11] Here we see the emergence of a distinct approach. What Appleby describes is a new kind of public figure, an administrator who has a special set of skills which has to do with public business. Yet, the phrase "skillful contrivance" does not have an open, public ring to it.

To get a fuller sense of what Appleby, and public administration, is about, it is useful to quote him at length:

> In administration, there are certain fundamental principles of general application, analogous to those characterizing any science, which must be observed if the end of administration, efficiency in operations, is to be secured, and these principles are to be determined and their significance made known only by the rigid application of scientific method in their investigations.[12]

BOX 1.4 The Line Between Public and Private: The Case of the Federal Reserve

The panic of 1907 revealed that American banks were engaging in unsound practices. The relationship between assets, loans and liquidity was not carefully watched or managed. Questionable and speculative investing were the order of the day, and the public lost confidence in the banks. This was not good business.

The Congress responded, slowly, by forming the Federal Reserve Board (called "the Fed") in 1913. Its responsibilities were mainly limited to policing banking practices to assure customers that their deposits and loans were safe. Later, in 1932, the United States economy was taken off the gold standard, and by default the Fed was given a greater role in regulating the money supply. Still later, in 1971, the United States stopped converting foreign-held dollars into gold, and again by default the Fed was given a greater role in regulating the price and supply of money. It is now a powerful government agency, some say the most powerful in the national government.

The interesting thing about the Fed is its structure. As illustrated in the accompanying diagram, at the top of the Federal Reserve System is the Board of Governors, seven members appointed by the president and confirmed by the Senate (from these the chair and vice chair are appointed by the president with the "consent" of the Senate). This is clearly a public agency. The members are chosen by elected officials. They have a budget which appears in the Budget of the United States. They hire a staff which is subject to government personnel regulations.

At the bottom of the Federal Reserve System are the member banks. These are the federally chartered banks. You may have a Guaranteed Student Loan or a checking account from one of these banks. These are clearly private businesses. They have shareholders. They try to make a profit.

In the middle, things get confusing. The Federal Reserve Banks are really the regional offices of the Fed. There are twelve such regional banks, operating twenty-five branches. Each of these banks is run by nine directors. Three of the directors are to be from the banking industry. They are elected by top officers of the member banks. Three of the directors are to be from business. They too are elected by top officers of the member banks. And three of the directors are to be from the "public." These are appointed by the Fed. The Fed also approves appointments of the top officers of the Reserve Banks, as well as their salaries. In addition, virtually all members of the Fed are recruited from these positions.

Now back to the Fed. They do their work through the Open Market Committees. Here they make decisions about the speed at which the money supply should increase, and the rate of interest to apply within the banking industry (the "discount rate"). These are important decisions for the economy, and they have important political consequences as well. (It was widely charged that the Fed allowed the economy to get worse so that Ronald Reagan's 1980 election would be assured.) Their deliberations are secret, and no one has ever publicly told what goes on in their meetings.

The Open Market Committees are made up of the seven members of the Fed, plus five representatives of the Federal Reserve Banks. In practice, the top official from each of the twelve reserve banks is privy to Open Market Committee deliberations.

As it turns out, it is just not clear if the Federal Reserve Banks, and even the Open Market Committees, are public or private agencies. In their functions they look a lot like public agencies. In their selection of members and closed deliberations they look a lot like private businesses. Of course the confusion is a bit deliberate. The intention was to preserve a private banking industry, yet to instill some public confidence and preserve some public controls. Yet the political hand should not rest too firmly on the money supply. The organizational problem was solved by having a governmental framework for the private banking activities.

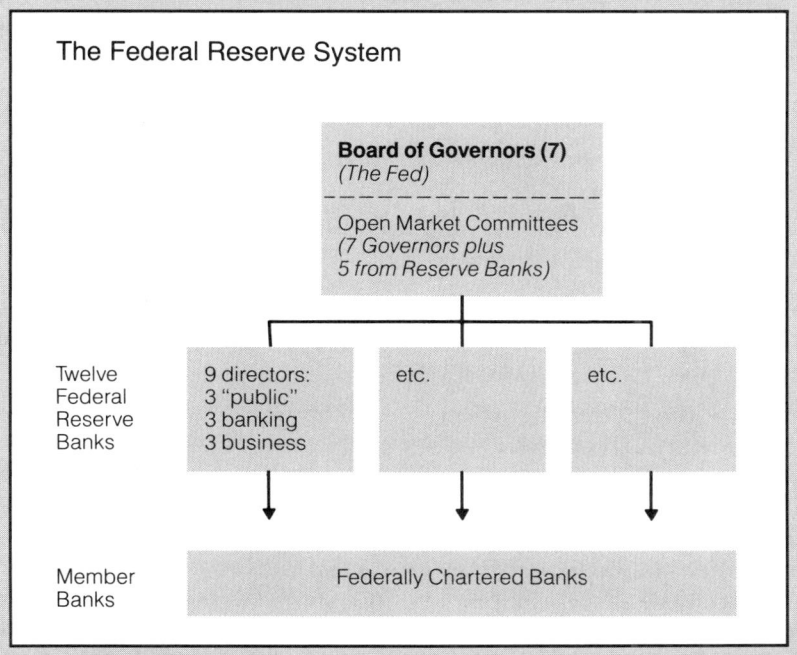

The definition of public administration, according to Appleby, ignores the public altogether. The tendency is to concentrate wholly on administration. It is an administration which revolves around "efficiency in operation." Given these biases, it is easy to conclude that the study of public administration can best be made by the "rigid application" of the "scientific method."

We believe that to use Appleby's definition encourages a misunderstanding about public administration. Although we are not making an argument for inefficiency, we believe that the study of public administration is much more than the search for efficiency. In public matters it is usually difficult to know what efficiency is, or even if that is the proper measure to use. The public, in other words, is often more and different than any kind of dollars-and-cents accounting. If, for example, one of the benefits of a decision-making process being more open to the citizens is that the citizens are less alienated or come to have more confidence in government, how are we to judge that process? How can we use the scientific method to weigh what might be a very expensive decision against the benefits to citizens who made that decision? As you can see, we are back to the clash between *administration* and *public*.

Newer Definitions

In the last several years, the definition of public administration has changed. In its latest incarnation, this is what we find. *Public Administration*:

1. is cooperative group effort in a public setting
2. covers all three branches — executive, legislative, and judicial — and their interrelationships
3. has an important role in the formulation of public policy and is thus a part of the political process
4. is different in significant ways from private administration
5. is closely associated with numerous private groups and individuals in providing services to the community.[13]

While this newer definition is certainly more inclusive than earlier ones, there are ways in which it is not adequate. What emerges from this is a great merging of public and private, while maintaining that private and public administration are different. As our society becomes filled up with huge, complex organizations, it becomes more and more difficult to separate the public from the private ones. Yet, it is just that separation which is so necessary for public administration. We live in an age in which private organizations have a powerful effect on the public. The boundaries between the private and the public become blurred, and public administration becomes closed off from the people. This newer definition may be a reflection of things to come.

FIGURE 1.3 What Do Public Administrators Do?

City of Seattle
EMPLOYMENT BULLETIN

FILING CLOSES MARCH 24, 1988, FOR,
Department of Community Development Position of

HOUSING   DEVELOPMENT   PROJECT   COORDINATOR

SALARY
(Ordinance Title: Program Coordinator II) Begins at $2,456 per month, increases in six months to $2,557, then in annual increments to $2,660 - $2,759 - $2,867 per month.

POSITION DESCRIPTION
This position reports to the manager of the Project Management Section in the Housing Division and is responsible for coordinating a variety of locally and federally funded housing development projects. Specific duties include: prepare housing development packages; set loan terms and conditions using a variety of financing techniques; develop and maintain administrative and finance plans for an assigned housing program such as Non-Profit Assistance, Rental Rehabilitation or Housing Development Grant; inform property owners of City and other lender requirements for development of low-income housing projects; assess project feasibility and make recommendations for financial assistance; negotiate project plans and financial requirements with developers and lenders; coordinate review of plans and specifications; assure project compliance with regulations and requirements; establish and monitor schedules for all project phases including planning, design and construction; prepare reports; work with community groups, non-profit agencies and private citizens to develop low-income projects; prepare and deliver presentations to community groups, developers, lenders and government officials; and perform related duties as required.

WHO MAY APPLY
Applications will be accepted from anyone who meets the following minimum qualifications:

```
MINIMUM QUALIFICATIONS
Education:    A baccalaureate degree in business or public
administration, urban planning, architecture, engineering, economics
or a related field.
Experience:   Two years of professional experience in housing
development or housing program development, including one year working
directly with local or federal housing programs.
Substitution: Additional qualifying experience may substitute for the
required education on the basis that one year of experience equals two
years of education.
```

SELECTION PROCESS
This is a competitive selection process. Applicants must submit the standard application forms, a personal resume which includes the dates of employment (month/year to month/year), the company/agency worked for, the hours worked per week and the functions performed for each job listed.

HOW TO APPLY
Submit your complete application package to the Personnel Department at the address shown below by not later than **Thursday, March 24, 1988.** All application materials are available at the Personnel Department.

What should make public administration special is the word "public," which ties administration to people. The people, by acting together, by acting politically, should dominate the administrative dynamic. It is our belief that the current conflict is less between public and private administration and more between public administration and politics. We offer the following example.

Over the years, we have produced a significant amount of high-level radioactive waste. The problem, of course, is that the radioactive half-life of this waste runs into the tens of thousands of years, and while it exists it is a hazard to our health. The question is: Where do we put the stuff? There is a scientific answer. It is important to find a location where there is granite which goes deep into the earth. This rock will help ensure the radioactive waste will be contained. Science tells us a workable answer is ready to administer now.

One of the ideal places for the waste is in Vermont. We should, rationally, dump our hot waste there. But, Vermont has a long-standing democratic tradition of town meetings. These meetings are the voice of the people, and the people spoke and voted overwhelmingly against the idea. Vermont is not on the final list from which a site will be chosen. But the state of Washington is, even though the rock there is basalt, which is riddled with small cracks; the site is near a major river; and the location involves more lengthy and dangerous travel for the wastes. Washington is not a strong political voice in national politics, and it is not clear what the public there wants. As the book progresses, we shall follow the ways in which public administration has tried to take over political functions, and how successful it has been.

SUMMARY

In this chapter we began with the premise that it is important to define terms in order to be clear about what is being discussed. Yet, from the first we saw that there was a conflict in the very words "public" and "administration" when we tried to put them together. This dichotomy will serve to help us better understand the field when we get into later chapters. We saw that people differ in the ways in which they understand the roots of the field (academic or practical) and even how academics act and conduct research. Finally, we turned to the major components of the study of public administration and reviewed definitions. There are many ways to understand the field, and it is important not to stop at a narrow and possibly misleading focus.

All of these conflicts and differences are important because each of our lives is continually affected by public administration and public administrators. From a global level, such as the State Department and Defense Department officials who contribute to arms control policy, to a remarkable number of events in our everyday lives, such as traffic control and safe air travel, decisions made and carried out by public organizations are the key to what happens. The study of public administration may hold the key to the shape (and therefore the quality) of our futures.

What follows, then, is a book about public administration. In it, we will review how we have gotten where we are, what the research shows us about how we got here, and where we might be headed. There will be theoretical material as well as practical advice. The problems in public administration are pointed out for two reasons. First, because public administration is in transition, the problems will tell you where the field is still open to question and to change. Second, in addressing these problems you will decide what you believe is important about public administration. Whether you become a professional public administrator or not, these are questions that you will have to confront as a citizen living in an age of organizations.

NOTES

1. See Eric Partridge, *Origins* (London: Routledge and Kegan Paul, 1958); and the *Oxford English Dictionary,* compact edition (Oxford: Oxford University Press, 1971).
2. This convention was first proposed by Dwight Waldo.
3. Dwight Waldo has contributed a great deal to how we might conceptualize the field. Refer to his book, *The Study of Public Administration* (New York: Random House, 1955).
4. Woodrow Wilson, "The Study of Administration," *Political Science Quarterly* 2 (June 1887), pp. 197–220. This has been reprinted in many collections.
5. Examples of policy studies can be found in Thomas R. Dye, *Understanding Public Policy* (Englewood Cliffs: Prentice-Hall, 1975); James E. Anderson, *Public Policy Making* (New York: Praeger, 1975) (both available in recent editions); and David Nachmias, ed., *The Practice of Policy Evaluation* (New York: St. Martin's, 1980). Professional journals such as *Public Administration Review* and *Policy Studies Journal* regularly discuss policy issues.
6. The example is from Laurence E. Lynn, Jr., *Managing the Public's Business: The Job of the Government Executive* (New York: Basic Books, 1981), pp. 26–27.

7. We adapt this definition of knowledge, and important parts of our approach, from Larry D. Spence. See his *The Politics of Social Knowledge* (University Park, Pa.: The Pennsylvania State University Press, 1978), p. 27 and passim.
8. Marshall Dimock, "The Meaning and Scope of Public Administration," in John Gaus, Leonard D. White, and Marshall Dimock, eds., *The Frontiers of Public Administration* (Chicago: University of Chicago Press, 1935), p. 1.
9. See James J. Martin, *Men Against the State* (Colorado Springs: Ralph Myles, 1958).
10. Leonard White, *Introduction to the Study of Public Administration* (New York: Macmillan, 1948), pp. 3–4.
11. Paul Appleby, *Big Democracy*, quoted in White, ibid., p. 8.
12. Quoted by Leonard White, "The Meaning of Principles in Public Administration," in Gaus et al., op. cit., p. 13.
13. Felix Nigro and Lloyd Nigro, *Modern Public Administration,* 6th ed., (New York: Harper & Row, 1984), p. 11.

CHAPTER TWO

Politics and Administration: The Context

> They may be every bit as intelligent as you say, but I'd feel a whole lot better about them if just one of them had run for sheriff once.
> — *Speaker of the House Sam Rayburn, Commenting to Vice-President Lyndon Johnson about Kennedy's cabinet appointees.*

There is a tendency to isolate whatever is being studied. In that way, so the logic goes, one is able to get a clear sense of the subject. Regrettably, the study of public administration cannot be isolated. Public administration in the United States both reflects and is sometimes in a dialectical relationship with its context. To understand American public administration, one must understand America.

Organizations do not exist floating around in space. They exist in a time and a place. To understand organizations, it is necessary to know where they came from and the environment in which they operate. One way to find this context is to describe the political culture of the society. A political culture includes prevailing ideology; basic orientations toward the self, others, and economic relationships; and political traditions. The people who enter public administration and politics bring these shared ideas with them. To know about the context is to begin to know the restrictions as well as the opportunities of our public administration.[1]

It is important to remember that one of the key contexts of public administration is how we think about public administration. The ideas we have about the role of administration in the United States help form how administrators act and what they can do. Our judgments, then, are part of the environment of public administration.

What follows is a description of the world our public organizations live in. We will start with liberalism, then describe the Constitution, and then discuss political relationships between administrative agencies and other parts of political systems.

Liberalism

The United States is, fundamentally, a liberal nation. By *liberal*, we are *not* talking about the liberal-conservative split played out by our political parties; we mean instead the political philosophy that is shared and debated by almost all Americans. Considering that the opposite of liberal is illiberal, and trying to think of what illiberal might be, will help you see that most of us, most of the time, are liberals.

The basis of our liberalism comes from the seventeenth-century thinkers John Locke and Thomas Hobbes.[2] Although the particulars of their thought differ, much of what they wrote about and discussed serve as the key issues in our political, social, and economic debates. The following list of traits seems so matter of fact that it is easy to miss their significance. Yet, it is just these traits which form the context of our public organizations.

1. *Individualism.*

Each of us understands, intuitively, that individualism is the underlying dynamic in our culture. We set out on our own to seek fame and glory. The emphasis is on the individual, from the structure of public schools to advancement in the workplace. It is so much a part of our society that we often cannot understand it until we study another culture. The Japanese, Native Americans, and Arabs, to name a few, are instructive examples of people who see themselves, their relations with others, and their roles in organizations quite differently than we do. (See Box 2.1.)

2. *Capitalism.*

Capitalism is an economic extension of individualism. One of our guiding myths centers on individual entrepreneurs who, with a good idea and a great deal of effort, succeed in the marketplace. In this founding myth, the marketplace is unregulated by the government, thus giving everyone an equal chance to succeed, leaving the public to sort the good products from the bad ones. This kind of capitalism gives the economy a vitality that so many Americans admire.[3]

Although it is true that there is a degree of individualism in our economic system, it is necessary to realize two things. First, from almost the beginning, the government has had an important say about what goes on in the marketplace. From legislation to Supreme Court rulings, the government has been involved in our economy. Indeed, the origins of capitalism lie in active government interventions to create markets. They are not "natural."[4]

Second, it is accurate to use the phrase "corporate capitalism" to describe our economic system, because it is dominated by huge, complex organizations.[5] So, for example, although it is still possible for two people to begin Apple Computer in a garage, it is foolish to forget that they had to fight for a place in the world of IBM and Digital. In the fight, the original two founders left Apple. They left rich, but they left. Now, of course, Apple is a big corporation.

> **BOX 2.1** Another View of American Individualism
>
> Professor Hu, from the People's Republic of China (PRC), accepted an appointment as a visiting scholar at an American university. Several faculty members took him on an automobile tour of the university town. At one point they drove past a lake and stopped to look at the water skiers.
>
> Professor Hu was less interested in the skiers than with the houses built on the lakefront for its entire perimeter, except for a small park and boat ramp. He asked, "Why are these houses built on the lake? Who lives in them?" One of his guides replied, "No one in particular. The people here own the land, and build houses to live in. My wife and I just bought a waterfront lot last year, and we should put up a house this summer."
>
> Professor Hu still did not understand. "How is it that you can own the land next to the lake? Do these people own the lake too?"
>
> "No, we are in a public park. Anyone can use this ramp to put a boat on the lake. We have some parks where everyone goes to use places like this, but most land is owned by individuals."
>
> Professor Hu pursued the point. "Is this land expensive? How long does it take a person to earn enough money to buy one of these houses?"
>
> "These houses sell for around $200,000."
>
> Professor Hu's eyes widened, then he put his hand to his mouth as he thought for a moment. "I see," he said, looking as though he had found out something very important about Americans.

3. *Individual Rights, including Freedom of Speech, Press, and Religion.*

In the Constitution and Bill of Rights, we are guaranteed certain freedoms. People who enter public administration share these ideas much the way Jefferson intended in his reference in the Declaration of Independence: "We hold these truths to be self-evident." They form part of the context of our public organizations, and both provide and prevent what those organizations can do.

For example, a vigorous and commercial press distinguishes our public administration from that of most of the world. American public organizations must operate "in the sunshine" for the most part; their actions are regularly held up for scrutiny and ridicule. This situation is distinct from the context in which public administrations operate in most of the world.

Another important example concerns protections against unwarranted seizure of property or freedom by the state. Individuals are afforded extensive hearings and rights of appeal in the administrative process so that the state cannot easily trample on their rights. This adds a great deal of "red tape" to public administration, but it also gives individuals a voice they have few other places in the world.[6]

4. *Rule of Law.*

People know what the rules are and generally understand and accept how the rules are made. At least, the *belief* in the rule of law is important. We can see possible conflict for those in public administration. With the rule of law, a person in public service is expected to treat everyone equally, because we are all, theoretically, equal before the law. However, this seems to contradict the idea of individualism — all of us believing we are special. The conflict goes still further, as Marshall Dimock describes:

> The central problem arising from this nexus of law and administration is this: how to make government more responsible to standards that take the form of law as enforced by the courts, and in so doing afford proper protection to individual and economic rights, while at the same time making the performance of government more efficient and enterprising, thus assuring the continued vitality of both the private enterprise system and representative government.[7]

Later in the chapter we will look at relationships among people and institutions that argue about, make, and enforce the laws. These are at the center of the way politics and administration operate in America.

5. *Majority Rule versus Minority Rights.*

This is one of the basic conflicts with which our public organizations must deal. We, as a political culture, firmly believe that the majority should rule, but that the minority must have certain rights. It is a question of *which* rights the minority should have and *what* matters the majority should rule that causes so much trouble. It is often our public organizations that are at the point of these tensions.

6. *Government-Antigovernment Feelings.*

There has been a series of great swings toward and away from government taking an active role in the everyday affairs of citizens. The first great swing toward a very active role of the national government was when Franklin Roosevelt attempted to stop the Great Depression during the 1930s. In the late 1940s a number of laws passed limiting the way government agencies could act and grow, and the 1950s passed with few major initiatives. Another great swing toward activism took place during the 1960s under Lyndon Johnson.

In 1980 and 1984 voters elected and reelected Ronald Reagan. He campaigned on the idea that government could be cut back without harming the "truly needy." Yet there were mixed messages from the voters. Polls showed that a majority of voters favored the policy positions of Reagan's opponents, but they voted for Reagan for other reasons. It is doubtful whether citizens supported specific cuts in government, although they did respond to Reagan's message that, somehow, government should be doing a better job. But there is no question about Reagan's ideas about government. Although he worked to cut back many social services and federal aid to areas like education, he was also willing to invade people's lives by mandatory drug testing. That contradiction seems typical of our government-antigovernment feelings.

It seems clear that we will never have a small, do-little government like we had before the New Deal, but it is also clear that we Americans have mixed feelings about what we think is appropriate for the government to do. For example, the so-called tax revolt of the 1970s and early 1980s involved voter initiatives and referenda to limit the taxing powers of state governments, particularly in California, Massachusetts, and Michigan. Yet most citizens are pleased with the services they receive from government, and similar measures failed in the mid-1980s.[8] This adds an element of uncertainty to the jobs of those who work in our public administrations.

These six points, then, form the general ideological context for American public administration. It should be remembered that not only do organizations exist in this context, the people in the organizations are products of these ideas and tensions. These people are, to put it another way, themselves a part of the context. They come to their jobs with strong feelings about individualism, the rule of law, and the rest. That they grew up in liberal America means that the context of public administration is their mind-set.

We shall see later in the book how these beliefs influence our organizations. Now, we will go to the specifics of how our government is organized.

The Constitution

In the broadest sense, the legal basis of public administration is the Constitution. There are two elements of the Constitution that are important to this discussion. One is the separation of powers and the other is the invention of federalism. Both of these share a similar source: The writers of the Constitution knew that the people of the new nation would not accept a government with highly centralized power.[9] The Constitution calls for at least some separation and decentralization of power. The states and most local governments continue the tradition of the separation of powers, and all are involved in federalism.

The Separation of Powers

First, the Constitution *separates* powers. We are all familiar with the three branches of government and what each does. The Congress has the legislative powers, the president has executive powers, and the Supreme Court and other federal courts have judicial powers. Also, the Constitution staggers and varies the times and methods of how people are selected for office. In the original provisions the president was elected by members of the electoral college (who were not simple reflections of popular votes) for a four-year term; members of the House of Representatives were popularly elected to two-year terms; a third of the Senate was chosen by state legislatures every two years for six-year terms; and justices were appointed for life. All were to come from different electoral constituencies, and some of the diversity is still preserved. The Framers did it that way so that there would never be an entirely new group of people in charge of running the government. If madness were to seize the government, it had to be an unusually persistent madness.

The separation of powers has several important results for public administration. First, there are administrative agencies in each of the branches of government. Most are in the executive branch (the Department of Defense, the Department of Agriculture, and so on), and this is the case for state governments as well. Many local governments adopt a council and manager form of government, where the legislature hires a professional administrator to run various agencies, but administrative powers in local governments still depend upon state law.

The size of executive agencies is impressive. In 1901, there were about 231,000 employees of the federal government. In 1930, just before governmental expansion during the New Deal, the number of federal employees had more than doubled to 590,000, only a moderate increase. In 1949, in the post–World War II, post–New Deal period, the number of employees reached 3.7 million, a much more than moderate rise. By the 1980s, federal employment had leveled off at about 2,840,000.

That almost-three-million number is deceiving. In 1975, more than 8.8 million people were employed by local governments, and more than 3,250,000 people were employed by state governments. In short, the way we organize to enable the executive to faithfully execute the law of the land is to rely on hiring people, and these people are public administrators. While this may not be the only way to do things, or even the best way, it has certainly come to be the way we do it.

Other administrative agencies are creatures of the Congress (the Gen-

TABLE 2.1 How Many People Work in Government?

State & Local Government

	State	Local
Alabama	76,219	145,362
Alaska	24,462	22,149
Arizona	51,826	124,485
Arkansas	42,932	80,269
California	327,441	1,134,829
Colorado	59,154	136,123
Connecticut	57,112	105,982
Delaware	19,860	16,885
Florida	131,256	425,391
Georgia	95,835	252,729
Hawaii	46,685	12,691
Idaho	18,556	39,715
Illinois	148,983	467,402
Indiana	91,942	214,494
Iowa	56,517	130,539
Kansas	52,182	116,111
Kentucky	69,608	113,620
Louisiana	100,656	166,374
Maine	24,149	43,975
Maryland	90,391	161,660
Massachusetts	87,439	215,212
Michigan	149,066	379,551
Minnesota	74,434	181,666
Mississippi	49,886	105,789
Missouri	72,778	187,132
Montana	20,712	36,773
Nebraska	35,023	78,001
Nevada	14,605	35,497
New Hampshire	20,809	35,515
New Jersey	101,821	318,570
New Mexico	41,131	52,893
New York	284,874	867,464
North Carolina	102,049	269,576
North Dakota	19,335	34,979
Ohio	151,328	430,665
Oklahoma	73,047	123,869
Oregon	54,465	114,094
Pennsylvania	143,718	395,286
Rhode Island	27,736	27,456
South Carolina	70,119	117,409
South Dakota	16,315	32,591
Tennessee	77,777	170,549
Texas	220,855	658,786

TABLE 2.1 continued

	State	Local
Utah	36,645	60,359
Vermont	12,100	18,438
Virginia	117,155	213,343
Washington	96,788	157,231
West Virginia	42,531	65,373
Wisconsin	85,609	219,143
Wyoming	12,391	31,124
Dist. of Col.	0	50,221
Total, State & Local	3,898,307	9,595,340

National Government	
Civilian agency	1,088,992
Defense	1,037,113
Postal Service	736,852
Total, National	2,862,957
Total, All Govts	**16,356,604**

Sources: *Book of the States, 1986–7,* and *Budget of the United States, 1987*

eral Accounting Office, the Government Printing Office, the Library of Congress, and so on), and counting various committee and legislators' staffs, about 30,000 nonelected people work for the Congress. Most state governments have similar important offices under the control of the legislatures. The staffs of legislative bodies help them function. These people manage the affairs of the people we elect to make laws. In many ways, they perform the functions of the legislature.

There are basically three functions of those in legislative administration. First, they help the lawmakers formulate policies and draft proposed legislation. Second, they are often the link between the lawmaker and his or her constituents. It is the administrator who often hears a complaint first, and it is the administrator who often actually tries to solve a particular problem. Legislative administrators are the link between the lawmaker and other branches of government. (The dynamics of this relationship are discussed later in the chapter.) For example, legislative administrators often oversee activities in the executive branch and evaluate programs put in place by the legislature. It is fair to say that the functioning of the legislative branch depends on these people for its administration. And, although the administrator may float from one job to another within the legislative offices, the administrator may have more seniority than the lawmaker he or she is working for. With that seniority and experience comes power.

The judicial branch also contains administrative units. For instance, there is an Administrative Office of the United States Courts, and most states have a similar bureaucracy. Many people are employed as clerks and other staff members of courts. Also, the Justice Department, headed by the Attorney General, is part of the executive branch but is involved heavily in the details of the judicial branch.

Those in the judicial administration do the job of "managing" our courts. They do everything from budgeting and management of clerical and support personnel, to handling the court's calendar and its public relations, to helping take care of jurors and witnesses and making plans about how to handle the courts' increasingly large case load.

When we think about the court and trials, we think about judges, lawyers, justice, particular cases, and perhaps juries. What we must also now consider is that there are administrators who are constantly working to make all of that happen. While it is common knowledge that there are too few judges to handle the volume of cases, we should realize that if we do have more judges we will also need to increase the number of administrators who help run the judicial branch.

There are several other types of administrative agencies in the national government that do not fit neatly into the classification of executive, legislative, and judicial branches. Some of these agencies were created to administer specific services or administer to specific groups of people. Among these are the Veteran's Administration, the Social Security Administration, and the Environmental Protection Agency. Their top administrators are appointed by, and accountable to, the president, with oversight and some control by the Congress.

Other agencies are more deliberately independent, such as the independent regulatory commissions. These usually have jurisdiction over some area of economic activity. Examples are the Securities and Exchange Commission, the National Labor Relations Board, and the Interstate Commerce Commission. More about these later in the chapter.

Still other agencies take the form of government-owned corporations (the Postal Service, the Tennessee Valley Authority, and the Federal Deposit Insurance Corporation are examples). The point is there are many forms (recall the example of the Federal Reserve system in Chapter 1) of organization in the federal government. Local and state governments exhibit similar diversity of forms. Special governments, such as school districts, irrigation districts, conservation districts, mosquito control districts, and public ports, offer still more variety in the forms of public administrations. The variety is a sign of political diversity. The more diverse and vital a political system, the greater its assortment of administrative forms. In many ways our organizations look alike, which suggests some kinds of limitations on our politics. In other ways the variety of organizations is staggering.

Second, the separation of powers works to put complex cross-pressures on administrative agencies. Each of the branches of government contributes something to the laws administered by agencies and to the procedures employed. Administrative participation in policy-making is extensive and complicated. We devote a section to the subject later in this chapter. For now, we want to point out how the separation of powers results in a curious mixing of styles of administration, depicted in Table 2.3. Each of the branches has a different approach to administration. The executive takes a managerial view, the legislative takes a political view, and the judicial takes a legal view, and each of these has different implications for the most important values in administration, the way organizations are structured, and the ways individuals are treated.

Imagine being the director of a county hospital. Your immediate boss would be the county. Funding would come from a variety of state and federal sources. Billings would also come from public and private insurance companies. Drugs would be controlled by national drug regulations, and many patient rights are legal ones which are decided in the courts. Most of the hospital's employees are licensed by the state. Many of the legal rights become political fights (like abortion), many drug regulations become legal and political (like experimental drugs to treat cancer and acquired immune deficiency syndrome, AIDS), and many organizational problems become political (you would have to justify a budget to the county, and services to the community always draw the attention of political groups). Different branches and levels of government constantly overlap, and, from the standpoint of a single agency, are often in conflict.

This means that public administration includes an almost bewildering assortment of structures, forms, and practices. And yet the Framers intended that government be diverse. They came to believe that they could keep what they treasured only by limiting the scope and effect of politics. In this sense, the revolution they fought was not made but prevented. The separation of powers embodied in the Constitution is intended to preserve individual rights in a liberal order and to keep government limited. These come at a cost, as we have suggested. To make most important things private, it is difficult to find a meaningful place that is public; and when administration is added to public, much of what we call political becomes part of the administrative process.

Federalism

The second great political invention of the Framers of the Constitution was *federalism*. One problem faced by the Framers was this: to construct a form of government that would not be overly centralized but which could still rule over a very large territory. The Framers believed older solutions

TABLE 2.2 Major Forms and Functions of U.S. Bureaucracy

Bureaucratic Form	Examples of Form	Major Functions
Executive Department (all levels)	State Department, Education Department, Defense Department	Principally implement tasks assigned, with some advisory and regulatory duties
Executive Offices of President, Governor, or Mayor (all levels)	Office of Management and Budget, National Security Council, Council of Economic Advisers	Principally advisory roles for chief executive
Foundations (mainly federal level)	National Science Foundation	Promotion of research through grants; some advisory roles
Institutions and Institutes (mainly federal)	Smithsonian Institution, National Cancer Institute (HHS), Foreign Service Institute (State), Institutes for Environmental Research (Commerce)	Promotion of research in-house and through grants; education and teaching function
Independent Agencies (all levels)	ACTION (headed by one person), CIA (headed by one person), Veterans Administration (headed by one person), Merit Systems Protection Board (committee governed), Transportation Safety Board (committee governed)	Perform a wide variety of executive quasi-judicial, quasi-legislative, and advisory functions *outside* formal executive departments — either single-headed or committee-governed
Commissions on Claims (mainly federal)	Indian Claims Commission, Foreign Claims Settlement Commission	Largely judicial functions
Regulatory Agencies (all levels)	Interstate Commerce Commission, Federal Trade Commission, Nuclear Regulatory Commission	Largely regulatory functions
Government Corporations (all levels)	Tennessee Valley Authority, U.S. Railway Association, Federal Prisons Industries, Inc., Federal Crop Insurance Corporation, St. Lawrence Seaway Development Corporation	Carry out a wide variety of functions either within an executive department or independent of the executive branch; may be mixed public-private ownership

Boards, Councils, and Committees (all levels)	Federal Regional Councils, Federal Records Council, Water Resources Councils	Largely coordinative and advisory duties
Advisory Bodies (all levels)	National Historical Publications Commission, Advisory Board of St. Lawrence Seaway Development, Advisory Council on Vocational Education	Advisory group of primarily private citizens but legally constituted permanent bodies
Intergovernment Units (all levels)	Advisory Commission on Intergovernment Relations, Great Lakes River Basin Commission, Ozarks Regional Commission, Local Council of Government	National and regional planninng, coordinating, and advisory bodies
Joint Executive-Congressional Units (all levels)	Migratory Bird Conservation Commission, Advisory Commission on Low Income Housing	Primarily advise both legislature and executive
Legislative Organizations (all levels)	General Accounting Office, State Auditor, County Auditor	Primarily advisor, research, and oversight role for legislature
Special Districts (local only)	School District, Water and Sewer District, Fire District	Perform a wide range of county and municipal services independent of general government
Private Organizations, funded and set up by government (all levels)	Rand Corporation, Institute for Defense Analysis, MITRE, Los Alamos Labs, County Hospitals	Independent units funded almost entirely by government and chartered by governor to perform specific types of contractual service
Public Organizations, privately funded with mixed public-private directorship and highly autonomous (all levels)	Federal Reserve Board, Corporation for Public Broadcasting, Legal Services Corporation	Autonomous public units, largely privately supported, with a wide variety of tasks

Source: Richard J. Stillman II, *The American Bureaucracy* (Chicago, Nelson-Hall, Inc., 1987), pp. 60–61.

TABLE 2.3 The Separation of Powers and Approaches to Administration

Branch	Approach to Administration	Origins and Values	Structure of Organization	View of the Individual
Executive	Managerial	Civil service reform of the late 19th century; values effectiveness, efficiency, economy	Hierarchy and bureaucracy, businesslike execution of policies set by elected officials; values political neutrality, merit, and neutral competence	Impersonal, subordinated to overarching values of effectiveness, efficiency, economy
Legislative	Political	Constitutional intent to avoid combined and arbitrary powers; value representativeness, political responsiveness through elected officials.	Political pluralism, structures that mirror values and conflicts among citizens. "Let ambition counteract ambition."	People have "interests," shared with other members of identifiable groups
Judiciary	Legal	Administrative Procedures Act of 1946, earlier civil rights cases; values Procedural Due Process, Individual Rights in Bill of Rights and 14th Amendment, Equity.	Use adversary procedures; stress independence and impartiality of presiding official	Each is a unique person under unique circumstances

Source: Based on David H. Rosenbloom, "Public Administration Theory and the Separation of Powers," *Public Administration Review* 43 (May/June, 1983), pp. 219–227. Reprinted by permission.

were unsuited for a large number of people in a large area or were too centralized. The solution was federalism.

Technically, federalism has to do with how power is divided.[10] In a federal system more than one government exercises power in a single territory. Each of the governments has powers the others cannot take away. In the United States, those powers most necessary to unite a nation reside in the central government:[11]

1. The power to raise and support armies, to declare war, to suppress insurrections, to repel invasions, to make treaties, and to send and receive ambassadors
2. The power to regulate commerce both at home and abroad
3. The power to collect taxes and duties
4. The power to coin money and regulate its value, to punish counterfeiting, to make bankruptcy laws, and to enact copyright and patent laws

The states also have certain powers. They have the power to create local governments, to control commerce within their borders, to establish electoral districts, to regulate marriage and divorce, political parties, the public morals, and the like.

Some powers are shared. For example, both the national and state governments may tax, build roads, and regulate public utilities and public safety.

This may sound like a reasonably clear-cut division of power, but in reality it is anything but that. Among the 80,000 or so government entities in the United States, relations are quite complicated. There are many public bureaus in these governments that have overlapping and often conflicting interests. Let us give a short example. We live in a house on the corner of a busy street. There should be a traffic light at the corner, because of the number of kids who cross on their way to and from school. We talked to the mayor about it (this is a small town), who talked with the road department. Everyone agreed there should be a light. However, the city has no control because the road is part of a state route, and the state bureaucracy will not put a light here. The city maintains the road, but the state controls it.

Most issues in federalism are like that. Relations among the governments are not strictly hierarchical but are rather mixed (see Box 2.2). And some of the most important aspects of federalism have to do with money. Who pays for what? If the national government helps the states build highways, do they also get to say how fast everyone may drive? Money and power are never much separated in public administration. We will discuss the fiscal side of federalism in Chapter 12.

Federalism viewed from the national perspective involves getting other levels of government to work toward national objectives. Of the total

BOX 2.2 Federalism and Federal Water

California's San Joaquin Valley includes five of the top ten agricultural counties in the nation. Agriculture is big business there. The area has rich soil, but the arid climate restricts the amount of agriculture that can be done without irrigation. In central California, the politics of federalism often revolve around water.

In 1952 agricultural interests successfully organized a local government, the Westlands Water District, on the west side of the valley. Its objective was to import water into the area, mainly through the use of federal dollars. Eventually the district built or participated in building a series of dams, canals, and pumping stations to bring water from all over eastern California and the valley to irrigate the crops. The earliest projects, a reservoir and canal, were financed with 55 percent local funds and the balance in federal funds. More recent large projects were mainly financed with federal funds, with heavy cooperation from Pacific Gas and Electric company, which also operates dams and power stations in the area. The intergovernmental structure operating the water system is quite complicated.

The Westlands Water District ran into trouble in 1986. It seems that in the water and in the soil are salts and dissolved metals, such as selenium. Continued irrigation causes these minerals to build up in the soil, and unless something is done the ground will be poisoned. In the 1970s a drain was constructed by the water district, with federal funds through the Interior Department's Bureau of Reclamation, which took the water from the fields and sent it north toward San Francisco Bay. Farmers installed drain tiles in their fields to carry the waters to the drain.

Federal money only allowed for completion of about half of the drain, and so the water only flowed as far as the Kesterson National Wildlife Refuge. It is administered by the Interior Department's U.S. Fish and Wildlife Service. The Fish and Wildlife Service told the Bureau of Reclamation it can no longer dump water in Kesterson, since the water, which carried the poisonous materials from the fields, was killing or deforming birds and fish. The Bureau of Reclamation told the Westlands Water District its members could no longer dump water into the drain, the equivalent of taking the land out of production.

The battle is likely to go on for another 10 years, the likely time needed for the Westlands Water District to again convince federal and perhaps state officials that agriculture needs their help and then to construct the rest of the drain. But now the drain probably cannot dump water into San Francisco Bay. Several local and state agencies

> responsible for the quality of bay water have already voiced opposition to the plan. An additional water purification plant, likely to cost around $4 billion, will be needed to make the water clean enough to dump into the bay. It is not clear who will pay for it.

federal domestic budget, only about 6 or 7 percent consists of services actually performed by the national government. The rest is spent on grants to state and local governments, administration, and coordination of national objectives. The question for national objectives follows fairly narrow partisan interests, however. Other federal political systems use intergovernmental grants to equalize government resources between rich and poor areas in the country; in the United States intergovernmental grants actually exacerbate such differences.[12]

Federalism viewed from the local level is a more complicated issue.[13] It is here that officials experience the network of higher government programs that affect citizens. One study showed that a town of 80,000 was the focus of twenty-five different federal programs spending about $100 million, and the programs were not coordinated. Although from the federal perspective local officials may not be entirely reliable to carry out national objectives, the local view usually holds that the money spent is needed, but should be more carefully tailored to local needs.

Local officials are poorly understood in the nation's capital. The usual picture is of a poorly managed, insensitive (or at least conservative) and probably corrupt government. Although this has been true of many local governments, it is a distorted picture. State governments have more frequent contact with local governments and have a correspondingly higher opinion of local capacities. Even though states do require many activities of local governments without giving the needed resources, state aid to localities comes with many fewer strings than does federal aid.

The local public administrator is usually the official who must get things done in a federal system. Regular contact among officials of other governments is a central piece of the job. Since the emphasis is on performing services, issues often expand to include agreements among different governments to perform services (such as emergency services communications, as in a "911" system), explore new trends and forces (such as local responses to diminishing federal dollars), and even to create new governments (such as the creation of a regional body to oversee water quality).

The International City Management Association offers the following advice to local managers involved in federalism issues:

1. Objectives — Reevaluate the scale of your city or county and other local governments in your area, especially for intergovernmental service agreements and transfers of functions. Strengthen political and financial support for your council of governments so that regional decisions are made regionally.
2. Actors — The effective local government manager probably is not the principal actor, but he or she should constantly encourage those with leading and supporting roles — mayors, county board chairpersons, city and county department heads, planning directors, state highway professionals, and others — to keep on top of legislation, policy changes, and other elements of the ebb and flow of day-to-day local government.
3. Means — There are many means of increasing the effectiveness of local government inter-governmental relations, but the most promising ones . . . seem to be intergovernmental service agreements, transfers of functions, and both short- and long-range plans. . . .[14]

Federalism, then, provides an interesting context for our public administration. It helps create a situation in which public organizations may fight among themselves for power. That struggle has at least two results. First, it is difficult to have a clear division of responsibilities. Political forces are never far removed from administrative acts, meaning that ours can never be the most bureaucratically efficient system (see Box 2.3). Second, if federalism works well, there should be a great deal of experimentation at the local level. In theory, we should be a nation of small organizational experiments. However, that is not always the case. The national government is as likely to be innovative as any local or state government. In any event, the context of federalism has a powerful effect on our public administrators.

Political Relationships

Public administrators exist in a web of political relationships that affect the policies they enact and their day-to-day operations. Figure 2.1 presents a simplified view of these relationships at the national level. The major institutions of policy-making are, of course, the Congress and the executive branch, but we have to make several distinctions to understand how these institutions affect the daily concerns of public administrators.

Public administrators are, of course, affected by their superiors in the executive branch. Other relationships inside the government, but outside their particular departments and agencies, are important as well. Members of Congress have responsibilities to exercise *oversight* of bureaucracy. Working mainly through committees, members of the Congress will ask

BOX 2.3 Managing the Details of Federalism — A Horror Story*

In June 1970 Flint civic leaders traveled to Washington to seek special HUD funding for an urban-renewal project that would redevelop 38 acres in the center of Flint. This area, known as Doyle, was the most blighted area of the city. More than 85 percent of its residents were black, possessing the lowest per-capita income in the city. At least half of the existing housing units were deteriorated or dilapidated, and most were owned by absentee landlords. The Doyle area contained the greatest population density in the city and experienced the highest incidence of crime.

Secretary George Romney himself assured his Flint visitors that $5 million of urban-renewal funds would be reserved for the development of the Doyle area. The civic leaders returned home, satisfied that they had obtained a federal commitment to accomplish a much-needed, and widely supported, community project. Little did they know that the secretary's approval was only to initiate a seemingly unending series of bureaucratic delays, in which the fate of the Doyle project was batted back and forth between the city and the HUD area office.

A month after the secretary's decision, the city of Flint submitted a planning application. HUD quickly responded, announcing in August that $5 million had been reserved for this project, with only one contingency — the city's submittal of a final application and HUD's approval.

The community development staff, working closely with the citizens' district council representing the area, immediately began to prepare a development plan for Doyle that would be the basis for a final application. After preparing the plan, holding requisite public hearings, following all appropriate procedures, and making final revisions, the city submitted its final application to HUD in June 1971. The process was conducted by the city in a period of less than ten months — near-record time for a project of this magnitude.

Apparently, HUD was not impressed. The plan, it said, did not meet recently developed criteria. HUD made a series of demands: first, more data on the relocation housing opportunities for displaced residents: the city complied. Then, more information about the city's affirmative action program. The city provided this information. Finally, HUD required a formal commitment from the Board of Education to build a new school in the Doyle area. After considerable debate between the city, the board, and the HUD area office, a document was prepared that everyone felt comfortable signing. By this time, it was early 1972, and most concerned individuals in the city felt confident the project would soon be approved — but not so.

Without warning, the HUD Detroit area office announced that there were problems. Instead of approving the rebuilding of homes in which existing residents could relocate, thereby maintaining the existing racial pattern — a premise on which the original Doyle plan was based — HUD now wanted to reduce racial impaction. To do so required a new plan which would ensure a different racial and income mix in the new housing proposed for the area.

So, in early 1972, the city went back to the drawing board. In less than six months the city was prepared to submit a new plan according to the latest HUD requirements. Accordingly, the director of community development and his staff put the requisite ten copies of the final application in a box and personally delivered them to the HUD area office in Detroit. Expecting immediate approval, they were shocked and angered when HUD officials told them they could not accept the box of plans because they did not comply with the most recently passed legislation covering the payment of relocation benefits to displaced residents. The city was told that it would now have to amend the project budget to ensure that the city would pay the relocation benefits which the federal government would have paid under the old regulations.

Back in Flint, the City Council, after long debate, finally agreed to appropriate $250,000 from the city's Public Improvement Fund to meet the new financial requirement. With this authorization, the city in June 1972 resubmitted its third "final" application.

This time, HUD accepted the application. Then, because HUD was beginning a new fiscal year, it did nothing. For nearly four months it did not react to the application. When the agency finally responded, it was bad news again. This time, HUD officials announced that during the period they had been reviewing the Doyle application Flint's "workable program" had expired, and that no new programs could be approved until a new workable program had been submitted and approved.

Three months of work by the city staff produced a new workable program in January 1973. The document was submitted and subsequently approved by HUD. Now, certainly, the Doyle project would be approved, the money would be forthcoming, and the city could get on with this major public improvement. No such luck! In late January, HUD in Washington announced that it was placing a moratorium on all federal subsidies for the construction of low and moderate income housing. This was a serious blow to the Doyle project, because a major objective of the project was the construction of 150 units of low and moderate income housing using federal subsidies. Without these subsidies the housing could not be built and the project, despite almost thirty months' planning, was effectively dead.

Community leaders were not prepared to give up on this project after so much time and energy had gone into it. They decided again to go directly to the top, and arranged a meeting with a representative of the new secretary of housing and urban development, James Lynn. In April 1973 a contingent of civic leaders met with the under secretary of HUD to examine alternative ways to get the Doyle project under way. The results of the meeting boiled down to this: HUD would approve the project if the city could demonstrate an ability to relocate residents displaced by the project and guarantee that 50 percent of the newly constructed units would be available to low and moderate income residents.

Back in Flint, civic leaders met with the City Council to determine if these requirements could be met. It was clear, given the city's budget situation, that the city itself would not be able to subsidize the low and moderate income housing. After much agonizing, the Mott Foundation agreed to replace the federal government as the provider of subsidies under a locally run program. This major commitment, combined with a relocation plan, allowed the city to make its fifth "final" application to HUD.

At last, all the existing, past, and future regulations appeared to have been met. The Doyle project was finally approved in June 1973, three years after its inception. Ironically, this program was the last, or one of the last, urban-renewal programs ever approved by HUD. As of July 1, 1973, the federal urban-renewal program was terminated by the Nixon administration. The Community Development Act of 1974 placed future urban-renewal programs within community-development bloc grants administered by a whole new set of rules and regulations.

*Source: Brian W. Rapp and Frank M. Pattitucci, *Managing Local Government for Improved Performance* (Boulder, Col.: Westview Press, 1977), pp. 224–226.

questions, review budgets, and add provisions to laws intended to affect the behavior of public administrators. Figure 2.1 simplifies an important part of these relationships — it is usually a hired staff member of a committee or member of Congress's office that makes the contacts with public administrators.

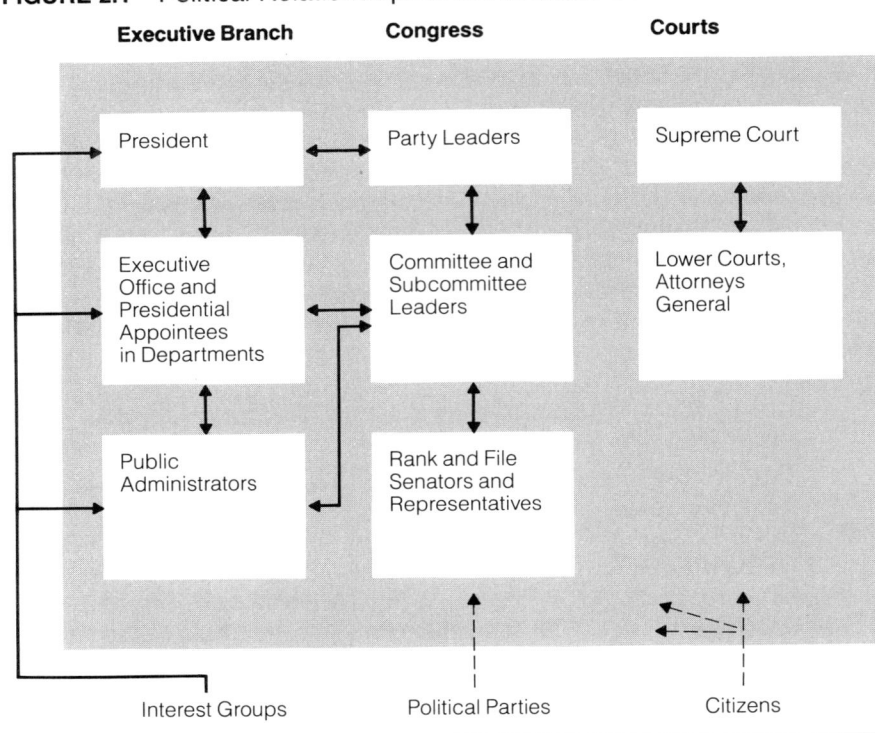

FIGURE 2.1 Political Relationships in the National Government

Look at it this way. Say you, an ordinary citizen, are receiving disability checks from the Social Security Administration and using the money to go to school. One month your check does not arrive on time. The school and your landlord want to be paid. What do you do? It seems sensible to first call Social Security and ask what happened. They may tell you that your case is under review, and until the review is complete payments have been suspended. Now who do you call? Your representative in Congress is the best bet. A staff person in the office will call Social Security, and you will get a much quicker response. And, unless policy has recently changed, you will get your check. Congress's oversight functions allow it to perform such casework for citizens.

But ordinary citizens do not get involved in administration (or government in general) very often. Organized citizens do. Put yourself in their shoes: imagine that you run a feedlot. You make money by buying cattle, feeding them grain for two months, and then selling the cattle. The more weight you put on the cattle, the more money you will make. One of the ways you enable cattle to gain a lot of weight is to add antibiotics and hormones to the grain. But then a public administrator in the Food and Drug Administration makes a rule limiting the types and amounts of these additives you can use in your grain. This will raise your costs and your cattle will not gain as much weight. What do you do?

It turns out that you belong to an association of feedlot owners, and the association employs people whose job it is to watch what the government is thinking of doing concerning your business. The association found out (by reading the *Federal Register,* the magazine that lists new rules proposed by the government) about the changes and notified you. The association requested a hearing on the proposed rules, and they have lined up an impressive array of supporters. Several members of Congress are complaining about the change. Officials in other parts of government, such as the U.S. Department of Agriculture, will write letters saying the change is not necessary and would hurt your business, and so on. Your association, a registered interest group, costs a bit to belong to each year, but you need it to make sure that government remains responsive to your interests. It is worth the expense.

Many political relationships in government are like that. There is a triangular relationship among people representing organized interests, public administrators in particular agencies, and members of Congress that sit on important committees. These people regularly deal with each other and each other's issues. They often know each other on a first-name basis, and they conduct business.[15]

This does not mean that ordinary citizens have little say in government. They do, as long as they are organized. So they form consumer groups, environmental groups, or find particular interests they share with a lot of other people and join groups to influence government actions. These groups often seek to open government up to citizens and successfully lobby to pass laws allowing citizens to get information, find out about intended agency actions, and attend hearings where agencies are required to get community opinions before proceeding with a decision. These groups compete with other groups to have a say in public policy. Political scientists have compiled descriptions of these political relationships to help explain the context of policy-making that surrounds public administrators. Box 2.4 contains a representative list of propositions about the policy process.

Political parties have a role in these political relationships, but it is a minor one. They are influential in helping to pick political appointees, but have little other influence. Once elected to Congress, a member belongs to the internal congressional political party, but public administrators are only indirectly affected.

Political relationships in local communities are much the same, although altered to fit the scale.[16] Local public administrators pay particular attention to elected officials (who are closer to department operations than in national or state government), the business community (by no means a single interest — their demands vary according to type of business, national or local focus, and so on), local government employees (particularly unions), the press, civic associations (taxpayer groups, welfare rights or-

BOX 2.4 The Policy Process in the United States

This list of propositions describes the policy-making process in the national government. It conveys the idea that policy comes from a pluralistic, incremental decision-making process shaped by competition among organized interests. It also suggests that much of what we mean by public policy is not terribly public.*

1. Events in society are interpreted in different ways by different people at different times.
2. Many problems may result from the same event.
3. People have varying degrees of access to the policy process in government.
4. Not all public problems are acted on in government.
5. Many private problems are acted on in government.
6. Many private problems are acted on in government as though they were public problems.
7. Most problems aren't solved by government though many are acted on there.
8. Policymakers are not faced with a *given* problem.
9. Most decision making is based on little information and poor communication.
10. Programs often reflect an attainable consensus rather than a substantive conviction.
11. Problems and demands are constantly being defined and redefined in the policy process.
12. Policymakers sometimes define problems for people who have not defined problems for themselves.
13. Many programs are developed and implemented without the problems ever having been clearly defined.
14. Most people do not maintain interest in other people's problems.
15. Most people do not prefer large change.
16. Most people cannot identify a public policy.
17. All policy systems have a bias.
18. No ideal policy system exists apart from the preferences of the architect of that system.
19. Most decision making is incremental in nature.

*Source: Randall B. Ripley and Grace A. Franklin, *Congress, the Bureaucracy, and Public Policy* rev. ed. (Homewood, Ill.: The Dorsey Press, 1980), p. 4.

ganizations, youth athletic associations, for example), the poor, and so on. Relations with these groups are crucial, and the International City Management Association advises top managers to seek answers to the following questions in order to facilitate community relations:

1. How can the important groups in my community be identified and their influence — for good or ill — be assessed?
2. How can I best solicit their help and support?
3. How can these partial special interests be encouraged to see and work for the betterment of the broad public interest?
4. Are there any groups that I am too closely identified with or too far removed from? How should I properly readjust and maintain these relationships to further the public interest as a whole?[17]

For top managers in local governments, most of their time is spent interacting with these groups and key elected officials. A typical day's schedule of such a manager is depicted in Box 2.5.

This discussion shows that administrators are involved with a great deal of political activity. We should point out that these activities are of a particular type. The feedlot owner and the local administrators see the political world through organizations. An important question to ask is this: Are organizations an adequate substitute for personal involvement in politics? This aspect of the organizational society allows people to go about their jobs with few demands on their time for politics, but this may be a heavy cost. It may, for example, keep us from facing central political conflicts in our society by having bureaucracies administer to the poor, the jobless, the aged, and so on.[18]

Administrative Policy-Making

Bureaucracies play an important role in making policy decisions.[19] For the most powerful and wealthy groups, such as the banking community, administrative agencies provide a direct conduit to government power. (See the description of the Federal Reserve System in Chapter 1.) For citizens in lower classes, administrative agencies may be less directly responsive, but they are often established to provide at least a symbolic presence in policy-making. In this section we will describe the sources of bureaucratic power and the way agencies get involved in policy-making.

Although elected officials have the constitutional authority to make policy, officials in bureaucracies have powerful resources with which to influence policy. The most important is their expertise. Elected officials cannot be well versed in every matter before a legislature. They even have trouble knowing enough about one or two areas of particular concern to them. Moreover, elected officials do not have the time to devote to detailed study of many subjects. They turn to people in their own offices and in

BOX 2.5 A Local Public Manager's Agenda for a Day*

8:00 a.m.	Arrives at work to polish off leftover paperwork/dictation from yesterday.
9:15 a.m.	Meets with mayor to review next week's council agenda prior to its publication.
10:00 a.m.	Local business group offers ideas on newly proposed industrial park on east side.
10:45 a.m.	City engineer and city treasurer join group to brief them on construction/financial details of site development.
11:30 a.m.	Police chief and personnel officer review a pending grievance against the department by a member of the city employees' union.
12:15 p.m.	Leaves ten minutes late for luncheon speech at League of Women Voters' monthly meeting to urge their help with the water bond campaign.
1:30 p.m.	Back again for more discussion with the police chief on same topic discussed in the morning.
2:15 p.m.	Rides with public works director to inspect north side residents' complaints of "smells" from nearby city dump — mentally drafts responses to their council members and neighborhood group on return to office.
3:15 p.m.	Returns stack-up of phone calls at office.
3:45 p.m.	Talks with local newspaper reporter about the importance to the city of next month's special water bond vote.
4:10 p.m.	Free time that was scheduled to review several pending budget items is interrupted by visit from two council members.
5:20 p.m.	Goes home for dinner.
7:10 p.m.	Leaves to attend meeting of south side citizen association, a predominately poor black group that the manager wants to involve more closely in community public housing planning.
11:00 p.m.	Home to bed at last!

*Source: International City Management Association, *The Effective Local Government Manager* (Washington, D.C.: ICMA, 1983), p. 35.

administrative agencies for advice. Often the advice includes drafting of legislation.

Elected officials also have little time or expertise in administrative matters. The implementation of policy is just as important as its enunciation, but that is often left entirely to bureaucracies. If an elected official seeks to redirect government policy, the available options are limited. Indeed, the existing agencies represent the range of available options, unless new offices or cancellations of programs are attractive alternatives.

Agencies are particularly influential when the expertise of their members is of critical use to society. Scientists, physicians, and military officers are obvious examples. The lay public, and most elected officials, rarely master these very technical areas. Some of these technical professions are highly respected, particularly when they contribute to spectacular achievements such as putting people on the moon or finding a cure for disease.

The expertise of administrative officials is recognized in the duties assigned to bureaucracies. Legislation is often vague, and the details are assigned to administrative agencies. This applies to both critical decisions, such as establishing the criteria by which the Federal Communications Commission (FCC) decides how many television or radio stations are permitted in an area, and routine decisions, such as awarding government contracts, applying agency rules to individual cases, and so on.

Some policy areas offer administrative agencies particularly wide discretion. The Central Intelligence Agency (CIA), for example, plans and carries out military operations without the knowledge of Congress, and if its director is to be believed, without the knowledge of the president. During President Reagan's first term the CIA organized an operation to mine harbors in Nicaragua, without first telling the Congress. The president apparently did not know the details of the operation. At first the CIA director insisted before a congressional committee that the CIA was not involved in the operation. Later he "changed his testimony" and was asked to sign an agreement promising to give "timely notice" of future significant operations. In Reagan's second term, the CIA was again involved in operations objectionable to Congress, its director again denied CIA participation before a congressional committee, and then "changed his testimony." It turned out that the CIA had been involved with illegally funding military operations in Central America for nine months, but did not feel the "timely notice" provision of the earlier agreement required them to tell the Congress, and the president swore he did not know it was going on. Although the example is extreme, this shows an agency can have extensive discretion over its actions.

Local police officials also exercise a great deal of discretion. It is not outlandish to claim that a police officer could not get more than a mile from the station in a day's shift if all traffic laws were precisely enforced. They must decide which rules to enforce and which not to enforce. As an example of the power this discretion may have over policy, police in one New Jersey town ticketed illegally parked cars in what they claimed was "only enforcing existing laws." All members of the city council received tickets; it turned out the police were dissatisfied with their salaries and vigorously enforced parking rules while city council meetings were in session. The action did result in larger-than-usual salary increases for the police officers.

Administrative officials need to add something else to their use of expertise and discretion in order to affect policy — they have to mobilize public support for their policy positions. Interest groups are important, since a group that supports an agency's work will communicate that support to legislators. The general public is less important. It is inattentive to the more detailed concerns of agencies. A bureaucracy's clientele, the people who receive its services, are its natural constituency. The Environmental Protection Agency (EPA), for example, is watched closely and vigorously supported by many environmental and some industry groups. The State Department, on the other hand, serves few citizens directly and must instead try to influence general public opinion.

An agency lacking a clearly organized constituency can organize one. The Department of Agriculture helped to organize the American Farm Bureau Federation, one of the most powerful agricultural interest groups. Local school administrators are often instrumental in organizing parent-teacher associations and school parents' organizations. The support cuts two ways, however. The Labor Department is widely regarded as being a political "captive" of organized labor. It is not very influential in times when the fortunes of organized labor decline, such as in the late 1970s and the 1980s.

It is fair to say that these ties between groups and administrative agencies are another form of representation in government. The elected officials represent geographic groupings of citizens, whereas agency representation is based on a citizen's role in the economy and membership in groups based on those roles. This means that politics and administration are closely connected in the United States, but they are connected in a way that is open to organizations, not individuals.

Administrative officials who want to be influential in policy will need excellent working relationships with legislators. Agencies live and die by legislation. Law is fundamental to the authority and actions of administrative agencies, and yearly appropriations establish how much money an agency may spend. In this sense the best friend, and the worst enemy, an agency can have is the chair of the relevant committees in Congress. The agency can have no better lobbyist when budgets and legislation are being considered. The agency can then deliver important services to the constituents of the legislators, give contracts to companies in particular legislative districts, and so on.

The "public" of administrative agencies also includes other executive branch bureaucracies. Good relations with a budget office are highly desirable, since the budget office exercises its own expertise and discretion and may advise elected officials to continue, cut, or increase an agency's budget. Some agencies are simply better at wielding administrative power than others. City utilities departments, for example, are often virtually autonomous, defying central administrative attempts to control their budgets and activities. This is usually because the administrators in those departments develop their own procedures that are difficult for outsiders to understand, a deliberate attempt to defy administrative oversight.

Relations with other administrative agencies depend a great deal on the degree of overlap between responsibilities of agencies. For example, who gathers intelligence for foreign policy considerations? There are separate, powerful intelligence agencies in the Army, the Navy, the CIA, the State Department, and the Defense Department. The intelligence-gathering offices of the State Department are almost constantly under criticism from legislators who believe other agencies do (or could do) a better job.

This discussion of the sources of bureaucratic influence on policy suggests that agencies are different political actors than people. When agencies are involved in policy-making, the decision processes are highly hierarchical, professionals are much more influential than ordinary citizens, and important decisions are often made in secret. This may be politics, but it should not be mistaken for an open, public-oriented approach to democracy.

Waves and Fads: The Constantly Changing Opinions

Within the broad themes we have just described, the practice of public administration changes from generation to generation. Affected by both politics and the reflections of public administrators, actions and ideas come and go in waves and fads. Certainly, the political culture of the 1960s had a dramatic effect on public administration. The changes cut both ways. First and most obviously, there were the civil rights and antiwar movements. No longer could the old-style, top-down type of administration be accepted as adequate. The flow of command, legitimate and legal, from top to bottom, was challenged by people who fought racial discrimination and the war in Vietnam.

Much of our culture seemed to loosen up during those times. People in our society who had been systematically discriminated against or simply ignored, the minorities, the underprivileged, women, made their cases forcefully that changes must be made. Laws were passed and agencies were created in order to administer justice. Grass-roots attempts were begun to change the way things were done. Social legislation was passed, and administrators were hired to do everything from giving children a needed head start to retraining people who needed jobs. People were sent into communities to help rebuild neighborhoods.

One of the interesting aspects of this challenge to authority is that the number of agencies increased to meet the demands being made on the government. In a strange way, the problem and the solution seemed to be the same thing: government administration was the focus of what was wrong and what was right. Those in government felt damned if they did and damned if they didn't.

By the 1970s, another series of changes began. The country seemed to be in a dual slump. First, the economy was in what was known as the Great Recession. Economic growth had stopped, and inflation increased rapidly. Second, faith in the government was not high. Richard Nixon convinced few people that he was not guilty of criminal activity, and Jimmy Carter convinced few more that he could handle the important domestic issues dominating the news. Furthermore, we could not convince Iran to give us back the fifty-two hostages held for more than a year.

In that atmosphere, administration retreated. Politicians who claimed that government programs were wrong — and partly to blame — were elected to office, and they did not ask administrators to take the lead in finding new solutions. Social programs were no longer popular, and resisting authority gave way to trying to make do in depressing times. One interesting issue that emerged during this period had to do with the air we breathed and the food we ate — the good earth itself. The EPA was set up to protect us from poisoning ourselves.

With the EPA we have a familiar American theme come into play — science, and its relationship to both democracy and administration. For example, science can tell us what automobile exhaust can do to the environment and to each of us. Yet, any economist can tell us just how necessary the automobile industry is to the economic strength of the country, and any citizen can tell us about the freedom his or her car represents. Science, then, is just one more variable in the politics of this public agency (see Box 2.6). There is little question that science is a powerful tool; yet, we have no clear notion where that tool belongs when it comes to public administration. The standards of science are not the standards of democracy, yet many governmental decisions involve scientific issues. This is another example of how we lack a clear sense of how the public fits in with administration.

The fact is that political taste has everything to do with public administration. For example, in times of serious ecological lobbying, off-shore drilling for oil was halted. In more recent times, the drilling has been resumed. Also, in the early days of nuclear reactors there was a rush to build them. Currently, almost all new construction has stopped.

It is clear that the direction of administration depends a great deal on the particular kind of person elected president. Ronald Reagan's election and reelection brought people into government who wanted to cut back

BOX 2.6 The Politics of Reaching a Scientific Decision

The ASARCO Corporation operated a copper smelter in Tacoma, Washington. The smelter was an old employer in the city, and even formed its own city around the plant to provide municipal services to employees. The technology of the plant was outdated, and the only way it was able to turn a small profit was by smelting high-arsenic copper ore and selling the arsenic as a by-product.

The arsenic also went into the air and water of the surrounding communities. Many smelter workers had arsenic blood levels well above toxic levels (although the body establishes a tolerance to arsenic, so that gradual increases in the level of exposure are usually not toxic to an individual), and children on Vashon Island, across a stretch of Puget Sound, had arsenic levels well above federal limits.

Each year ASARCO was notified by the Environmental Protection Agency (EPA) that its arsenic emissions were above permissible levels. Each year ASARCO applied for a variance from the standards, and as a result of pressure from the local community and Congress, the variances were granted. Each year the company successfully argued that no studies demonstrated a tie between the emissions and health problems. During the late 1970s and the early 1980s, the debate heated up to the point where environmentalists were demanding the plant be closed, and ASARCO was threatening to leave. Finally, a law passed the Congress requiring the EPA to set a clear standard of emissions, based on scientific evidence concerning health effects, opinions of the area's citizens, and economic effects on the community. The EPA was given a deadline for establishing the standards.

EPA director William Ruckleshaus, a native of the Northwest, found the deadline disconcerting. Public opinion and scientific findings were difficult enough to blend, and the Congress expected it to be done on a very tight schedule. According to the scientists, there was simply not enough time to produce a definitive study. According to the political groups interested in the issue, it would take even longer to reach a compromise.

The EPA was able to do some studies and construct mathematical models of the dispersion and effects of arsenic. The studies were heavily criticized by ASARCO officials. Next the EPA scheduled a series of public meetings to explain their findings to the public and ask for citizen input into the proper trade-offs between public health and the strength of the economy. Very few people showed up at the meetings, and EPA officials expressed their dismay.

Two years after the legislation had passed, ASARCO announced they were closing the Tacoma smelter. They blamed the closure on cumbersome government regulations and began shipping the ore to a smelter in Japan.

FIGURE 2.2 The 1980s' "Supply-Side" View of Bureaucracy

	Supply-Side (1980s)	Demand-Side (pre-1980s)
Size of Bureaucracy	Sharply reduced	Expanded to meet public/special interest needs
Federal Role	Sharply restricted and expanded state/local roles	Feds take lead in most policy fields
Regulation of Business	As much deregulation as possible to free up business	Strong public sector role in private sector on behalf of consumers and citizens
Source of Policy Direction	Top-down — from chief executive — with centralized controls	Bottom-up — from legislative and special interest groups
Operational Emphasis	Operating functions with "bottom line results"	Emphasis upon staff functions (planning, policy analysis, data collection, etc.) and critical of business practices
Key Personnel Staff	Reliance on temporary appointees drawn from business or "new-right" supply-siders	Career professionals committed to the public interest and application of expertise to public problems
Agency Policy Development and Management Approach	Tolerant of risk-taking, entrepreneurship, contracting-out for public services, and voluntary approaches	Emphasis upon consensus building, conciliation, "muddling-through" coupled with professionalism, planning, analysis, evaluation, etc.
Political/Administrative Relationships	Sharp split in roles of political policy making and careerist administrators	Cooperative relationships between political appointees and careerists
Reliance upon Ideology for Governance of Bureaucracy	Heavy reliance on supply-side theory and economic methodology	Little or none — pragmatic orientation most often used
Ideal Public Bureaucrat	David Stockman, Reagan's 1st OMB director	David E. Lilienthal, builder of TVA

Source: Richard J. Stillman II, *The American Bureaucracy* (Chicago, Nelson-Hall, Inc., 1987), pp. 259–260.

the federal administration, and to privatize much of public administration. Although he was in part successful (major cuts occurred in aid to state and local governments, and in federal grants in such areas as energy, health care, and education, which are referred to as federal discretionary spending), it is interesting to note that the federal budget continues to grow. (Figures are given in Chapter 12.)

All of this is a long way of saying that *within* our liberal political and constitutional context, we can expect variations on our basic administrative themes. Indeed, in times of great tensions there may even be some significant change. But, in the final analysis, we stay pretty much within the boundaries of what we know as business as usual. The liberals in the 1960s increased the administration of social services; the conservatives of the 1980s increased the administration of our national defense.

Academics

The context of public administration includes those who write about it. To put it differently, those who control the definition of public administration have a certain amount of power over the field itself. We can expect that as "worldly" changes occur, so too will academic explanations. The academic world provides spokespeople for almost any imaginable position, and academics are often called upon to serve those who seek power.

As we shall see in the next two chapters, there are serious disagreements about the proper role and scope of administration in a democracy. The range of opinion is from those who favor a strict bureaucratic structure,[20] following the idea that elected officials make policy and bureaucracies implement policy; to the not-quite-so-strict structure,[21] such as those described in our chapter on organization psychology; to a politicized structure,[22] where advocates say administration should be guided by regular personal contact with citizens; to a private structure,[23] whose advocates claim the private sector can do nearly any job better than government; to a scientific structure,[24] based on the idea that most important questions are technical, rather than political; to no structure at all,[25] a position described by philosophical anarchists. Opinions are strongly divided on how to learn about public administration.[26] These matters of theory are important — how an individual finally thinks about something has a direct effect on how that individual acts.

These variations of positions are meaningful to academics. In many ways, it defines their politics, their brand of social science, their position in the field of public administration, and their friends. As we have seen, how we think about public administration, that is, what we believe is the proper role of our public organizations, forms one of the most important contexts of public administration. The very acts of studying public administration and making decisions on how to view it become the basis of future actions.

BOX 2.7 "Privatization" and Public Administration

In the early 1980s the idea of "privatization" became politically popular. Partly a response to tight budgets, its core idea is that the "private sector" can better handle many of the responsibilities now shouldered by government.

Privatization comes in many forms. One popular scheme is to have profit-making companies provide public services on a contractual basis. A private garbage carrier, for instance, may be able to do the job with a smaller, nonunion payroll and save the taxpayers money, and cost the jobs of many public workers.

Education vouchers are another form of privatization. Each citizen would pay taxes and receive a certificate good for education. The certificates could be "spent" at either public or private schools. Some versions of the plan even enable people without children (as well as parents) to sell the vouchers. The argument is that consumers have something more akin to a market choice as to the type and quality of education for their children. There are even serious debates about private prison systems (where the state hands convicted felons over to a corporation for incarceration).

One perplexing part of privatization is that the private sector also includes the not-for-profit organizations currently delivering about half of the nonincome assistance human services in America. Most schemes for privatization seek to have something like a market, with money changing hands between vendors and consumers, take place. Yet the not-for-profit sector exists mainly because the goods they provide go to people who cannot make economic demands. These organizations are at the receiving end of many intergovernmental programs, and cutbacks during the Reagan administration cut their budgets by over 20 percent.

Privatization seems to mean two things, then. At first look it is a way to save money, mainly by having nongovernmental organizations work on certain public purposes. The savings, if any, would usually come in the form of lower-paid workers, smaller public work forces, and in some cases diminished administrative overhead. Public administrators rightly see this movement as an attack on their profession.

Privatization can also mean new forms of organizations and new forms of cooperation among levels of government and organizations in communities, some of which may operate for profit. But in this second sense, privatization is a misleading word. What it really should mean is publicization, finding ways to define and perform public services closer to the public. As the 1980s show, public debates over public purposes are not very adept at sorting out what is properly public and what is properly private. A public administration has not emerged from the debate.

SUMMARY

In this chapter, we began to explore the political context of public administration in the United States. Liberalism is the broadest level of generalization. We reviewed those principles, such as individualism, capitalism, and personal freedoms, which we rarely discuss simply because we consider them "givens" in our society.

The next level is the constitutional arrangement of our government. There, we saw how power is separated and divided, and how this reaches deeply into the workings of day-to-day administrative issues. Federalism is another core constitutional principle in America, and we offered views of federalism from the top and the bottom of the system. These combine to produce a number of administrations and to serve different public (and often private) groups. To put it in a little different way, public administrations may have different interests and may fight among themselves.

Getting more specific about the political context of administration, we then mentioned the political relationships surrounding public agencies. Other parts of government, interest groups, and citizens weigh heavily in the concerns of public administrators.

Finally, we looked at the changing waves and opinions that affect the conduct of public administration. The ideas of the time do affect the way government operates.

Two important issues are suggested in this overview of political context. The first is not terribly obvious, but needs to be mentioned. As we noted earlier, one way of defining public administration has to do with people coming together, deciding to do things, and having an administration execute the public's business. In this chapter, we saw that millions of people are doing the public's business, and that there are many forms and relationships in which they perform this business.

The question is *not*: Are these people doing a good job? It is right to assume that most of our public administrators, most of the time, are doing well. The question, instead, is this: Are huge public administrations the best way to do what needs to be done? The dynamic is a familiar one. Beginning with the basic separation of powers, we have the Congress pass laws and the president administer them. Most laws imply administration. However, if we took politics and the division of power more seriously, would it not be possible to decentralize to the point of having decision making given back to citizens and have today's administration limited to those things less public in scope? For example, certain aspects of national defense may not work best if totally decentralized. The idea of having North Dakotans or Montanans govern the missiles beneath their prairies may unsettle foreign governments and New Yorkers. Yet, it is entirely possible to decentralize many aspects of national defense, as well as public housing and welfare programs in which recipients would get together and decide how the money would be divided and used.

We are not at all suggesting that public administration be done away with or handed over to private enterprise. We are asking whether we have good answers to the big questions. What we are questioning is the set of ideas that leads us to the point where laws are written and passed that *need* to be administered. We are asking if citizens could again become an active part of the governing and decision-making process.

The second issue may be the strangest problem of all. It seems as if administration in general, and public administration in particular, has become a part of its own context. Our lives are filled with activities of the government. There is surprisingly little that we do that is not regulated by one or more of our governing bodies. The sense that we are so regulated and administered reflects on the regulators and administrators, no matter how well they perform their jobs. Public administration is, in many ways, creating a big part of its own environment. The environment, to put it another way, is shaping itself to the demands of administration.

As we saw in Chapter 1, the root meanings of the words public and administration seem to be at odds. Where public is open, administration is closed, and so on. In this chapter, we began to see that the political and cultural setting of the United States helped support that split. The nature of our liberalism contains mixed messages about government and individualism. We can speculate that the split between public and administration is one we need to know about because it is ingrained in our political lives.

Later, when we study organization theory, we can see this dynamic more clearly. For now it is enough to say that when Dwight Waldo asks us to speculate about the relationship of public administration to its current culture, he is asking an important and difficult question.

NOTES

1. Dwight Waldo, "The Administrative State Revisited," reprint no. 12 (Berkeley, Calif.: Institute of Governmental Studies, 1965), p. 23.
2. The important work by John Locke is his *Second Treatise of Government* (many editions available). In it, he imagines the beginnings of the liberal state coming from an *almost* perfect state of nature. Our greed is its chief defect. In Thomas Hobbes' *Leviathan* (many editions available) he imagines the beginnings of the liberal state coming from a state of nature in which the life of a person was "nasty, brutish, and short." Each of these early English liberals was reacting against feudal society. There is legitimate debate about who we are most like: Hobbes or Locke. A thorough discussion on the power of liberalism

in America is made in Louis Hartz, *The Liberal Tradition in America* (New York: Harcourt, Brace and World, 1955).

3. This can be seen in Adam Smith's *Wealth of Nations*, written in 1776. More recent versions of the ideas are available in William E. Simon, *A Time for Truth* (New York: McGraw-Hill, 1978); and George Gilder, *Wealth and Poverty* (New York: Basic Books, 1981).

4. On the origins of capitalism, see Karl Polanyi, *The Great Transformation* (Boston: Beacon Press, 1957).

5. There has been a lively debate over the importance of economic concentration in America. See John Kenneth Galbraith, *The New Industrial State* (Boston: Houghton Mifflin, 1967); James Barber, *The American Corporation* (1971); and Thomas Dye, *Who's Running America?* (Boston: Duxbury Press, 1976).

6. See Herbert Kaufman, *Red Tape: Its Origins, Uses, and Abuses* (Washington, D.C.: Brookings Institution, 1977).

7. Marshall Dimock, *Law and Dynamic Administration* (New York: Praeger, 1980), p. 8.

8. This evidence is summarized in Charles T. Goodsell, *The Case for Bureaucracy*, 2nd ed. (Chatham, N.J.: Chatham House, 1985).

9. The point invites controversy. Those who say the Articles "failed" are in the majority, yet the belief was not widely shared among the last government under the Articles; the Framers were sent to fix the Articles, not to do away with them. See Merrill Jensen, *The New Nation* (New York: Alfred J. Knopf, 1962); and Jackson T. Main, *The Antifederalists* (Chapel Hill: University of North Carolina Press, 1961).

10. See Martin Diamond, *What the Framers Meant by Federalism*, in Robert A. Goldwin, ed., *A Nation of States* (Chicago: Rand McNally, 1974), pp. 25–41; and also in Laurence J. O'Toole, *American Intergovernmental Relations* (Washington, D.C.: Congressional Quarterly Press, 1985), pp. 28–35.

11. See the Constitution, Article I, Sec. 8, particularly the last line of Sec. 8. This section also includes the "commerce" clause. See the Tenth and Fourteenth Amendments to the Constitution. See also *McCulloch v. Maryland* (1819), implying that in federalism disputes the national government is supreme — but remember it took a civil war to settle that issue, and issues of state power versus national supremacy are still being debated.

12. U.S. Advisory Commission on Intergovernmental Relations, *An Agenda for American Federalism* (Washington, D.C.: ACIR, 1981), pp. 104–6.

13. This section relies on The International City Management Associa-

tion (ICMA), *The Effective Local Government Manager* (Washington, D.C.: ICMA, 1983), pp. 180–192.
14. Ibid., p. 190.
15. The regular relationships among particular sets of interest groups, members of Congress, and members of the bureaucracy are often called "subgovernments." See Randall B. Ripley and Grace A Franklin, *Congress, the Bureaucracy, and Public Policy*, rev. ed. (Homewood, Ill.: The Dorsey, Press, 1980). On political relationships of bureaucracies, see Francis Rourke, *Bureaucracy, Politics, and Public Policy*, 3rd ed. (Boston: Little, Brown, 1984).
16. This section is based upon ICMA, op. cit., Chaps. 2 and 3.
17. Ibid., p. 42.
18. Gideon Sjoberg, Richard A. Brymer, and Buford Farris, "Bureaucracy and the Lower Class," in Francis E. Rourke, *Bureaucratic Power in National Policymaking*, 4th ed. (Boston: Little, Brown, 1986), pp. 293–306.
19. This section is based on Francis E. Rourke, *Bureaucracy, Politics, and Public Policy*, 3rd ed. (Boston: Little, Brown, 1984).
20. For an advocate of strict bureaucratic structure, see Donald J. Devine, "The Challenge To Federal Employees Today," *Labor Law Journal*, 3 (July 1981), pp. 387–394.
21. For descriptions of not-so-strict bureaucratic structures, see Warren Bennis, *Changing Organizations* (New York: McGraw-Hill, 1966); and Robert T. Golembiewski, *Renewing Organizations: The Laboratory Approach to Planned Change* (Itasca, Minn.: Peacock, 1972).
22. For advocates of a politicized structure, compare Michael M. Harmon, *Action Theory for Public Administration* (New York: Longman, 1981); and Vincent Ostrom, *The Intellectual Crisis in American Public Administration* (University, Ala.: University of Alabama Press, 1973).
23. A strong advocate of privatization is found in E. S. Savas, *Privatizing the Public Sector* (Chatham, N.J.: Chatham House, 1982). Useful conceptual clarification is found in Ted Kolderie, "The Two Different Concepts of Privatization," *Public Administration Review* 46 (July/August 1986), no. 4, pp. 285–291.
24. On science and organizations, see Charles G. Schoderbek, et al., *Management Systems*, rev. ed. (Dallas, Tex.: Business Publications, 1980), especially the discussion of "the manager-scientist symbiosis," pp. 285–288.
25. For a partisan overview, see Frederick C. Thayer, *An End to Hierarchy! An End to Competition! Organizing the Politics and Economics of Survival* (New York: Franklin Watts, 1973).

26. See the recent exchange between Howard E. McCurdy and Robert E. Cleary, "Why Can't We Resolve the Research Issue in Public Administration?" *Public Administration Review* 44 (January/February 1984), no. 1, pp. 49–55; and the response, Jay D. White, "On the Growth of Knowledge in Public Administration," *Public Administration Review* 46 (January/February 1986), no. 1, pp. 15–24.

CHAPTER THREE

Organization Theory

> Division of work and integrated organization
> are the bootstraps by which mankind lifts itself
> in the process of civilization.
>
> — *Luther Gulick*

One of the important points we want to make is that in order to understand the basis of how and what we think, it is important to study our past. When we study the roots of words or the history of ideas, we often see how certain things we take for granted came into being. To put it another way, we are able to see our biases in sharper focus.

In this chapter, we will do two things. First, we will go back into our intellectual past and review the public-administration split discussed in Chapter 1. Second, there will be a discussion of the twentieth-century beginnings of organization theory. Current practices have developed from earlier theory, and it is surprising how many of the earlier basic biases are still held. Although we certainly know more and different things than were known 50 years ago, it is often disconcerting when we realize how little the issues have changed.

Public/Administration

The public/administration split was most notably articulated by the American academic, college president, and later president of the United States, Woodrow Wilson. Writing during the last quarter of the last century, Wilson put his sense of public administration in the context of the times.

"Like a lusty child," he wrote, "government with us has expanded in nature and grown great in stature, but has also become awkward in movement. The vigor and increase of its life has been altogether out of proportion to its skill in living."[1]

This kind of expansion of both government and society called for "more careful administrative adjustments." One of the things of interest to us, and something that has much to do with our own thinking, is just what this administration meant to Wilson.

In the classic statement, Wilson wrote,

> The field of administration is the field of business. It is removed from the hurry and strife of politics. . . . It is part of political life only as the methods of the counting house are a part of the life of society; only as machinery is part of the manufactured product. . . . The object of administrative study is to rescue executive methods from the confusion and costliness of empirical experiment and set them upon foundations laid deep in stable principle.[2]

What we find here are two biases that have come to us almost untouched. The first concerns politics; somehow, we mistrust politics because it is full of "hurry and strife." Second, we have the desire to "set" our public administration (which is business) upon stable principle. As we know, stable principles came to be understood as scientific principles. Wilson was quite clear, "Administrative questions are not political questions. Although politics sets the tasks for administration, it should not be suffered to manipulate its offices. . . . This discrimination between administration and politics is now, happily, too obvious to need further discussion."[3]

It is important to stop for a moment and notice the *direction* of Wilson's thought. For Wilson, and in part because of the times in which he lived and wrote, it was common sense for him to protect the public administration from politics. Given the perspective of our truly big government today, the administration of the various governments in this country when Wilson wrote was neither large nor powerful. It would have been an act of great speculation for him to have written about protecting the political process from the administrative process. However, this is just what we may be coming to in our age.

It was Wilson's wish that the "neutral" bureaucracy be allowed to perform its business. To quote: "Bureaucracy can exist only where the whole service of the state is removed from the common political life of the people, its chief as well as its rank and file. Its motives, its objectives, its policy, its standards, must be bureaucratic."[4]

Although it would be wrong to believe that Wilson wanted to create a huge bureaucracy of what we now stereotype as "bureaucrats," what he did want to create seems unrealistic (see also Box 3.1):

> The ideal for us is a civil service cultured and self-sufficient enough to act with sense and vigor, and yet so intimately connected with the popular thought, by means of elections and constant public counsel, as to find arbitrariness or class spirit quite

> **BOX 3.1 The New Wilsonians**
>
> An interesting form of the Wilsonian dichotomy has come to us in the form of "The Blacksburg Manifesto." This collection of ideas illustrates an important shift in public administration since the time of Wilson. The change has come in the role of public bureaucracy, and has taken on the tasks of what was once seen as the role of government.
>
> The Public Administration, according to the manifesto, must be viewed as a social asset instead of a liability. Indeed, those in the public bureaucracy are in an enviable position to judge the public interest and the constitutionality of a policy program. It is argued that "agencies are repositories, and their staffs are trustees of, specialized knowledge, historical experience, time-tested wisdom, and most importantly, some degree of consensus as to the public interest relevant to particular societal function."
>
> The task of the Public Administration now becomes "to share in governing wisely and well in the Constitutional order."
>
> The argument is fully developed in John A. Rohr, *To Run a Constitution: The Legitimacy of the Administrative State* (Lawrence, Kan.: University Press of Kansas, 1986).

out of the question. . . . The problem is to make public opinion efficient without suffering it to be meddlesome.[5]

To follow the thought of Woodrow Wilson is to begin to understand many of our own biases. He clearly articulated just how public and administration might be separated. Indeed, it was his sense that administration (bureaucracy) needed to be "removed" from the "common political life of the people." As we know, the results of that "removal" can be very mixed. To remove the public is certainly one way to eliminate the tension implied in public/administration. Given the cultural context of liberalism and democracy, it is safe to assume that to take away the public would have a profound effect on the way we live. Without the public, our governmental organizations would be closed to us. They would be less and less responsive to our needs and more demanding of our resources.

To begin to address these questions we must turn to organization theory, the group of theories about what bureaucracy might look like in isolation, and what effect these theories may have on their environment.

Max Weber (Administration)

Max Weber died in 1920, but there are many ways in which today's organization theorists have yet to catch up with Weber's insights. His ideas about bureaucracy, and the effects of bureaucracy on society, have set the course of the field in which we work. Max Weber, among his other intellectual work, has supplied us with the foundation of modern organization thought.

Sadly, Weber had a difficult life. Born to a religious, humanitarian, self-denying mother, and a harsh, strict, firm, self-righteous, authoritarian father, the young Weber grew up amidst a psychic war. He lived at home until he was twenty-nine. Weber was described as "Immensely hard working, impeccably honest, dedicated, serious, methodical, he drove himself with an inner vehemence that left him an insomniac for years and dead at the age of fifty-six."[6] He was hospitalized several times for psychological problems.

Weber's past is highly suggestive, which is exactly the reason we mentioned it.[7] There is a place in social science for the study of the relationship of an individual personality and the world he or she perceives and analyzes. Certainly the tensions Weber was brought up with can be seen repeated in his work.

In order to best understand Weber's work on bureaucracy it is necessary to step back for a moment and see what he understood as existing prior to social organization. One of the central focuses in Weber's thought was the idea that the legitimacy of the state was based on authority. He reasoned that if we could understand authority it would be possible to trace, in a broad sense, what motivated people — and see more clearly how and why they acted and organized the way they did. According to Weber, there were three types of authority: traditional, charismatic, and legal-rational. Each type represented a distinct way of relating to and then ordering the world. Each had a special style and dynamic that dominated its cultural setting. It will be helpful to get a sense of Weber's three types of authority.

A royal family, a matriarchy, and a patriarchy are examples of authority based on tradition. A tribal leader or a queen would be chosen by traditional methods. There is a sense of history and the past that is a dynamic part of such a society and that informs much of how society is organized. We have less and less of this type of authority as the world becomes "modernized."

Charismatic authority comes from people's perceptions of the personal strength, magnetism, or aura in a single individual. Prophets and heroes are the most obvious types of charismatic leaders. There can be a range of what we mean by charismatic leaders. In our century, for example, many people found John Kennedy charismatic. He had a flair, an energy, possibly even a vision that people wanted to follow. A sense of urgency arose that the world might become a better place. Also charismatic, but in our view monstrous, was Adolf Hitler. What we need to know is that charismatic authority has the potential of breaking traditional authority apart.

Purely charismatic leaders have a small group of advisers and a large, unorganized following, each follower feeling personally beloved by the leader. As in the case of traditional authority, charismatic authority is vulnerable to modernization (or, in Weber's terms, legal-rational bureaucracy). Weber was able to show us that a charismatic leader may actually set up a bureaucratic structure and may, ironically, be progressively ruled by that structure.

The third type of authority is the legal-rational. It is the one we are most familiar with and dominates the modern world. Legal-rational authority can be thought of most easily as a closed system of regulations and a hierarchy of roles that combine into what we can recognize as a bureaucracy. Unlike the other two kinds of authority, in this arrangement modern loyalty is devoted to impersonal and functional purposes. It should be no surprise that process is so central to most discussions of organizations. Indeed, the focus on process goes beyond organizations because "Behind the functional purposes, of course, 'ideas of cultural values' usually stand." A bureaucracy has "impersonal and functional purpose."[8]

Weber imagined an *ideal* bureaucracy that can never exist; it provided a way for him to describe the essences of an actual bureaucratic structure. It is important to keep in mind that Weber never believed that the ideal could be achieved. It might be better to think of it as an idealized bureaucracy. For it to exist, the nature of human beings would have to change, and the world in which we live would have to cease changing. Neither of these things is going to happen. Weber did not want an ideal bureaucracy to exist. In an essay "Politics as a Vocation," he explained the dangers of a bureaucratized world.

The use of an ideal form is an effective way of explaining the dynamics of a structure. What follows are the key elements of a bureaucracy:

1. There is a division of labor and there is functional specialization. Labor is divided by skills and authority, and the responsibility of each position is defined by law and administrative regulation.
2. Each position, each job and each office, is independent of its occupant. The job is permanent and may be filled by any number of different individuals. There are two important outcomes of this. First, the ongoing nature of the bureaucracy is important and, second, human labor must become interchangeable.
3. Authority becomes more centralized and hierarchical. There is a clear-cut vertical chain of command. At each stage in the organization

there are superiors and subordinates. As one goes up the authority scale, there is great status, power, pay, and more subordinates. The ideal-typical bureaucracy is shaped like a pyramid.

4. The bureaucracy is structured by rules and procedures. General rules help ensure against acts of personal discretion and help promote predictability and impersonality both in internal affairs and when dealing with the general public. All employees act in accordance with the legal definitions of their jobs.
5. For the sake of organizational continuity, there is the maintenance of files and other records. Red tape, to put it in an ungenerous way, is the life-blood of bureaucracy.

This ideal-typical bureaucracy, which represents so much of how we have come to visualize organizations in the modern world, is not value-neutral. "The decisive reason for the advance of bureaucratic organization," writes Weber, "has always been its purely technical superiority over any other form or organization. The fully developed bureaucratic mechanism compares with other organizations exactly as does the machine with nonmechanical modes of production."[9]

The bias is clear: The rationally conceived (i.e., the most efficient) bureaucracy is superior. As we shall see later in our review of more current organization theory, data do not support Weber's claim. Also, for our purposes it is important to note that a bureaucratic structure has almost everything to do with administration and very little to do with the public. In spite of this and the possible elimination of the public, there are those who still believe that a well-running bureaucratic organization is the superior way to organize (see Box 3.2).

When we introduced Weber, we mentioned that certain kinds of authority have effects that permeate society. Let us follow this thought through legal-rational authority. According to Weber, bureaucracy appeals to the "settled orientation of man for keeping to the habitual rules and regulations that continue to exist independently of documents."[10] This "settled orientation" is a particularly interesting benefit, given Thomas Hobbes' liberal notion of how hostile and unpredictable people can be. According to Weber, one of the effects of bureaucracy is its ability to help make life's relations conform, to a great degree, to knowable patterns.

But it is here, somewhere in this settled orientation and knowable patterns, that the bureaucratic dynamic takes over.

> Once it is fully established, bureaucracy is among those social structures which are hardest to destroy. Bureaucracy is *the* means of carrying "community action" over into rationally ordered "societal action." Therefore, as an instrument for "socializing" rela-

> **BOX 3.2** Hierarchy and Professionals
>
> It is not unusual for an organization to solve its problems by instituting fairly standard, top-down, bureaucratic structure on its members. An interesting example is what happened to the air-traffic controllers.
>
> The controllers are professional people who are highly trained to make on-the-spot, second-to-second decisions without having to consult with a supervisor. In 1981, the controllers went out on strike. One of their central complaints was that new technology, technology to make their work more effective and less stressful, was not adopted by their employer, the Federal Aviation Administration (FAA). The FAA, they charged, would rather keep traditional control over employees than adopt technology that would make the skies safer but result in less control for FAA officials. In the end, we found the charges were true. (See Box 10.3 and Box 13.4).
>
> President Ronald Reagan fired those air-traffic controllers who went out on strike. A new generation of controllers had to be trained and hired. One of the results was that during the first six months of 1985, the FAA reported 54 incidents in which planes maneuvered on runways and taxiways in such a way as to end up in hazardous situations. That was a 31.6 percent increase over such incidents the year before.
>
> The response of the controllers' boss, Donald Engen, was predictable. First, by a special telephone setup he said that there should be better communications between controllers, aircraft, and so on. Second, he assigned a supervisor to routinely assist the controller, during busy periods, "to provide an extra set of eyes."
>
> Put differently, hierarchy returned to America's air-traffic control towers.

tions of power, bureaucracy has been and is a power instrument of the first order.[11]

What Weber suggests, and what seems to be an accurate assessment of the dynamic, is something like this: As a bureaucracy grows and becomes more powerful, it turns on the society that created it and reorders that society.[12] The society is reordered into the categories of stability and rationality, something a bureaucratic structure can most easily deal with. In our context, administration would try hard to push the sloppiness of the public out of existence.

Max Weber (Politics)

If one simply read Weber on bureaucracy, it would be easy to assume that the ideal-typical bureaucracy was his ideal for the way a government should organize. But buried in that essay, Weber plants the seed of doubt about bureaucracy. He writes,

> Under normal conditions, the power position of a fully developed bureaucracy is always over-powering. The "political master" finds himself in the position of the "dilettante" who stands opposite the "expert." . . . Every bureaucracy seeks to increase the superiority of the professionally informed by keeping their knowledge and intentions discrete.[13]

What is suggested is that there is an ongoing tension between the bureaucracy and politics. Each operates according to a different dynamic, and the conflict is continuous.

In a remarkable essay titled "Politics as a Vocation," Weber indicates his preference for politics.[14] The first, and most obvious, difference between Weber's essay on bureaucracy and his essay on politics is language. Although it was possible for him to describe an ideal bureaucracy in precise detail, it was not possible for him to do that for politics. There is a rational structure to a bureaucracy, but politics can only be described in surprisingly passionate (and, it follows, imprecise) language.

The differences between the two are great: A bureaucrat is permanent, the politician is temporary; the bureaucrat administers from a closed set of rules, the politician is a leader open to ever-changing pressures and needs. "To take a stand, to be passionate . . . is the politician's element. . . . The honor of the political leader, of the leading statesman . . . lies precisely in an exclusive *personal* responsibility for what he does, a responsibility he cannot and must not reject or transfer."[15] Weber continues to describe political activities with such words as faith, courage, and honor.

One need only go back and review the traits of a bureaucracy — the impersonality, administrative rules, records and files, functional specialization, settled orientation, and so on — to see how different Weber believed it was from politics. It is a tension we cannot ignore.

Frederick Winslow Taylor

For most people, it is difficult to read *The Principles of Scientific Management* by Frederick Winslow Taylor. Not only does it read like a crude way to make a profit, it also taps into some deep sense inside us to which we choose not to admit. Taylor's aims of efficiency, productivity, rationality, and profit are not unknown to our contemporary organization thinkers. In part because Taylor was the first to present these aims as a whole dynamic, much of what he says seems heavy-handed. But, there is much to be learned from him.

It is important to know a little about the time in which he worked. Taylor was born in 1856 and died in 1915. During that time, great and hard changes took place in the United States. The West was opening, the Civil War was fought, there was a constantly expanding economy and mechanization of industry, there were almost limitless natural resources, and huge fortunes were made. Also, labor was abused by management, labor unions were coming into existence, there were terrible depressions, and labor-management disputes were the bloodiest in our history. Society seemed on the brink of a class war.

It was in this environment that Taylor did his thinking and working. His social concern was to bring harmony to the people, and his method of revolution was his plan of scientific management. This should not be read as a foolish, idle dream. Taylor was a dead-serious revolutionary; he wanted a mental revolution, a revolution of the spirit. He believed that if all people accepted his system the antagonisms would stop and social solidarity and world peace would naturally follow.

The Congress of the United States took him seriously enough to investigate him. It is interesting to imagine an organization theorist — one who advocated much more control by management — being called to testify before the Congress because he or she may be too radical.

Frederick Taylor was the first to write about management in organization theory. He helped create the context of our current thought, and it is important that we understand what he believed.

The Method

"In the past," Taylor wrote, "the man has been first, in the future the system will be first."[16] To recall the earlier discussion about authority, Taylor fits well into the shift of authority from more traditional ways to the more modern. The change was meant to be widespread; "these principles are certain to come into general use practically throughout the civilized world, sooner or later [and] the sooner they come the better for all the people."[17] During the 1920s scientific management became a worldwide movement. After the Communists took over Russia, Lenin had Taylor's work translated into Russian.

The problem of the world, according to Taylor, was that workers were not productive.

> Underworking, that is deliberately working slowly so as to avoid doing a full day's work, "soldiering," as it was called in this country, "hanging it out," as it is called in England . . . is almost uni-

versal in industrial establishments . . . and the writer asserts without fear of contradiction that this constitutes the greatest evil with which the working people of both England and America are now afflicted.[18]

Taylor was truly horrified by what he understood to be systematic inefficiency and the inability of managers to do anything about it. He believed that natural laziness, group pressure, and ignorance about the best way to do a job caused inefficiency. It was Taylor's belief that science could cure this "greatest evil." Taylor wrote that

There is always one method and one implement which is quicker and better than any of the rest. And this one best method and one best implement can only be discovered or developed through a scientific study and analyses of all the methods and implements in use, together with accurate, minute, motion and time study. This involves the gradual substituting of science for rule of thumb.[19]

What Taylor is suggesting is nothing less than taking apart every task, understanding every movement, and timing each action until the most efficient method of doing something is proven. "The development of a science . . . involves the establishment of many rules, laws and formulas which replace the judgment of the individual workman and which can be effectively used only after having been systematically recorded, indexed, etc. . . . *every single act of every workman can be reduced to a science.*"[20]

Taylor's plan can be divided into four categories. First, each element of each person's work comes under the dictates of scientific experiment. This means, among other things, a whole new category of employee, the efficiency expert. Second, each person must be scientifically selected and trained. No longer could an individual choose his or her own work and training. Dwight Waldo summarizes it this way, "for any given task there is, theoretically, one person, or at least one type of person, better suited by measurable qualities than all others."[21] Third, Taylor believed that managers and workers must cooperate fully to ensure that the principles of science are fully developed and carried out. Fourth, and finally, according to his plan, managers must take much more responsibility for the work that is done.

What Taylor gave us is a neat overview of how to increase efficiency and cooperation based on universal principles. One of the interesting aspects of what we have just seen is that what Taylor proposed has a familiar and reasonable ring to it. How, in good faith, could we be against what sounds so rational? Of course, current thought has added a psychological element to the efficiency equation, but there is more than a touch of Taylor in much of our modern organization theory.

How It Works

Frederick Taylor was more than a theorist. He set about to demonstrate that his systems worked. In order to see how it worked, it is helpful to know how Taylor thought about those peopled systems.

"All of us," he wrote, "are grown-up children."[22] Given that opinion, it is easy to see that when Taylor thinks about changing things he thinks in terms of teachers and children. To Taylor, the teacher who gets the "best" results is the one who gives the most definite and clear-cut tasks. "Each day a definite, clear-cut task is set by the teacher before each scholar, stating that he must learn just so much of the subject, and it is only by this means that proper, systematic progress can be made by the students."[23]

The way scientific management (school, life) works is like this: Each worker (child) is given a clear-cut task every morning by his or her supervisor (teacher) who, it follows, is someone else's child. Each task, too, is part of a larger plan and is to be designed according to principles of what Taylor calls science. There is always one best plan.

Taylor does not ignore the critical issue of motivation. Given the materialist values of our liberalism, motivation is not difficult to find. With improved efficiency and productivity will come higher wages and more things to consume. One of the notable elements of Taylor's ideas is that workers would get more money for more productivity. That was not always the case.

In his most famous experiment, Taylor demonstrated how to increase the productivity of people who loaded pig iron onto a railroad car. We can best see how Taylor's method works by reading his description of the experiment. First, Taylor knew the type of worker he was looking for: "the pig iron handler is not an extraordinary man difficult to find, he is merely a man more or less of the type of an ox, heavy both mentally and physically."[24] (See Box 3.3.)

Taylor calls for an organizational revolution which, we must understand, will also lead to a revolution in the surrounding society. The whole idea of breaking up each job into motions, putting a stopwatch to each motion, and reconceptualizing and reorganizing work according to the principles of science was truly a great change. Over and over Taylor called for more responsible workers and managers and was always confident that these people could do a "good" job.

> The idea [is] of taking one man after another and training him under a competent teacher into new working habits until he continually and habitually works in accordance with scientific laws, which have been developed by someone else . . . The man suited to handling pig iron is too stupid to properly train himself.[26]

It is here that we begin to see the change go from an organizational

FIGURE 3.1 Frederick Taylor's View of Workers

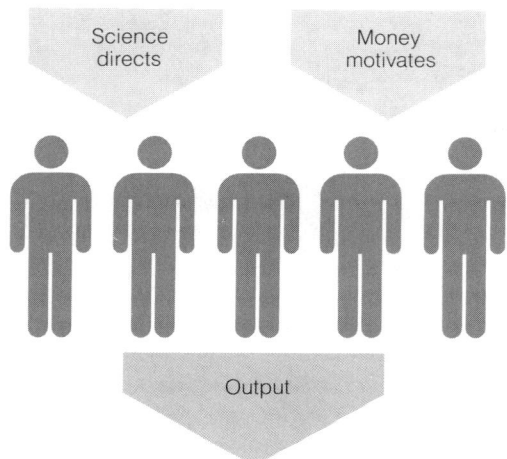

one to a societal one. The new organization is dependent on a new hierarchy of workers.[27] What is now needed is

> One set of men, who are engaged in the development of the science of laboring through time study . . . another set of men, mostly skilled laborers themselves, who are teachers . . . another set of toolroom men who provided them with the proper implements to keep them in perfect order, and another set of clerks who planned the work well in advance, moved the men with the least loss of time from one place to another, and properly recorded each man's earnings, etc.[28]

What Taylor suggested, without yet having a name for it, was a technocracy; a society run by the elites of technology. One reason why Taylor is so helpful is that he explains how to set up this new elite in an undisguised way. What he saw was an inefficient, sloppy organizational world in which workers and management were at war. He honestly believed that he could solve those problems in a rational, if not wholly scientific, way.

Dwight Waldo has summed up the work of Taylor quite well.

> Both public administration and scientific management stood midway between the eighteenth — and nineteenth — century

BOX 3.3 Taylor and a Man Called Schmidt

Taylor writes of the man he was going to experiment with: "He also had the reputation of being exceedingly 'close,' that is, of placing a very high value on a dollar. As one man whom we talked to about him said, 'A penny looks about the size of a cart wheel to him.' This man we will call Schmidt.

"The task before us, then, narrowed itself down to getting Schmidt to handle 47 tons of pig iron per day and *making him glad to do it*. This was done as follows.

'Schmidt, are you a high-priced man?'

'Vell, I don't know vat you mean.'

'... What I want to find out is whether you are a high-priced man or one of these cheap fellows here. What I want to find out is whether you want to earn $1.85 a day or whether you are satisfied with $1.15, just the same as all those cheap fellows are getting.'

'Did I want $1.85 a day? Vas dot a high-priced man? Vell, yes, I vas a high-priced man.'

'Oh, you're aggravating me. Of course you want $1.85 a day — everyone wants it! You know perfectly well that has very little to do with your being a high-priced man. For goodness sake, answer the questions, and don't waste any more of my time. Now come over here. You see that pile of pig iron?'

'Yes.'

'You see the car?'

'Yes.'

'Well, if you are a high-priced man, you will load that pig iron on that car tomorrow for $1.85. Now wake up and answer my question. Tell me whether you are a high-priced man or not.'

'Vell — did I got $1.85 for loading dot pig iron on dot car tomorrow?'

'Yes, of course you do. . . .'

'Vell, dot's all right. I could load dot pig iron on the car tomorrow for $1.85 and I get it every day, don't I? . . .'

'Now hold on, hold on. You know as well as I do that *a high-priced man has to do exactly as he's told* from morning to night. . . . You will do exactly as this man tells you tomorrow, from morning till night. When he tells you to pick up a pig and walk, you pick it up and walk, and when he tells you to sit down and rest, you sit down. You do that right straight through the day. And what's more, no back talk. . . . Do you understand that? When this man tells you to walk, you walk; when he tells you to sit down, you sit down, and you don't talk back to him. . . .'

> This seems to be rather rough talk. And indeed it would be if applied to an educated mechanic, or even an intelligent laborer. With a man of the mentally sluggish type of Schmidt, it is *appropriate and not unkind,* since it is effective in fixing his attention on the high wages which he wants and away from what, if it were called to attention, he would probably consider impossibly hard work."[25]

notion of a natural harmony of nature and the "wide-open world" conceived in certain recent philosophies. There *is* a harmony of nature, but it does not bring the greatest good of the greatest number simply by not being disturbed — that is the wrong interpretation. Man must *discover* this harmony, and impose his will upon it. No, not "impose," the laws of nature will suffer no interference. But by a cosmic stroke of good fortune the Laws of Nature and the Real Will of man will coincide![29]

With cosmic good fortune, Frederick Winslow Taylor decided that the best and most efficient organization could adhere to the laws of nature as discovered by time and motion studies. While the rest of this book will deal with how far thought has come from this seemingly out-of-date notion, it should be remembered that there are people who still do time and motion studies.

If one believes that science is at the heart of administration, then it is safe to say that there could never be a public administration. Science has always been concentrated on administration. It has, and continues, to focus on the internal workings of organizations and ways in which those organizations can be made to be more efficient and effective. The concerns of public — of citizens and democracy — are not the concerns of science and technology. So, to concentrate on science is to argue that there might be an administration, but it might never be a public administration. (See Box 3.4.)

Early Principles

The early writers of public administration set about to discover the operating principles of management according to the ideas of Frederick Taylor. In his 1926 book *Introduction to the Study of Public Administration*, Leonard White wrote that at the heart of administration was the notion that it was possible to discover, scientifically, the best management procedures.

> **BOX 3.4** The Science of Administration Revisited
>
> The quest to use science to remove administration from the strife of politics has not been abandoned. The search is now carried on under the name of "management science" and related techniques, the application of optimizing methods to administrative concerns.
>
> Stuart Nagel, who describes the use of these techniques in policy evaluation, makes the following distinctions:
>
>> The basic methodology in finding an optimum *choice* among discrete alternatives involves determining the benefits and costs for each alternative, and then determining which alternative produces the most benefits minus costs. . . . The basic methodology in finding an optimum policy *level* involves determining the relation between an increase in the policy and whatever goal one is seeking to optimize. . . . The basic methodology in finding an optimum *mix* in allocating scarce resources involves first determining the relation between (1) the amount of allocation to each alternative activity or place, and (2) the amount of benefits received."*
>
> The techniques for studying such optimizing solutions to problems include operations research, decision sciences, and other methods that are normally taught in business schools and departments of economics. The courses are called quantitative analysis, operations management, and the like. While some applications note the limits on analysis imposed by politics,† most do not. The clear implication is that there are many issues and problems in public administration that can be addressed and solved by techniques geared to finding the most rational use of scarce resources.
>
> *Stuart S. Nagel, *Policy Evaluation: Making Optimum Decisions*, (New York: Praeger, 1982) pp. xiv–xv. See also Edith Stokey and Richard Zeckhauser, *A Primer for Policy Analysis* (New York: Norton, 1978); and Michael J. White, et al., *Managing Public Systems* (North Scituate, Mass.: Wadsworth, 1980).
> †See Stephen R. Rosenthal, *Managing Government Operations* (Glenview, Ill.: Scott, Foresman, 1982).

White also split politics from administration and believed that public administration was a value-free pursuit. Other early writers, names important in the history of ideas about organizations, who carried on in this vein, were Henry Fayol and F. W. Willoughby.

The strongest set of early principles of administration came about in the mid-1930s. The social context was the response of the government to the Depression. As we saw earlier, the size of the administration grew enormously during those years, as government became involved with more areas of American life. Because the government was not really set up for such a massive effort, a President's Committee on Governmental Reorganization was formed. A member of that committee, Luther Gulick, decided that it was necessary to try and translate the principles of administration theory into principles of administrative practice. Given his intellectual context, he landed somewhere between Max Weber's ideal-typical bureaucracy and Frederick Taylor's scientific management.

The task Gulick set for himself was limited. For example, he was not concerned with what went on at the lower end of the bureaucracy, nor did he write about the increasing effect of bureaucratization on people. He was concerned with and wrote about what he believed to be the management activities common to all organizations. He was interested in the role of the administrators in organizational structure.

The reorganization committee published a book of essays, and the lead essay, by Gulick, was titled "Notes on the Theory of Organization."[30] In it, he gave the world POSDCORB — an acronym which most all public administrators have heard of. POSDCORB was Gulick's attempt to describe what executives do.

1. **P**lanning. An executive should plan what is to be done, and how it is to be done, by the organization. These should be general, not overly specific plans.
2. **O**rganizing. There needs to be a formal structure of power and authority defined and coordinated for specific purposes to specific ends.
3. **S**taffing. The executive must set up a system to bring in and train a staff and make certain that there are good working conditions.
4. **D**irecting. The executive makes decisions. He or she must give both general and specific directions so that the decisions can be carried out.
5. **C**oordinating. It is necessary that all parts of the organization work together toward the same goals.
6. **R**eporting. The executive keeps those to whom he or she is responsible informed. It means, by implication, that the executive and those around him or her must be well informed, that records need to be kept, research needs to be done, and the like.
7. **B**udgeting. Fiscal planning, accounting, and control make up budgeting.

These activities are *staff* activities. Generally speaking, the "staff" are those people in an organization who do supportive activities. They are not directly involved in making the product or delivering the service for which the agency is organized; this is the sphere of the *line* workers. Although

Gulick's POSDCORB was not all-inclusive (for example, there might be an *E* added for *evaluation*[31]), it is fair to say that the acronym is good and easy advice for any beginner. It is also fair to say that the emphasis is entirely on administration, and the single-sided notion of a particular type of efficiency. The idea of public simply does not appear.

Another set of principles proposed by Gulick revolves around ways to organize work. He wrote that each position could be characterized in these four ways: (1) the *purpose* served by each position, (2) the *process* used, (3) the *persons* or *things* dealt with, and (4) the *places* in which the work is done. These four categories have been less and less descriptive of what actually goes on in the "real" world.

In the introduction to Gulick's work, we said that he combined the theoretical work of Weber and the detailed work of Taylor. Without going into much detail, but to give you a sense of what the intellectual operating principles of organization theory were in the 1930s, here are the things Gulick believed essential for an efficient organization. There should be *unity of command, hierarchy, functional specialization, narrow span of control, authority parallel with responsibility,* and a *rational organizational arrangement.*[32]

It would be wrong to leave the impression that Gulick believed that he solved the problems of organizations in government. He did write about the strengths and weaknesses of what he was proposing. What we need to remember is that his advice as well as his assessments were all written for those who ran organizations. It was Luther Gulick who helped make the study of organization and public administration applicable to the everyday world. His principles have become part of our heritage.

Problems with Principles

Although what Gulick wrote has been influential, it has also been discredited. Such diverse thinkers as Herbert Simon and Dwight Waldo have pointed out problems with the principles proposed by Gulick. Waldo showed that the kind of "empirical" work that was the basis of Gulick's studies was not reliable. Mostly, Gulick relied on what people said about their work; more reliable data come from what others observe. One great difference is that the ability to theorize comes more easily from an observer than from someone just sharing an experience.

Herbert Simon was particularly active, and successful, in showing the shortcomings of Gulick's work. Simon went beyond Waldo's critique of the scientific validity of the work and attacked the principles themselves.[33] According to Simon, the principles were merely public administration proverbs that, if one took them seriously, were mutually exclusive. He shows, for example, that to limit the span of control (which is good), also increases the amount of red tape (which is bad). Or, to arrange an organization in a true hierarchy, with the pyramid coming rapidly to a peak, is to require a supervisor to oversee too many employees, and thus his or her control is weakened. These kinds of problems are present in the early proverbs of public administration; but, what is important here, is that, wrong as they may be, Gulick's principles are still taught. Even Simon credited Gulick with creating "criteria for describing and diagnosing administrative situations."[34]

Another challenge to the entire classical school of organizational thought was being formulated in the late 1920s and early 1930s. We will only introduce it here, but later we will devote an entire chapter to it. It was a move to include human beings in the study of organizations. In the late 1930s the human relations school of thought was begun.

The Hawthorne Studies

There is little doubt that the classical school of organization theory and public administration holds a certain appeal to the rational part of our emotions. After all, there is a certain clarity and elegance in the notions of an organization set up with a clear logic and run according to rules and regulations that fit well into that logic. It is also comforting to assume that there is a scientific basis for running organizations.

The problems, of course, are too great to ignore. The science is bad science, and there is an almost complete misunderstanding of human beings underlying the classical school of thought. In 1927, a one-time medical student turned psychologist-philosopher and his student-assistant at the Harvard School of Business began a five-year study to learn how people behaved in organizations. What Elton Mayo and F. J. Roethlisberger found has changed how we understand organizations.[35] Before we go on, note that much of what you are to read will seem like common sense. It is common sense in large part because Mayo and Roethlisberger did what they did. What we take for granted now had not yet been conceptualized when they began their work.

Their study took place in a relay assembly plant of the Western Electric Company in Chicago. What Mayo and Roethlisberger believed was that there was a range of human motivations, in addition to the economic one, that could be at work in an organizational setting. They set out to see what motivated the workers and they made two fundamental discoveries. Their experiments were as easy as they were interesting. For example, in one experiment they kept changing the physical surroundings of a group of women who were assembling telephone relays. The assumptions were that better working conditions would lead to higher output and poorer working conditions would lead to lower output. This simple cause-and-effect relationship seems not much beyond the thinking of Taylor.

The women being studied had better lighting and poorer lighting, more work space and less work space, more rest breaks and fewer rest breaks, and so on. Mayo and Roethlisberger's findings were surprising:

The production levels of the women went up after *every* change in working conditions. It did not matter if the change was positive or negative. The finding called into question much of what was believed at the time.

What the researchers discovered was that the workers were responding to the attention being paid to them and not the working conditions. It is what we now call the *Hawthorne effect*. An outcome of the discovery of this effect was the field of industrial psychology and the use of psychologists in organizations. We will return to the psychologists in a later chapter. Refer to Box 3.5 for more about the Hawthorne studies.

The second important discovery was that informal social structures had a strong effect on both women's and men's work groups. It was learned that the physical conditions of the workers were of secondary importance to the role of the informal group structure. There was pressure in the group to conform to that group's production levels as opposed to the production levels set for them by management. The workers understood themselves as being members of the group and responded to management in those terms. The kind of economic individualism of the classical theorist was wrong.

To anticipate the developments in organizational theory, there are critiques of the human relations school we should at least introduce here. First, the human relations people did not take into account the genuine, long-range differences — and problems — between workers and management. It is simply wrong to believe that these differences will disappear if management makes the workers feel more important. The second problem is that the human relations theorists almost completely ignored the effects of the formal structure on the worker, including the structure of the economic individual, which, although not as important as once believed, still exists. What people earned, both absolutely, and compared to others, still matters. As we have mentioned throughout the book, structure does have an effect. The human relations people failed to take that into account.

BOX 3.5 The Hawthorne Studies and Social Science

Some things aren't true even if they did happen.

The Hawthorne studies are widely regarded as a dramatic breakthrough in organization theory. They added two important ideas to our thinking about organizations:

1. Informal relations among workers are important for building morale. Cohesive work groups encourage higher productivity, and there are ways managers can encourage this.

2. Workers react to attention paid them. "The Hawthorne effect" is a widely used phrase that means people respond not only to a change in working conditions but also to the process of being observed. There are ways managers can pay attention to workers that will make for happier, more productive workers.

These "lessons" have been accepted as fact for two generations. They are the basis for the human relations approach to organizations, and they spawned a huge industry in human relations consultants. The ideas also put a great deal of control and responsibility in the hands of managers who are supposed to organize human relations for greater productivity.

Recent reinterpretations of the Hawthorne studies have isolated new variables for attention. One author argued that the people at Hawthorne responded to feedback on their rates of outputs and pay increases for higher rates of output. Another author argued that straightforward discipline, exercised through the firing of two workers, made the Hawthorne employees work harder. Again, these are things managers can control.*

Something entirely different may have happened at Hawthorne. Students should read the detailed account of the experiments available in *Management and the Worker,* by Dickson and Roethlisberger.† Although the original researchers noted that experimenters and managers at Hawthorne elicited the cooperation of workers, this process of cooperation was not considered as a separate variable. From the standpoint of the workers, an effective transfer of authority occurred. They were consulted frequently and actually voted on the physical surroundings of work, the conditions of work, and various amenities such as breaks. Their advice was usually taken and they were treated as if their ideas were important. The real lesson of Hawthorne may be that hierarchy hurts organizations.

Such a conclusion could never make it into the management literature of the 1930s. A search for a more public form of administration will require another look at accepted facts.

---

*See H. M. Parsons, "What Caused the Hawthorne Effect?", *Administration and Society* 10, (November 1978) no. 4, pp. 259–284; and R. H. Franke and J. D. Kaul, "The Hawthorne Experiment: First Statistical Interpretation," *American Sociological Review* 43, (October 1978) no. 5, pp. 623–642.

†P. Dickson and K. Roethlisberger, *Management and the Worker* (Cambridge, Mass.: Harvard University Press, 1939). See also P. Blumberg, *Industrial Democracy: The Sociology of Participation* (New York: Schocken Books, 1973), Chap. 2.

Another problem is simply a reflection of how times have changed since 1927. The human relations school did not anticipate the effect that increased, and increasingly complex, technology would have on the workers. A greater sense of isolation has been created with the impersonality of complex technology. "User-friendly" machines are, after all, still machines.[36]

A last "problem" was brought about by a new school of thinkers. The *organizational humanists* have tried to understand the factors in the complete organizational picture that affect workers' psychological and social health (the subject of Chapter 5). They began to focus on such topics as the intrinsic interest of work and how work may satisfy the worker. These thinkers really take us to modern organization theory and are the subject of the next chapter. Also, it is important to note that without the human relations school, the humanists would have no base from which to work.

Human Relations and Authority

Chester Barnard, a president of the New Jersey Bell Telephone Company, helped advance thinking about organizations when he published *The Functions of the Executive* in 1938. What Barnard did was give us a much more realistic view of what really goes on in formal organizations. Because of his work whole new subfields of organizational thought, such as decision-making and communications theory, were created.

The individual, according to Barnard, has only a limited amount of power. A person can do only so much when acting alone. Quite naturally, people gather in groups in order to do more things, and to get more things done. An increase in goods or services is possible only because of cooperation.[37] This development means that a whole new social and personal dynamic is set in motion.

The *cooperation*, which is the *process of interaction*, must be invented. This new, invented, way of acting will bring about a change in both the motivations and interests of those involved. Barnard theorizes that there are two ways to measure this new cooperation. The first is *effectiveness*, which is social in character, and the second is *efficiency*, which relates to the satisfaction of individual matters and is more personal in nature.

For an organization to survive, it must be able to maintain itself in relationship to its environment and, equally important, be able to maintain the satisfaction of those individuals within the organization. There are no more important functions of the executive than those.

It is especially important to note, given our interest in public/administration, that Barnard reminds us that any organization exists in a social environment. He is exceptional because he insists that something important goes on between an organization and its total environment. Too many theorists miss this point as they concentrate on how to improve the inner workings of an organization.

This is not to suggest that Barnard was not interested in how an organization worked and how to make it work better. Indeed, his three major contributions come in the areas of communications, decision making, and authority. We will take these three areas up in that order.

If Barnard is correct and the base of an organization is cooperation, one of the key components of the organization will be communication. Unless people can be heard and understood, one would hardly expect that an organization could survive. According to Barnard, four conditions need to be met in order for an individual to accept a communication as authoritative. First, the person must understand the communication; second, *at the time of his or her decision,* that person must believe that what is to be done is consistent with the purpose of the organization; third, *at the time of his or her decision,* that person must believe that what is to be done is compatible with his or her personal interest; and fourth, that person is mentally and physically able to comply with the communication.

What Barnard has done with this idea of communications is to describe the world of organizations in ways that mirror the world as we know it. No longer is an organization simply a group of people with stopwatches who are trying to discover the "one best way" to do a job. According to Barnard, we have an invented situation in which many individuals, each with personal and social motives, try to cooperate in order to get things done. Given the limitations of language and the complexities of each person in each situation, it seems remarkable that anything ever gets accomplished.

Our world is, of course, a monument to the fact that things are constantly getting done and getting made. Barnard gives us two reasons why this is the case. First, most orders comply with the four conditions he says must be met and, second, there is something called a "zone of indifference" in which many communications take place.[38] This zone is an interesting invention. Barnard argues that we do not bother to think about a whole range of everyday occurrences; they are so normal and accepted that we simply *do* them without being told. It is in the best interest of the executive to maintain this zone of indifference in order to keep communications (i.e., commands) clear, authoritative, and acceptable.

Communications are important because they carry decisions and information from the top down as well as from the bottom up in an organization.[39] Thinking about decisions provides us with an interesting insight into both Barnard and into complex organizations. Decision making is a complicated task of means and ends, "facts" and personality, logic, and timing. To make a good decision is to "exhilarate"; but, a good decision must forever be adjusted, rearranged, and reevaluated. Barnard gives us a picture of the executive as an individual who has a seemingly impossible, but potentially fulfilling, set of functions; this executive is nothing like Weber's bureaucrat or Taylor's technocrat.

In Barnard's theory, both communications and decision making rest on his idea of the legitimacy of authority. This idea represents a real contribution to the way we understand the authority concept. Barnard wrote that authority did not automatically lie in a formal position in the organization, a position that could be occupied by anyone. Indeed, he turned the traditional formulation upside down. Authority is the property of the individual who *received* the order. Authority is *granted* if the order is obeyed. Authority, instead of being a tool of the executive, becomes a limitation on the executive; those who receive orders always have a veto. Authority is most naturally granted to those with greater ability or talent, but no authority should be granted until it is clear that the individual giving the order is ultimately responsible to the organization.

Chester Barnard gave us a much better understanding of how an organization works than did his predecessors. Life in an organization does depend upon communications and how decisions are made and carried out. We know how difficult communication can be simply by thinking about the problems we have making ourselves understood by our friends. We can also see how the zone of indifference works by listing the habits and routines we do unthinkingly.

FIGURE 3.2 The Zone of Indifference

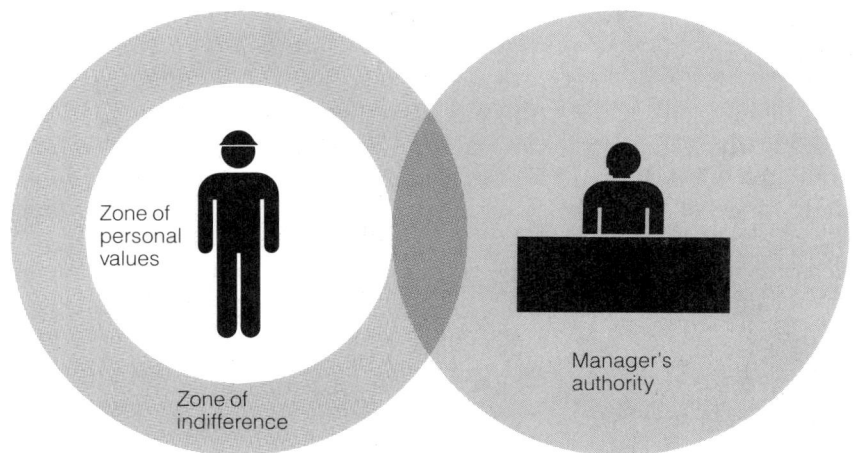

There is one last part of Barnard's thought that is important to note. It is something that he failed to tell us but is implied in what he wrote. From his description of how an organization works, one can assume that *once* that system of cooperation is set up it is almost impossible to change. Certainly the executive cannot change the basic process, nor can any other person or groups of persons. We must go back to Weber's insight to see the truly conservative nature of organizations; a bureaucracy, once set up, is one of the most difficult kinds of social structure to change or destroy.

We want to emphasize that choices are available in the making of organizations. (See Box 3.6.) Only one writer of this period, except for the anarchists, wrote about organizations that revolve around another dynamic. The writer, Mary Parker Follett, was one of the few who took the public part of public vs. administration more seriously than the administration part.

Mary Parker Follett: A Public Emphasis

Mary Parker Follett was of the same generation as Max Weber, Woodrow Wilson, and Frederick Winslow Taylor. She was an American who lived from 1868 to 1933. Follett was strongly opposed to the basic assumptions of scientific management and worked against them all of her professional life.[40] Her epistemological starting point, and the way she followed out the implications, were both daring and dazzling.

Follett wrote both too late and too early. She was too late because Taylor's work was already being accepted, and she was too early because the problems of scientific management were not yet self-evident. Her writing was lost in a crease of time, meaning that, although we can be inspired by her work, it is necessary to redo it to put it into our present context.

As we saw, the basis of scientific management was the belief that the gathering of data would lead to the discovery of the one best way to perform a task. This view assumed that a fact was constant over time; that a fact today was the same fact yesterday and would be the same fact tomorrow. Such a static notion of the world was one that Mary Parker Follett could not accept. She believed these two things about facts: first, they did not remain stationary, and second, they had no value in themselves but take on value.

"The value of every fact," she wrote, "depends on its positions in the whole world-process, [and] is bound up in its multitudinous relations. . . . Facts must be understood as the whole situation, considering whatever sentiments, beliefs, ideals that enter into it."[41] The world, and that certainly includes the organized part of it, is not frozen; it is always changing and evolving.

BOX 3.6 The Public Orientation of Police Hierarchies

How should a police department be organized? The way particular governments answer that question says a great deal about the role of the public in public administration.

People who study police departments say that the most effective organizations choose a style based on community expectations. A central job of police leadership is to gauge the attitudes of the public toward police, a job that entails judging who is "the public" police serve. It could be that business organizations and service clubs are the most influential in some cities and towns; in others, neighborhood associations may be politically important. In any case, the model of police organization should not be in open conflict with community expectations.

Gerald Sprecher and James Banovetz, writing for the International City Management Association,* suggest that two models of police organization predominate. The models are summarized below. The legalistic model is closest to Max Weber's ideal-typical bureaucracy; the service model incorporates recent administrative thinking on the need to control and improve the image of public organizations. Defining, studying, and responding to the public becomes a component of administrators' work.

Legalistic Model

1. Highly specialized with great division of labor and a centralized style of command.

2. Stresses rules, policies and procedures and obedience thereto.

3. Primary operational thrust is reactive — suppression and apprehension.

4. Impersonal attitude toward public and its problems.

5. Selection of personnel based solely on achievement and criteria: tests, education, and past accomplishments.

Service Model

1. Generalized approach with less division of labor and a decentralized style of command.

2. Stresses individual discretion and trust of individual decision making.

3. Primary operational thrust is proactive — prevention and deterrence.

4. Personally involved with public and its problems.

5. Selection of personnel based on tests, achievement, and ascriptive criteria with voluntary recognition of need to recruit minorities and different types of people.

> 6. Stresses influence of authority to accomplish tasks.
> 7. Narrowing the role of employees.
> 8. Exemplary conduct of employees based on threat, external control, and enforcement of rules.
>
> 6. Stresses influence of persuasion with subtle use of authority to accomplish tasks.
> 7. Expansion of rule of employees.
> 8. Exemplary conduct of employees based on training, self-control, and individual responsibility.
>
> *James M. Banovetz, ed., *Small Cities and Counties: A Guide to Managing Services* (Washington, D.C.: International City Management Association, 1984), Chap. 8.

This is not to deny that there are things people agree on, nor does it mean that these things are not important. Follett believed that facts are important so that people can agree as quickly as possible on what the real questions and differences between them are. Never did she believe that scientific data were either the answer or were capable of leading to answers of important problems.

The elimination of experts logically follows. She sarcastically writes about the human dynamic behind scientific experts. "For the people, it is assumed, will gladly agree to become automata when we show them all the things — nice, solid, objective *things* — they can have by abandoning their own experience in favor of a superior race of men called experts."[42] The choice she presents, the choice of being automata versus being human beings, is a stark one. What she suggests is that a person can become an expert not by being a specialist in one small area, but because of "his insight into the relationship of his specialty to the whole."

It is in relationships that Follett finds the basic dynamic that runs the world. "In human relations . . . this is obvious: I never react to you but to you-plus-me; or to be more accurate, it is I-plus-you reacting to you-plus-me. 'I' can never influence 'you' because you have already influenced me; that is, in the very process of meeting, we both become something different."[43] Although this may sound like an accepted psychological truism, it is both more than and different from that. For what Follett wants is an organization to draw on the kind of creative energy produced by that kind of dynamic. In the context of our discussion, Follett calls for a *public* administration.

"I asked a man once to join a committee I was organizing," she wrote, "and he replied he would be very glad to come and give his advice. I didn't want him — and didn't have him. I asked another man and he said he would like very much to come and learn but that he couldn't contribute anything. I didn't have him either."[44] To Follett, individuals who *participate* in administration make it public. Her message cannot be more clear than this: "The *process* of production is as important for the welfare of society as the product of production."[45] "Progress," she continues, "implies respect for the creative process, not the created thing; the created thing is forever and forever being left behind us . . . we must allow no mechanism to come between our spiritual source and our life."[46]

One of the remarkable aspects of Follett's work is that she makes a compelling argument for just the things others ignore. Taylor tells us that we will be happy if we earn more and can in turn consume more. The organizational form follows that informing idea. Follett is able to turn that around and show us an entirely different informing idea . . . and an entirely different organizational dynamic. She is the greatest of our *public* administration thinkers.

SUMMARY

We have reviewed the classic organization theorists. Mostly, the dynamic has been to make organizations "rational," so that they can produce more things. As we shall see, that is still the way most organization theorists understand their work. There are ways in which these thinkers have influenced the way we think and write about organizations. While some of their work seems very dated, we have yet to work beyond some of their basic biases. Organization theory is a young body of thought. Both Taylor and Weber wrote in this century, and their ideas are still at the root of how we conceptualize organizations. The material in this chapter provides a good basis for our understanding of modern organizations.

NOTES

1. Woodrow Wilson, *The Study of Administration* (Indianapolis: Bobbs-Merrill, reprint no. PS244 from *The Academy of Political Science*, 1887), p. 487.
2. Ibid., pp. 493–494.
3. Ibid., pp. 494–495.
4. Ibid., pp. 500–501.

5. Ibid., pp. 501 and 499.
6. Randall Collins and Michael Markowsky, *The Discovery of Society* (New York: Random House, 1972), p. 99.
7. For the relationship between mental illness and politics, see James Glass, *Delusion: Internal Dimensions of Political Life* (Chicago: University of Chicago Press, 1985).
8. Hans Gerth and C. Wright Mills, eds., *From Max Weber: Essays in Sociology* (New York: Oxford University Press, 1956), p. 199.
9. Ibid., p. 214.
10. Ibid., p. 229.
11. Ibid., p. 228.
12. For example, look at Jacques Ellul, *The Technological Society* (New York: Vintage, 1964); Dwight Waldo, *The Administrative State* (New York: Ronald, 1948); Hannah Arendt, *The Human Condition* (Chicago: University of Chicago Press); Floyd Matson, *The Broken Image: Man, Science and Society* (Garden City, N.Y.: Doubleday).
13. Gerth and Mills, op. cit., pp. 232–233.
14. One way to imagine the dynamic is to see bureaucracy as the idealized form of Weber's father and politics as the idealized form of Weber's mother. Although nickel psychology is never worth much more than fun, there is a strange truth to the above formulation.
15. See "Politics as a Vocation" in Gerth and Mills, op. cit., p. 95.
16. This is Taylor, quoted by Waldo, op. cit., p. 51.
17. Frederick Winslow Taylor, *The Principles of Scientific Management* (New York: W. W. Norton, 1967), p. 29.
18. Ibid., pp. 13–14.
19. Ibid., p. 25.
20. Ibid., pp. 37–38, 64. Emphasis added.
21. Waldo, op. cit., p. 59.
22. Taylor, op. cit., p. 120.
23. Ibid., p. 37.
24. Ibid., p. 137.
25. Ibid., pp. 44–47. Emphasis added.
26. Ibid., p. 63.
27. See Judy Merkle, "The Taylor Strategy: Organizational Innovation and Class Structure," *Berkeley Journal of Sociology*, 13 (March, 1968), pp. 59–81.
28. Taylor, op. cit., p. 70.

29. Waldo, op. cit., pp. 58–59.
30. Luther H. Gulick and Lyndell Urwick, eds., *Papers on the Science of Administration* (New York: Institute of Public Administration, 1937), pp. 3–4 and 30–31.
31. For the "E" see Orville F. Poland, "Why Does Public Administration Ignore Evaluation," *Public Administration Review* 31, (March–April 1971), no. 2, p. 202.
32. Gulick and Urwick, op. cit., pp. 1–46.
33. Herbert Simon, *Administrative Behavior*, 3rd ed. (New York: Macmillan, 1976), see Chap. 2.
34. Ibid., p. 36.
35. The key book is F. J. Roethlisberger and William J. Dickson, *Management and the Worker* (Cambridge, Mass.: Harvard University Press, 1939).
36. For example, one might look at Robert Blauner, *Alienation and Freedom: The Factory Worker and His Industry* (Chicago: University of Chicago Press, 1964), or Edgar Schein, *Organizational Psychology*, 2nd ed. (Englewood Cliffs, N.J.: Prentice-Hall, 1970).
37. Chester Barnard, *The Functions of the Executive* (Cambridge, Mass.: Harvard University Press, 1968), pp. 60–61.
38. Ibid., pp. 167–169.
39. Ibid., Chap. 13, "The Environment of Decision," pp. 185–199.
40. Mary Parker Follett, *The New State* (New York: Longmans, Green, 1923), and *Creative Experience* (New York: Longmans, Green, 1924).
41. Follett, *Creative Experience*, op. cit., pp. 12–13.
42. Ibid., pp. 3–4.
43. Ibid., pp. 62–63. This is much like Alfred Schutz, *The Phenomenology of the Social World* (Evanston, Ill.: Northwestern University Press, 1967).
44. Follett, *The New State*, op. cit., p. 29.
45. Quoted in Bertram Gross, *Managing of Organizations: The Administrative Struggle*, vol. 1 (New York: The Free Press, 1964), p. 159.
46. Follett, *The New State*, op. cit., pp. 98–99.

CHAPTER FOUR

Modern Organization Theories

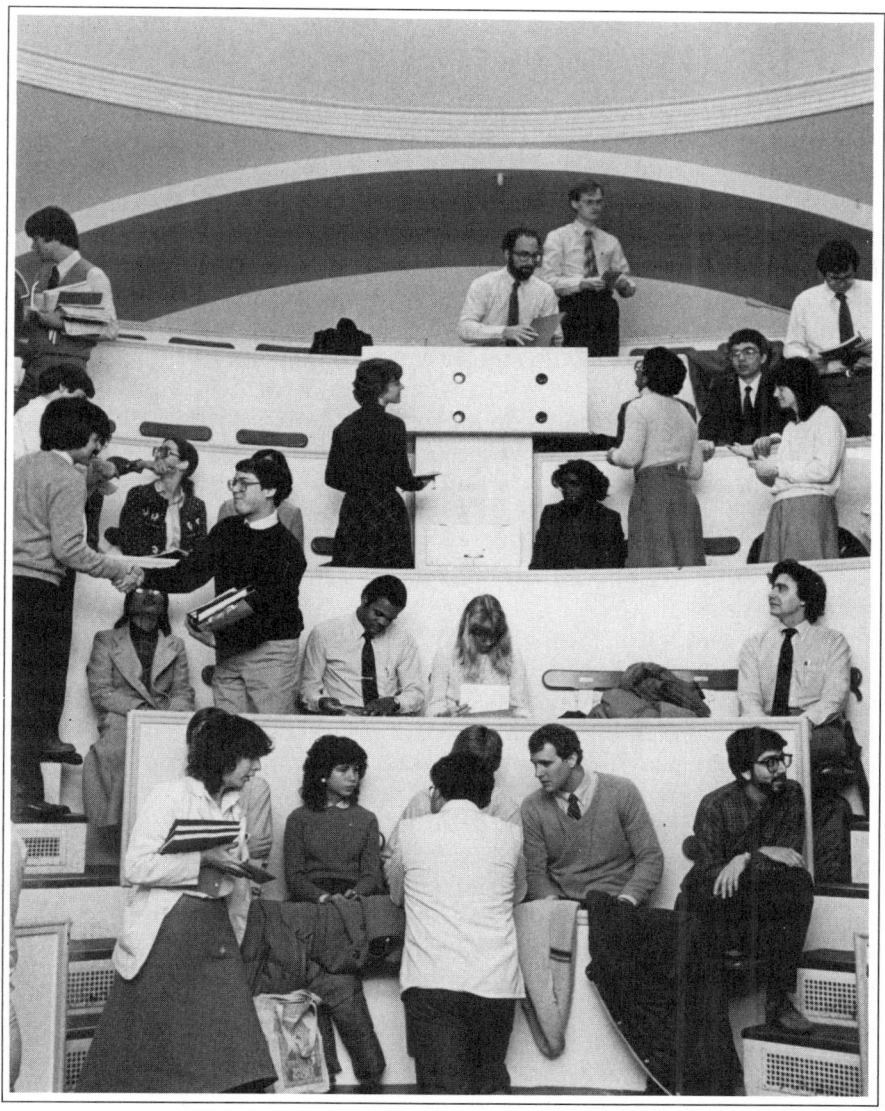

> If this civilization is to survive, we must obtain
> a new understanding of human motivation
> and behavior in . . . organizations —
> an understanding which can be simply
> but effectively practiced.
>
> — *Fritz J. Roethlisberger*

The United States went through a great deal during the thirty years between 1940 and 1970. During World War II, Japanese-Americans were sent to "relocation" camps; they were, essentially, arrested and put into prisons simply because they were Japanese-Americans. Then the war ended in Europe, and we dropped the bomb — twice — on Japan. The economy enjoyed a postwar boom, but we also fought wars in Korea and Vietnam. Socially, the fifties were quiet and the sixties were loud.

The Cold War began shortly after World War II and affected political life within the United States. Committees in both houses of the Congress, with the help of the Attorney General and the Federal Bureau of Investigation, destroyed lives in their paranoid search for communists. The civil rights movement gathered strength in the late 1950s and through the 1960s.

Science and technology roared ahead. A polio vaccine was discovered, the interstate highway system was built, and agriculture became productive almost beyond imagination. Technological advances became social forms. Television emerged as a cultural fact and changed how we viewed political candidates. Computers entered our lives, and each of us became numbers on many lists. Some engineers were able to take people to the moon and back. Others helped to construct horrific nuclear arsenals, and some tried to develop "peaceful" uses of nuclear technology.

With all these events and advances, plus the war in Vietnam, it seemed as if every part of our society had come unglued by the end of the 1960s. There was a name for this feeling: "Future Shock."[1] It was not so much that changes were occurring, it was the rate of change that was new. It was as if the kinds of changes that had taken most of a lifetime to occur were now happening every decade, even faster.

Organization Theory

It should be no surprise that during these thirty years, public administration and organization theory expanded and diversified almost as much as the culture in which it existed. Organization theory, the way in which we think about and design organizations, split into many different areas. In this chapter, we will discuss some of the important areas of organizational theory so that you will have a solid understanding for what follows in later chapters.

The two writers who most readily represent the split in organization theory are Herbert Simon and Dwight Waldo. They are also the "names" in the field who emerged during the 1940s. Both are still productive scholars.[2]

Herbert Simon

In the mid-1940s, Herbert Simon wrote an essay titled "The Proverbs of Administration."[3] It was a response to approaches to administration like POSDCORB. It was Simon's contention that, although proverbs are quotable, they will not hold up to scientific examination. "It is the purpose of this paper," he wrote, "to substantiate this sweeping criticism of administrative theory and to present some suggestion . . . as to how the existing dilemma can be solved."[4]

Simon was out to change how we thought about organizations. Proverbs, and he believed that just about all organization theories up to then were merely proverbs, simply were not sufficient. What we needed was a much more systematic and, he hoped, scientific way to study and analyze and ultimately to change organizations.

The theorist Simon admired most was Chester Barnard. Much of Simon's book *Administrative Behavior* is an effort to apply what is found in Barnard's *The Functions of the Executive* to the world of organizational behavior.[5] The important questions for Simon revolved around how decisions were made. Although he rejected the one-best-way formula for decision making, he did not at all reject efficiency. He shared Frederick Taylor's understanding of efficiency, i.e., getting the largest result for a given application of resources, but had a deeper understanding of how to pursue it. Simon sees human beings as only semipredictable. Where for Taylor employees responded solely to economic incentives, Simon understood that all people in organizations are much more than the sum of their economic parts. This led him to examine all kinds of problems concerning how decisions are made and communicated in complex organizations.

Simon's basic insight is that people are not entirely rational, and that this affects their behavior in organizations. We discuss this at length in

> **BOX 4.1 Herbert Simon and the Proverbs of Administration**
>
> Early works in organization theory emphasized principles of management. The idea was that the principles offered clear guides to managers, and that if transferred to the public sector, would result in the improvement of government operations. Among the principles were:
>
> > *Departmentalization by Major Functions.* The amount of specialization inherent in a particular division of labor will make some arrangements of like specializations more effective than others.
> >
> > *Exception Principle.* Routine matters should not be dealt with regularly by superiors, but should be delegated to an appropriate level.
> >
> > *Span of Control.* The division of labor determines the complexity of the supervisory task. The span refers to the appropriate number of subordinates that can be effectively overseen.
>
> Herbert Simon showed that for virtually every principle there is a counterprinciple, rendering them useless even for teaching people about management. For example, Simon pointed to the following difficulty with the principle of "unity of command":
>
> > If unity of command . . . is observed, the decisions of a person at any point in the administrative hierarchy are subject to influence through only one channel of authority; and if his decisions are of a kind that requires expertise in more than one field of knowledge, then advisory and informational services must be relied upon to supply those premises which lie in a field not recognized by the mode of specialization in the organization.
>
> After a series of similar observations, Simon concludes: "One is left with a choice between equally eminent theorists of administration, without any evidential basis for making that choice." Simon's work marks the beginning of the application of the techniques of modern social science to the study of management and organizations.
>
> Source: Herbert A. Simon, *Administrative Behavior* (New York: Macmillan, 1957).

Chapter 13, but the basic idea can be stated simply: people have limited cognitive capacity. They can only remember so much at one time, can only respond to so many pieces of information, and their behavior in organizations will, therefore, reflect only part of what they and others know. People cannot expect to act according to clear calculations about means and ends; that is, they cannot expect to be fully rational.

By arguing that people are not wholly rational, it is up to Simon to find a new basis for decision making, and possibly for organizations. Simon understands rationality to involve "complete knowledge and anticipation of the consequences that will follow on each choice . . . [and] a choice among all possible alternative behaviors."[6] Rationality, from this definition, does seem well beyond any of us. Simon then points us in a new direction: "The central concern of administrative theory is with the boundary between the rational and the nonrational aspects of human social behavior."[7] It is, in many ways, a provocative and interesting thought. The "boundary between" is that area between intended rationality and everyday emotion. It is an area in which "human beings . . . have not the wit to maximize."[8]

Any decision maker would be empirically wrong, according to Simon, if he or she tried to apply a rational model to human beings. The decision maker simply cannot expect to have the "perfect" choice, and, therefore, must be satisfied with choices that are good enough. Simon, in essence, rejects the Taylor supervisor who would "maximize" and urges us to accept the administrator who would "satisfice."

Decision making is an area that will need its own chapter (Chapter 13). But it is important for us to know just how important Simon's work was and where he took it. In the beginning, Simon took us away from the comforts of rationality and into much of the real life of how people act in organizations. Simon helped to point us toward such topics as organizational communications and leadership, natural parts of organizational behavior that need to be understood.

What is interesting is that Simon did not stay in that boundary between the rational and the nonrational. He chose to move to the rational side of the boundary and to work in the world of computers, simulations, and formal models.[9] It was Simon's idea that organizations could help make up for people's deficiencies in rationality. He believed that the role of the organization theorist was to devise operational techniques and then teach those techniques to members of organizations in order to help them become more rational.

We know, simply from everyday experience, that computers are a fact of our organizational world. The basic counting operations necessary for organizations — keeping track of budgets and people, their paychecks, their equipment, and so on — are now routinely done with computers, but it goes much further. Elaborate mathematical models help not only predict but also help influence actions taken by organizations. The amount of data available to decision makers seems almost limitless given the storage capacity of computers. That the quality of many decisions does not seem to have improved any is beside the point for now. The point is that, for much of organization theory, an interest in human frailty has been transformed into a search for answers in this technology.

Dwight Waldo

One way to think about the work of Herbert Simon is that he concentrated on how to make organizations more efficient. Dwight Waldo was less interested in the internal workings of a public organization than he was in just what public administration in the United States meant. In the opening paragraph of *The Administrative State*, Waldo writes,

> If they are to be understood, political theories must be construed in relation to their material environment and ideological framework. The political theories of American public administration are not exceptions. For, despite occasional claims that public administration is a science of universal validity, American public administration has evolved political theories unmistakably related to unique economic, social, governmental, and ideological facts.[10]

What Waldo suggests is that when we try to understand public administration, we must come to terms with the motives that underlie organizations, the dynamics driving them, the social values with which organizational values collide, and the values that they encourage.

In Chapter 2, there is a discussion of the environment of public administration. In part because of the influence of Waldo, we must take that discussion seriously. Public organizations are a fact of our everyday life. If we concentrate merely on *how* these organizations work and do not bother to try and understand what they *mean*, then public administration can simply get out of control.

Waldo worked in a government agency during World War II and is an example of a point that needs to be made. The question of what organizations mean is not merely a question for theorists; it is equally a question for practitioners. Although everyday problems of organizational life are constantly pressing every practitioner, it is not enough of a reason to let other questions be answered by academics. People in the public service must concern themselves with what their actions mean.

As we learned in the 1960s, concentrating on doing one's job in a public organization may not be enough. We will take up this theme at the

> **BOX 4.2** Organizational Values and Social Values
>
> The Bureau of Indian Affairs (BIA), an agency within the Department of the Interior, is responsible for government relations with and administration of policies affecting Native American tribes. This simple statement of responsibilities masks a bewildering range of social issues that are part of BIA administrative responsibiliaties.
>
> It is still less than 100 years since the last battles between tribes of Native Americans and the United States Army. There are many Native Americans still living whose parents and grandparents gave them eyewitness accounts of those events. And there are still survivors from the days of the Dawes Commission, which enacted a plan to "civilize" Native Americans by substituting individual for tribal ownership and use for land — and selling parcels not claimed by individuals to whites. Although fewer shots are now fired, Native Americans are still being sent to jail in disputes over the fishing rights guaranteed tribes as part of peace treaties written in the last century.
>
> Underlying the BIA's administrative charge is this history of military conquest, government policies aimed at destroying Native American cultures, and continued disputes with white groups, such as sport and commercial fisheries. Although many officials of tribes work with BIA officials and regard them as representing their concerns in Washington, this is only because other government agencies (mainly within the Interior Department) are, in comparison, hostile to the tribes. It is hard to understand government-tribal relations without memory of conquest, cultural conflict, and continuing clash of values.

end of the chapter. For now, it is necessary only to understand that one of the important splits in organization theory is between those who concentrate on how organizations might run more efficiently and those who think about what organizations mean in their economic, social, political, and ideological contexts.

There are people who try to work between the ideas of Simon and Waldo. One such person is Charles Lindblom. In an article titled "The Science of Muddling Through," Lindblom offers a description of how decisions are made in public organizations.[11] This essay has been influential, in part because it fits so well in pluralist theory. Lindblom argues that decision making is divided into two approaches. One is called the *rational comprehensive* method. A decision maker who uses this method tries to find out everything before making a decision: clarification of objectives, all the factors that determine how each alternative will affect the objectives, and so on. In this way the decision maker tries to make the best decision. It is Lindblom's contention that this approach works *only* with relatively simple problems. After all, the variables in complex problems overwhelm what we can "rationally" deal with. According to Lindblom, most of the literature of public administration dealt with the simple (rational) decision making and ignored the complex decision making. It is the approach to complex decision making that Lindblom takes up.

This approach is called *successive limited comparisons* (also known as "incremental" decision making, or just plain "muddling through"). With this method, when complex decisions must be made, the decision makers do the best they can with the information they have. The details of the method can be found in Chapter 13. What is important in this context is what Lindblom has to say about the method, why it makes sense for public administrators in the United States.

First, he writes, "Successive limited comparisons, is, then, indeed a method or a system; it is not a failure of method for which administrators ought to apologize.... I suspect that in so far as there is a system in what is known as 'muddling through,' this method is it." Essentially, Lindblom is arguing that there is no one best way to make a decision; indeed, there is not only one kind of rationality. This last point, of course, is in direct contradiction to Simon.

Second, Lindblom explains muddling through this way:

> It is a matter of common observation that in Western democracies public administrators and policy analysts in general do largely limit their analyses to incremental or marginal differences in policies that are chosen to differ only incrementally.... Democracies change their policies almost entirely through incremental adjustments. Policy does not move in leaps and bounds.

So public administrators simply do not seriously look at things they believe to be politically unacceptable. Yet, how can we be sure their judgment is reasonable? Lindblom assures us, "Almost every interest has its watchdog."[12] In other words, there is an appropriate way to make decisions in public organizations according to the political ideology of that country. But his western bias is clear; there is no reason to assume that "watchdogism" is a part of every ideology.

It is Lindblom's argument that muddling through is the actual method decision makers in the United States use. They should recognize it as a method and try to get better at it. Right or wrong, he at least begins to take Waldo's concerns into consideration.

Reconceptualizing Organizations

In the early 1950s, David Easton wrote about politics as a system. His book, *The Political System*, changed the way many political scientists study politics.[13] In 1960, John Pfiffner and Frank Sherwood brought the systems concept to organizations and were able to integrate many different approaches in *Administrative Organization*.[14] Systems theory took hold as the most popular innovation in organization theory in the postwar period.

A system is a collection of parts with prescribed interactions; a system has specific goals or general purposes. There are all kinds of systems, and systems theory is used in a remarkable number of places. For example, political scientists study national politics as a political system, organization theorists study huge organizations as systems, and some psychotherapists study families as systems. The systems approach is simply a framework for study.

A closed system is the easiest to understand. Big Ben, the English clock tower, is a machine. It can also be described as a closed system. There are inputs (someone has to wind it), there are processes within (the clockworks), there are outputs (it tells the time and rings its chimes), and there is feedback (mechanical governors that regulate the speed of the clockworks). Inputs, processes, outputs, and feedback. Simple. Yet in the real world there are very few closed systems. Even machines need tending from the outside, and all need inputs of energy from the outside.

Open systems are more dynamic and more complicated than closed systems. Instead of a machine metaphor, open systems correspond to an organic metaphor. There are still the familiar input, processes, output, and feedback, but there are important additions of environment and boundary (between the organism and the environment). In an earthquake, or when someone forgets to wind Big Ben, we find out that it too is an open system. The environment matters.

Figure 4.1 depicts an organization as an open system. There is an inside and an outside to the organization. We can see that the organization gets certain things from the outside (the inputs), transforms them (the process), and sends certain things back to the outside (the outputs). The output is monitored (the feedback) to see if it meets standards, and this information affects the various parts of the organization. And the environment matters. There are outsiders in a position to threaten or support the organization.

Figure 4.1 is greatly simplified. For example, there is not one single process within the postal service. They have different operations for local mail, long-distance mail, parcel and overnight mail delivery, and so on. The managers have to be concerned with personnel management, budgeting, the efficiency of operations, and several other things besides. The

FIGURE 4.1 The U.S. Postal Service as an Open System

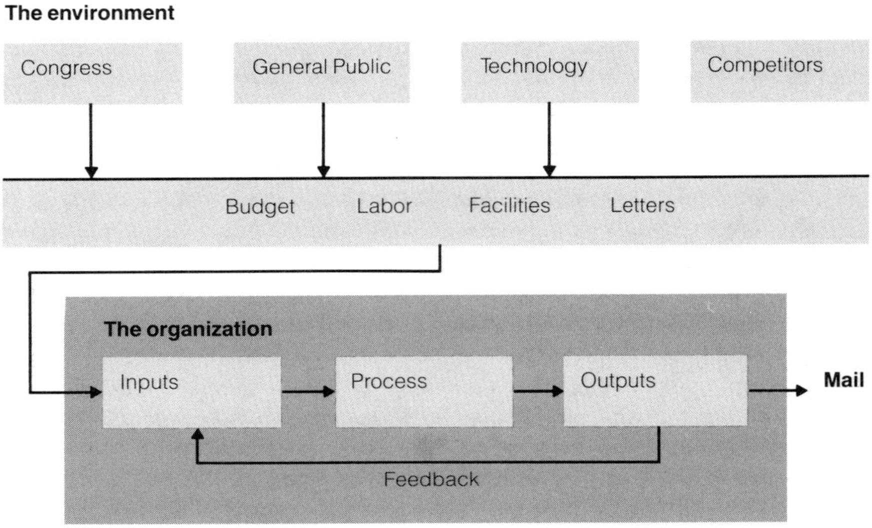

The environment

Congress → General Public → Technology → Competitors

Budget — Labor — Facilities — Letters

The organization

Inputs → Process → Outputs → **Mail**

Feedback

outputs affect how the environment treats the organization. Each of these elements of postal operations could be depicted as a subsystem, and the diagram could be expanded to show how the various subsystems fit together. There are no rules about how simple or complicated the design of a system should be. It should be specific enough to help people fulfill their purposes in making a system.

With open systems theory, organization theory, in a real sense, has progressed from mechanics to biology. L. T. Hobhouse wrote, "The life of society and the life of an individual do resemble each other in certain respects, and the term 'organic' is as justly applicable to one as to the other. For an organism is a whole consisting of interdependent parts. Each part lives and functions and grows by subserving the life of the whole."[15] It is important that organic not be confused with human, for an organic organization has special traits that should not be thought of as human traits. But the fact is that organic is a much more serious and complicated metaphor than a machine. By using an open systems approach, the study of organizations has gotten more sophisticated.

In their book *The Social Psychology of Organizations*, Daniel Katz and Robert Kahn speak of an organization in terms of energy: how energy is brought into the organization, how it is used and transformed while it is there, and how much is produced in the form of goods and services.[16] This tracing of energy allows one to study practically every aspect of an organization's operations. As we do this, remember that this energy flow is going through a variation of the input, processes, output, and feedback loop discussed earlier.

If we follow the energy, we would naturally look at the boundaries between the open system and its environment in order to check the inflow of energy. There should be a continual monitoring of the environment so that the organization will be neither overwhelmed nor forgotten. By studying the internal workings of the system, one could find out how energy was used. For example, people in organizations would want to know how much time and effort was spent on producing the goods or services, and how much was spent on maintaining the organization. It is possible to find out if the output was the one intended, and if it was efficiently produced (the most product for the least energy). With feedback, the whole process begins again. With each output, the open system environment is changed, and its previous calculations must be reviewed.

The idea of energy flow, energy exchange, and energy transformation provides a way not only to understand how things work, but also a way to measure if work is done efficiently and effectively. An open systems approach seems sensible when an organization's environment is a threatening one. It calls for a continual evaluation of the changes in its environment. As the environment changes, the organizational response can change accordingly.

Metaphors are, we must remember, just metaphors. A closed system is not *really* a machine, and vice versa. Nor is an open system *really* an organism. Katz and Kahn go to some lengths in describing the "catabolic and anabolic processes of tissue breakdown and restoration within the body, ... external conditions of humidity and temperature, ... [and] the endocrine glands [as] a regulatory mechanism for preserving an evenness of psychological functions."[17] Organizations do not simply appear on earth; they are not natural but artificial. Human beings thought them up and make them go or stop. People in organizations may seem glum or happy or whatever, but it is impossible to find an "organizational endocrine gland" anywhere. To see too little in a metaphor is to miss its poetry and miss its ability to teach. To see too much is to misunderstand reality.

This is not to say that open systems theory and the organic metaphor are somehow wrong. They are both helpful ways of looking at and understanding much of our surroundings. The problems are (1) to take it too literally is misleading, and (2) if you see everything as a system, then nothing is (in the same way that if we call every part of a house a wall, then there are no floors). Open system metaphors give us a useful way to study organizations, but they are not the only way and are not always the best way. Remember that in the history of organization theory, open systems theory was a great invention.[18]

Organizations and the Environment

As the social, economic, political, cultural, and ideological environment changes, so too should the shape of organizations. Up to this point we have not discussed much about organizational design; i.e., about what an organization would actually look like if we drew a picture of it. We know that Weber's ideal-typical bureaucracy was a hierarchical arrangement with one person at the top and an increasing number as you went down. But we also know that there are many different ways of organizing. In principle, the United States Army and an academic department in a college are not arranged the same way. Academics claim to be collegial; privates and generals do not.

The question is, then, can we make generalizations about which kind of organization will work best? F. E. Emery and E. L. Trist have suggested that there are differing ideal organizational forms for differing types of environments.[19] They argue that an organization must be able to reduce uncertainty to its lowest possible costs. This means that it must be capable of either controlling its surroundings or guiding actions of others, or at least predicting events. How well an organization functions depends upon its ability to do these things with the lowest possible cost to its resources.

One of the interesting elements of this theory is the emphasis on the organization's ability to change its openness or closedness according to its environment. For example, to be efficient in a static environment, an organization need not assume a form that would require the spending of many resources for change. There would be little reason to invest in continually studying and anticipating change in a static environment. The most efficient organization, in an environment of little change and little challenge, would be one that was closed and that concentrated on internal matters.[20] The following are four ideal-typical combinations of environment and organizational form suggested by Emery and Trist.

PLACID-RANDOMIZED ENVIRONMENT. In this organizational environment, there are no connections between the various segments; actions occur almost at random. There are no lasting coordinated threats to the supremacy of the organization. Thus, the organization can be formed into units of smaller size to handle individual problems as they might arise. There is no need for an elaborate scheme capable of devising complex strategies; all that is required is that tactics be devised to handle each new situation. One can think of tribes of Indians before Europeans settled in the Americas. The white settlers who wanted the Native American's land became a "lasting coordinated" threat.

PLACID-CLUSTERED ENVIRONMENT. In this environment, the organization is faced with many more difficult problems and is much more complex than the preceding one. In the placid-clustered environment, there is some connection among different segments of society. For example, the

FIGURE 4.2 The Environment and Organization

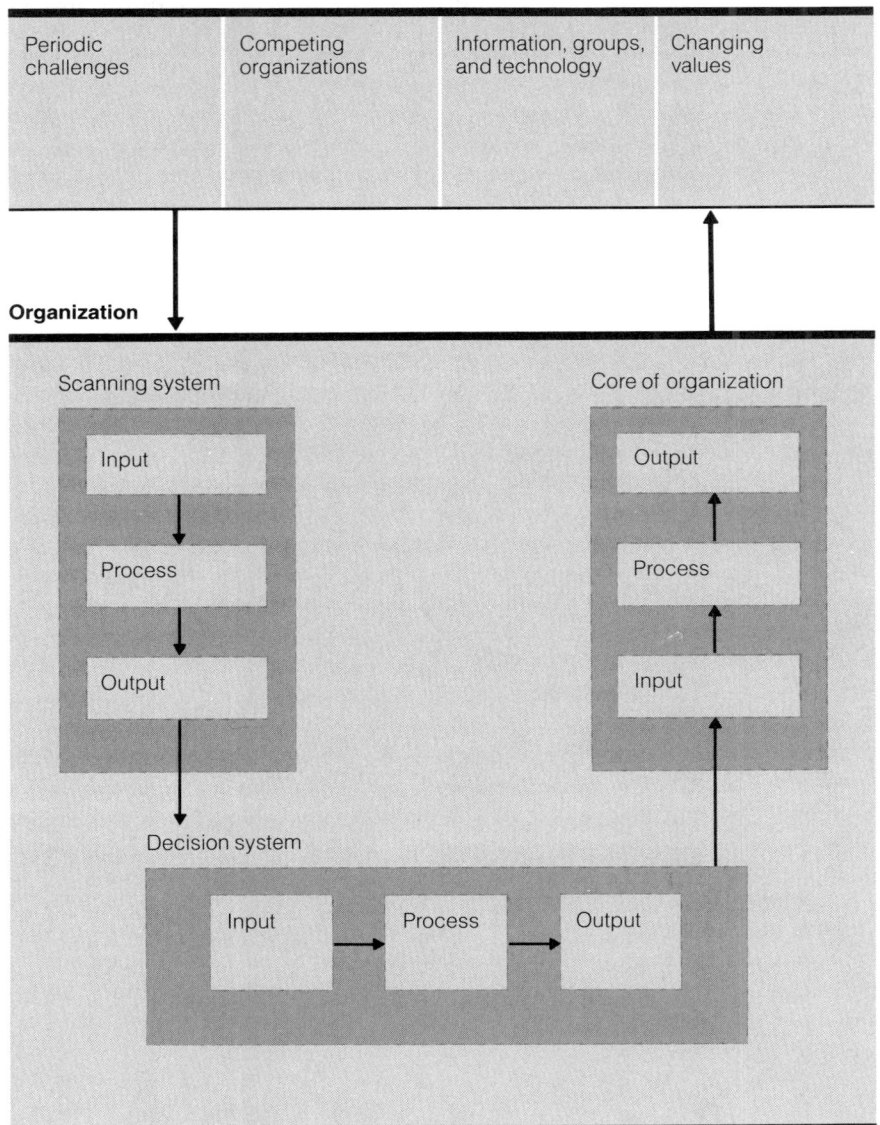

Adapted from Peter Schoderbek et al., *Management Systems,* 3d. ed. (Plano, Texas, Business Publications, Inc., 1985), p. 204.

people who wanted to rally the colonies to break away from the British needed to organize the various segments of society. The New England clergy had to get the merchants, farmers, and lawyers to join together to be as organized as the British.

In order to survive in this kind of environment, an organization has to devise strategies that will last over time. This is much different than merely dealing with problems as they arise. Survival becomes linked with information, with what the organization knows about its surroundings. Energy and resources must be used to find out what to avoid or what is unavoidable. As this organization grows in size, it becomes hierarchical, with a tendency toward centralized control and coordination. For the new government to survive, there were certain powers it had to have and to use in order to deal with potentially hostile elements in the environment. It had, for example, to control the currency, commerce, the army, and foreign relations in order to keep power.

There are various ways in which this kind of organization is able to protect itself. An organization may try to clothe (or infuse) itself with overriding social values. That way, it is able to argue that an attack on it is an attack on some social verity. In some cases, professional organizations will emerge to ensure and protect the status of the organization involved. In still other cases, institutionalization will occur. An organization becomes an institution through the embodiment of organizational values that relate them to the wider society.

Although institutionalization does stabilize an organization in the placid-clustered environment, real problems arise when new values arise. An organization, if institutionalized, not only subsumes the value of a society but becomes an authoritative allocator of those values. One real problem is that the more powerful the organization is, the less likely it is to change. As we saw in the 1960s, change can be very slow if we institutionalize organizational forms that are not able to adapt to new environments.

DISTURBED-REACTIVE ENVIRONMENT. This environment is much more complicated than the first two. The segments of this environment are both interconnected and powerful; they form a continual threat to the organization. An organization is no longer faced with merely periodic challenges; now, it must consider what other ongoing organizations might know and do. Several organizations now compete for the same information and the same space; the survival of any organization is endangered at any given time. In this kind of environment, the forms of organizations must change. Organizations must be able to do more than simply devise clever strategies; they must be able to choose actions that, in part, will mislead and distract their competition. An organization must deal with plans and counterplans. These new forms of organizations must be flexible and decentralized. A premium is placed on the quality and speed of decisions at various peripheral points. Each part of the organization must have the power to operate more or less at will; each must have the ability to make and meet competitive challenges.

One way to understand the different kinds of organizational thinking and forms can be seen in the evolution of the automobile industry. In the placid-clustered environment, Henry Ford could invent the assembly line and say to new car buyers: "You can have any color model-T you want, as long as it's black." Today, color is only one of an amazing number of options — how many doors, what kind of transmission, radio, engine, windows, etc. The question is: How can any manufacturer produce exactly the right number of cars, with the exact options wanted by individual buyers? The answer is to decentralize to the point of the purchaser. In the future, the buyer will sit at a computer and type in exactly what he or she wants. The order will go directly to the plant where the right color car with the right array of options will be made. In theory, the car will be delivered to the buyer within two weeks, and the manufacturer will produce exactly the right number of the right cars.

TURBULENT FIELDS.   As in the third type, this environment is dynamic; however, its dynamism is a result of more than just the actions of the component organizations. In this case, the whole field is moving. No single organization is capable of dealing with this environment. Given the complexity of action and the multiple areas where actions might arise, the amount of information needed to understand what is happening is well out of the reach of any organization operating alone. The result is a deepening interdependence of many parts. Each part must rely more and more heavily on research and development of new things and new ideas. Because the areas of uncertainty are vast, the result of any organization's action is increasingly unpredictable. Organizational forms in this environment must assume the same flexible characteristics as those in a disturbed-reactive environment, only more so.

The computer industry is probably the most turbulent field right now. Small, innovative companies are constantly pushing the state of the art beyond what we thought was possible. Generations of computers are measured not in years but in months. The bigger companies — IBM, Digital, Apple — are doing the best they can to decentralize and *act* like smaller companies, at least in areas like new product development. The first Apple computer was built in a garage; the MacIntosh computer was built by a small work group trying to recreate the garage mentality. Computer companies, in order to stay alive, must center their work around research and design.

There are, of course, different ways to think about the *best* form an organization might take. Joan Woodward believes that "technology" is a good way to choose the appropriate form or structure an organization should take.[21] By that she means that different tasks (or technologies) need different types of organizational structure. So, for example, bureaucracy appeared to be the best form of organization for routine operations, while temporary work groups, decentralization, and emphasis on interpersonal processes appeared to work best for nonroutine operations. Put a little differently, the kind of work that is to be done might have a most appropriate form of structure.[22]

Recent Organization Theory

These innovations in organization theory, new concerns with rationality and efficiency, the cultural surroundings, open systems, and the details of organizational environments, are impressive. We are better at describing organizations than ever before. Yet, for all the research and writing on organizations, there are some important things we do not know about organizations.

The most critical question for public administration is this: What does organization theory have to do with the main concerns of public administration? The split represented by Simon and Waldo is still there. One set of concerns has to do with getting things done — delivering services — and getting them done efficiently. The other set of concerns has to do with the larger effects of public administration.

For the most part, organization theory has not addressed either concern very well. In the remainder of this section, we will look at how services are delivered efficiently. We will conclude the chapter with a discussion of the relation of organization theory to broader social and political questions.

Organization theory's focus on efficiency has been extremely narrow, probably because too much of the field is focused just on business organizations. There, it may be enough to figure out how to best compete in the airline business or to make and market the lowest-priced cookies, but these lessons are not always immediately relevant to public administration. The detailed march of social science through the intricacies of systems theory has not provided clear guides to building and running organizations. In fact, the most popular, influential, and best-selling organization theory in the private sector looks remarkably similar to the older proverbs of administration. In their book *In Search of Excellence,* Thomas Peters and Robert Waterman write about the best-run companies in the United States.[23] These companies:

1. Have a bias for action; a preference for doing something — anything — rather than sending a question through cycles of analyses and committee reports.

2. Stay close to their customers, learning their preferences and catering to them.

3. Exhibit autonomy and entrepreneurship, breaking the corporation into small companies and encouraging them to think independently and competitively.
4. Find productivity through people, creating for all employees the awareness that their best efforts are essential and that they will share in the rewards of the company's success.
5. Are hands-on, value-driven; executives keep in touch with the firm's essential business.
6. Stick to the knitting, remaining with the business the company knows best.
7. Have simple form, lean staff; few administrative layers, few people at the upper levels.
8. Have simultaneous loose-tight properties, fostering a climate where there is dedication to the central values of the company combined with tolerance for all employees who accept those values.

Of course, these broad guidelines are all easier said than done, and the people who do them just "seem to have a sense" of them. They get it from experience and leaders with that sense; they do not get it from research.

Public organizations deal with public policy. Their environment is filled with the political relationships described in Chapter 2. There has not been much work in organization theory about the relation between these political realities and organizational forms. This probably has a lot to do with the origins of the fields of public policy studies and organization theory.[24] Organization theory arose in a time when social science in general was concerned with processes in society and organizations, whereas public policy studies came about when concerns had shifted to purposes of organizations and social groups. Each has been more concerned with the routine questions of their disciplines than with the places where the two might overlap — and that is where public organizations do their work.

In Chapter 5, we will see how organizational psychologists think about the problem of organizational form. These theorists, who are direct descendants of the human relations people we discussed in Chapter 3, care a great deal about the psychological health of the individual worker. A psychologically healthy worker, they contend, is a productive worker. To that end, they propose the breaking up of the bureaucratic organization and various methods of integrating the individual into the organization. They are less involved with the old-fashioned suggestion box and more concerned with sensitivity groups (a kind of group therapy for co-workers).

These newer methods of understanding and changing the underlying psychological processes of organizations were just beginning to become popular during the mid to late 1960s. They caused a shift in the way we think about organizations and are important enough to study in detail later. The point here is that if you begin with the psychological health of

BOX 4.3 Thinking about New Organizational Forms

Simple hierarchies, as depicted in illustrations in Chapters 1 and 9, are based on fairly simple assumptions about the way people fit into organizations. New organizational forms are based on new assumptions. Some contemporary organization theorists picture future organizations in constant flux, changing form as judgments and forces emerge from other-than-hierarchical interactions among organization members. It is indeed difficult to picture something that has not yet been seen.

One theorist includes the following propositions in his description of a new way of making organizations:*

1. The primary focus or unit of analysis in the theory is the face-to-face encounter between people, rather than the group, the nation, or the "system."
2. People are by nature active rather than passive, and social rather than atomistic. This means they must have a measure of autonomy in determining their actions, and that their actions must correspond to their context.
3. This active-social nature of people means considerable attention is directed to the subjective meanings people attach to their actions and those of others — these everyday meanings are the basis of knowledge in the organization.
4. The selection of organization decision rules is the most important aspect of determining structure. A structure that takes account of the active-social nature of people relies on negotiated meanings arrived at by consensus rather than by hierarchy, bargaining, voting, and contract.
5. Consensual organizations require that each actor bear moral responsibility for his or her actions — the institution and its actions cannot be viewed apart from the intersubjective processes people use to define and take action. The legitimacy of organization actions must be established and sustained in face-to-face encounters between people.

This picture of organizations is impossible to put on a chart, but in many ways it fits in with important ideas we have about public administration. It focuses on people doing things, delivering services; in short, it tries to look at actions in a practical way. Second, it makes a great deal of room for individual citizens, and citizens collectively, to talk about what organizations do and how they do it. It tries to make a very public sense of public administration. But as we have seen in earlier chapters, these ideas about public administration are not entirely clear, and so this new organization form will show up, if at all, in practice before on paper.

*Adapted from Michael M. Harmon, *Action Theory for Public Administration* (New York: Longman, 1981).

the worker, you naturally move to different kinds of organizational forms. To remain powerful, the psychologist must keep the focus on the individual psyche. Although the psychologists are dismayed by the suggestions that the environment and/or the task of the organization may play a dominant role in structure, that has not stopped them from commanding the attention of many in the field.

The Larger Questions

It is possible to spend a great deal of time — indeed, a lifetime — looking into the determinants of internal structures of bureaucracies. But remember, there is a split in organization theory. To return to the other side of the split, the question of form becomes wholly political by trying to answer just one question: How does a closed organizational form like a bureaucracy fit into a democratic state? Later in the book we will look at how policies are made, and what happens when people try to put policies into effect. But the question here is more basic: Even if the policy is a wonderful one, what if the citizens it affects are not directly involved in the process of making that policy? In a democratic state, could the argument be made that a less efficient policy that is democratically made would better serve the citizens than an efficient policy not democratically made?[25] In a sense, these were the questions being asked at the end of the 1960s. It is appropriate to take up the ideas of Dwight Waldo again.

In 1968, Waldo wrote an article titled "Public Administration in a Time of Revolution."[26] With the war in Vietnam, the civil rights movement, the leftist movements that were radically against large organizations and large government, the women's movement, sex, drugs, and rock 'n roll, it truly felt like a time of revolution. Waldo, who twenty years earlier had written about the importance of understanding the relationships of public administration to its environment, tried to focus the field on what was going on and how people might respond.

Briefly, Waldo felt that the following "items" helped add up to a revolutionary time. There were revolutions in science and technology, as well as a growing reaction *against* science and technology. Indeed, in one of the great speeches leading to the years of violence at the University of California at Berkeley, Mario Savio asked people to "throw their bodies on the gears, and stop the machine." There was, at the time, a revolutionary increase in the means of violence, and a counterrevolutionary movement against the use of violence. There was a crisis in relations and a reaction against gradualism in solving problems. There was a severe generation gap, an urban revolution, an increase in crime, and a revolution in morals and values.[27]

The first question Waldo asks public administrators is this: Did we help cause these problems? His answer is simple enough: Of course we did. It was Waldo's sense that the problems extended beyond those of public administration. "Since our civilization is so deeply organizational and technological, the revolt often seems and in a sense is against civilization itself." The twist is that these very organizations and technologies have produced an enormous amount of riches. The success became a part of the problem, as it seemed absurd to have poverty and discrimination with such great wealth.

Public administration is, in part, responsible for much of the wealth. For example, Waldo writes that technical assistance has made United States' agriculture one of the great revolutionary forces of this century. Something as common as state and interstate highways have brought about huge changes in life-styles and outlooks. There are public administrators who try to ensure we have clean air and water; who try to deal with the problems of the inner city; who try to put us in space; who try to set standards of professionalism; and who try to respond to the pressures for equality.

In the first chapter, we introduced the idea that there was an ongoing question about the proper role of public administration in the United States. Woodrow Wilson argued that it should be neutral; that it should be "above" politics. Mary Parker Follett argued that it should be democratized. Many modern theorists, like Herbert Simon, seem to argue that the job of public administrators is to seek the highest level of efficiency possible; that is, to become sophisticated enough to make "rational" decisions. During the late 1960s, these questions were brought up again.

Here is one side of the argument: "The idea . . . of civil service neutrality has served its purposes, and real dangers *are* created by abandoning it. . . . The proper role of a bureaucracy is to act as a stabilizing force in the midst of vertiginous change . . . by acting in its routinized, mechanical, ponderous way it helps society keep its cool."[28] This, as we know, is a view of public administration that has been powerful since people first began to systematically consider public administration. It is socially comforting to be able to count on a stable, unchanging, routinized public service.

"Having admitted that this point of view has some force and validity," writes Waldo, "let me say that on the balance I reject it. . . . I'm going to take the position that we ought to respond more consciously, more *self-consciously,* to the revolutions of our day." Waldo offers some advice:

> Certainly we have been aware of the *problem* of adjusting organizations to the people in them, and have worked toward solutions. . . . We hoped and assumed the two objectives of efficiency and humanity were congruent. . . . However, in my opinion we have advanced very little in making public bureaucracies acceptable and efficient in working with many of our clienteles. . . . I think that experimentation in new organizational styles is in order. Some of the new organizations and procedures won't fit any of the approved patterns and traditional textbooks.

It is important to remember that the call for change in those very institutions that many believed were to protect the status quo was serious advice. It called for a complete rethinking of much that was going on. There is, it seems, a series of interesting and sometimes critically important questions that comes out of the study of why and how we should organize. As we have seen, there is little agreement on what questions we should ask. Although many of the theorists of organizations seem to turn inward and first ask what are essentially efficiency questions, it is not altogether clear that efficiency should be the overriding virtue in a democratic country. But, everyone does agree that how we organize is central to much of what we do.

SUMMARY

We began the chapter with the early works of Herbert Simon and Dwight Waldo. These thinkers represent the split in organization theory, a split between concerns for efficiency and concerns for the (democratic) environment of the organization. We reviewed several types of organization theories that responded to the split. Lindblom's "muddling through" attempted to answer questions about efficient conduct of organizations and democratic politics. It is still the most widely accepted version of how these things fit together.

Systems theory and descriptions of the environments of organizations attempted to construct a powerful description of the parts of organizations, and most importantly, of the way the parts fit together. These are powerful descriptive tools, and they add a great deal to our understandings of organizations. The more detailed they get, however, the more questions of efficiency take the place of questions about democracy.

Finally, we returned to the "larger questions" of how public administration fits in a democratic society and argued that the split in organization theory is as deep as ever. By 1970, Herbert Simon was giving lectures to the Rand Corporation explaining his mathematical models. He would later win a Nobel Prize for his work. At the same time, Dwight Waldo was trying to come to terms with the relationship between real world events and public administration. In his efforts, he uses the works of Albert Camus, and writes this warning: "It is possible that historians of the future will puzzle over our fascination with 'technology' while alarm bells were ringing in all directions."

NOTES

1. See Alvin Toffler, *Future Shock* (New York: Random House, 1970).
2. As a historical note, we would like to clarify the lineage of organization theory. Although Max Weber (discussed in Chapter 3) was a turn-of-the-century thinker, he was not influential in the United States at that time. His works were not translated into English until 1940. They did somewhat influence administrative thinking through the translated works of Henry Fayol.
3. Herbert Simon, "The Proverbs of Administration," *Public Administration Review* 6 (Winter 1946), pp. 53–67.
4. Ibid., p. 53.
5. Herbert A. Simon, *Administrative Behavior* (New York: Macmillan, 1957); and Chester Barnard, *The Functions of the Executive* (Cambridge, Mass.: Harvard University Press, 1938).
6. Herbert Simon, op. cit., p. 81.
7. Ibid., p. xxiv.
8. Ibid.
9. For example, see Simon's *The New Science of Management Decision* (New York: Harper & Row, 1970).
10. Dwight Waldo, *The Administrative State: A Study of the Political Theory of American Public Administration* (New York: Ronald Press, 1948), p. 3.
11. Charles E. Lindblom, "The Science of Muddling Through," *Public Administration Review* 19 (Spring 1959), pp. 79–88. See also Charles E. Lindblom and David K. Cohen, *Usable Knowledge: Social Science and Social Problem Solving* (New Haven: Yale University Press, 1979).
12. Ibid., pp. 84–85.

13. David Easton, *The Political System: An Inquiry into the State of Political Science* (New York: Knopf, 1953). Several methodological points were ambiguous in this work, clarified in his later *A Framework for Political Analysis* (Englewood Cliffs, N.J.: Prentice-Hall, 1965).
14. John Pfiffner and Frank Sherwood, *Administrative Organization* (Englewood Cliffs, N.J.: Prentice-Hall, 1960).
15. Leonard Hobhouse, *Social Evolution and Political Theory* (New York: Columbia University Press, 1922), p. 82; quoted in Robert Boguslaw, *The New Utopians* (Englewood Cliffs, N.J.: Prentice-Hall, 1965), p. 41.
16. Daniel Katz and Robert L. Kahn, *The Social Psychology of Organizations* (New York: John Wiley, 1966).
17. Ibid., p. 23.
18. On systems theory, see Charles G. Schoderbek et al., *Management Systems: Conceptual Considerations,* rev. ed. (Dallas: Business Publications, 1980); and James D. Thompson, *Organizations in Action* (New York: McGraw-Hill, 1967). For a critical view of the use of systems theory, see Ida Hoos, *Systems Analysis in Public Policy: A Critique* (Berkeley: University of California Press, 1972).
19. This section relies heavily on F. E. Emery and E. L. Trist, "The Causal Texture of Organizational Environments," *Human Relations* 18 (November 1965), pp. 21–32.
20. A concise summary of the theory, in propositional form, is offered in James D. Thompson, op. cit.
21. Joan Woodward, *Industrial Organization: Theory and Practice* (London: Oxford University Press, 1965).
22. A lively debate took place over the role of technology in determining organizational form. An excellent overview is found in Arthur G. Bedian, *Organizations: Theory and Analysis* (Hinsdale, Ill.: Dryden Press, 1980), Chapter 8.
23. From Thomas J. Peters and Robert H. Waterman, Jr., *In Search of Excellence: Lessons from America's Best-Run Companies* (New York: Warner, 1984).
24. See Warren F. Ilchman and Norman T. Uphoff, "Public Policy and Organizational Theory," in Richard H. Hall and Robert E. Quinn, *Organizational Theory and Public Policy* (Beverly Hills: Sage Publications, 1983), pp. 23–36.
25. There is often confusion over the term *democracy.* James Madison clarified the point in *The Federalist Papers,* Number 10. He wrote, "The two real points of difference between a democracy and a republic are: first, the delegation of the government, in the latter, to a small number of citizens elected by the rest; secondly, the greater number of citizens and greater sphere of country over which the latter may be

extended." So no one gets too close to power, because representatives wield it, and because so many different interests abound, none is able to dominate the representatives. In an important way, our republic was meant to work by limiting access to politics. However, Madison did expect more direct political controls on bureaucracy, as described in *The Federalist Papers,* Numbers 68 through 77.

26. The following comes from Dwight Waldo, "Public Administration in a Time of Revolution," *Public Administration Review* 28 (July/August 1968), pp. 362–368.

27. Such a list cannot convey the way participants saw these events. Several documents from the time are useful: *The Pentagon Papers, The White House Transcripts, The Skolnick Report,* and *Why Men Rebel* indicate the main concerns of the time. This is how far it went: The White House was advocating a plan to have the FBI and the CIA spy on and keep files on citizens deemed subversive (the qualification of some subversives was supporting the presidential candidate of the opposition party). The head of the FBI, J. Edgar Hoover, agreed to go along with the program as long as the White House officials would put it in writing. They would not, and the plan died.

28. Waldo, "Time of Revolution." The following quotations are also from this essay.

CHAPTER FIVE

Organization Psychology

> The human "motors" of the group and the organization have to be checked periodically, just as does the motor of an automobile. Without proper maintenance, all will fail.
>
> — *Chris Argyris*

To repeat a major theme of the book: The tension between what it means to be public and what it means to administer goes to the heart of much of the discipline of public administration. Themes such as openness and closedness, democracy and efficiency, equality and expertise are in constant tension when we think about the public service in the United States. The tension is clearest when we look at the links between psychology and organizations.

Since the 1920s, psychology has been a part of the workplace. As we saw earlier, industrial psychologists helped to redirect theories of organization with the Hawthorne experiments. Fritz Roethlisberger summarized the importance of the new views:

> Workers are not isolated, unrelated individuals; they are social animals and should be treated as such.... If [this idea] were systematically practiced, it would revolutionize present-day personnel work.... If this civilization is to survive, we must obtain a new understanding of human motivation and behavior ... an understanding which can be simply but effectively practiced.[1]

It is important to take organizational psychologists seriously. They have become some of the most prominent of our theorists. What they have to say is at the cutting edge of how we think about organizations. It is also important to think seriously about what organization psychology means for public administration. For example, many of the ideas in organization psychology come from private industry, where the main goal is to make individuals more productive so that companies can increase their incomes. As we saw in earlier chapters, the constitutional differences between public and private organizations may require important changes when they borrow ideas from each other.

We will see that organization psychologists propose visions of organizations and of people in organizations that seem to hold the promise of unqualified good. We are given the sense that individuals can become healthier, more productive, even more fully human; that organizations can become more productive and more democratic. We will have to closely examine these visions of health and democracy to see if they are appropriate for our political idea of what a public administration means.

Major Themes in Organization Psychology

Before we look at specific ideas about people and organizations, let us consider where a psychological approach to organizations begins. Even more so than areas in earlier chapters, such as organization theory, organization psychology is very much an applied behavioral science. There is a strong commitment in the field to both ongoing research and applying findings to actual situations. As you may have already discovered in psychology classes, the discipline stresses the use of experimentation, rigorous models for testing hypotheses, statistical correlations and tests of significance, and replication and peer review. The applied side of the discipline is similarly stringent. Organization psychologists are seriously trying to build a science of behavior in organizations. They have an important insight: If we are to develop a science of administration, it has to focus where people and organizations meet.

The starting point in organization psychology is, of course, the individual psyche.[2] Individuals are the essential building blocks of organizations. Without them offices, machines, and information have no meaning and certainly no action. Yet, individuals are enormously complicated. Why do people act the way they do? The simplest act of an individual may involve motivation, perception, memory, calculation, learning, and emotion. The act probably occurs in close proximity to other complicated individuals and involves the way people see themselves and others.

To understand people in organizations, organization theorists have tried to answer the following questions:

1. *Is there a consistent underlying structure to human personalities?*

If people are psychologically similar, it may be possible to build organizations that encourage the best efforts of individuals and at the same time satisfy important personal needs. The similarities in personalities immediately translate into practical applications. Later in the chapter we will discuss Abraham Maslow's "hierarchy of needs," an attempt to describe such an underlying personality structure.

2. *What motivates people in the workplace?*

This is the practical side of the first question. As we saw in the earlier chapters on organization theory, it is possible to see organizations in a number of ways: as a set of economic relationships, as another form of social cooperation, or as sets of political relationships. The theories of human motivation implied by each of these views differ remarkably. For instance, should the organization offer anything more than increased pay when more productivity is sought from a worker? The answer depends on whether we see workers as valuing money, status, challenge, power, or combinations of these things. The major approaches to motivation are summarized in Chapter 9, but we should recognize that these insights come from the organization psychologists.

We should remember one qualification when talking about the structure of personalities, human motivation, and related topics. The organization psychologists are talking about things we cannot actually see. No one really knows what goes on in a person's head. The human brain is poorly understood. Yet there are things that need to be done with the cooperation of other people. To help understand these practical matters, an organization psychologist will propose a theory of motivation. Some way of testing the theory will be devised, and if the results do not discourage its maker, the theory will be described in journals, books, training seminars, and eventually be applied in organizations. Yet motivation remains an intangible thing. Because of the underlying complexity of human beings, the theories will work only in some places, only with some workers, only with some job technologies. Understanding these distinctions consumes a great deal of the time of organization psychologists.

3. *How do people process information and learn?*

This concern of organization psychologists greatly influences our understanding of decision making (Chapter 13) and negotiations (Chapter 10). Essentially, people perceive a great deal, yet their perceptions are affected by emotions, existing ideas and expectations, roles in organizations, and inherent limitations of the human mind.

Psychological tests are important technical developments in this area. Is it possible to predict who the best workers will be? To predict who will have a job-related injury? To appraise individual performance in a way that enhances learning and performance? The measurement of such individual abilities, or psychometrics, is an important contribution of organization psychologists. Some of this work is discussed in Chapter 8 (personnel administration), when we discuss testing.

4. *How do group relationships affect individual behavior?*

People in organizations are almost always part of a group. There will be hierarchical groupings among supervisors and subordinates, small task-related work groups, and informal groups developed alongside the official organization structure. Organization psychologists study behavior within and between groups to understand ways that behavior in groups contributes to, and detracts from, organization goals. Some of this work is reviewed in Chapters 7 (leadership) and 9 (management practices).

This brief introduction suggests that the work of organization psychologists affects nearly every area of public administration theory and practice. What follows is a discussion of the most influential ideas public administration has borrowed from the organization psychologists.

The Human Side

Douglas McGregor proposed that there are two kinds of organizations. One he called Theory X, the other he called Theory Y.[3] According to McGregor, the "old" kind of organization was the X kind. The main assumptions in this form of organization are:

1. Management is responsible for organizing the elements of productive enterprise — money, material, equipment, and people — in the interest of economic ends.
2. Management is responsible for directing people's efforts, motivating them, controlling their actions, and modifying their behavior to fit the needs of the organization.
3. People will be passive, and even resist organizational needs, unless management persuades, rewards, punishes, and controls their activities.

To put these assumptions a little differently, the job of management is to harness human activity to organizational needs. Behind these assumptions about organization are five underlying ideas about workers. They are:

1. The average worker is by nature indolent. He or she will work as little as possible.
2. The average worker dislikes responsibility and prefers to be led. He or she lacks ambition.
3. The worker is inherently self-centered and indifferent to organizational needs.
4. The worker is by nature resistant to change.
5. The average worker is gullible, not very bright, the ready dupe of the charlatan and the demagogue.

This list of traits may bring Frederick Winslow Taylor to mind, and his discussion of the pig-iron carrier Schmidt. One of the interesting things about McGregor is the way he decides to attack the Theory X organization. He writes that social scientists have, indeed, found that workers act about like Theory X assumes they will act. But, and here is the rub, they act that way *not* because of their basic nature, but because of "the nature of industrial organizations, of management philosophy, policy, and practice." What has gotten confused, according to McGregor, is what is the cause and what is the effect.

McGregor suggests a kind of hierarchy of needs (we will take this claim up more seriously in the discussion of Abraham Maslow) in which he proposes that we all have physiological, safety, social, ego, and self-fulfillment needs. It is up to management to see to it that *all* of the worker's needs are fulfilled. In order to do this, a new kind of organization is needed. McGregor calls it Theory Y, and it rests on the following four assumptions:

1. Management is responsible for organizing the elements of productive enterprise — money, materials, equipment, people — in the interest of economic ends.
2. People are *not* by nature passive or resistant to organizational needs. They have become so as a result of experience in organizations.
3. The motivation, the potential for development, the capacity for assuming responsibility, the readiness to direct behavior toward organizational goals are all present in people. Management does not put them there. It is a responsibility of management to make it possible for people to recognize and develop these human characteristics for themselves.
4. The essential task of management is to arrange organizational conditions and methods of operation so that people can achieve their

---

BOX 5.1   Theory Y and Management

Most modern management and budgeting techniques assume a Theory Y organization. They will just not work in a Theory X context. Management by objectives (MBO), for instance, relies heavily on setting clear goals that organization members can agree to and implement rather independently. Progress toward goals is monitored by milestones rather than apparent level of effort that supervisors can observe on a day-to-day basis. Ideas for and implementation of improvement must come from many levels of employees. Without this overall commitment to participation and independently reaching the organization's goals — without Theory Y — MBO becomes just another way to watch over disgruntled employees.

Zero-base budgeting and related techniques allow substantial delegation of budget decisions. The initial ranking of programs and later evaluation of achievements assume that employees at virtually all levels of an organization share goals. Without these shared goals — without Theory Y — individuals are able to pursue their own objectives, often at the cost of the organization's goals.

There is no simple method for creating a Theory Y organization; but there is widespread agreement on the costs of maintaining a Theory X organization. Most modern management techniques will not fit into the old style of organization.

own goals *best* by directing *their own* efforts toward organizational objectives.

It was McGregor's belief that getting to Theory Y was not going to be easy. People were too accustomed to Theory X, and there would be efforts to somehow graft Theory Y onto a Theory X organization; that is, for management to act interested in the autonomy of workers but still keep rigid control of policy and process. But, McGregor believes that it is necessary to get to a genuine "industrial citizenship," and that to concentrate on the "human side" of enterprise would lead not only to substantially more materialistic achievements but also to "the good society."

In this brief comparison between types of organizations we see the scope of modern organization psychology. The main concern is, of course, getting people to work hard toward organizational objectives. This is the great concern of leaders and managers. There are much wider concerns in McGregor's work, too. He is saying that administration may have positive or negative effects on the public and that positive effects may include "the good society" and "industrial citizenship." These are political claims, self-consciously tied to organization psychology and theory.

Changing Values

Let us skip ahead chronologically and look at a list of particular features of this new thinking. The list is from an essay by Robert Tannenbaum and Sheldon Davis[4] and is a good summary of the kinds of changes necessary if we wish to go from Theory X to Theory Y. The changes are:

> Away from a view of man as essentially bad toward a view of him as basically good.
>
> Away from avoidance or negative evaluation of individuals toward confirming them as human beings.
>
> Away from a view of individuals as fixed toward seeing them as being in process.
>
> Away from resisting and fearing individual differences toward accepting and utilizing them.
>
> Away from utilizing an individual primarily with reference to his job description toward viewing him as a whole person.
>
> Away from walling off the expression of feelings toward making possible both appropriate expression and effective use.
>
> Away from gamesmanship and game playing toward authentic behavior.
>
> Away from the use of status for maintaining power and personal prestige toward use of status for organizationally relevant purposes.
>
> Away from distrusting people toward trusting them.

Away from avoiding facing others with relevant data toward making appropriate confrontation.

Away from avoidance of risk taking toward willingness to risk.

Away from a view of process work as being unproductive effort toward seeing it as essential to effective task accomplishment.

Away from primary emphasis on competition toward a much greater emphasis on collaboration.

As you can see, these are powerful changes in both organizations and in the surrounding society. The organization theorists understand that in order to remake organizations in a better mold, they will have to change a great deal more than organizations. For a comparison, recall the discussion of bureaucracy and Max Weber in Chapter 3. The ideal-typical bureaucratic values may change society, but the change may be undesirable. Here the organization theorists are making a radical turn on the values of bureaucratic theory, yet they are by no means antibureaucratic. They are trying to build effective organizations that can do the jobs of bureaucracies yet encourage "better" social values.

We can get a closer look at their sense of these better values by looking at the work of Chris Argyris.[5] He argues that organizations generally treat their employees like children, but that they should treat them like adults.

Argyris makes the following comparisons: An infant is passive, an adult is active; an infant is dependent on others, an adult is relatively independent; an infant has only a few types of reactions or behavior, an adult has many; an infant has shallow, brief, and erratic interests, an adult has intense, long-term, and coherent commitments; an infant has brief and unconnected jobs, an adult has long-term challenges that link the past with the future; an infant is in a low place in the status of society, an adult is in a high place; and, finally, the infant is impulsive and not very self-aware, and the adult is both self-aware and self-controlled.

A person cannot act like an adult if he or she is put in a childlike situation. According to Argyris, the organizational context must change so that an adult will be free to act like an adult. Basically, he calls for the following four changes. First, organizations must provide jobs that are complex, not simple. In other words, the individual must be freed from task specialization in order to be involved in a psychologically rewarding complex task. Second, the individual must assume the responsibility to make decisions. Third, the individual must be able to work well within a group and be capable of helping make group decisions. And finally, the individual must be given the opportunity to work with various levels of the organization.

The implications of Argyris's work cover many areas. As we mentioned, the new organization will look less and less like the ideal-typical bureaucracy of Max Weber. It will be a place more suited to adults than to children, and it will encourage development of the best attributes of

BOX 5.2 Individual and Organization Problems*

What happens when members of an organization acknowledge they have a problem and seek outside help? If they advertise for a consultant to diagnose their problem, they are likely to get responses from organization psychologists.

In the 1960s the State Department was known as "foggy bottom" because of its unfathomable bureaucratic procedures. Critics in and out of the department cited overly cautious and voluminous reports from field officers. Important information often was lost in the avalanche of paper. An elaborate hierarchy was constructed to sift through the field information, but without desired results.

Finally, the department sought outside help. Academics from Yale and Harvard were invited to look at the organization, diagnose the roots of the problem, and suggest ways to improve it. One consultant, using a wide range of theories, embarked on a ten-year relationship with the department, suggesting small steps for improvement and conducting studies to monitor the outcomes of the changes. Another consultant, an organization psychologist, spent a little over two weeks in the department and produced a diagnosis of the organization's culture.

The report insisted that organization members were treated like children instead of adults. Of course, childlike behavior results from such treatment. This was why, the report suggested, subordinates refuse to make judgments about what is and what is not important and simply send all information up the hierarchy. The department paid $3500 for the report.

Department officials did not know what to do with the report. It is one thing to characterize relationships; it is another to show how to change them. As the longer-term studies demonstrated, State Department pressures were not generated solely from within. An elaborate network of other organizations in the national government was in an intense competition for State Department responsibilities. Intelligence agencies in various departments and hostile congressional committees made the price of individual failure very high. Individuals within the State Department tended to cover every possible problem in their reports to make sure that the eventual events were somehow covered and, in cases of foreign policy disasters, that others could be blamed.

Since then State Department officials have been careful to hire consultants with a wide range of tools at their disposal. The organization's problems are a mix of organizational relationships and politics.

*Source: Donald Warwick, *A Theory of Public Bureaucracy: Politics, Personality, and Organization in the State Department* (Cambridge: Harvard University Press, 1975).

humans. On the face of it, a society full of such organizations would provide much better places to work and be a better place to live.

So far we have discussed a vision of a better organization, and of a better society, without getting too specific. If the organization psychologists have anything to offer, it will have to make sense to people who do things in organizations. The work of Eric Berne gives an example of translating the vision into advice.[6]

According to Berne, there are basically three categories of human action (or, to be accurate, human ego states). They are adult, child, and parent. Each of these states is characterized by certain behavior, words, and body language. For example, the parent nurtures, restricts, and blames; the adult processes information, thinks, then acts and plans; the child invents, acts on impulse, and loves. According to Berne, we each have all of these types of "tape" in our head. By using transactional analysis when looking at human interaction, a person can tell which "tape" is playing. The analyst can see, for example, if a person is acting and feeling like he or she did as a child. If, to put it differently, that old tape is playing.

When doing transactional analysis, the analyst must be aware of the various "games" that the individuals are playing. According to Berne, a person who wants to be punished will do a poor job and the boss will point it out. The game is called "Kick Me." There are, as you can imagine, many games, and many levels to these games.

At the end of every interaction in these games, there is a "stroke." The strokes come in many forms and may be either positive, make a person feel good, or negative, make a person feel bad. But what it is important to understand is that the stroke produces a feeling that the game player is accustomed to. So, in the Kick Me game, we can assume that the person making the mistakes grew up expecting those kinds of strokes from his or her parents. Put in the language of transactional analysis, the parents set the rules and the person is following that old script.

In these scripts, there are more fundamental kinds of transactions (those many levels of the games). These interactions are based on how an individual understands him- or herself and others. They are called life positions, and they are as follows:

1. I'm OK, you're OK. In this position, the individual is confident about self and trusting about others. The scripts lead to success, friends, and happiness.
2. I'm OK, you're not OK. This person belittles others and has an exaggerated amount of self-confidence.
3. I'm not OK, you're OK. The script calls for the individual to complain a great deal and to be depressed.
4. I'm not OK, you're not OK. In the words of transactional analysis, this person's script is aimed at "giving up." Nothing positive is ever expected, from oneself or from others. It is a continual case of "missing the boat."

Transactional analysis (TA) was a growth industry in the 1970s and remains a very popular method of understanding the psychological individual in an organizational setting.[7] Once a person has learned the vocabulary, it is a fairly easy method to apply, which makes it a tool managers are quick to pick up. The following lessons come from TA. First, the best managers do not play games. In order to do this, a manager needs to learn the games people play and to stop playing when he or she recognizes what is going on. Second, the best managers think about the best way to act and then act that way. The most effective manager does not always act like an adult. The manager may be a parent, or even a child, if that is most appropriate. Finally, the best manager understands that different people need different strokes. What works for one person may not work for another.

Notice how the role of manager has changed, going all the way from Theory X, to an attempt at Theory Y, and now TA. The manager becomes something of a therapist, administering not only to the measurable needs of the organization but also to deep-seated needs of individuals in the organization. In the next section we take a closer look at those needs of individuals, because much of the work of the organization psychologists emanates from an understanding of the individual psyche.

The Individual Hierarchy

There is a kind of irony here: The basis of the psychologists' criticism of the ill effects of the bureaucratic hierarchy is a belief in a personal hierarchy. This personal one is the hierarchy of human needs, best articulated by Abraham Maslow.[8]

The concept of a hierarchy of needs is based on a kind of common sense. Maslow contends that in order for an individual to realize his or her full potential, he or she must have certain needs met. Not only that, these needs can be ranked (see Figure 5.1). The needs, from the bottom up, are: physiological, safety and security, social, esteem (for the self and by others), and so on. The logic is that we will not be very interested in self-respect, for example, until we have satisfied our physical needs. An empty stomach is much more immediate than our need to be esteemed, according to the theory.

When all of these needs have been met, it is possible for an individual to work toward becoming self-actualized. Since each individual has different capacities, self-actualization comes to mean many things. In its simplest form, it means a person becomes what he or she is capable of becoming. The self-actualized individual is at the top of the psychological health scale. Being self-actualized is, we are told, the ultimate individual end of where the organization psychologists want to take us.

This has three immediate implications. First, Maslow shows it is possible to equate various needs with concrete aspects of our workplace. These connections are displayed in Figure 5.1. Again, the theory says that

FIGURE 5.1 Maslow's Hierarchy of Needs

Need Levels	General Factors	Organizational Factors
Self-Actualization	• Growth • Achievement • Advancement	• Challenging job • Achievement in work • Job growth
Ego, Status, and Esteem	• Recognition • Status • Self-esteem	• Job title/Peer recognition • Merit pay increase • Work itself/Responsibility
Social	• Companionship • Affection • Friendship	• Quality of supervision • Compatible work group • Professional friendships
Safety and Security	• Stability • Personal safety	• Safe working conditions • Job security • General salary increases
Physiological	• Food • Shelter	• Base salary • Working conditions

Adapted from John M. Invancevich, Andrew D. Szilogyi, Jr., and Marc. J. Wallace, Jr., *Organizational Behavior and Performance* (Santa Monica, Calif.: Goodyear, 1977) p. 105.

before a worker can become creative, the quality of supervision, peer recognition, base salary, and so on, have to be taken care of.

Second, Maslow is talking about moving to a new kind of organization and a new kind of person. The self-actualized person experiences an "ongoing actualization of potentials, capacities and talents, as fulfillment of mission (or call, fate, destiny, or vocation), as a fuller knowledge of, and acceptance of, the person's intrinsic nature, as an increasing trend toward unity, integration or energy within the person."[9] It follows that this self-actualized individual has positive wants and not harmful ones. The self-actualizer is self-directed.

It goes much beyond this. The self-actualizer moves a little beyond what we may be familiar with. Maslow writes that self-actualizers "have so much to teach that sometimes they seem almost like a different breed of human being."[10] The psychologically healthy person, the psychologically complete person, seems to transcend.

These periods of transcendence are called "peak experiences" and self-actualizers have these experiences as a matter of course. Those who are not self-actualized have these experiences only rarely. Peak experiences are those times during which a situation is viewed as a whole, when one's perception is relatively "ego-transcending," and when the individual has a sense of self-validation.

The people Maslow talks about are the "doers, achievers, drivers." The benefits are clear: "The potential energy an individual has available to him will be a function of the degree of self-esteem; the higher the self-esteem, the greater the potential energy." In a book entitled *Eupsychian Management,* Maslow writes that this increased energy will lead to higher organizational productivity.[11]

Third, Maslow gives a vision of organization and society being better off through the application of psychology. Maslow is explicit about this:

> In a still larger sense it can be said this way: that democracy needs absolutely for its own existence people who can think for themselves, make their own judgments, and, finally, who can vote for themselves — that is, who can rule themselves and help rule their country. . . . Therefore, any man who really wants to help his country, who is devoted to it, and who would sacrifice for it and take upon his own shoulder the responsibility for its improvement must, if he is to be logical, carry this whole philosophy into his work.[12]

Rearranging Organizations

One of the great appeals of the organization psychologists is that they have been able to break down the way we think about traditional hierarchical arrangements. The ideal-typical bureaucracy of Max Weber has been their steady target. We have gone from the time of large organizations to the era of complex organizations. The complexity has, in part, to do with their form, but the main emphasis has been on psychology.

Since the basis of this thinking is psychological, the emphasis is on process. Organizations now turn, in part, on the process of interaction of the employees. Although we take that as a truism, it is interesting to see the kind of "structure" that is implied.

Organizational Development (OD)

OD is one way to translate the insights of the organization psychologists into organizational change. A typical OD program has seven objectives:[13]

1. To increase the level of trust and support among organizational members.
2. To increase the incidence of confrontation of organizational problems, both within groups and among groups, in contrast to sweeping problems under the rug.
3. To create an environment in which authority of assigned roles is augmented by authority based on knowledge and skill.
4. To increase the openness of communication laterally, vertically, and diagonally.
5. To increase the level of personal enthusiasm and satisfaction in the organization.
6. To find synergistic solutions to problems with greater frequency. (Synergistic solutions are creative solutions in which 2 plus 2 equals something more than 4, and through which all parties gain more through cooperation than through conflict.)
7. To increase the level of self and group responsibility in planning and implementation.

The basic assumptions behind the list are self-consciously borrowed from Theory Y. But, OD goes further and is much more specific about group and system dynamics. There is also practical advice on how to get change to occur. OD efforts need both research and a "change agent." We can see the new role of research and change agents by going through a simple example of how OD works.

In the first phase, people in the organization have to learn what OD is and what problems it might help to solve. The top executives and OD consultants gather data, diagnose the problems of the organization, and check their results, again, at the top level. In the second phase the data gathering, diagnosis, and feedback continue, but now mid-level people are brought in to see if key line and staff people agree with the diagnoses of their superiors and consultants.

From that time on, the lower reaches of the organization are included. Teams are formed that cut across hierarchical divisions. These teams, following the lead of the earlier work, do their own data gathering, diagnosis of organizational problems, and so on. Often managers attend group meetings with other, unfamiliar, portions of the organization, to help them obtain a wider picture of the organization.

The heart of OD is in these learning teams, and the heart of the teams is the consultant who directs the process. The consultant is the expert in organization psychology and OD, and the interaction within teams is the method of applying the insights of psychology. One objective of the team process is to teach individuals how to learn. For learning to take place, individuals must (1) have the desire to learn, (2) "unfreeze" old behavior patterns (similar to our earlier encounter with the games people play), (3) get involved in the teams, and (4) receive feedback on their new forms of behavior.[14]

OD presents a dramatic and interesting way in which people can come together and learn how to work together. If the diagnoses of organizational difficulties are sufficiently clear, the leaders of the OD effort have a direction in which to go. When we consider the persuasive and even coercive powers of group pressure, we can appreciate the thinking behind the process even more. With the weight of organizational goals providing the power for the consultant running the group sessions, and the power of the process that consultant sets in motion, it is difficult to imagine how any single individual could challenge or resist. Indeed, one common outcome of OD efforts is to get rid of people who do not fit into the organization. This is to be done in a positive way, without casting aspersions on the people who leave, but they leave.

This last aspect of OD is a clear sign that the technique comes from the private sector, where it is very popular. It is not difficult to understand why; OD focuses on "unfreezing" unproductive behavior, involves people in teamwork, allows the organization to adapt to new situations, and the people in organizations to adapt to new projects. The language and concepts evoke images of openness, productivity, and participation. Indeed, within an organizational context, OD sounds a lot like the language of freedom. Yet public managers and leaders do not have the power to fire and transfer employees at will. Employees can only be released for "cause," and it is difficult to justify firing an employee because "she didn't fit into the team." As we have said before, the transfer of techniques from the private to the public sector must be done with care and attention to the real differences between the two. We will have more to say about this in the conclusion to this chapter.

There is one more important vision to be taken from the organization psychologists. In an interesting argument, Warren Bennis believes that the processes we have been discussing — the greater recognition of the role of psychology in organizations, new pressures for and methods of change — will, inevitably, lead us to democracy. We will take this up in the following section.

Postbureaucracy

According to most organization psychologists, there is a great need for change in our organizations. In order for individuals to be more healthy and for organizations to be more productive, traditional bureaucratic structure must be broken up. Going one step further, Warren Bennis says that there are additional reasons why bureaucracies cannot survive.[15] They are the reasons of our modern world. According to Bennis, a bureaucracy cannot survive because (1) it is surrounded by rapid and expected change; (2) organizations have grown to extreme complexity, beyond the control of traditional forms of organization; and (3) the complexity of modern technology requires highly specialized competence.

When added to the needs of the human psyche, these environmental conditions create too much of a strain on traditional bureaucratic structures. These structures are not able to respond quickly enough, and their very survival is at stake. The proper response, says Bennis, is for organizations to become more complex and less hierarchical. The structure must break down so that smaller groups of individuals, teams, are able to constantly monitor the environment and react to it appropriately. In short, complexity requires a decentralized response, not a centralized hierarchy.

These decentralized organizations have some important characteristics. They are smaller, more adaptive, more specialized, and more temporary than bureaucratic ones. They are built to cope with change. Bennis lists six requirements for these new organizations — requirements for training from organizational psychologists.

First, we must train for change. Individuals must learn to tolerate ambiguity, to cooperate with others, to adapt to temporary situations. This is a problem with individual attitudes. Second, we must employ "systems counselors" to help diagnose and treat organizational problems. These are people with special competence in understanding the workings of complex organizations. They are in-house consultants, to put it another way. Managers ignore the insights of organization psychologists, Bennis warns, and so the insights must be built into the organization. Third, incentives will need to be changed to correspond to the higher reaches of the needs hierarchy — toward more recognition of professional activity. Fourth, there is a need for continuing socialization of adults. The organizations of the future are responsible, says Bennis, for creating good citizens. Organizations do this anyway — they must take responsibility for it and do it right. Fifth, organizations need to develop problem-solving teams. The era of the loner and the maverick achiever is over. Finally, organizations need to find a way to develop and inculcate supraorganizational goals. In a decentralized, complex organization, individuals must carry the goals within themselves, since there is little direct supervision of middle managers who put the goals to work.

With these developments, says Bennis, we have moved from the era of bureaucratic organization to one of democratic organization. Individuals can find freedom, challenge, and personal growth, and new forms of citizenship within organizations.

Organization Psychology and Public Administration

So far in this chapter we have shown that organization psychologists have affected most areas of public administration. Their work informs virtually every chapter of this book. Their findings make sense too. There is good reason to believe that individuals in organizations need to be in a better work environment. There is good reason to believe that bureaucratic organizations will change, become more complex, and perhaps become much less rigid in order to handle a variety of new situations.

Yet there are several questions to ask about the work of the organization psychologists. To return to a central theme of the book, what does it mean to have a public administration? Are there political claims in the work of the organization psychologists? Do we as citizens, and, for about one-third of our readers, we as public administrators, find those to be appropriate political claims?

Consider the basic approach of organization psychologists. The new vision of individuals in the organization is a psychological one. Beneath our acting self is a hidden, needy psychological self. This hidden self becomes very important, and the work that goes into this hidden self also becomes important. The process of discovering this psychological side of individuals is expected to be very productive, since a psychologically healthy worker is a productive worker. Treat workers like adults and they will work better.

The whole line of argument is compelling, but the language and direction of psychology may not be appropriate for public administration. It is, after all, the language of pathology and the dynamic of a patient-doctor relationship. If we define our problems as a disease, we go looking for doctors who can fix them, by using their tools and by advising us on how to live. In so doing, we may be turning to a profession and possibly an elite to solve what might be public, political problems.

The language of organization psychology gives the impression that the individual and the organization are somehow on equal terms, as if the good of all is kept in mind. But make no mistake about it, in techniques like OD, in the order of treatment of organizational disorders, the organization comes first. What happens when the good of the individual comes into conflict with the good of the organization? The organization is stronger than any of its individuals. The organization psychologist is working to produce a healthy organization, which will provide the environment for a healthy adult. The order of treatment will not work unless the organization is a healthy one. The organization must have its way.

Within organizations, there is a clear sense of who comes first in the work of organization psychologists. In the arguments of Maslow and Argyris, we see an emphasis on the rise of a superior person, the self-actualizer. The case is made that the organization needs to be reinvented so that the "cream" rises to the top. Maslow writes:

> We arrange things in such a fashion that the boss or leader or general or successful person tends to be put on the defensive. But should this be so in a perfectly mobile and ideal society in which cream does rise to the top, and contrariwise that which rises to the top is therefore cream?[16]

It is one thing to call for an ideal society; it is quite another to call for automatic respect for those in positions of power.

In his book *The Bureaucratic Experience*, Ralph Hummel argues that large modern organizations strip away and replace the psyches of their members. He writes:

> In a bureaucracy, the individual must live up to external standards. If there is a conflict, he or she can be sacrificed — the strength of bureaucracy as a control institution cannot. . . . The fact is that many functionaries "become" their organization. They are the identity it gives them. They cease being private persons with private personalities. If they internalize bureaucracy's external norms, they never also internalize the right to make normative demands on their surroundings. In their public identity they become dependent on the organization because they internalize a set of norms the actual and only origin of which is external.[17]

Hummel goes on to argue that organization psychologists construct a neat fit between the self and organization by in effect denying that there is or ever was a self. The individual is instead defined only in terms an organization can understand and use. For example, the hierarchy of needs does not square with our political history, as we noted earlier; but it does make sense within organizations. The organization can give things to individuals, roughly in the order depicted in the hierarchy of needs. The worker needs his or her superior for a sense of self-esteem, or any of the other higher levels of need. The definition of self-esteem is almost wholly made in organizational terms. Organizations, then, create a dependency in employees by attacking, and perhaps destroying, the social personality. When conflict between individuals and organizations arises, OD or other persuasive techniques are used to reset the system along more official, and more "healthy" lines.

Hummel's arguments are disturbing, but need to be taken seriously. Psychology is a central part of theories of public administration, but it remains to be seen whether psychologists have found an adequate answer for how the public fits into administration.

> **BOX 5.3** Personal Values and Hierarchies
>
> Sociologists like to study the values people have, mainly to keep track of how they change over time. The most basic values regard orientation toward ideas like personal freedom, individual rights, psychological comfort, societal order, and so on. Researchers usually refer to these ideas as fitting into personal value hierarchies.
>
> The hierarchies differ remarkably. A large part of the American citizenry thinks that personal freedom and individual rights are the most important values, ranking well above societal order. Another large group values psychological comfort highly, and since they rank personal freedom much lower than the first group, these people are apparently aware that the freedom to choose can be discomforting. A third large group values religion and societal order most highly, ranking individual rights very low.
>
> It is difficult to fit these three broad types into a single type of organization role. Indeed, it is difficult to fit some of these people into any organizations. Measurements of values hierarchies suggest that theories of shared needs exaggerate our similarities.

We began with the idea of finding a healthy person. In order to do that, we were given the proposition that to be most healthy, we must fulfill a hierarchy of needs. There is no evidence that human beings operate by this hierarchy.[18] There is no agreement on the workings of human motivation, and the best researchers can offer are rough rules of thumb (see the discussion in Chapter 9). If, for example, psychological needs and motivation were acknowledged as the most basic of human needs, we would expect to find political states organized around that fact. We know, of course, that this is not the case. We even have a state in our union that is unambiguous in its understanding of needs. On its license plate is the motto: "Live Free or Die." The language of modern psychology may be misleading on much that is political.

This is not to say the organization psychologists are wrong in their critique of bureaucracy and relationships in organizations. There are reasons to suspect these are repressive. But we go in the wrong direction when we start with the bias of individual pathology. The idea that the first step of intervention is into the worker's psychological self, with the accompanying attention to process, is the triumph of the personal in what should be a public world. When we think about public we think about appearing and speaking and listening and acting in front of — and with — others.[19] It is exactly in this realm that the "public" person must be judged. When we think about administration in public terms, then we may want to think of arrangements in which each of us is able to stand up and

> **BOX 5.4** Computers and the Future of Organization Psychology*
>
> The next generation of computers will be capable of a kind of logic, even thinking, that is not possible today. Computer engineers call this capability *artificial intelligence* (AI).
>
> Today's computers can calculate according to logic programmed into them. AI computers will be able to make logical inferences based on a series of calculations; that is, they will be able to make judgments and, for instance, evaluate a series of events from several points of view. Many of the judgments now performed by humans in organizations and the professions will be done more quickly, cheaply, and accurately by machines. Already many medical diagnoses can be done much more accurately by machines. Large brokerage firms use many AI programs to keep track of markets and plan investment strategies. Full-scale AI applications may be less than a decade away.
>
> Organization psychology will take on new meaning under AI. Many of the judgments now performed by mid-level managers will be done by machines. The need to respond to a complicated environment will be there, and machines will do a better job of it than people. There will be a greater need to feed information to the machines, and so a greater proportion of jobs will be lower paid, lower skilled, and demand less of the overall capabilities of the individual. The people who program the machines, who engage in conversations with them, and who carry out the plans will most likely be highly skilled, highly paid, and speak in a language quite different from the rest of the organization members — and the rest of the citizenry.
>
> It is rightly said that information is power. As machines of the not-so-distant future amplify the uses and application of information, the uses and application of power will also be amplified. It is not at all clear that we have strong enough traditions of a public administration to deal with these forces democratically.
>
> *See the discussion of computing and information technology, in *Public Administration Review* 46, (November 1986), special issue on public management information systems.

be seen, heard, and counted. It may be a mistake to adopt the private sector truism that the people in an organization are a resource that needs to be managed. The people, both inside and outside of the organization, may be much more than that.

The pull, then, in public administration, would be away from the turning in of the psychologists and to the making public of both administrators and citizens. There is, of course, the possibility that a side result of such a change might be a new definition of a healthy organization and of a healthy individual. But we think it is clear that, if we recall our public-administration split, psychology goes to the far side of the administrative scale when instead we may want to search for public answers.

Looking at the larger picture, the organizations of the future will surely be different, but the picture offered by organization psychologists does not necessarily add up to democracy. Nor do they assure us that administrators will be taken over by the public. A good case can be made that administration will become less and less public, and that the logic of this new administration leads not to democracy but to a new elite.

SUMMARY

In this chapter, we have seen the evolution of psychology as applied to the workplace. As early as the Hawthorne experiments, industrial psychologists have had an increasingly significant impact on how we think about organizations. It was understood almost from the start that the psychologists sought to increase organizational output by focusing on the individual psyche. The psychologists were able to offer critiques of organizations that helped show how personal growth may be limited in an organizational setting. Naturally, the psychologists also provided models for greater interpersonal interaction, better mental health, and increased organizational efficiency.

Moving from the mechanical model to organic models, organization psychologists also suggested ways in which to reconceptualize and redesign organizations. Put differently, these theorists tried to break up the hierarchical models of bureaucracy that the earlier theorists had developed. These newer models, they argued, were geared for the rapidly changing modern context as well as for a much healthier environment for the employee.

Certainly these thinkers have provided interesting and, in many ways, accurate critiques of large bureaucratic and complex organizations. What they have written is the wave of the present and may well be the wave of the future. We need to note, however, that the demands of public administration are often different from the demands of private organizations. Although it may be wholly reasonable for private organizations to want to direct individuals' efforts in order to increase productivity, we believe that this focus on the individual runs counter to the "public" part of our public organizations. It may be that what is efficient for private organizations is totally inappropriate for public administration.

NOTES

1. F. J. Roethlisberger, *Management and Morale* (Cambridge: Harvard University Press, 1941), p. 26.
2. Excellent introductions to various aspects of organization psychology are offered in Wayne Cascio, *Applied Psychology in Personnel Management,* 2nd ed. (Reston, Va.: Reston, 1982); Don Mankin et al., *Classics of Industrial and Organizational Psychology* (Oak Park, Ill.: Moore, 1980); and William Eddy and W. W. Burke, eds., *Behavioral Science and the Manager's Role* (La Jolla, Calif.: University Associates, 1980). This section relies heavily on William B. Eddy, *Public Organization Behavior and Development* (Cambridge, Mass.: Winthrop, 1981), Chapters 2–5.
3. Douglas M. McGregor, *The Human Side of Enterprise* (New York: McGraw-Hill, 1960).
4. Robert Tannenbaum and Sheldon Davis, "Values, Man and Organizations," in Warren Schmidt, ed., *Organizational Frontier and Human Values* (Belmont, Ca.: Wadsworth, 1970), pp. 131–145.
5. Chris Argyris, *Integrating the Individual and the Organization* (New York: John Wiley, 1964); *Personality and Organization* (New York: Harper & Row, 1957); and "Organizational Man: Rational *and* Self-Actualizing?" *Public Administration Review* 33, no. 4 (July/August, 1973).
6. This section is based on Eric Berne, *Games People Play* (New York: Grove Press, 1964), and *Transactional Analysis in Psychotherapy* (New York: Ballantine Books, 1973).
7. See M. James, *The OK Boss* (Reading, Mass.: Addison-Wesley, 1975).
8. Abraham Maslow, *Toward a Psychology of Being* (Princeton, N.J.: Van Nostrand Reinhold, 1962).
9. Ibid., p. 23.
10. Ibid., p. 67.
11. Abraham Maslow, *Eupsychian Management* (Homewood, Ill.: Richard D. Irwin, 1965).
12. Ibid., pp. 61–62.
13. The list is from Wendell French, "Organizational Development: Objectives, Assumptions, and Strategies," *California Management Review* 12, no. 2, 1969.
14. This part is based on Warren Bennis and Edgar Schein, *Personality and Organizational Change* (New York: John Wiley, 1965), p. 49.

15. For an accessible statement, see Warren Bennis, "Organizations of the Future," *Personnel Administration* (September/October 1967); for a more detailed treatment, see Warren Bennis and Phillip Slater, *The Temporary Society* (New York: Harper & Row, 1968).
16. Maslow, *Eupsychian Management,* op. cit., p. 137.
17. Ralph Hummel, *The Bureaucratic Experience,* 2nd ed. (New York: St. Martin's, 1982), p. 106.
18. For example, one might look at Dorothy Lee, *Freedom and Culture* (New York: Spectrum Books, 1959); or Hannah Arendt, *The Human Condition* (Garden City, N.Y.: Anchor Books, 1959); and *Eichman in Jerusalem: A Report on the Banality of Evil* (New York: Viking Press, 1965).
19. This is discussed at length in Arendt, *The Human Condition,* op. cit.

CHAPTER SIX

The Civil Service

> What is representative government, anyhow?
> ... Say, the people's voice is smothered by the cursed civil service law; it is the root of all evil in our government.... First, this great and glorious country was built up by political parties; second, parties can't hold together if their workers don't get the offices when they win; third, if the parties go to pieces, the government they built up must go to pieces, too; fourth, then there'll be hell to pay.
>
> — *George Washington Plunkitt,*
> *Tammany Hall Ward Boss*

This chapter is about those people who work in our public organizations and how those organizations handle their workers. It is also, in part, about how the civil service has evolved in the United States and how that evolution continues. We will review the Reagan administration, and make judgments about the changes in our public organizations during his presidency.

The pressing business of the current literature on civil service concerns unionization of public employees, criteria for establishing pay, and whether public employees should be allowed to strike.[1] The whole subject of the public interest is at stake in the debate, and it is easy to see why. For example, we expect our garbage to be picked up several times a week. That, for us, is in the public interest. For those who pick up the garbage, it is necessary to make enough money to provide for their families. Again, a stable working class is in our public interest.

But what happens in a time of economic decline, when the city has tight budgets and the garbage collectors' wages do not keep up with inflation? How can we let public employees become members of a lower class while continuing to do their work? That would be socially disruptive and morally wrong. The garbage workers should strike. But, it is also clear that we still want our garbage collected. It would be socially disruptive, morally wrong, and smell bad if it was not collected. Where is the public interest now? How did we get ourselves in this particular kind of mess?

> **BOX 6.1** The Public Interest and Public Employee Strikes
>
> In 1986 two strikes occurred, almost simultaneously, that symbolized the uneasy position of the contemporary civil service. In Philadelphia 12,000 blue-collar workers, many of them garbage collectors, went out on strike. Their union wanted the same wage and benefit package earlier granted to other city workers, and wanted also to limit the city's use of contracted services that take the place of union workers. The city did not trust the union leadership and demanded an audit of the union health care trust fund.
>
> In Detroit 7000 workers, including sewage plant workers and garbage collectors, walked out over money. Workers wanted a 26 percent increase over three years, arguing they needed to catch up from earlier years when no raises were granted. The city offered 2 percent the first year, and remaining years based on ability to pay. The city projected a modest budget surplus for the year.
>
> City officials in both Philadelphia and Detroit felt squeezed by the twin pressures of tight budgets and a loss of federal aid under the Reagan administration. The economic outlook for the subsequent two years was not strong in either city, and further cuts in federal aid had been proposed in Washington. In both cases the cities' position was closest to the final settlement, and the trend these strikes symbolize is not lost on government employees: They are being asked to bear the brunt of tight budgets and diminishing federal aid.

To best understand where we are, we need to go back to where we have been. In the case of the civil service, and how we view public employees in the United States, that means going back to the early days of the Constitution.

The Federalists and Andrew Jackson

The earliest years of the new American government were peaceful, at least as far as the civil service was concerned. The Federalists' main concerns were with establishing a government, working out the rudimentary details of the separation of powers, and getting on with the business of commerce and diplomatic relations. George Washington's presence quieted many questions that would otherwise have caused bitter conflict. The Congress trusted Washington to choose his own advisors, today's cabinet secretaries, and to remove them when he felt like it. The departments of government were his to run. Although Washington did once go to the Congress to discuss his thoughts on various policy matters, their disorganized response prompted him to present only complete proposals and not involve the Congress in earlier stages of policies.[2]

The Federalist view of a civil service is often characterized as elitist, but they had reasons for their positions. They were the Founders; their supporters were the best-educated and most experienced in running organizations; it was obvious who should fill the few positions in a federal service. Patronage and merit were not distinct concepts to them.

The Federalists, at least in their early years, did not have to cope with the divisions among political parties while setting up the government. Political parties were not at all recognized in the Constitution, and virtually all the Founders regarded parties as the worst sort of influence on politics. Jefferson, later to be the opposition party leader and the first non-Federalist president, wrote: "If I could not go to heaven but with a party, I would not go there at all."

But the environment changed. There were more cities, and in the cities there were more people. Better transportation helped connect the increasingly urban population. The steamboat and the steam locomotive began to replace the oxcart and river raft. Railroads spread west, while the east experienced what Frederick Jackson Turner called an "epidemic of canal building." The United States was beginning to industrialize and bureaucratize. Between 1830 and 1850 a great shaping and sophistication of industry took place. There was, in the words of one writer, a "transition from mother and daughter power to water and steam power." This, in part, changed the economy from household manufacture to the factory system.

Although the love of equality, the love of competition, and the ideal of the self-made man still held in the west, it was in constant tension with the economic centralizing and growth in the well-populated east. Put differently, the kind of environment the Federalists had planned for, an environment that could more easily come under the control of a centralized power, was developing. But they had not counted on these disparate interests forming continuous factions — political parties.

Andrew Jackson was elected president in this new environment. With his election, the Federalists were really through. Jackson was the "people's" president. He was the leader of "King Mob." Although it would seem that a dramatic change might have taken place when he got to Washington, it did not happen.

First, Jackson set the tone for the times by being a strong president. He came to office with the leadership ideas of a soldier. He was a strong defender of the Union. Jackson became president forty years after the office had been established. He well understood that the president was head of the executive branch. As the private business of the United States increased, so too did the business of the president.

In the final account, Jackson depended upon experience to solve problems. As Leonard White pointed out in his book *The Federalists,* the Jacksonians "had nothing to guide them beyond what Hamilton had said in the *Federalist Papers*"; and, we should add, what the Federalists had done in practice. Given these intellectual limits, and in response to the growing, more sophisticated environment, the Jacksonians enlarged the authority of the executive. The growth took an expected bureaucratic form. The key to the times was growth, not change.

With Jackson's emphasis on centralization came his attempt to democratize the civil service. He wanted his people in the public service, and we call the concept rotation in office. In principle, it meant that those in the public service could be replaced by any new president. Jackson liked the notion of rotation in office for several reasons. First, he believed that most government jobs could be handled by common people. There is some kind of logic about reasonable people accepting reasonable jobs and doing reasonably well. Second, it was a democratic idea. He recognized that the Federalists' idea of a highly educated elite in the civil service was undemocratic. Third, there was nothing to stop Jackson from appointing his people, because there were no qualifying examinations or job security for public employees. Fourth, there was a powerful anti-intellectual spirit during Jackson's presidency. Finally, and possibly most important, political parties were becoming highly organized. To remain powerful, this political machinery needed to reward its personnel, and these rewards came more and more from civil service jobs.

What we have to note is that Jackson's ideas were much more powerful — in this case — than his actions. The *idea* of rotation in office, which became the spoils system about a decade later, was really an idea to Jackson. He did not use his power to create a spoils system. The most careful estimate is that between a fifth and a tenth of all federal officeholders were removed during Jackson's administration, and many of those for good reason. To put it a different way, Andrew Jackson removed no greater proportion of officeholders than did Thomas Jefferson when he took office.

What was created soon after Jackson was a kind of dual public service. One part consisted of career people, the other of political appointees. It is not difficult to understand why the period from about 1840 until 1860 saw the establishment of the spoils system: The country truly was divided. The divisions that led to the Civil War also made governance next to impossible. Elected officials in the national government needed patronage to assemble a governing coalition in Washington.

The story in the cities was quite different. The recent emergence of parties coincided with the influx of immigrants, and party officials lost no time organizing the new armies of voters. A generous view of the matter was that it took some time for people to fully understand and deal with the increased power of parties, wealth of citizens, and size of public administration. To most it looked like corruption, pure and simple.

BOX 6.2   A Story of Machine Politics*

The Tammany Democratic political machine controlled New York City politics from before the Civil War until the election of Mayor LaGuardia in 1934. One Tammany ward boss, George Washington Plunkitt, was very frank about the workings of the machine.

Plunkitt saw virtue in his actions. He said, "Everybody is talkin' these days about Tammany men growin' rich on graft, but nobody thinks of drawin' the distinction between honest graft and dishonest graft . . . My party's in power in the city, and it's goin' to undertake a lot of public improvements. Well, I'm tipped off, say, that they're going to lay out a new park at a certain place. I see my opportunity and I take it. I go to that place and I buy up all the land I can. . . . Ain't it perfectly honest to charge a good price and make a profit on my investment and foresight? Of course, it is. Well, that's honest graft."

Plunkitt's New York City politics were also ethnic politics. He said "The Irish were born to rule, and they're the honestest people in the world. Show me the Irishman who would steal a roof off an almshouse! He don't exist. Of course, if an Irishman had the political pull and the roof was much worn, he might get the city authorities to put on a new one and get the contract for himself, and buy the old roof at a bargain — but that's honest graft.

Plunkitt understood power, and worked to get more of it for the party and, of course, for himself. "I acknowledge that you can't keep an organization together without patronage. Men ain't in politics for nothin'. They want to get somethin' out of it." The main "somethin'" was city jobs, which the party controlled. But they also kept power by convincing people to vote for them. "What tells in holdin' your grip on your district is to go right down among the poor families and help them in the different ways they need help. . . . If a family is burned out I don't ask whether they are Republicans or Democrats. . . . I just get quarters for them, buy clothes for them if their clothes were burned up, and fix them up till they get things runnin' again. It's philanthropy, but it's politics, too — mighty good politics. . . . The poor are the most grateful people in the world, and, let me tell you, they have more friends in their neighborhoods than the rich have in theirs."

*Source: William L. Riordon, *Plunkitt of Tammany Hall: A Series of Very Plain Talks on Very Practical Politics* (New York: Dutton, 1963).

Reform

Although there had been some attempts to reform the public bureaucracy (for example, in 1814, army surgeons had to take an examination, and ten years later examinations were required of navy surgeons), nothing serious happened until after the Civil War.

In the 1860s, a Republican representative from Rhode Island, Thomas Allen Jenckes, systematically studied administration in America, Europe, and Asia. Jenckes liked centralized administration and called for reforms. He admired the highly centralized Prussian civil service, the French scheme that allowed a few ministers to control hundreds of thousands of bureaucrats, and China's well-organized treasury department.

Representative Jenckes believed that: (1) open and competitive examinations should be used, (2) the appointing power should be taken over by an independent agency, and (3) the agency should be empowered to "conduct trials or hearings in cases of inefficiency and misconduct and to pass sentences of suspension or removal."[3] Jenckes's reform ideas were twenty years ahead of their time.

President Grant tried to get some reform passed and actually did sign the first national civil service reform bill, but under political pressure gave up on its implementation. President Hayes had a study produced that showed in great detail the tremendous amount of graft in government. Yet Hayes could produce no reform. The National Civil Service Reform League was created to lobby for change. Change finally did come, but only because graft and the spoils system had gotten out of hand.

The "gotten-out-of-hand" story is fairly dramatic. In 1880, Charles J. Guiteau supported James Garfield for president. Garfield won, and Guiteau wrote the president-elect a letter, explaining that because of his support, Guiteau wanted the consulship at Paris. Indeed, that was the only consulship he would accept. Guiteau got no consulship at all. As a way of expressing his anger, Guiteau shot and killed James Garfield. The United States had a dead president, and the Pendleton Act was passed in 1883. The Pendleton Act reformed the national civil service.

From 1883 to now, we have a history of reform. Before going into the reform, it is necessary to think about the choices that had already been made. In those choices lie many of the tensions of our civil service. The attempt of Jackson to politicize and centralize the administration ended in its centralization. Later efforts at professionalization and improving management added to the bureaucratization of the civil service. Out of the tensions between the Federalist view and the Jacksonian view came an approach to civil service that we are not entirely reconciled to.

We seem constantly bothered by the desire for decentralization as well as centralization; we want a competent, professional civil service, as well as a civil service responsive to the popular will; we believe in democracy, but we also demand an efficient public service. While all of these tensions

> **BOX 6.3** Guiteau's Letter to Garfield*
>
> Charles Guiteau wrote the following letter to the newly elected president, James A. Garfield:
>
> *March 26, 1881*
>
> *Gen. Garfield:*
>
> *I understand from Col. Hooker of the Nat'l committee that I am to have a consulship. I hope it is the consulship at Paris, as that is the only one I care to take. Wish you would send in my name for the consulship at Paris. Mr. Walker, the present consul, has no claim on you for the office, I think as the men that did the business last fall are the ones to be remembered.*
>
> *Very Respectfully,*
>
> *Charles J. Guiteau*
>
> *Source: From the U.S. Office of Personnel Management, Washington, D.C., quoted in Jay M. Shafritz et al., *Personnel Management in Government: Politics and Process*, 3rd ed. (New York: Marcel Dekker, 1986), p. 4.

are being played out, it is important to remember that much of what we are feeling is part of our history. By 1883, the administration part of public administration was legally set in motion.

The Pendleton Act

The Pendleton Act helped put the public service on the merit system. It provided for selection of employees by open competitive examination; it protected employees against political pressures; it set up the Civil Service Commission, a semi-independent commission, to oversee the merit system, charging it to implement the provisions of the act. Many current practices in merit systems, competitive examinations, the "rule of three" (the three most qualified applicants are interviewed for a position), etc., were part of the Pendleton Act.

Given the political context, it is not surprising that the Pendleton Act did not cover all civil servants. In fact, only 10 percent of federal employees were affected. However, the act provided that presidents could include additional positions in the merit system. Presidents "blanketed in" whole groups of workers, so that by 1908 almost two-thirds of those in the federal service were under a merit system. More than 90 percent are covered now.

Histories of reform often emphasize the federal experience, but the local governments exemplify the main forces working on public bureaucracies in the last century. The main targets of reform there were the city bosses, the heads of political parties who may or may not hold elective office, but who held most political power in a locality. These bosses, operating under what is called "machine politics," openly traded jobs and other benefits for political support. These organizations were usually focused on particular ethnic groups, mainly Irish, and were remarkably successful in getting out the votes in sufficient numbers to win offices for the party.[4]

However, the city bosses were not routed by the reformers. Instead, the environment of local politics changed. Machine politics has always been a working-class phenomenon. The jobs the party was able to control were most often in the basic services such as trash collection, water and sewer works, and road crews. The middle classes were the political support behind reformers, and fewer of them were tempted by the lower-paying jobs that required little formal education. The machines did fall as the "good government" forces rose, but the change was, in large part, a result of a shrinking working class and a growing middle class. The work force was trading the blue for the white collar.

The development can be seen in the evolution of local government structures, too. There was a movement from the weak executive model to more professionalized forms, such as council-manager and others that employ a chief administrator. The problem with the older forms was that they let politics get in the way of efficiency. A typical weak executive government also has citizens elect many of the administrative officials. Counties, in particular, often separately elect council members or commissioners, a sheriff, an assessor, a treasurer, a county clerk, a prosecuting attorney, and even a coroner. Many officials are relatively independent, and decentralized administration simply is designed to favor political responsiveness over centralized efficiency. The long ballot is done away with in the newer forms, and the less numerous council members select the professional administrator who runs the executive departments. This centralized style of administration is endorsed by most good government reformers and such professional associations as the International City Management Association.

Although some of the change was in response to demands by reformers, most changes were the result of policy failures. Also, the nature of the work force was changing. The growing middle class — a white-collar class — began to respond to crises by a call for greater organizational efficiency. It was the call for increased efficiency, as well as the fear of scandal, that

> **BOX 6.4** The Meaning of Merit
>
> Nearly every government in America officially employs a merit system in its civil service. The U.S. Office of Personnel Management says a merit system makes sense because:
>
> 1. Hiring is nonpolitical, and so government is open to all citizens. This results in a more representative and responsive government.
> 2. Employment is based on fairness, effectiveness, and efficiency. This increases productivity and improves citizens' confidence in government.
> 3. The merit system strives to improve employee performance and permits separations only for inadequate performance. Thus wholesale turnover and discontinuity of service is prevented, from which a high level of experience and expertise is developed.
> 4. The stress on openness and competition makes a career in government attractive.
> 5. Merit system provisions simplify personnel systems, making government administration cost less and enhancing compliance with federal, state, and local laws concerning equal treatment.
>
> On closer inspection, merit systems do not solve every problem of a civil service. There remains important conflict between competition and openness to all groups in society. It is not at all clear that efficiency and effectiveness are bound so closely to fairness and democracy.
>
> The history of the idea of merit points to some of these tensions. The Federalists genuinely argued that their class included the people best suited for government service. After all, they had the best education and experience for the job. The Jacksonians added the idea of openness and representation, but coupled with centralization of administration. Their idea was that the common person could be meritorious, too. During the Civil War period and even after the war, advocates of patronage cited the benefits of a work force that must perform in order to keep their jobs. In some parts of the east and midwest the argument is still made that a snowplow driver who can be replaced at any time will more quickly follow an order to get to the plow at 3:00 a.m.
>
> The modern idea of merit, that it is in inherent conflict with patronage, became national policy in late 1938. Franklin D. Roosevelt signed an order announcing the rigid separation of merit and patronage — after his own very numerous appointees had been

> transferred into the career civil service. To this day the most carefully crafted civil service exams rank most white applicants highly, whereas very few blacks pass. The idea that merit systems bring these things together — efficiency and democracy, openness and competition, expertise and performance — remains unfulfilled.

led to the passage of the Pendleton Act. Merit systems were adopted for the first time by the national government. It was a time of the growing bureaucratization and professionalization of organizations in the United States.

The latest set of federal reforms embodies the current thinking on merit systems at all levels of government. The Civil Service Reform Act of 1978 (CSRA) abolished the U.S. Civil Service Commission and put in its place two offices. The first office is the Office of Personnel Management (OPM) and is headed by a director appointed by the president. Its function is to help the president manage the personnel resources of government, much as the Office of Management and Budget prepares and oversees the president's budget. The second office, the Merit System Protection Board (MSPB), retains the independent structure of the Civil Service Commission, but its duties are now limited to hearing appeals of adverse actions, reviewing OPM regulations for threats to the merit system, and investigating complaints of improper personnel practices. There were also reforms in the treatment of unionized employees, to be described in Chapter 10. The overall emphasis is on giving the executive the tools to manage the government. In the list of values that merit systems support, efficiency has clearly come out on top.

People in the Public Service

Before getting into the details of personnel administration (the subject of Chapter 8), it is necessary to know just who we are talking about. Except for members of the military, government employees are known by their positions. In the federal service, for instance, employees are ranked in grades, the General Service (GS) and the Wage Service (WS) grades, the latter for blue-collar workers. The GS grades go from GS-1 (the lowest) to GS-18, with the top three grades, the most prestigious and highest-paid positions, constituting the Senior Executive Service. College graduates generally start at GS-7, whereas people with graduate degrees start at about GS-11. Substantial power begins at GS-14. Table 6.1 lists the num-

> **BOX 6.5** Political Activity and Government Employees
>
> The Pendleton Act of 1883 sought to protect employees from coercion to give political service or tribute. The Hatch Act, passed in 1939, went much further toward defining the dos and don'ts of political activity for government employees. Most states have similar provisions, covering virtually all public employees. Here are some of the things a government employee may *not* do:
>
> Be a candidate for nomination or election to a partisan political office, and any nonpartisan office must not conflict with job responsibilities.
>
> Campaign for or against a political party or candidate in an election for public or party office.
>
> Serve as an officer of a political party or on a committee for any party.
>
> Solicit, receive, or in any way handle political contributions for partisan political purposes, nor contribute to any political cause while on government property.
>
> Take an active part in managing a political campaign (not even sell tickets for fund-raising dinners).
>
> Work at election polls on behalf of a party or partisan candidate.
>
> Distribute campaign material.
>
> Serve in any official capacity at a party convention.
>
> Address a convention, rally, or caucus or similar gathering on partisan contests or issues.
>
> Use their automobile to transport voters to the polls on behalf of partisan candidates or organizations.

ber of people in each grade and the average and aggregate salaries for those grades.

Who are these people? Where do they come from? Those with any knowledge of how power is divided in American society will not be at all surprised at which people occupy which end of the GS scale.

When compared to the population in general, high-level administrators in the federal government disproportionately represent white males from middle- and upper-class families. According to the 1980 census, the total federal service is made up of 78 percent whites and 22 percent minorities, about the same as the general population. However, the higher

TABLE 6.1 Employees and Pay in the Federal Government

GRADE AND STEP DISTRIBUTION
General Schedule (including merit pay as of March 31, 1985)

Grade	Aggregate Salary	Average Salary	Total Employment	1	2	3	4	5	6	7	8	9	10	No Step	Merit Pay
01	18,398,316	9,523	1,932	1,742	38	9	25	21	9	7	5	15	47	14	
02	160,915,955	10,748	14,972	12,518	599	264	301	301	119	111	111	104	398	146	
03	916,099,761	12,236	74,871	40,290	8,072	4,714	5,631	3,370	2,046	2,019	1,441	1,511	4,893	884	
04	2,301,537,204	14,272	161,259	46,810	17,704	13,843	20,138	12,690	9,158	10,039	8,872	5,373	14,818	1,814	
05	3,240,227,291	16,289	198,916	42,292	18,098	16,685	24,164	19,841	15,050	15,753	14,722	9,607	19,630	3,074	
06	1,711,490,890	18,467	92,677	9,813	6,332	8,093	12,320	9,636	11,044	10,504	9,028	5,412	9,706	789	
07	2,805,847,900	20,227	138,720	32,654	10,649	10,697	15,622	14,196	11,011	13,297	10,322	6,871	11,618	1,783	
08	677,835,386	22,885	29,619	2,506	1,851	2,468	3,978	3,214	3,148	3,775	2,583	2,536	3,181	379	
09	3,612,576,391	24,508	147,401	35,200	16,048	13,197	19,059	13,874	10,473	11,556	8,439	6,803	11,388	1,363	
10	841,549,898	27,632	30,456	2,538	2,555	2,315	4,311	3,888	3,563	3,725	2,271	1,865	3,139	286	
11	5,171,936,401	29,772	173,718	28,340	22,795	16,484	24,881	19,646	13,845	14,785	9,211	7,645	14,783	1,303	
12	6,410,114,319	36,082	177,654	20,143	17,991	15,613	25,565	21,869	17,265	18,064	12,773	9,832	17,072	1,467	
13	5,112,995,141	43,523	117,478	5,502	5,015	5,158	8,244	7,138	6,517	7,089	5,144	4,067	6,801	56,121	56,169
14	3,103,562,852	51,714	60,013	1,831	1,474	1,338	2,346	2,347	2,433	2,734	1,569	1,213	1,986	40,742	40,600
15	1,833,205,237	61,505	29,806	286	275	360	699	584	681	697	487	406	775	24,556	24,553
16	49,133,166	67,957	723	23	20	29	128	146	115	81	94	87			
17	9,961,500	68,700	155	15	13	14	30	68							
18	5,015,100	68,700	73	73											
Total	37,982,362,708	26,187	1,450,433	282,576	129,529	111,313	167,447	132,830	106,471	114,236	87,072	63,347	120,235	135,321	121,322

Average grade: 8.39 Median grade: 9

Source: *Federal Employees' Almanac 1986* (Falls Church, Va.: Federal Employees' Digest, 1986).

civil service positions are 95 percent white; of the whites in higher positions, only about 5 percent are women. It is not hard to understand how these white males came to fill most of the more important positions. These men enjoyed the advantages of growing up with money, education, and a cosmopolitan view of the world. Many went to private high schools and prestigious colleges and graduate schools.[5]

Children of professionals and executives who went into government work were most likely to reach positions of GS-16 to GS-18. The children of farmers and blue-collar workers who went into government work — and were able to work their way to the higher-level positions — generally could reach GS-14 and GS-15. Those who started their careers as professionals were most likely to reach the highest positions in the bureaucracy. About one-third of the professionals at the top of our public service began as lawyers or scientists.

BOX 6.6 The Senior Executive Service

The Civil Service Reform Act of 1978 established the Senior Executive Service (SES). The three top levels of the general service grade, GS-16 to GS-18, were converted into what was intended to be a more prestigious, more professional, and more competent cadre of top managers in the national government. The SES is designed much like the top levels of the British and Canadian public services. These career administrators are expected to be neutrally competent, serving Democrat and Republican politicians with equal devotion. They are also expected to be able to change agencies and assignments, carrying their rank more in the person than in the position.

One of the key ideas behind the SES is that the reform would make top government managers more productive. Their bosses, political appointees, would set goals and expectations and write performance evaluations. The superior performers get bonuses, up to $20,000 per year, and the weaker performers are encouraged to leave. Critics charged this amounted to politicizing the senior reaches of the civil service, since the political people writing performance appraisals might be more partisan than competent.

At the inception of SES, top managers had a strong incentive to join. It appeared that about half of SES members would receive bonuses. The first year they did, but Congress cut the bonuses in subsequent years. For those who did not join, but elected to stay in their GS-16, 17, or 18 position, career progression was over. A bit disgruntled, 96 percent of officials in those top grades signed up.

These top-level decision makers have certain traits and attitudes in common.[6] They are group workers, not individualists. They accept the restrictions of huge, complex organizations, and generally understand and willingly accept the need for coordination and cooperation. They have high ideals and believe that they are responsible for programs with high social value. The authority they work with comes from outside of themselves. This is an interesting public administration statement; their authority is from the public.

Although they are idealists, these high-level administrators rarely seem to reflect on abstract ideals. For example, the ideas of justice, democracy, or freedom are not topics they are likely to ponder. What they do think about are particulars. These decision makers stick to their subjects; they concentrate on how to improve education, or public health, or whatever. These attitudes are not at all surprising. These appointees are careful politically; they believe in the institutions of government, and think that rules of the political game should be played fairly. Mostly, they have liberal democratic values, and they favor free speech, due process, equality, and so on. Yet, not-so-subtle changes occur as these people go through their careers. Those at the highest levels of bureaucracy, with the longest time in the public service, are less likely to express respect for democratic values or to believe that the political process offers a meaningful opportunity to change public policy than their younger colleagues.[7]

We might speculate about why the people at the top of the bureaucratic structure have those attitudes. Have they become isolated from the public? Have they simply learned how to operate in a bureaucracy without close contact with those for whom they work? Do the "best" survive, or is it those who are clever bureaucrats? What have these people learned about the way power and democratic principles fit together? We can only speculate.

Professionalism

The work of public servants is difficult to classify, since there are so many types of work done. A comprehensive list would more than fill this book. One trend that helps us to understand the life of a public servant is the growing professionalism in public organizations.[8]

In general terms, a profession is a reasonably clear-cut occupational field that requires higher education and offers a lifetime career. Professions perform several functions:

1. They stake a territory. Lawyers try to gain control over legal issues, engineers try to gain control over technical issues, education administrators try to control curriculum and logistics of schools, all according to standards set within their professions. A profession does not gain recognition if others are allowed to have an authoritative opinion in the conduct of their field.

2. They form a corps with substantial control over the operation of an agency primarily employing them, especially in the policy area. They try to dominate employment in the organizations in which they work. The standards of a profession can be enforced only when the personnel in an agency belong to the profession.
3. They control entry into the profession, which influences who gets the jobs. Entry into professional organizations is primarily on the basis of credentials. These credentials claim the person shares the standards and training enabling them to understand and exercise authority within the professional territory.
4. They establish a career system. This is largely because of the nature of professional work. In their purest form, professionals believe that their work has an intrinsic value expressed in the notion of a "calling" or vocation; they believe in the ideal of service, of the responsibility and right to protect their part of the social fabric against the effects of politics and markets.

We associate power with knowledge in bureaucracies, and professions seek to define which knowledge becomes operational. They mark off a range of behavior that is the "correct" way to do things. This means that politics, the public side of public administration, is threatening to professionalism. Of course, professionals engage in politics — they lobby, cajole officials, and try to exercise political influence — but they do it to protect their right to define the appropriate knowledge within their specialization.

We should not make the mistake of confusing rank with professional standing, or of equating staff functions with professionals. There is no separation between managers and workers along professional lines. That varies from organization to organization. It is important to see professionalism as a shift in the method of organizing; it represents the increasing organization of society along with more sophisticated organization of administrative agencies. It is a move away from strict bureaucratic hierarchy, toward an administration of technocratic politics where specialists have the initiative for charting and directing government programs. The trend is vigorous in the private sector as well.

Since knowledge is the stock in trade of professionals, their training is very important. Most people are familiar with the basic outlines of medical and legal training, the titular professions. Medical and law schools teach students to heal people and to interpret law, respectively, but they by no means stop there. In medical schools, for instance, students come out ready to set up a business, but not to practice medicine. More experience in hospitals is necessary first. In the top law schools, students are taught the law, but they must take intensive "cram" courses to pass state bar exams. This is because, just as in medical and other professional schools, they do not just teach the techniques of working in the profession. They spend a great deal of time teaching the concepts for reasoning rather than a mass of facts.

Perhaps the primary purpose of professional education is socialization, the transmission of attitudes and philosophies of the professional community. It is a way to ensure that something more than a degree is shared by members of a profession, and it is certainly necessary if they are to exert influence in today's organizations. To exercise their power, the commodity of knowledge must be authoritative, and so the professionals themselves must be produced by the organizations that transmit the knowledge.

There is a context to the way professionals come by their influence. To some extent, they have authority thrust upon them. Legislators honestly do not know what to do with most programs. They give the job of making many decisions and running the programs to people who have some specialized knowledge.

Professionals are also typical products of a modern industrial society. In the attempt to wed applied science and technology with organization, there is a need to plan and administer. The larger the organizations, the greater the need to rationalize and create an elaborate division of labor. Professionals provide one important basis for deciding who gets to exercise authority and, by implication, occupy the highest reaches of organizations.

There are fears that professionals constitute an attack on public control of government. Professional decision making is essentially bureaucratic and not highly visible to the public. Frederick Mosher says we have a democracy that is three times removed from a direct democracy: Once removed by letting elected representatives make decisions; twice removed by letting political appointees make decisions for representatives; and thrice removed by letting professionals in a career service make decisions. Professions differ in their public accessibility, of course. In the search for knowledge, and status for individual professionals, the public in public administration becomes smaller.

Representative Bureaucracy

White males have always dominated the federal service. In the 1960s many people came to see this as a problem. Laws were passed and executive orders signed calling for equality in employment opportunity. The policy of affirmative action, where hiring practices seek to change the domination of white males in civil service, was adopted at this time. Out of this popular concern that individuals receive equal opportunity came a kind of equal opportunity concept for public administration. The concept is called representative bureaucracy.[9]

The idea of a "representative bureaucracy" is not an easy one. It may be simple, but it is not easy. In the broadest, most simple way, a representative bureaucracy is one that includes, in the proper proportions, the various groups in society. For example, the bureaucracy in the United States should include men, women, Asians, blacks, whites, Native Americans, gays, the physically handicapped, people of all religious beliefs, and some with no belief at all.

Since the mid-1960s, some effort has been made to change, and the changes are far from complete. One study showed that affirmative action had *no* effect on employment of blacks, and only some effect on women.[10] During the 1980s, these changes are taking place slowly, if at all. But, the idea of representative bureaucracy is not the same as equality of opportunity. It may be misleading to discuss a representative bureaucracy at all. These notions take us back to the ideas of public and administration, of democracy, and to the ideas of Max Weber.

According to Weber, it *does not matter* who holds any position in any bureaucracy, as long as that person is qualified to do the work. The task of each position is defined beforehand, and all the employee is hired to do is what has been defined. Put differently, although it may be important in terms of equality that anyone may hold the job who is qualified, it should make no difference in terms of what is done on the job. A white social worker, by law, has to use the same set of rules to determine eligibility for services as any other social worker, no matter who the client is.

Representation is a political term. We elect someone to represent us. A person who might have the same skin color or sexual preference and pass an examination to get a job with the civil service really represents no one. To argue, even implicitly, that a woman bureaucrat represents all women is to somehow believe that all women are the same politically. The fact is, in a bureaucratic setting, a bureaucrat is a bureaucrat.

What the term representative bureaucracy does is remind us how the lines between politics and the public service have somehow been wiped out. It feeds into our bias that the bureaucracy has become politicized. It may be that, overall, the opposite is true: Bureaucracy is taking over our political life.

As we write this book, the problems of the Iran/Contra affair are becoming public. The process of discovering all of what went on will, it appears, take years. We know what happened, we just do not know all of the players, dates, and amounts of money and war materials involved. We know this: The Congress (the political process) passed a bill that cut off

---

BOX 6.7 How Are People Recruited to Civil Service?

Merit systems rely on competitive selection procedures to fill available positions. At least, that is the official policy. The actual practice of most governments falls far short of that ideal. In the federal service in 1985, for instance, only 20 percent of newly hired people were on a competitive basis.

There are several factors at work here. Sadly, the most prevalent is the "wired" job — the announcement of a vacancy is a mere formality, since the people doing the hiring know who they want in the position. Yet this is not a case of widespread corruption. Instead, it is an indication that the competitive process is less than ideal at selecting workers who can do the best work and meet equal opportunity guidelines in a timely fashion. Civil service registers, the list of people who took exams, age quickly and the best candidates find other work. The veterans' preference (a 5 percent advantage, 10 for disabled veterans; in at least one state it is an absolute advantage where the employer must hire any minimally qualified vet before others) means that, in lean times, most competitive jobs will go to veterans if registers were used. The vets doing very well on the tests are almost exclusively white males, which makes equal opportunity guidelines difficult to meet.

A survey of local governments suggests that prospective employers resort to many recruiting devices to get the right people to the job interview.* Virtually all governments advertise in local papers and professional publications. About 85 percent send notices to minority, female, and other special interest organizations. About 80 percent publicly announce job-related exams, and well over half rely on school career offices, state and private employment agencies, and referrals from current employees.

Once people apply for positions, over 90 percent of the governments surveyed test their performance skills, and over 75 percent test job knowledge and job-related physical agility. Less than half test for writing ability, aptitude, or ability to use the English language. A few, less than 20 percent, use a personality test.

For actual selection criteria, virtually all are guided by training and experience. Over 80 percent check references and level of education. Over 25 percent use polygraph tests for some employees, and a few, less than 10 percent, actually use a lottery method of selecting qualified workers for some positions.

All of this is time consuming. For management positions, only about 13 percent are filled within one month. Most take greater than six weeks to fill, with about 25 percent taking more than two months. For clerical positions, two thirds are filled within one month, but a sizable portion take more than six weeks.

The Municipal Yearbook, 1986 (Chicago: International City Management Association, 1986), pp. 45–49.

aid to the Contras. High-ranking public officials (administrators) broke the law and sent money to the Contras. Some of that money came from selling arms to Iran.

The political process was bypassed by the administrative process. No amount of representative bureaucracy would have prevented this from happening. It had to do with the mentality of the people in the bureaucracy, not with their color, age, or sex.

We need to rethink what we want. Although representative bureaucracy has a pious ring to it, there are unsolved problems. We can agree, hopefully, we do, that equal opportunity should be a fact. We can agree that every citizen should have the opportunity to have a good education. These things will open up the public service to more people, which fits our political principles. But, hiring different people does not change the structure. Equal opportunity is not representation, it is a statement about who should be allowed to compete for positions in an organization. As Mary Parker Follett showed us, the dynamics of politics are dramatically different than the processes of bureaucracies. Organizational dynamics are greater than the sum of organizational parts.

Appointees

Although we do not have the spoils system anymore, that does not mean presidents, governors, and mayors have no say in higher-level appointments. Indeed, political appointments have become increasingly important during the past few years. Before giving examples of how that is so, it may be helpful to discuss the general types of jobs in the government bureaucracy. Basically, people in the civil service may be lumped together in these three ways: politicos, amphibians, and career officials.[11]

The "politicos" have gotten where they are in government by working on a successful political campaign. The more important they were in the campaign, the more powerful their position will be. Generally, they work on the administration's overall political strategy and spend a great deal of their time working with the various groups in the government in order to build winning coalitions for their programs. They do not last long in government positions.

The "amphibians" are generally not important campaign workers, but they do some work for the successful candidate. They possess two important qualities: They are of the correct political persuasion, and they have expertise within a substantive policy field. These people are hired to do work within their area of expertise. Like the politicos, their service in government positions is temporary.

The career officials are in continuous government service. The majority of professional-level bureaucrats are career officers. They provide the continuity of government, they have the institutional memory of the bureaucratic process, they are the experts in their fields. As we saw, they generally have academic or professional credentials beyond the baccalaureate.

We are most interested in the appointees, the politicos and the amphibians in this section. They can serve an executive in two ways. First, they can identify with the president's priorities and help get the administration's programs passed by Congress. Second, they can try to take charge of the bureaucracy and make it yield the results the president wants. The helpfulness of the appointees depends absolutely on who is appointed.

For example, President Jimmy Carter seemed to prefer appointing people with great expertise. One of the results of this bias was that his appointees were much more comfortable with the career officials than with the people directly involved with electoral politics, like senators and representatives and their staffs. To put that in a different way, Carter's appointees were not as helpful to him as they might have been. Because of their expertise, and their closeness to the policy people in the bureaucracy, their loyalty to the president's program was suspect, and their political usefulness was limited. The Carter people were simply too much policy professionals. They were too involved in the agenda of their own agency.

The appointees of Ronald Reagan could not have been more different. It is important that we review what has gone on in some detail. Since the election of John Kennedy in 1960, the appointment power of the president has increased a great deal. Kennedy began the change in the appointment process by taking it away from political party control and putting it into the White House. When he was elected, he had a small staff who chose about 250 people to the high-level positions that required confirmation by the Senate.

Ten years later, Richard Nixon had extended the process to thousands of appointees at all levels of the bureaucracy. Another ten years later, Ronald Reagan both changed and expanded the process. First the person in charge of personnel, E. Pendleton James (is there need to comment on the irony of the name Pendleton?), was named one of the twelve assistants to the president, the highest rank ever given to a personnel director. It is also instructive to note that the personnel director in charge of appointees was higher in the administration hierarchy than the head of the Office of Personnel Management.

Further, James was given an office in the White House, regular access to the president, and a staff that at its peak numbered almost a hundred. What we have, in a sense, is American history coming back around on itself. President Reagan used the power to appoint with a decided twist. Not only was it important that the appointee be active in the campaign — that would include *most* Republicans — but it was also important that the person be in ideological sympathy with Reagan.

Although Reagan did appoint cabinet members who understood and practiced politics well (one exception was James Watt), most people below

FIGURE 6.1 Merit and patronage are not entirely separate

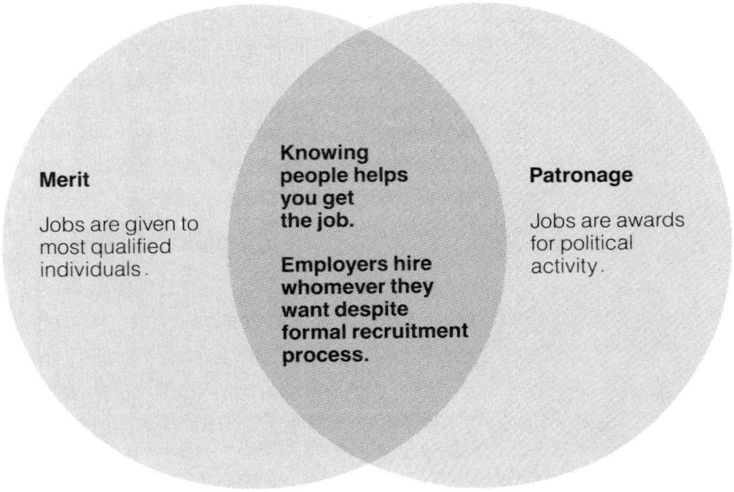

Merit

Jobs are given to most qualified individuals.

Knowing people helps you get the job.

Employers hire whomever they want despite formal recruitment process.

Patronage

Jobs are awards for political activity.

cabinet rank were selected because they were true believers. Not only that, their expertise did not seem to matter much, nor did their experience in government.

Reagan was elected, in part, because he said he would reduce the size of the federal government and do more for free enterprise. So, Anne Burford was appointed the head of the EPA, when her only prior experience with the agency was fighting it. James Harris, a state senator from Indiana, had challenged the federal strip-mine laws. Reagan appointed Harris as head of Interior's office of surface mining. Thus Harris was in charge of "enforcing" federal strip-mine laws.

The argument is that this power to appoint is the only way a president can get his way with the federal bureaucracy. To compare the effectiveness of Carter and Reagan, it would seem apparent that an ideological loyalty oath is of some use.

There is, as we know, an "on the other hand" with some of the Reagan appointees. Although ideological purity is important, it is not the only thing. So, Richard Allen, the national security adviser, had only a brief stay in office because he accepted gifts from a foreign government. Paul Thayer, a Deputy Secretary of Defense, was convicted of obstruction of justice after being investigated for illegal stock trading. Rita Lavelle, an EPA assistant administrator in charge of the "superfund" toxic waste cleanup money, was convicted of perjury and obstructing a congressional investigation into her decisions on superfund projects. Both Thayer and Lavelle were sentenced to prison. As a final example, Marianne Mele Hall was appointed to be chairperson of the Copyright Royalty Tribunal, a good job that pays $70,000 a year. She did not hold the job long. Ms. Hall resigned when it became public that she had edited a racist tract.

It is clear that President Reagan has used the appointment power in the grand tradition of those who believed in rotation in office or the spoils system. What Andrew Jackson was accused of, Ronald Reagan did. Is this defensible? Should the president use the power to appoint in such an aggressive way?

Jimmy Carter chose competent people who turned out to be little or no help to him. Ronald Reagan chose people for different reasons and had a great deal of success changing the way government acted.[12] He also chose people who were an embarrassment. At least one hundred appointees have left under an ethical and/or legal cloud. Should a president have the power to appoint people like that? What does it do to the ideal of professionalism, to a career service, that we at least periodically desire?

The examples from the Reagan presidency are striking. At this point, it appears that no presidency matches Reagan's more closely than that of Richard Nixon. In both cases, it appears that the law was broken at the highest levels of administration. What is interesting to note is how the press seemed to attack Nixon and not attack Reagan. Why? Certainly a case can be made that selling arms to terrorists is at least as bad (and maybe even worse) than breaking into Democratic National Headquarters. How has Reagan escaped the kind of criticism that Nixon got?

Beyond moral questions, beyond the power and freedom of the press, or the politics of Washington, D.C., is the answer: The American public like Ronald Reagan more than they liked Richard Nixon. There have been critics of Reagan all along who have suggested that a president who does not know what is going on in the White House will eventually get into trouble. People did not want to hear that. As we write, we can only speculate about how much they will now be willing to hear. It is clear that we cannot separate administration from the political process.

What needs to be acknowledged are all of those mixed feelings we have. Of course we do not want crooks in the public service, but neither do we want a bunch of appointed experts running our lives from Washington. We want a highly professional and very dedicated public service, just as we want to elect a president who can keep campaign promises.

For all of the changes Reagan introduced, it may well be that the most far-reaching one is his invention of a kind of ideological spoils system. The effect on the morale of the public service has been devastating. The top goal of the civil service system, to attract and retain first-rate government employees, has been supplanted by short-term policy preferences.[13]

The Personnel Question

There are more issues that revolve around personnel in the civil service. Subsequent chapters will go into detail on leadership of government organizations, personnel administration, management of programs, and labor unions. Some of these will describe whole other categories of workers. Although the issues will involve the public interest, the people are mostly jobholders in a government bureaucracy.

The heart of our problems with the personnel in public service is exactly the problem of the differences between public and administration. For every public instinct we have, we also have an administrative instinct. Do we want a huge administrative structure to "efficiently" take care of our business, or do we want more of a voice, and are we willing to do more of the work? We are on the track of an increasingly large administrative structure; what our political culture has failed to do is figure out a public solution.

SUMMARY

The early parts of this chapter introduced the origins and development of the civil service. The Federalists, not surprisingly, were our first high-ranking bureaucrats. They had been deeply involved in the Revolutionary War and instrumental in writing the Constitution, and they helped make up the political, social, and economic elite of the times. In no small way, they were the initial American government.

The first major change came with the election of Andrew Jackson. Jackson "opened up" the public service. He believed that almost anyone could be a part of the civil service, and that the president had the right to appoint whomever he wanted to office. Jackson also believed that there should be rotation in office, that no public servant should necessarily serve for life. Furthermore, he wanted every new president to have the opportunity to select his friends and supporters to the public service. Jackson had the reputation of being the great populizer of patronage and of democratizing the public administration.

As the civil service became more corrupt, calls for civil service reform became more numerous. When President Garfield was shot and killed over a patronage matter, it seemed time for change. Finally, in 1883, the Pendleton Act was passed in an effort to reform the civil service. The act instituted the selection of employees by open competitive examination, protected employees against political pressures, and set up the Civil Service Commission to oversee the merit system and to implement the various provisions of the act. Much of the history of the civil service in the

United States has been that of expanding the basic principles of the Pendleton Act.

At the local level, civil service reform targeted city bosses and machine politics. While bosses and machine politics did take care of lower classes and immigrants, as the middle classes grew, so too did the call for reform. A larger white-collar population brought with it reform for local governments.

We noted that the make-up of the civil service does not reflect the make-up of the population. For example, the high-level administrators in the federal government disproportionately represent white males from middle- and upper-middle-class families. The higher level civil service positions are 95 percent white, and of the whites in these higher positions, only 5 percent are women. Privilege and position seem to correlate. Furthermore, like a great many people in other parts of society, those in the civil service want to achieve a higher status by professionalizing. Thus, professional schools and organizations now produce and protect the emerging professionals in our public administration.

In the last part of the chapter, we reviewed the move for a representative bureaucracy, and how presidents since John Kennedy have handled — and expanded — the civil service. What we found, in part, is that the tensions mentioned in the first chapter are clearly illustrated in the example of the civil service. We want an efficient civil service to be responsive to our public mood, open to everyone, and as democratic as possible. Given our criteria for efficiency, it seems impossible to have both an efficient and a democratic civil service.

NOTES

1. Among the journals that keep you abreast of developments in civil service issues are *The Review of Public Personnel Administration, Public Personnel Management, The Bureaucrat,* and *Public Administration Review.*
2. Several excellent histories of the early civil service are available. See Jay M. Shafritz, *Public Personnel Management: The Heritage of Civil Service Reform* (New York: Praeger, 1975); Paul P. Van Riper, *History of the United States Civil Service* (Evanston, Ill.: Row, Peterson, 1958); Matthew A. Crenson, *The Federal Machine: Beginnings of Bureaucracy in Jacksonian America* (Baltimore: Johns Hopkins University Press, 1975); and Leonard E. White's histories, *The Federalists* (New York: Macmillan, 1948), *The Jeffersonians* (New York: Macmillan, 1951), *The Jacksonians* (New York: Macmillan, 1954), and *The Republican Era* (New York: Macmillan, 1958).

3. H. H. Gerth and C. Wright Mills, *From Max Weber: Essays in Sociology* (New York: Oxford University Press, 1958), p. 215.

4. This section is drawn from Harold Zink, *City Bosses in the United States* (New York: Duke University Press, 1968), a reissue of the 1930 edition.

5. For examples, see Hugh Heclo, *A Government of Strangers* (Washington, D.C.: Brookings Institution, 1977).

6. Warren H. Schmidt and Barry Z. Posner, "Values and Expectations of Federal Service Executives," *Public Administration Review* 46 (September/October 1986), no. 5, pp. 447–454. See also W. L. Warner et al., *The American Federal Executive* (New Haven: Yale University Press, 1963), which accentuates the differences between the general public and public servants; Charles T. Goodsell, *The Case for Bureaucracy* (Chatham, N.J.: Chatham House, 1983); Chapter 5, contains a summary of evidence suggesting the differences are small; for more recent evidence, see Kenneth Meier, "Representative Bureaucracy: An Empirical Analysis," *American Political Science Review* 69 (June 1975), pp. 526–542; Lenneth Meier and Lloyd Nigro, "Representative Bureaucracy and Policy Preferences," *Public Administration Review* 36 (July/August 1976), pp. 458–469; and Hal G. Rainey et al., "Reward Expectancies and Other Work-Related Attitudes in Public and Private Organizations," *Review of Public Personnel Administration* 6 (Summer 1986), pp. 50–72.

7. B. L. Wynia, "Federal Bureaucrats' Attitudes Toward a Democratic Ideology," *Public Administration Review* 34 (March/April 1974).

8. This section is based upon Frederick C. Mosher, *Democracy and the Public Service* (New York: Oxford University Press, 1968); Frederick C. Mosher, "Professions in Public Service," *Public Administration Review* 38 (March/April 1978); Magali Sarfatti Larson, *The Rise of Professionalism* (Berkeley: University of California Press, 1977); and David Noble, *America by Design* (New York: Knopf, 1979).

9. See Samuel Krislov, *Representative Bureaucracy* (Englewood Cliffs, N.J.: Prentice-Hall, 1974); J. Donald Kingsley, *Representative Bureaucracy* (Yellow Springs, Ohio: Antioch Press, 1944); Samuel Krislov and David H. Rosenbloom, *Representative Bureaucracy and the American Political System* (New York: Praeger, 1983).

10. James E. Kellough and Susan Ann Kay, "Affirmative Action in the Federal Bureaucracy: An Impact Assessment," *Review of Public Personnel Administration* 6 (Spring 1986), no. 2, pp. 1–13.

11. Colin Campbell and Donald Naulls, "Politicos, Amphibians, and Career Officials: Three Bureaucratic Cultures Under Carter and Reagan." Paper presented at the annual meeting of the American Political Science Association, September, 1985.

12. Numerous examples of Reagan's influence in the regulatory process are provided in Susan J. Tolchin and Martin Tolchin, *Dismantling America: The Rush to Deregulate* (New York: Oxford University Press, 1983); and Kenneth J. Meier, *Regulation: Politics, Bureaucracy, and Economics* (New York: St. Martin's, 1985). See also John L. Palmer and Isabel V. Sawhill, eds., *The Reagan Experiment* (Washington, D.C.: The Urban Institute Press, 1982); George C. Eads and Michael Fix, eds., *Relief or Reform? Reagan's Regulatory Dilemma* (Washington, D.C.: The Urban Institute Press, 1984); and Lester M. Salamon and Michael S. Lund, eds., *The Reagan Presidency and the Governing of America* (Washington, D.C.: The Urban Institute Press, 1984).

13. See Bernard Rosen, "Crisis in the U.S. Civil Service," *Public Administration Review* 46 (May/June 1986), no. 3, pp. 207—214; and Charles H. Levine, "The Federal Government in the Year 2000: Administrative Legacies of the Reagan Years," *Public Administration Review* 46 (May/June 1986), no. 3, pp. 195–206.

CHAPTER SEVEN

Administrative Leadership

> The differences in requirements for successful leadership in different situations are more striking than the similarities.
>
> — *Douglas McGregor*

> The principle that explains the need for leadership in large governments (as in the private sector) may be stated as follows: the more subdivided and specialized an organization becomes and the more rules and procedures it is expected to follow, the more bureaucratic it becomes and consequently the more leadership it requires if internal inertia is to be activated into cooperative accomplishment. Further, it needs motivated employees, with interests in their work and some challenge in the form of flexibility and discretion if they are to put forth their best efforts.
>
> — *Marshall E. Dimock*

> There is nothing more difficult to carry out, nor more doubtful of success, nor more dangerous to handle, than to initiate a new order of things. For the reformer has enemies in all who profit by the old order, and lukewarm defenders in all those who would profit by the new order.
>
> — *Niccolo Machiavelli*

The fact of leaders and the idea of leadership have always been with us. Different social and political structures demand and produce different kinds of leaders. In Plato's *The Republic*, the guardian was forced away from his or her contemplation of important things in order to lead. In *The Prince*, Machiavelli suggested that for the good of Italy a person seek and hold leadership in ways that seem appalling. In our large, complex organizations people are promoted into roles of leadership for a wide variety of reasons.

In this chapter, we will look at the various elements of leadership. First we will discuss those things that go into the idea. Second, we will review the social science literature about leadership. Our systematic thinking about leadership has gone through several phases. Finally, we will put our current leadership into its political context.

Elements of Leadership

The etymological roots of the word *leader* help us begin our understanding. At one level, *lead* means "to guide," or "to make go." There is also another meaning that seems beside the point of leadership, but might not be. To lead also means "leading motive . . . a strongly marked melodic phrase." These definitions imply much of what we need to think about when we think about leadership.

First, leadership is not an isolated concept like "apple" or "beer." A leader is somehow connected with followers. It may be any kind of relationship, national, neighborhood, or bureaucratic, but it is a relationship. In it, some people are guided, or "made to go." A beer is a beer and an apple is an apple, even in isolation.

Second, power is an important part of what we mean by leadership. As we know, power itself has more than one definition. In a simple way, power happens when there is a relationship among people, and one or more of the people get their way. To push this definition to its logical conclusion, that would mean that all relationships are defined as power relationships.[1] We know that is not the case. If power defined everything, it would define nothing, just as calling all flat surfaces a "floor" destroys our ability to use the word. We offer two definitions of power to think about when considering leadership. They are (1) the ability of A to make B do something B would not have done, and (2) the ability of A to make B do something B could not have done.

The third part of leadership, in our modern world, is the whole notion of hierarchy. In Pfeffer's terms,

> Power is seen as deriving from the division of labor that occurs as task specialization is implemented in organizations. When the overall tasks of the organization are divided into smaller parts, it is inevitable that some tasks will come to be more important than others. Those persons and those units that have the responsibility for performing the more critical tasks in the organization have a natural advantage in developing and exercising power in the organization. Although individual skills and strategies can certainly affect the amount of power and the effectiveness with which it is used, power is first and foremost a structural phenomenon, and should be understood as such.[2]

BOX 7.1 Comparing Leadership in City Managers and School Superintendents*

The qualities of leadership vary by the leader's situation. Studies of leadership are thus likely to emphasize cases or comparisons to emphasize the effects of context on actions. In some ways city managers and school superintendents are quite similar: both are well-paid professionals who are responsible for administering important community enterprises. Both must respond to elected boards and face a curious mix of public apathy and anger on local issues.

The differences between their situations are considerable. The superintendents have a stronger sense of professional identification and rely more heavily on technical expertise. This helps give status and smooth conflicts in intraorganizational conflicts; but their city manager counterparts' continual use of political skills gives them considerably wider responses to expanded conflicts. Although each delivers a different service, the difference is not as great as might appear at first glance. Superintendents usually have to deal with conflict that focuses on peripheral issues rather than the quality of education. City managers usually face single-service issues, such as planning and zoning.

City managers are less able to lead policy initiatives because their board defers less to expertise and is responsive to more vocal constituents than is the case for superintendents. The distinction between lay board members and professionals is much stronger in school districts.

Finally, although both municipal governments and school districts are decentralized, important differences in structure are apparent. School districts are geographically decentralized while general-purpose governments are functionally decentralized. The department heads in a city often form close relations with relevant interest groups, and city managers find themselves harder pressed in political conflicts than do school superintendents.

There is a great deal of room for individual differences in leadership style and particular policy initiatives, but these basic differences between the organizations mean that the actions permitted leaders and their response to conflicts vary tremendously.

*This is based on a study by Harmon Zeigler, Ellen Kehoe, and Jane Reisman, *City Managers and School Superintendents: Response to Community Conflict* (New York, Praeger, 1985).

What Pfeffer has written certainly seems true. Yet, it merely describes without telling us any of the reasons. We do not know, for example, just why some persons and units are given more critical tasks. To know that might just tell us something about leadership. To say something is inevitable does not tell us why it is inevitable. What is important to note is that in our modern world, hierarchy and leadership do intersect. Hierarchy is one of the places in which leadership takes place. In a broader way, we can say that situations make a difference to leadership.

A fourth part of leadership is obedience. Leadership invites followership. Moreover, followers generally assume a certain kind of attitude. In a personal way, think of it like this: A person works for a boss, but follows a leader. A leader does more than simply occupy a position; he or she somehow inspires people to follow.

As we shall see later, a leader may have many tasks. In fulfilling those tasks, there are times when a leader may be more of a manager, or a boss, than a person who inspires followership. Indeed, one can imagine many different variations and additions to leadership. People in positions of authority often exhibit leadership, but other times followers simply grant people in those positions a certain amount of legitimate power. In other, very formal cases, someone may just "lead" and that person's leadership will not extend past the moment. This does not begin to exhaust the examples, but we must not forget our point here is that obedience and followership help fill out the meaning of leadership.

Qualities of leaders, such as knowledge, skills, and personality traits, make up the fifth part of leadership. A quick sample of presidents will help make the point. Jimmy Carter was an extraordinarily knowledgeable person. One of the stories about him was that, as governor of Georgia, he met many people running for the presidency. He quickly came to the conclusion that he was brighter and knew more than almost all of them. He was probably correct. Interestingly, one criticism of him was that he knew too much — got bogged down in the details of every matter — and failed to see the shape and meaning of whole policies.

Lyndon Johnson had remarkable skills of getting legislation through Congress. After serving so long and so successfully in the Senate, Johnson became president with all of his skills intact. He was able to get what he wanted from the Congress, but he seemed to have no way to regulate what he wanted. While only someone with his abilities could have passed the civil rights legislation and begun to seriously address the problems of the poor, Johnson used those same abilities to fight the war in Vietnam. He misled his followers about the war, and it came to be unpopular and politically divisive.

Finally, Ronald Reagan appears to have a wonderful personality. He seems to be the best kind of grandparent — comforting, nice, and easygoing. He was able to translate this into personal political triumphs and

FIGURE 7.1 Leadership

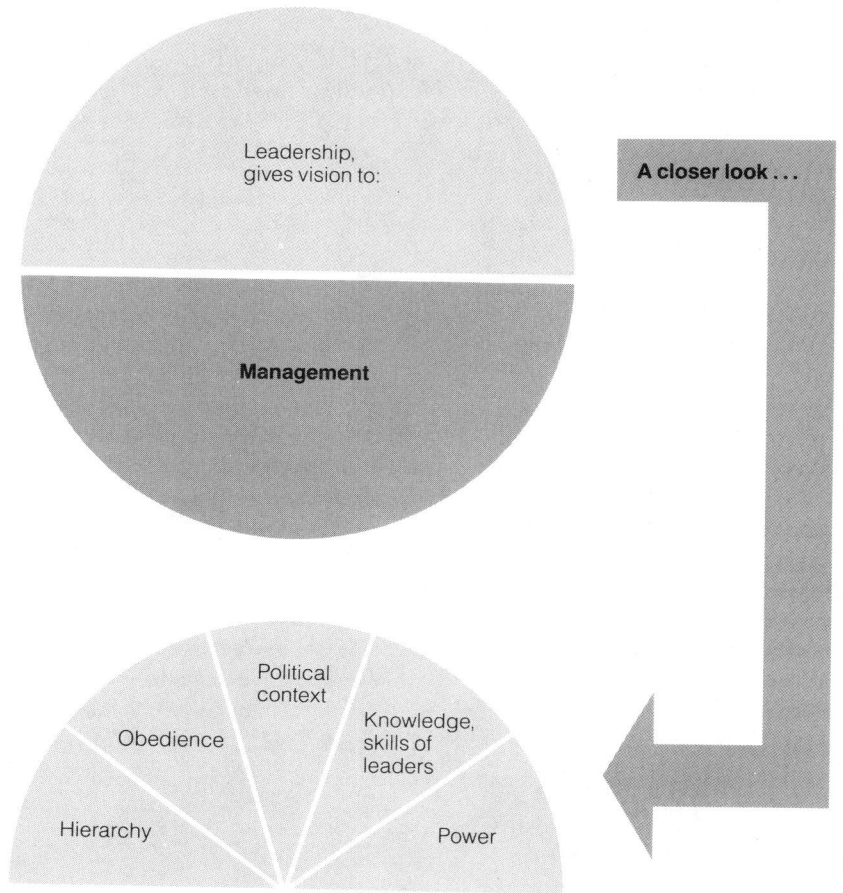

some significant legislation. Yet, the Iran/Contra affair shows that, just as knowledge cannot substitute for vision, personality cannot substitute for knowledge. Easygoing or not, there are serious questions about Reagan's ability to actually do the job of president.

The last point about leadership has to do with the political context. As we saw in Chapter 2, the administrative environment in the United States is a complex of federalism, the separation of powers, individualism, capitalism, and pluralism. Each state and each local setting is some combination of these themes. It is easier to speak only of administrative leadership. This means that the leadership positions are higher in organizations, resting in positions with a large amount of discretion in dealing with subordinates and policy questions. Although leadership is often understood to be a part of management (the subject of Chapter 8), we believe it is important enough to deserve a separate discussion. The various components we have discussed are represented in Figure 7.1. Like any subject that is, at least in part, at the whim of human action, there is a part of leadership that will always remain a mystery. The remainder of the chapter will discuss what we do know about leadership and provide a sense of where it may take public administration.

Administrative Leadership and Democratic Government

Before reviewing the research on leadership, it is important to get some idea about the place of organizations in our political thinking. The fact is that bureaucratic organizations occupy an uneasy place in our political thinking. Although it is clear that elected officials should be leaders, and it is a defensible notion that political appointees should be leaders, we are less certain about leadership as we go further down into bureaucracies. People who are elected or not far removed from elections have a certain authority. We are less willing to automatically be followers to those seemingly removed from our powers to reelect.

Yet, the manager of a school district transportation office will hear many public demands for changes in services. An elementary school principal will hear many demands about class assignments, playground supervision, and special programs. The manager of a local welfare office will hear demands from client groups and be sensitive to perceptions of the news media. All these administrators work under budget constraints in specific organization contexts. All must be concerned with the people who work in the organization. All must exercise judgment. All must lead.

The jobs of these officials suggest that when we think about leadership we also think about accountability. Given the context of bureaucratic organizations in the United States, we assume that someone will be watching bureaucracies, and that someone will be watching the watchers. These structures of accountability are an attempt to preserve democratic controls on the state while allowing the exercise of authority to deliver services. (The main accountability structures were discussed in Chapter 2.) In our administrative system there are often no clear lines of authority and no powerful controllers. When we look at leadership at the various levels, we often see ambiguity and the play of politics.

There is a wider context of administrative leadership that centers on the place of citizens and employees in the political system.[3] Peter Drucker writes that large organizations, particularly corporations, are poorly understood in American political thinking. Our political theories envision independent individuals in a society without many centers of power and wealth, except for one central government. But the realities have changed dramatically, and Drucker says that a new understanding of individual roles is needed.

For Drucker the corporation is the most important organization in American public life. Good managers must expand markets for goods and services, investments, and jobs. They must anticipate the needs of society. Also, they must see that the private sector provides for these needs, so that requirements for state action are kept to a minimum. Governments will always operate with expensive and elaborate procedures that make officials accountable to the electorate. With these higher administrative costs governments will be unable to make rational economic decisions (which are provided by markets).

Government organizations, in Drucker's scheme, will provide services where markets fail to perform adequately. Because these demands are political, they are more prone to errors of inefficiency. In many important ways, Drucker is a twentieth-century adaptation of James Madison. He believes that politics is limited and that people's wants are essentially private and can be best served by the wealth modern corporations can provide. It is Drucker's view that if citizens and employees see their place in this scheme, they can more readily share in the goals of an abundant and democratic society. Madison's fears of diabolical human nature remain, but roles in organizations give people clear guidance for exercising individual wills without encroaching on the rights of other citizens. The web of structure will help control the citizen.

As we saw in Chapter 3, there are different ways to understand leadership. Mary Parker Follett, for example, believed that democratic nations need democratic organizations. Democratic organizations would do away with some of the common traits of our current organizations. There would no longer be strict roles in organization life, nor would there be someone who was the absolute leader. Follett believed that authority and expertise would be constantly shifting, and so would leadership. It was her strong view that centers of power — both private organizations and government agencies — should not necessarily be accepted by citizens.

Although it is clear that the view of Drucker is closer than the vision of Follett to what we have today, the tension between the two is still very much alive. Since the 1960s, there have been many attempts, with varying degrees of success, to change our forms of leadership. In times of political uncertainty, the kind of leadership we want can easily become a primary public question.

BOX 7.2 The Deadly Sins in Public Administration*

Peter Drucker writes that we are not able to guarantee the success of public programs, but we do know how to make them fail. His six "deadly sins" lead to failure, he says, if two or more are followed simultaneously:

1. Have a lofty objective rather than clear performance targets.
2. Try to do several things at once so that efforts are not concentrated on top priorities.
3. Tackle problems by throwing a lot of people at them rather than by asking "What is the fewest number of people we need to accomplish this purpose?"
4. Do not experiment — decide on one way and do it on a grand scale.
5. Make sure you cannot learn from experience — do not feed back experience to expectations so that you can sort out strengths, weaknesses, limitations, and blind spots.
6. Do not abandon programs when objectives are met, when clientele changes, or when problems become less urgent.

Drucker claims the sins are committed regularly and are committed out of cowardice. A solid, objective attitude toward performance is a risky and courageous act, he says. In other writings he acknowledges the tensions on bureaucracies are imposed from without (from politics) rather than solid "business" decisions. This picture of the failures of public agencies is open to question, but the diagnosis is widely held.

*Source: "The Deadly Sins in Public Administration" *Public Administration Review* 40 (March/April 1980), no. 2, pp. 103–106.

Research on Leadership

There has been a great deal of research done on leadership, and it is necessary to introduce the work before we review it. As we noted earlier, not only is the situation of leadership always changing, leadership itself is in part a function of particular sets of human beings. Depending on your view of the world, one of these two statements is true: (1) Because of the number of variables involved, we have not yet discovered how to understand and predict all situations that require leadership or (2) given the unpredictable nature of human beings, we will never fully understand leadership.

Thus far the research on leadership has not produced powerful results. The reasons are numerous.[4] First, there is a lack of an overarching framework; there are too many seemingly unrelated studies. Second, most studies are done in private sector organizations or situations that have very little in common with modern administrative organizations. For example, one of the most widely cited articles in the literature is a study of Boy Scout troops' reactions to different leadership styles. Third, much of the literature consists of speculations about what leaders should do, rather than empirical studies of activities. The early POSDCORB writings of Luther Gulick were perhaps the first of these applied to public sector leadership theory.

The fourth bias has to do with size. Much of the literature concentrates on small groups and makes the assumption that management tasks are similar across all levels of organizations. Finally, most studies take a short-term view of leadership and focus on relations between leaders and followers. The overall questions of how leadership fits into an organized system have been neglected. It is not uncommon for writings on management systems to exclude the topic of leadership altogether.

To ignore what we know about leadership would be foolish. In truth, there are things we can learn from the research.

Who Makes a Good Leader?

The earliest approach to the study of leadership, and one that is still popular, is the search for traits of leaders.[5] Early studies reported that effective leaders possessed nervous and physical energy, technical mastery, enthusiasm, decisiveness, faith, and other general attributes. One list included physique (it is better to be tall and have a deep voice), technical skill (it is better to be able to do the job), perception, knowledge, memory, imagination (it is better to be able to think of new ideas), persistence, endurance, and courage.

These kinds of lists proliferated, but there was little consistency between them, and they lacked the power to explain leadership. In too many instances, leaders lacked some of the characteristics, whereas many followers had most of them. Reviews of trait literature[6] found that as few as 5 percent of cited traits were shared among studies, and that evidence suggests leaders are in fact very much like their followers. The personal qualities of leadership may be widely distributed among the population, and the search for distinctive traits, although still actively pursued,[7] has yet to bear fruit.

Where and When Do Leaders Emerge?

Another emphasis in leadership literature is on the situations in which leaders find themselves.[8] This approach emphasizes the contingencies of time, place, and pressures on the organization that elicit a response from leaders. Studies found that needs of the organization are perceived by more than just top officials, and that informal arrangements between subordinates may arise to take the place of unresponsive leadership. A study of leadership patterns in wartime found that different leaders emerged depending on whether the people were under fire, resting, or heading for home ports.

The situation literature has been directed to the question of how to choose a leadership style based on a particular situation. An ambitious attempt to provide such a leadership tool is provided by Vroom and Yetton,[9] represented as a decision tree in Figure 7.2. To select a leadership style, a series of questions (A through H) is asked, for which you must answer yes or no. The questions are displayed in a decision tree, and depending on the answer to each question, the trail of questions and answers is followed until a number is reached. The number describes the style appropriate to the situation, depending upon whether an individual or a group is being led.

This guide to leadership style, like others,[10] is a carefully thought out and impressive attempt to provide guidance to leaders. Yet, although there are situations in which the guidance is clear, in most cases a variety of styles is suggested. There are some approaches that are obviously inappropriate for some situations. Beyond these wrong approaches is where there can be no prearranged advice about what to do; it is here that leaders must choose what is best. If leadership could be correctly selected by

---

FIGURE 7.2 Choosing a Leadership Style

Questions to ask:

A. Is there a quality requirement such that one solution is likely to be more rational than another?
B. Do I have sufficient information to make a high-quality decision?
C. Is the problem structured already?
D. Is acceptance of decision by subordinates critical to effective implementation?
E. If I make the decision alone, will it be accepted by subordinates?
F. Do subordinates share the organizational goals to be attained in solving this problem?
G. Is conflict among subordinates likely in preferred solutions?
H. Do subordinates have sufficient information to make a high-quality decision?

FIGURE 7.2 Continued

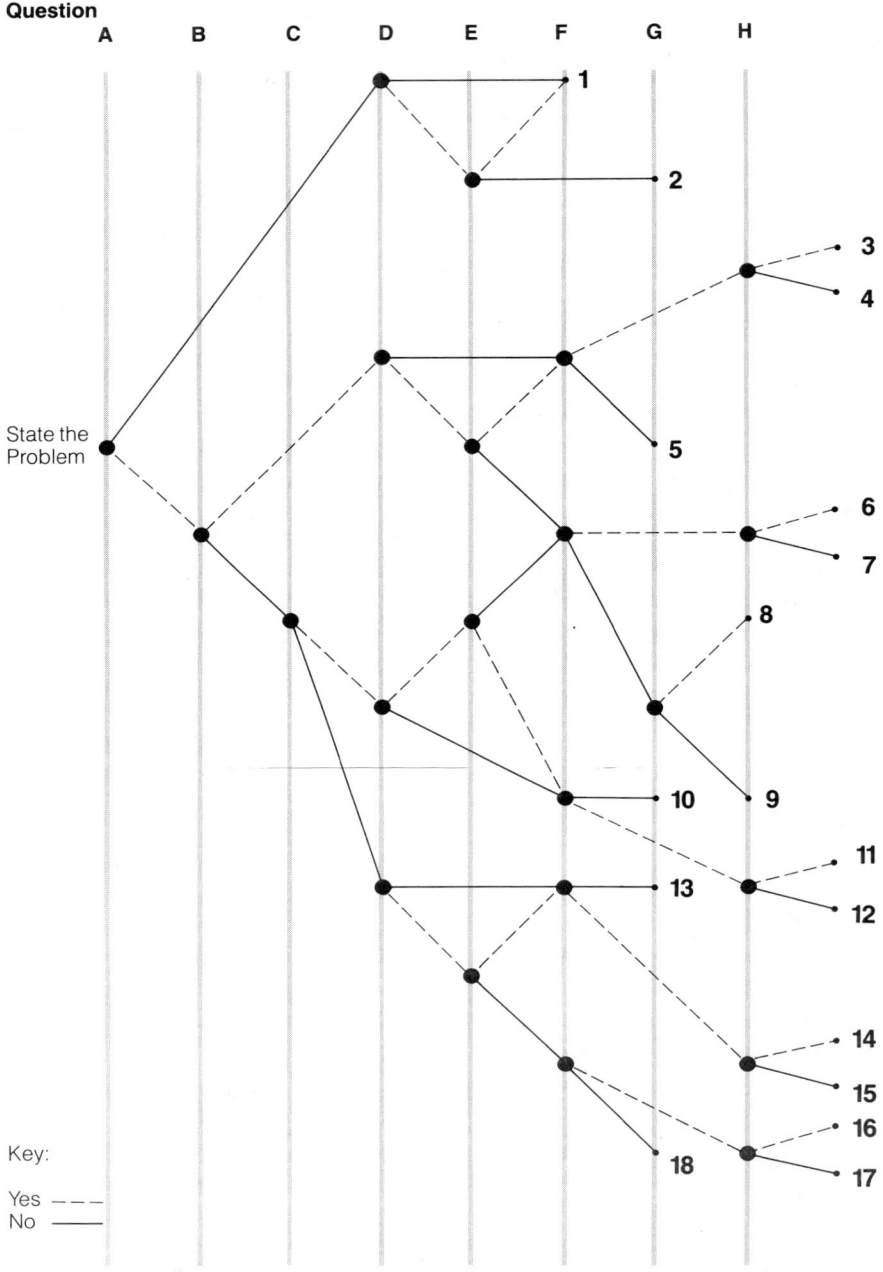

The meaning of the styles:

In situation	You use for a group	You use for an individual
1	A1, or A2, or C1, or C2, or G2	A1, or D1, or A2, or C1, or G1
2	G2	D1 or G1
3	A1, or A2, or C1, or C2, or G2	A1, or D1, or A2, or C1, or G1
4	A1, or A2, or C1, or C2, or G2	A1, or A2, or C1, or G1
5	A1, or A2, or C1, or C2	A1, or A2, or C1
6	G2	D1, or G1
7	G2	G1
8	C2	C1
9	C1 or C2	C1
10	A2, or C1, or C2	A2, or C1
11	A2, or C1, or C2, or G2	D1, or A2, or C1, or G1
12	A2, or C1, or C2, or G2	A2, or C1, or G1
13	C2	C1
14	C2 or G2	D1, or C1, or G1
15	C2 or G2	D1 or G1
16	G2	D1 or G1
17	G2	G1
18	C2	C1

The meaning of the leadership style codes (A1, A2, etc.):

A1 You solve the problem or make the decision yourself, using information available to you at the time.

A2 You obtain the necessary information from your subordinates, then decide the solution yourself. You may or may not tell your subordinates what the problem is in getting the information from them. The role played by your subordinates in making the decision is clearly one of providing the necessary information to you, rather than generating or evaluating alternative solutions.

C1 You share the problem with the relevant subordinates individually, getting their ideas and suggestions without bringing them together as a group. Then you make the decision, which may or may not reflect your subordinates' influence.

C2 You share the problem with your subordinates as a group, obtaining their collective ideas and suggestions. Then you make the decision, which may or may not reflect your subordinates' influence.

D1 You delegate the problem to your subordinate, providing any relevant information that you possess, but giving him or her responsibility for solving the problem. You may or may not request the subordinate to tell you what solution has been reached.

FIGURE 7.2 Continued

G1 You share the problem with your subordinate, and together you analyze the problem and arrive at a mutually agreeable solution.

G2 You share the problem with your subordinates as a group. Together you generate and evaluate alternatives and attempt to reach agreement on a solution. Your role is much like that of a chair. You do not try to influence the group to adopt your solution, and you are willing to accept and implement any solution that has the support of the entire group.

Source: David M. Hunter, *Supervisory Management,* 1981, pp. 225–226. Reprinted by permission of Prentice-Hall, Inc., Englewood Cliffs, NJ.

the numbers, then it would cease to be the highly valued and mysterious entity that it is.

What Does a Leader Do?

A third kind of leadership study is the functional approach.[11] In these kinds of studies, the focus is on the function the leader fills in the group or organization, and it can be argued that the functional approach attempts to encompass traits, situations, and a view of organizational goals. Many of the findings of this approach are summarized by Lynn:[12]

1. A specific sense of direction must be established by the leader. This may be a reiteration of positions of elected officials.
2. Leaders must be able to spend their time on the most important matters, rather than urgent but minor matters that can be delegated.
3. Distrust and anxiety in the organization must be minimized by following a process in decisions so that subordinates have a stake in them.
4. The substantive quality of decisions must be high. This will encourage trust from subordinates. Careful analysis and consideration of alternative approaches and arguments should be undertaken.
5. The work load must be managed so that it does not peak unreasonably and so that the number of different and conflicting directives is low.
6. Decision making should be as uncomplicated and free of burdensome paperwork as possible.

Lynn adds that straightforward management procedures are available to pursue these elements of leadership. Here we can see a trend we mentioned earlier. There is a desire to merge the skills of being a manager with the qualities of being a leader. To study the presidency is to understand that the essence of management and the essence of leadership may be quite different. Certainly it is possible to be a "good" leader and have almost none of the skills of a manager.

Leadership and Management

Let's return to our discussion of Lynn and management procedures. Among these procedures are a master calendar (listing dates by which specific instances of policy planning, budget and legislative submissions, and policy implementation are to be achieved), a planning guidance document (listing the assumptions, priorities, issues, and constraints that guide managers in the organizations), plans for what the agency intends to do and why, regular meetings at which managers can discuss the documents and agency affairs in a face-to-face context, decision memoranda that record decisions, and an appeals process so that subordinates may appeal unfavorable decisions.

A management by objectives (MBO) system, described in Chapter 11, is another way of pursuing these management details. It is at this point that the literature of leadership becomes the leadership of management. As we saw in Chapter 5, much work has been done by organizational psychologists in this area. The ideal leader, as we will see, becomes the master manager for the psychological well-being of the follower. This new leader-manager is able to inspire, motivate, listen, and so on, in order to have an effective organization and satisfied followers. This particular literature has much more to do with managing than with leading.

In this hazy area between management and leadership, some of the newest research is tied to some of the earliest. We have new studies about the traits of a good leader. For example, we find the leader has stamina (physical and mental energy), sensitivity, good judgment, intelligence, is articulate, and has the ability to think abstractly. Comparing this to the earlier list in this chapter, we see that studies of leadership traits have not come very far.

The direction of the management and leadership literature is clear: One of the ways to understand leadership is the special contribution an individual makes to the coordinated activities of others. Given this view, administrative leadership seems much like an act of management. Studies of leadership often end in studies of management simply because the practical act of running an organization involves so many variables. For example,[13]

1. The leader's personal preference or style.
2. The leader's skill in applying various leadership practices.
3. The leader's confidence in subordinates.

4. The leader's value system or the importance attached to organizational efficiency, personal growth of subordinates, policy goals, etc.
5. The leader's assessment of the situation of subordinates.
6. The leader's evaluation of possible undesirable side effects of a particular practice.

It might be interesting to imagine yourself as a leader of a public organization, and try to answer questions about the list above. How, for example, would you define your personal style, and do you have any sense if anyone would like it? Would it inspire followers? Would it hold up over time? In the end, would you have to depend on the power of your position in the organization to get a job done? If you have to depend on the power of a position, then you are more a manager than a leader.

Imagine, again, the number of variables involved with each of the above statements. If the above six points are an accurate beginning of what is involved with being a leader in an organization, then it is no great surprise that we have yet to fully understand the phenomenon. This we know: The more questions we ask about the leadership-management overlap, the more answers we get about management.

Leadership in Public Administration

We need to remember that administrative leaders in public organizations are under a particular set of pressures. Most of the problems encountered by these people are due to the complexities of politics. Public organizations must be responsive to constituents and constitutional controllers, and the ensuing conflicts can result in both innovation and ossification. James MacGregor Burns writes

> By responding to this conflict, by engaging the forces that play on and in the organization, by remaining sensitive to the distribution of power within the agency, bureaucratic leadership can be an important part of the broader forces of party, legislative, and executive leadership that bring change to the entire society. Public bureaucracies participate in genuine leadership if, recognizing that they themselves are instrumentalities to external ends, they respond to reciprocal relations with the individuals and the groups they exist to serve.[14]

For Burns, bureaucracies are an integral part of pluralist politics in America. They are a focus for conflict among groups and officials. Leaders judge the political forces and decide on appropriate responses. In this view of things, bureaucratic leadership is what we would think of as leadership.

There are competing ideas about the proper role of even high-ranking people in our public administration. Woodrow Wilson argued that administration should be split away from politics. That vision of the public service is a powerful one that people still believe. For Wilson, politics made problems for politicians but not for administrators. It was the task of administrators to merely do their jobs. In the following section, we will return to these competing views.

Future research on leadership will have to sort out these issues to find practical advice for officials in bureaucracies. It is possible that a richer, more in-depth study of individual experiences will provide insights that will lead to improvements in administrative leadership. Some studies of this type have been published.[15]

In his investigation into the factors explaining organizational response and survival, Herbert Kaufman presents the disquieting hypothesis that leadership, ability, intelligence, adaptability, and other indicators of critical qualities will not differentiate successful from unsuccessful organizations.[16] He hypothesizes that a probability function will better explain success. In short, he suggests that successful organizations may have just been lucky. If such is the case, then leadership studies are not very important. Indeed, if luck is the key to successful organizations, the whole field of public administration may need to undergo some serious rethinking.

Possibilities for Leadership

The research on leadership provides an assortment of information, some interesting data, and suggestions that might be helpful. There are, though, too many questions that do not seem to be addressed. Leadership, and especially the intersection of human creativity and organizational constraint, needs to be re-viewed. The problem of defining and providing administrative leadership stems from two important questions. The first question revolves around the relationship of our public organizations to our ideas about democracy. We are uncertain about who should lead. It is unclear if administrative leadership positions should be permanent or if they should follow election returns. Our political past does not help us answer the questions of how leadership is linked to power, obedience, politics, and knowledge.

Our tradition, as we suggested, gives us two ways to answer the questions of democracy and administration. We could understand organizations as purely instrumental. The top leaders — the president, or mayors, or governors, or school superintendents — simply use organizations to carry out their policies. Given this view, orders would be given and carried out. The individual roles in the organizations would be narrow and precise. Efficiency would be the main criterion for assessing the internal workings of the organization.

The other way to conceptualize organizations is to believe that they are the proper foci for democracy. This means that life in the organizations would be political. More time would be spent discussing purpose and means, and individual roles would be more variable. The nature of leadership would change. The idea of democratic practices would become as important as efficiency, so that decisions would not only be made in a different way, but the decisions themselves would probably be different. And, of course, citizens would have a more active role in the process.

The role of leadership in each of these views of organizations is very different. Until we sort out the relationship of democratic theory to public organizations, we will never be clear about what we want or expect from administrative leadership.

The second question about organizations concerns effectiveness. What makes an organization effective? How does an organization become and stay effective? Although a quick and simple answer is often offered ("The effective organization is one that achieves its goals at the least possible cost," or "The most productive organization is most effective"), organizational effectiveness has eluded researchers.[17] Reputable researchers do not agree on what indicators to use to measure effectiveness. We have a number of different indicators, and we are not even close to a consensus about which one is best.

Administrative leaders do not operate in a vacuum. There is seldom agreement within an organization on the content of goals. More than that, the leader is under complicated constraints involving the organization's environment, previous decisions and practices, personal qualities, styles and aspirations of decision makers, perceptions of the needs of the clientele, what the mores of society will allow, and on and on. W. Richard Scott writes about the literature on organizational effectiveness and its determinants:

> After reviewing a good deal of the literature on organizational effectiveness and its determinants, I have reached the conclusion that this topic is one about which we know less and less. There is disagreement about what properties or dimensions are encompassed by the concept of effectiveness. There is disagreement about who does or should set the criteria to be employed in assessing effectiveness. There is disagreement about what indicators are to be used in measuring effectiveness. And there is a disagreement about what features of organizations should be examined in accounting for observed differences in effectiveness.[18]

The leader in our public administration — the person who makes things go — is in a difficult situation. It appears as if the culture provides no answers to these questions: What is the proper role of leadership in public administration? What is the proper definition of effectiveness within that administration? It is clear that the "good" administrator makes judgments about these questions and "makes things go" according to his or her will. Anyone going into a leadership position in the public sector must have clear answers to problems left unanswered by our political tradition.

We will close the chapter by reviewing three pictures of the possibilities for leadership. It will help focus on the fact that to discuss leadership is to discuss individuals and their judgments. It will help us remember that although large, complex organizations tend to act in the same way — and certainly look alike from a distance — individuals assure that there is an enormous variety in the form and function of organizations.

Leadership as Attention to the Right Details

The dominant view of leadership is incorporated into systems theory; leaders make the pieces of a system fit together. Leaders are decision makers who set up communications systems that will bring the right information to their attention and provide continuous feedback on corrective actions. In this sense, communication is synonymous with control of the organization. As much as possible, such communication systems should be automatic so that the leader makes decisions only about new issues, unsolved conflicts, and critical policies.[19]

Of course, systems are just metaphors to describe relations among people in an organization. A leader will have several concerns in a new position. As we know, no single person can observe, hear, or read reports about everything that goes on in his or her organization. The leader's subordinate managers and employees must take care of part of this communication and do it in a way that is loyal to the leader so that the leader does not have to worry about everything that goes on. As we saw in Chapter 5, behavioral psychologists are full of advice about how a person can encourage loyalty from people working in lower parts of the hierarchy. But, this is an area of leading and managing that is too mechanistic for this discussion.

It would seem that we should be able to get a sense of who would be a good leader. That is not the case. Peter Drucker acknowledges that it is difficult to predict who the best managers will be.[20] According to him, the only adequate test is performance in the field, which, according to Drucker, is precisely the function of hierarchy. In theory, it works out just right. Those managers who demonstrate the qualities needed to take on greater responsibilities and lead others are promoted. Over time this brings many of the most talented to the top, not because we know what leadership is made of, but because there is sufficient consensus on the results and who is formally responsible for them. Put differently, the structure will select the best leaders.

We know, of course, that this is not the case. It is altogether possible that the most promising people never advance in large structures. Many, on principle, will not even work in them. It is quite true that "cream rises to the top" in milk, but we have no such assurance about the best people rising to the top of our complex organizations.

Leadership as Political Imagination

This view of leadership deals in large part with how a person views the political world. It has to do with the choices he or she makes, and what happens next. In a large and sweeping way, a leader may have great political imagination and be charismatic enough to change a whole society. Or, more to the point of what we have been discussing, a person may make a set of choices that the culture has already provided. Within those choices, a person may be able to change the way a whole school system operates or change the way a city goes about rebuilding its downtown.

The United States has a set of conflicting central values. Saudi Arabia has much less of a problem. It is an Islamic republic, and the Koran codifies most (but not all) social and political values. There, basic questions seldom come up. America is more of a salad bowl — many traditions and beliefs tossed into the same space, finding strength and vitality in the diversity, but defying attempts to find homogenizing values. One version was expressed by the Reagan administration. Their core values looked something like this:

1. Markets are the best way to make decisions about who gets what in America.
2. Government should interfere in markets as little as possible; its primary responsibility is to defend the nation's interests and territory.
3. The national government has grown beyond its proper reach; most of its functions should be taken over by state and local governments, where citizens can more easily control its scope and growth.

The Reagan administration was better than any previous modern presidency in selecting appointees who shared the core values, and most of its policy successes occurred administratively, not in new legislation. A lasting effect of this ideological hegemony is expected to be in the federal judiciary, where the Reagan administration was able to nominate half of all sitting judges.

Another version of this view of leadership is found in the "new public administration" (NPA), put forward by a group of academics in the late 1960s and early 1970s.[21] The core beliefs of the NPA are as follows:

1. Social equity should be the primary goal of the administrative state.
2. Social equity has not been sufficiently pursued, mainly because public officials represent special interests and impose values of efficiency and economy at the expense of equity.

FIGURE 7.3 The Continuum of Leadership Behavior

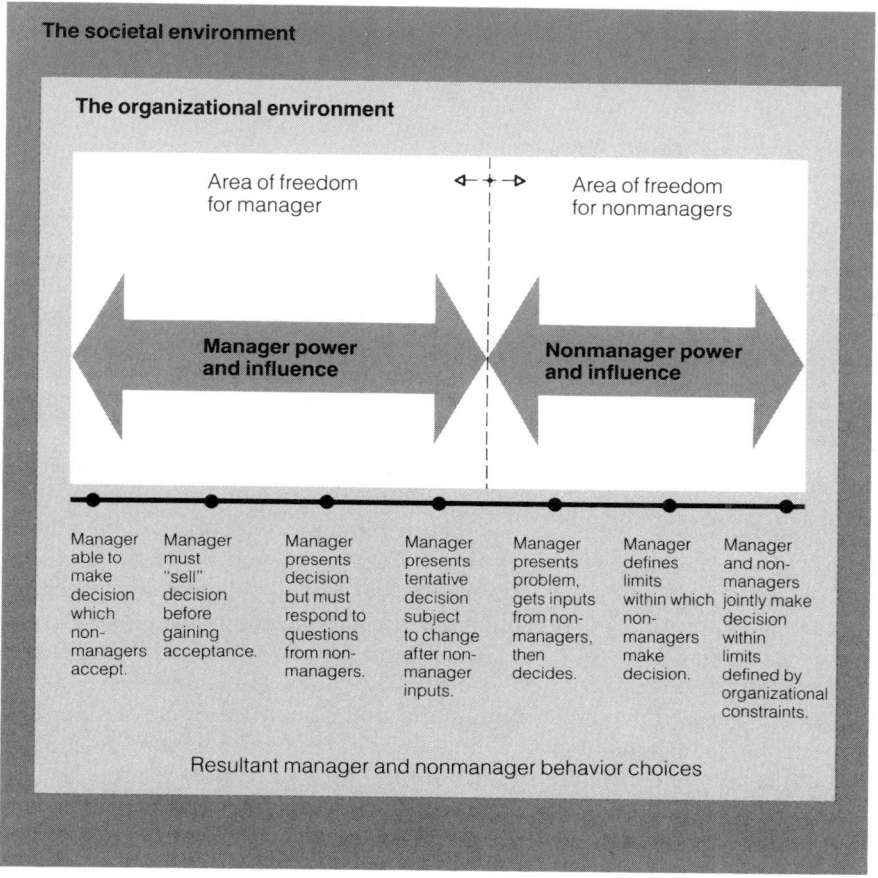

Reprinted with permission of the *Harvard Business Review*. An exhibit from "How to Choose a Leadership Pattern" by Robert Tannenbaum and Warren H. Schmidt (May–June 1973). Copyright © 1973 by the President and Fellows of Harvard College; all rights reserved.

3. Public administrators should be a political force for more democracy, less bureaucracy, and decentralized client-focused services.

To put the NPA in the context of our earlier discussion, advocacy should be the key to our public administration.

The comparison of the Reagan administration and the NPA suggests how different American ideals can be. Our political imagination has never been completely worked out — indeed, many of the central ideas are necessarily vague in order to solve difficult conflicts. Yet, it is exactly this vague set of ideas that allows people with different interpretations of our tradition to prosper.

Leadership as Creating Tensions

One of the facts of leadership is that most issues encountered by organizations are beyond the scope of one leader. How often can people be at once powerful and neutral, patient and decisive, setting new directions and encouraging loyalty, steeped in principles and adept at compromise? When we consider this kind of constant pressure, it is easy to understand why good leadership might turn, at least in part, on luck.

It could be that leadership is not an individual thing. There are visions of leadership that are more democratic, more group-oriented, and (of course) more difficult to describe than the common brands.

In an ambitious book, Michael Harmon[22] combined a variety of theories into a general approach to public administration that rejects the traditional practices represented by Weber's ideal-typical bureaucracy. Harmon argues that the value of human actions lies mainly in the process, not the outcomes of action. This is not so much a rejection of seeking outcomes as an attempt to go beyond the dichotomy between substance and process. Good decision processes should both enhance the well-being of participants and improve substantive outcomes. Harmon believes these things can happen if people understand and act with the knowledge they are personally responsible for their actions. This would be a huge change in the way we conceptualize organizational life. Since public agencies will remain in a subordinate position to legislative controllers, there will always be a tension between the controllers and the members of organizations. Leadership, in these instances, is provided by "mediating structures."[23] Leadership now takes the form of groups that continuously negotiate the tensions among decision-making levels.

This view of administration is less hierarchical than what we read in most of the literature. Harmon wants organizations to constantly take ongoing tensions into consideration. For example, system, individual, and client requirements must always be reviewed. At any point in time, a mix of legislators, workers, members of mediating structures, and citizens might be involved in the same issue. The mix, as well as the political mood, is always in flux. Leadership, in these cases, becomes a collective creation. Leadership looks like the management of tensions. The picture Harmon paints is one of politics, which is openly embraced by public administration.

Experience tells us that all of the research we have reviewed has a ring of truth to it. There is merit to what has been written. Yet, that same experience reminds us that there might be more to leadership than has met the social science eye. When we go back to the etymological roots, we can at least guess what has been missing. Part of the definition was this: "Leading motive . . . a strongly marked melodic phrase." It is possible that what makes followers is the melodic phrase that is made real by the leader. Good followers and good leaders somehow hear the same music and see the same vision. It may concern nothing bigger than how a day-care center is organized, or it may be sweeping enough to start a world war. But, it seems that all effective leaders are able to strike the right notes for their followers.

SUMMARY

A review of the definitions of leadership reveals that the concept is not precise, though it is essential. The different elements that are involved in leadership, such as power, the knowledge and skills of leaders, obedience, hierarchy, the political context, and its relation to management, are combined in a complicated mix. The things that leaders provide seem to be essential to administration.

Research on leadership reflects its complexity and importance. Different approaches to research include emphases on traits of leaders, on the situations of leaders in organization, and on the functions leaders should fulfill. The approaches to leadership reflect differences in political vision; whether, for instance, one sees politics as an integral part of administration or as a separate activity. Our review of leadership literature closed with the unsettling hypothesis that success in organizations may depend more on luck than on the qualities and actions of leaders. This does not mean that leadership studies are useless. It does mean there are important unanswered questions about authority and effectiveness in organizations. These are questions left unanswered by our political traditions, questions that leaders help people answer.

These observations brought the discussion of leadership back to politics. The political context of leadership is perhaps its most essential ingredient. Leaders bring political ideas and practices to organizations, but not all views of leadership want politics to happen within organizations.

NOTES

1. On fallacies of theories of power, see Larry D. Spence, *The Politics of Social Knowledge* (University Park, Pa.: Pennsylvania State University Press, 1978), pp. 13–21.

2. Jeffrey Pfeffer, *Power in Organizations* (Marshfield, Mass.: Pitman Publishing, 1981), pp. ix–x.
3. See Peter Drucker, *Management: Tasks, Responsibilities, Practices* (New York: Harper & Row, 1974).
4. Alan W. Lau, Arthur R. Newman, and Laurie A. Broedling, "The Nature of Managerial Work in the Public Sector," in James L. Perry and Kenneth L. Kraemer, eds., *Public Management: Public and Private Perspectives* (Palo Alto, Calif.: Mayfield, 1983), p. 200. See also Morgan W. McCall and Michael M. Lombardo, eds., *Leadership: Where Else Can We Go?* (Durham, N.C.: Duke University Press, 1978).
5. James B. Spotts, "The Problem of Leadership: A Look at Some Recent Findings of Behavioral Science Research," in William R. Lassey and Richard R. Fernandez, eds., *Leadership and Social Change* (La Jolla, Calif.: University Associates, 1976), pp. 46–47.
6. See Ralph M. Stogdill, *Handbook of Leadership* (New York: The Free Press, 1974).
7. See Richard Boyatzis, *The Competent Manager: A Model of Effective Performance* (New York: John Wiley & Sons, 1982).
8. James B. Spotts, op. cit., pp. 48–49.
9. V. H. Vroom and P. W. Yetton, *Leadership and Decision Making* (Pittsburgh: University of Pittsburgh Press, 1973), quoted in David M. Hunter, *Supervisory Management* (Reston, Va.: Reston Publishing, 1981), pp. 223–226.
10. Other popular guides to choosing a leadership style are Robert Tannenbaum and Warren H. Schmidt, "How To Choose A Leadership Pattern," *Harvard Business Review* 51 (May/June 1973); and Robert R. Blake and Jane S. Mouton, *The Managerial Grid* (Houston: Gulf Publishing, 1964).
11. James B. Spotts, op. cit., pp. 49–51.
12. Laurence E. Lynn, Jr., *Managing the Public's Business: The Job of the Government Executive* (New York: Basic Books, 1981), pp. 177–179.
13. James B. Spotts, op. cit., p. 61.
14. James MacGregor Burns, *Leadership* (New York: Harper & Row, 1978), pp. 301–302.
15. See Theodore W. Taylor, ed., *Federal Public Policy: Personal Accounts of Ten Senior Civil Service Executives* (Mt. Airy, Md.: Lomond Publications, 1984).
16. Herbert Kaufman, *Time, Chance, and Organizations* (Chatham, N.J.: Chatham House Publishers, 1985), pp. 68–69.
17. This section relies on Charles G. Schoderbek et al., *Management Systems: Conceptual Considerations*, rev. ed. (Dallas: Business Publications, 1980), Chapter 9.

18. Chester Barnard called this the core of "the executive functions." See his original discussion in *The Functions of the Executive* (Cambridge: Harvard University Press, 1938).
19. W. Richard Scott, "Effectiveness of Organizational Effectiveness Studies," in Paul S. Goodman, Johannes M. Penninger et al., *New Perspectives on Organizational Effectiveness* (San Francisco: Jossey-Bass, 1977), p. 63, quoted in ibid., p. 233.
20. Drucker, op. cit.
21. Frank Marini, ed., *Toward a New Public Administration: The Minnowbrook Perspective* (Scranton, Pa.: Chandler, 1971).
22. Michael M. Harmon, *Action Theory for Public Administration* (New York: Longman, 1981).
23. Ibid., p. 107.

CHAPTER EIGHT

Personnel Administration

> Thus most attempts to plan and coordinate the civil service system as a whole have been accepted only grudgingly, if at all, in Congress; by contrast, detailed administrative inventions on those personnel issues of particular interest to individual congressmen find ready acceptance on Capitol Hill.
>
> — *Hugh Heclo*

Running an agency, managing its people and material, and getting things done requires that someone pay attention to the details of hiring, training, and paying public employees. These and related tasks are commonly assigned to a personnel office. Personnel offices are often the center of controversy in the conflict between politics and public administration. A famous private manager, Robert Townsend, said the first thing he does to revitalize an organization is fire the entire personnel office.[1] When legislatures pass laws intended to make public employees work harder or be paid more fairly, the details are usually farmed out to a personnel office. Just what are personnel offices, and what do they do?

Structure, Functions, and Goals

Figures 8.1 and 8.2 are organization charts of personnel offices. Figure 8.1 is from a county government, and the boxes represent individual people. Most of the work of this office consists of sifting through applications for county jobs, testing job applicants, reviewing requests to change job descriptions, and doing special tasks assigned by the county council. One position, the "Quality Circle Facilitator," is a recent addition. It took the place of a person in charge of affirmative action and equal employment opportunity. Such changes are common: as county councils decide someone has to pay attention to a new idea, personnel offices are often asked to fill the gap. The work of equal employment opportunity and affirmative action still must be done, but these areas now are someone's part-time responsibilities as a new focus becomes paramount.

Figure 8.2 represents a personnel office in a larger government. Here the boxes represent offices instead of people, although some of the offices

FIGURE 8.1 A County Personnel Department

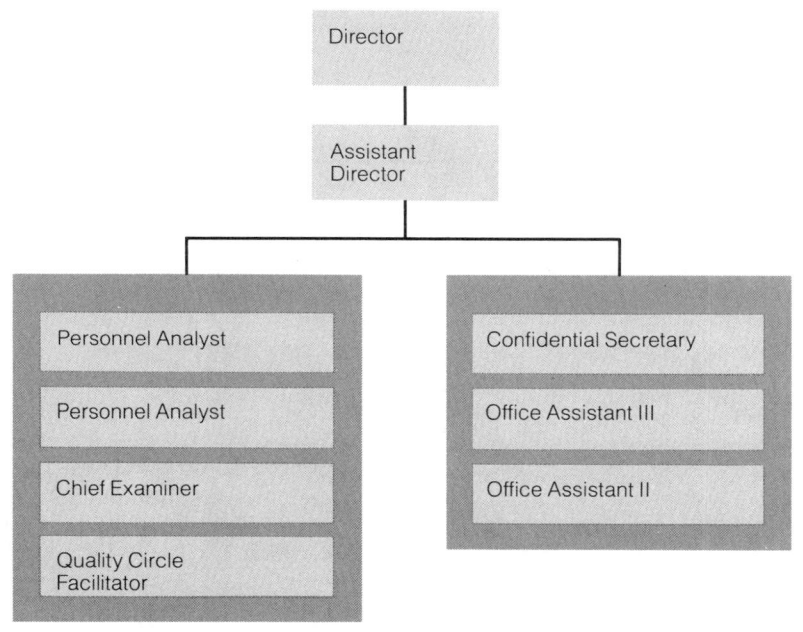

consist of just one person. A lot more is asked of this personnel office. People here are specialists in position classification, training, testing, and so on. The problems in running an agency expand with increases in size, and governments seek recourse through such specialists.

Both of the personnel offices depicted here are organized as staff offices, lodged in the executive branch. The purpose of a staff office is to enable executives, such as a president or a mayor, to control the budgets or personnel practices of agencies. Staff offices serve as the eyes and ears and accountants of executive officials. Under this form of organization, executives are trusted to manage the details of administration. Some governments still organize personnel matters under a commission or board, where appointed officials give policy guidance to a semiautonomous agency. Under this model executives are not entirely trusted to control the details of administration. The board organization of personnel functions originated in a time when the chief concern of lawmakers was to limit the use of patronage in staffing and setting personnel rules. Personnel com-

FIGURE 8.2 A State Personnel Department

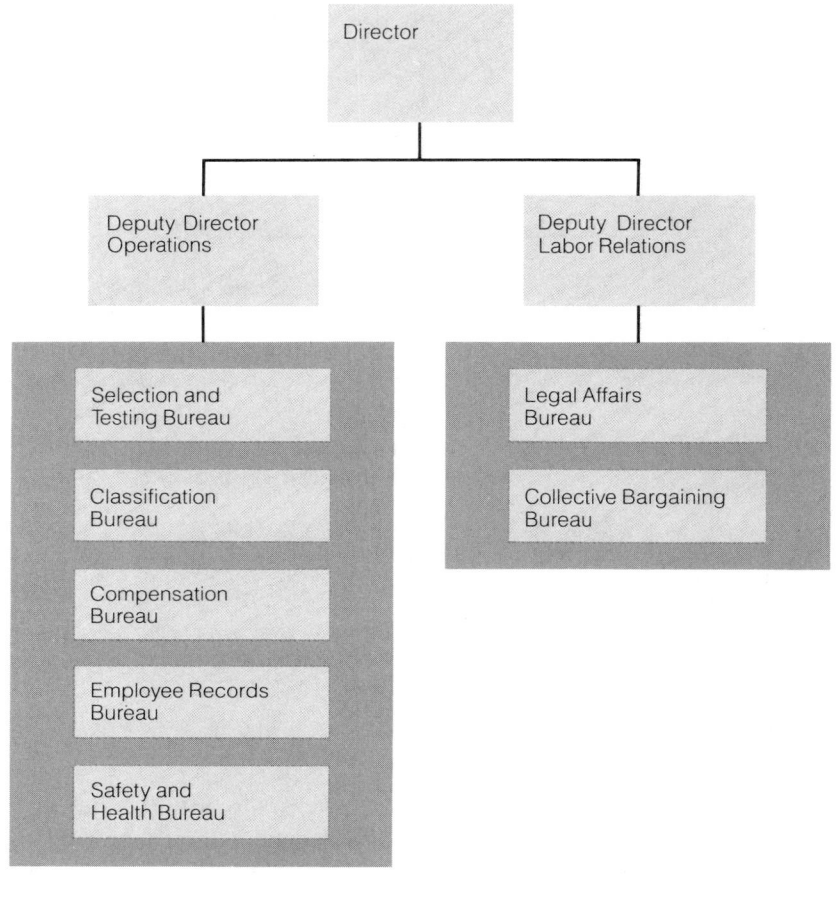

missions and boards are steadily being replaced by the staff office model of organization. The Civil Service Reform Act of 1978, discussed in Chapter 5, embodies this shift in thinking on the proper organization of personnel administration.

The people in these personnel offices are supposed to know about people in organizations, about the nuts and bolts of running a government. They are members of a staff organization, and their primary duty is to serve members of line organizations. For instance, if the managers of a public housing agency need to redefine positions in their agency in order to cope with a diminished budget, they may contact people in the personnel office for help in reclassifying positions and providing incentives to individual employees.

Providing service to line agencies is not so simple most of the time. The personnel office serves many masters. Most of their functions are the result of ad hoc changes in duties brought about by legislation, new procedures issued by budget offices, and court rulings. A manager in a public housing agency may ask for help from a personnel office, and may receive it. But the manager may also receive an audit of positions to ensure that employees are not being paid more than similarly classified employees in other agencies. There will probably be hiring and promotion guidelines to enhance the role of women and minorities in the government. The budget office may have imposed a hiring freeze with certain exceptions, and exceptions must be pleaded before the personnel office. The personnel office must serve the often conflicting masters of organizational purpose, fairness, and fiscal stress.

This is how the conflict between politics and public administration emerges in the personnel function. Courts, legislators, interest groups, and managers ask many things of government employees. Compromises are made, and the details of day-to-day operations are worked out. Personnel offices do this work, but they cannot be entirely neutral. For a number of reasons, the central needs of administration come first. Cost control and other budgetary requirements are the first priority. Consider this fact: When managers have to meet program goals, it is time to assess whether new activities or new people are needed; but when managers fail to meet budgetary limits and violate antideficiency laws, it can lead to criminal charges.

Maintaining the legitimacy of the personnel office is the second priority. Since a personnel office does not deliver a service to the public, but instead controls resources needed by service-oriented programs, a personnel official must attempt to build a spirit of cooperation with other agencies. Political officials and key managers must believe the personnel office has the ability and authority to carry out its central functions. The other functions of the personnel office must be subordinated to these top priorities. Some students of administration are uncomfortable with this set of priorities, and it has been said that in personnel administration we find the triumph of technique over purpose. A look at roles of managers and the details of personnel administration may show why.

Managers and Personnel Administration

Public managers make few if any of the rules that govern key areas of their jobs. In the areas of human resource flow and compensation, virtually all tools are controlled by a personnel office or commission. Managers have some latitude in selecting particular employees for promotion and transfer, disciplinary proceedings, overtime, and training. For the most part a clear line can be drawn between the tools readily available to the manager and those controlled by others, such as a personnel office. If it is a matter of interpersonal relations between manager and subordinate (coaching an employee, setting examples, thanking an employee) almost complete discretion rests with the manager. Tools which involve money and official recognition (performance pay, new titles to reflect additional duties) are controlled by the personnel office.

To acquire the cooperation of the people in a personnel office in the use of these tools, managers have to behave a certain way. Even before they get an idea about a change in staffing or promotion of a particular employee, managers need to keep in touch with personnel office people to be sure of their options and the way such changes must be handled. The schedules of the two agencies must be coordinated, and managers should not assume that the paper can be "walked through" and sped up to suit their needs. Managers need to be sensitive to the pressures on a personnel office. For instance, exceptions from standard hiring procedures may be technically available, but the personnel office may be under a great deal of pressure to limit their use. The proper forms must be filled out, and here the manager has to pay particular attention to the focus and level of detail considered appropriate in the personnel office. In general, there is no excuse for being unpleasantly surprised by snags in the personnel process. A manager needs to do the homework necessary for ensuring cooperation from the personnel office.

Managers are not without their own resources in this exchange with personnel offices. The latter rely on managers to carry out the details of most personnel systems. A manager who relies upon and accepts personnel office expertise in areas like hiring and promotions may well find an added measure of cooperation when position classification concerns come up. Managers should know they are just one constituency of a personnel office. The level of cooperation depends mainly on the degree to which goals are shared, something that does not occur spontaneously.

This discussion points to a crucial difference between personnel management and personnel administration. The former is mainly the job of managers who must achieve the goals of line agencies. The latter is mainly the job of personnel administrators who must see that managers come to share some of the goals of staff agencies. Both must respond to a variety of forces and make the compromises necessary to getting their respective jobs done.

BOX 8.1 Confessions of a State Personnel Director

The director of a state personnel department was having lunch with one of his former professors. It had been several years since his MPA studies, but he was still deeply concerned with central problems of the theory and practice of public administration. "A job like mine is really impossible to do well because no one agrees on what I am supposed to do. There are programs to run and deadlines to meet, but nine different interests think I should do it a different way." He went on to claim that "if academics really want to contribute to public administration, they will get their act together and build a theory of organizations that shows the importance of the perceptions and values of people who work in government."

His professor pointed out that academics seldom lead but rather report the theoretical developments of practitioners. This is radical, antihierarchical talk for the director of a major state staff agency, he added. The director pressed on. "I do a good job of bringing the technicians, the politicians, and the employee groups together, but we are missing out on so much of the creative energies of state employees. I have to pay attention to the heads of the most important legislative committees who believe that supervising a state employee is like running a bunch of field hands. Watch them close, push them hard, and send them home with their check — end of transaction. The unions play the same game, worrying about the number of members they have and that the employees get a fair shake on pay and working conditions. The political appointees are always surprised at employees who won't jump on the bandwagon for their policy ideas and get it done in two weeks. And my department is supposed to give them all the tools to get things done and keep everyone happy.

"I don't know how to make or spread the right theory," he continued, "but the pluralist idea doesn't work. As long as we have this organized warfare among groups, politicians will beat up on government and we won't be able to bring out the best in our employees. The politicians have to get over the idea that they own government agencies. And employees have to be given the responsibility to run things."

He sat and thought, and then went on. "You have to have dreams to keep up your energy level. I might see it come true in my lifetime."

The Nuts and Bolts of Personnel Administration

Figure 8.3 lists the technical functions of personnel administration. The focus is on managing positions in government agencies, but as we noted earlier the context of this management is highly politicized and personnel offices must be responsive to many constituencies. In this sense Figure 8.3 is an idealized representation of the work of personnel administration. The context complicates matters, as we shall see in the following sections.

Human Resources Planning

The literature on personnel administration is full of detailed advice on how to plan for personnel needs.[2] The logic goes something like this. Good management requires planning of all needed resources. Human beings are an important resource for organizations. Therefore, good management requires planning of human resource needs.

The budget is the essential resource of organizations. Nearly every dimension of personnel management is a function of budget purposes and amounts. It is not surprising, then, that planning for personnel needs looks a lot like the politics of budgeting. Although general budget levels may be predictable, it is difficult to predict how many positions will be available in particular agencies from year to year. Legislatures may place special requirements on agencies, leading to dramatic shifts in duties. Hiring freezes are common when revenues run short. In states where budgets are prepared on a biennial basis, revenue "shortfalls" of 20 percent in the second year are not unheard of. Such forces destroy the best plans.

Yet planning is essential. For example, in one state administrators were surprised when 25 percent of the computer systems analysts positions were vacant. They did not plan on it. Qualified people could not be recruited because the budget requests for agencies requiring computer systems analysts were not tied to estimates of the labor-market trends in the field. As a result, important work in agencies could not be done properly. Many examples of similar problems are easily found in school districts and local governments. Personnel costs commonly constitute more than 50 percent of an agency budget, up to 80 percent in labor-intensive functions such as teaching and firefighting. Government officials strongly desire to control and manage this key resource.

For more than a decade a common problem in many governments has been cutback management, which we discuss further in Chapter 9. Here is a brief list of the problems cutbacks pose for personnel resources:

> Payments are required for severance pay, retirement system withdrawals, and unemployment insurance charges
>
> Additional work is required to maintain a call-back roster

FIGURE 8.3 The Work of Public Personnel Administration

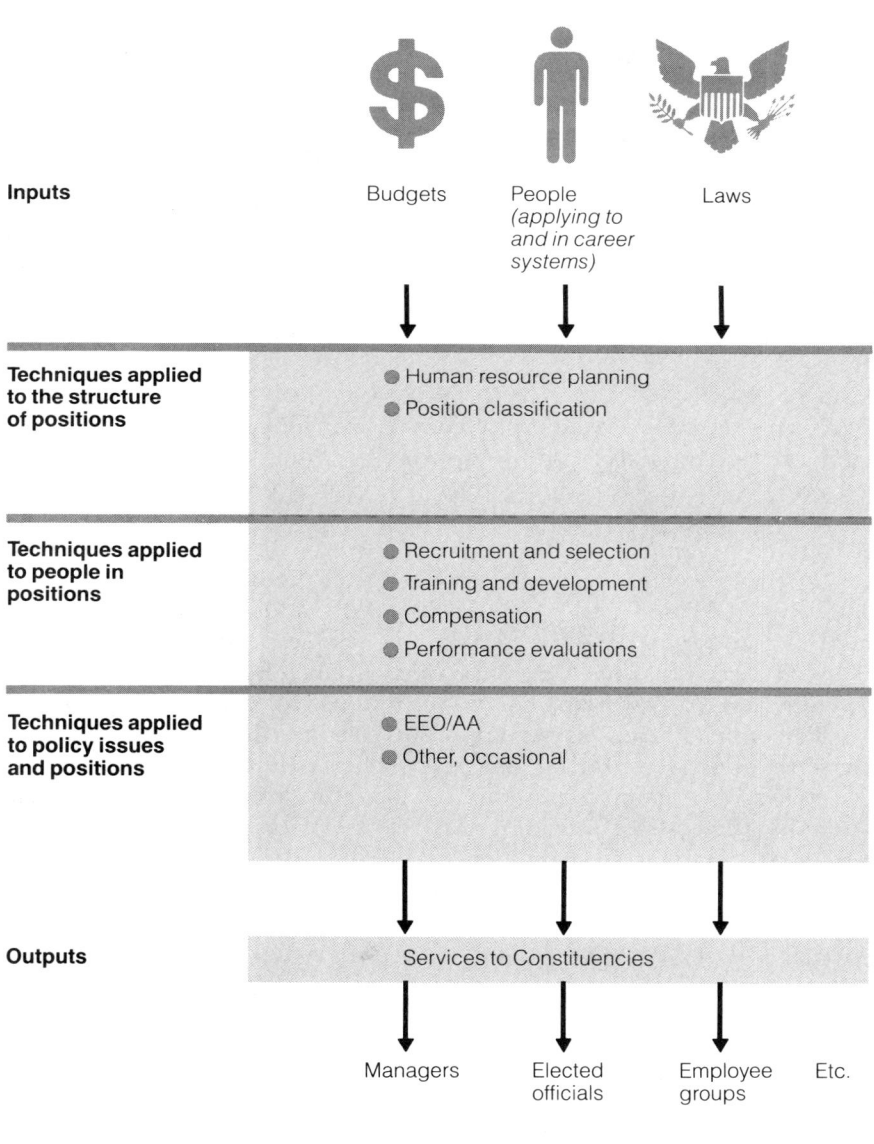

- Productivity may suffer as high-turnover jobs empty and agency morale plummets
- Since the last hired may be the first to be fired, plans to achieve equal employment opportunity and affirmative action (EEO/AA) and other goals may be subverted
- Extensive retraining may be necessary to equip employees for newly assigned duties.

Planning will not eliminate such problems, but it offers a chance to manage agencies and provide the best services possible to citizens.

What goes into a human resources plan? The ultimate goal is to fit resources to needs, but organization dynamics and politics severely complicate matters. We can break down the process into setting objectives for the plan, doing the work of planning, and carrying out the plan.

1. SETTING OBJECTIVES FOR HUMAN RESOURCES PLANS. Elected officials provide the overriding priorities by attaching budget limits to personnel resources. This top-down approach is discussed in Chapter 11, in the general discussion of budgeting. It is geared to macroeconomic and other broad goals of elected officials and pays scant attention to the details of running programs.

Agencies provide bottom-up objectives in the budget process. Their objectives are based partly on past levels of funding and staffing, and partly upon estimates of the numbers of people needed to do new and changed tasks. Collective bargaining sets parameters for pay, promotions, benefits, and many working conditions that use up personnel resources.

Personnel officials play an important role in sifting through and making sense of these conflicting objectives. They estimate the costs of tentative collective bargaining positions, calculate the "roll-up" costs of present positions (the costs of providing this year's services at next year's costs), issue staff reports to help budget and elected officials interpret pressing issues, and in general try to serve both budget controllers and department heads. Making the match between the conflicting sets of goals is the chief purpose of human resource planning.

2. PLANNING ACTIVITIES. A large number of factors influence whether a government can afford and will attract the workers it needs. There are legal requirements for hiring procedures (such as AA and EEO, requirements that positions first be offered to current employees, limits on the number of political appointments), job markets, changing technology of the workplace and professions, training programs to upgrade in-house skills, competing requests for scarce resources — all factors that are difficult to estimate accurately. A number of procedures and formulas are available to planners,[3] but the work is most often done by rules of thumb and professional judgments. Most government agencies make the tacit assumption that the right people will come to their door to apply for jobs.

The voluntary armed forces are a notable exception (they need to convince you that the Army is the place to "be all that you can be"), as are notices encouraging women and minorities to apply for specific positions. Agencies also use other techniques discussed below, such as job analysis, to make estimates of the skills available in the workforce.

3. CARRYING OUT HUMAN RESOURCE PLANS. Since human resource plans are not often technical masterpieces, but instead compromises achieved by people in personnel offices, they evolve constantly. Recruitment strategies may change, promotions and lateral transfers are used to acquire talent, RIFs (reductions in force — the government euphemism for layoffs) occur, special pay exceptions are granted as the circumstances appear to dictate. Personnel offices rely heavily on the techniques described below to carry out the plans.

Position Classification

Even a small government, employing only 150 people, must deal with the fundamental problems of hiring, paying, and evaluating employees in a way that ensures both equity and meeting the goals of the organization. Position classification is the basis for this work in virtually every government organization.

The management of government personnel resources begins with an emphasis on positions, not people. The idea is that jobs are designed to fit together in an organization which will survive the departure of individual officeholders. People are compensated on the basis of the worth of the position rather than the achievements or talents of the person. The notable exceptions to this focus in the United States are the military, where rank is given to the person regardless of the position occupied; the Foreign Service; and the Senior Executive Service.

The work of studying and comparing positions is called *job analysis*. When applied to a particular position, it results in a *position description*. A position description is written for each distinct collection of duties, a job. The people who write position descriptions follow a manual on how to use particular words to describe particular situations, so that the work of many different job analysts will yield similar results. When placed in an overall plan of position control, position descriptions are the basis of *position classification*.

To get an idea of how to do job analysis, look at the structure of position classification systems, the methods used to compare positions. The most popular method is some variant of what is called *factor comparison*. Several factors are used to analyze all positions. Here is a list from a local government:

> *Factor 1: Duties and Responsibilities.* The relative complexity of the work, its diversity, scope, effect, difficulty, level of judgment, originality, initiative, or other mental demands required by the work.

Factor 2: Independence of Action. The need to apply knowledge and make decisions independently as indicated by the type of supervision received; the relative variety and complexity of matters on which decisions are required; the relative frequency of decisions; and the consequences of error.

Factor 3: Personnel Management Responsibility. The extent to which the incumbent is required to plan, organize, direct, review, and appraise the work of others.

Factor 4: Working Relationships. The extent and purpose of interactions with others inside and outside of the organization, in terms of the importance and frequency of contacts.

Factor 5: Working Conditions. The physical characteristics of work and its environment, dexterity and exertion required, degree of risks, discomforts imposed upon the incumbent.

Factor 6: Necessary Worker Traits. The nature, variety, and level of knowledge, skills, and abilities required in performing the work.

Factor 7: Qualification Requirements. The training, experience, and other qualifications an applicant needs to bring to the work.

Each factor is carefully explained so that everyone doing job analysis uses the terms similarly. For instance, factor 2, independence of action, is broken down into the following:

1. Immediate supervision
2. Close supervision
3. General supervision
4. General guidance and direction
5. Broad policy guidance and direction

Each form of supervision is described in detail to distinguish it from the others. Key words are used to distinguish the various levels.

The format is followed for all seven factors. Points are usually given for each category within a factor, so that when the job analysis is complete, the numbers are simply added to achieve an overall score for the job. This total is used to place the position into an overall framework of classified positions. "Benchmark" jobs are written up so that job analysts can compare their work to that of others as a further check on accuracy of comparisons.

Initially, job descriptions are written by the people in positions or, in the case of a new position, by the supervisor. The work is audited by a position analyst. Most positions are audited periodically to update classification plans, a time when the personnel office is placed in a potentially adversary role to managers in line agencies.

There are other methods for classifying positions, but they all share one thing in common: They have to *look* fair and objective. The more objective a technique appears to be, the fewer objections encountered (see Box 8.2). This leads to attempts to restrict the judgments of position classifiers as much as possible, embodying them in techniques. The point guidechart method, pioneered by Hay and Associates, is perhaps the most popular such technique. Figure 8.4 is a sample point guidechart. One is constructed for each classification factor, and the job analyst simply has to apply the terms to the job. Some discretion in point assignment is left to the analyst, but not much.

Remember that governments use classification plans as the basis for compensation. When money is at stake, the legitimacy of a technique is vital. There is a great deal of pressure on people doing position classification to find authoritative techniques that government employees will respect and accept.

Recruitment and Selection

Personnel offices usually control the filling of vacancies in public agencies. Employment is a commitment of money, and the controls are remarkably similar to other spending controls. (Financial management is discussed in Chapter 12.)

BOX 8.2 Confidence in the New Classification System

In the mid-1970s, the state of Montana moved from a traditional position classification system to a factor-point system. The old method relied upon supervisors writing a narrative essay on every position, and personnel department people would compare whole jobs and rank them for uses in a pay plan. As the number of state-classified employees doubled between 1965 and 1975, the narrative classification system became unwieldy. It was simply impossible to make reliable comparisons among so many position narratives.

The new system was similar to the factor-point method recently adopted by the national government. Each job was analyzed according to nine separate factors. Each factor was subdivided into several categories constructed to carefully distinguish job responsibilities. Points were assigned to each category so that the ranking of jobs became more automatic. The new system was quite technical — judgments about the worth of jobs were built into the system of analysis rather than residing in specific employees of the personnel department.

The new system was the responsibility of the personnel department's classification office. The office requested each employee to write his or her own position description according to a set of guidelines to the factor-point system. Two supervisors were required to check each description. Final point totals and comparisons were made by panels of state employees selected by the classification office. Classification office people were proud of the new system because of the high quality of the work, the high level of employee and supervisor participation, and what they felt was an inherently defensible and reliable classification methodology. It was clearly a technical triumph and a vast improvement over the old system.

Problems began to appear as soon as the classification office published a draft class plan that included point totals for individual positions. Twenty-five percent of state employees found some reason to disagree with their classification (it had a direct bearing on pay) and appealed. The appeals process is a careful one where two position analysts and a review board study each case. Many state workers appealed their job classifications on the grounds that their positions were more responsible or dangerous than listed in the description, and these required job audits (a visit to the work site by a position analyst). On many positions the point totals fell just short of a higher pay level, and employees often complained that reasonable interpretations of the classification standards should give them the benefit of the doubt. Classification office people estimated that each appeal took approximately 12 hours to process. With over 1200 appeals to process, it would take seven people an entire year to process all claims. The classification office had five positions at the time.

The head of the classification office said that any system would encourage such discontent: "The new system is better for all the reasons the state does position classification. We will just have to bear these transition costs. It makes the job a lot harder to do." When asked why such a good system raises serious doubts in at least 25 percent of employees, he replied that "people support procedures mainly through routines. Some of the appeals are mistakes we made, but most of them are people sincerely trying to understand why they won't be getting paid a little more. Once they get used to it they will support it. I just hope to God we don't ever change again."

The classification appeals backlog took 5 years to clear. In the sixth year, a legislative commission on personnel and labor issues was formed to take a complete look at the state's personnel system. Among the commission's agenda items was a new position classification method, alleged to be the latest technology that ensured employee confidence and effective cost controls for the state.

FIGURE 8.4 Point-Guidechart Classification

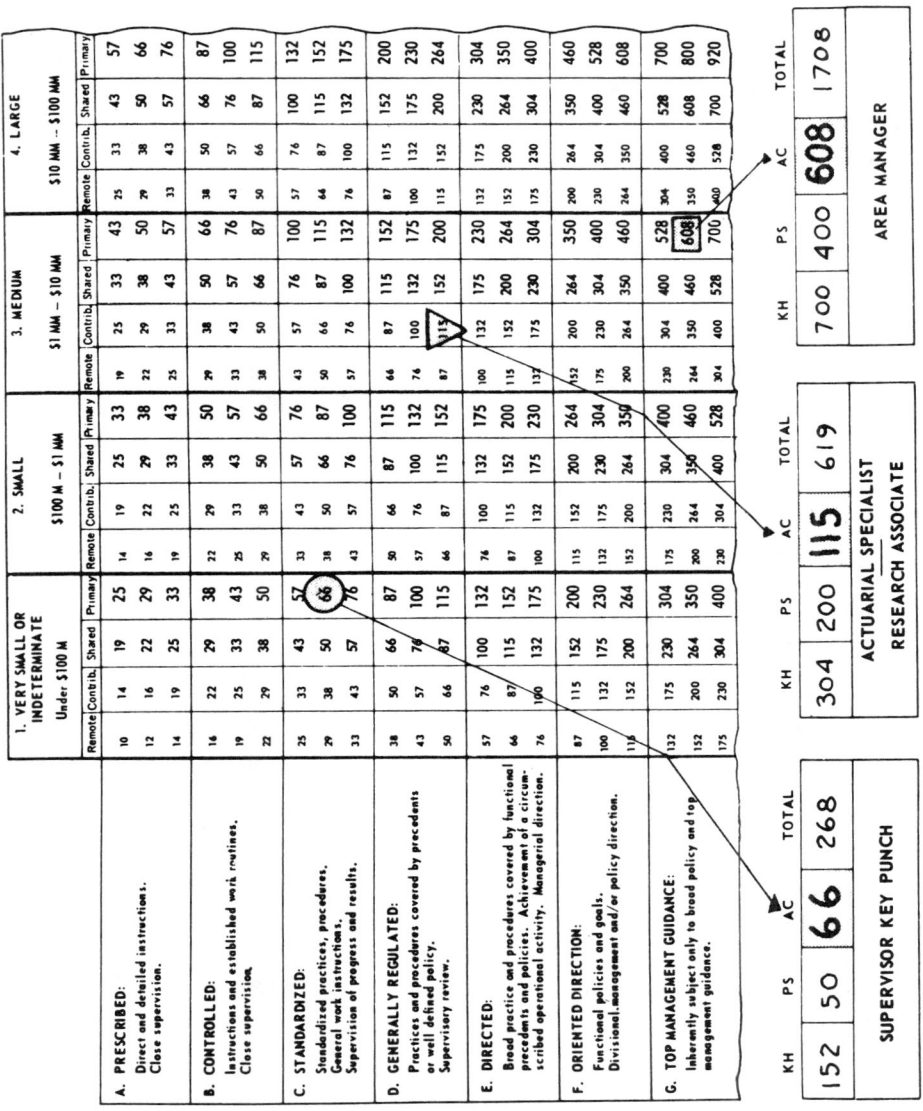

Source: State of Montana Department of Personnel, Salary System Design, July 1981. Chart prepared by Hay Associates Public Sector Group, Chicago, Ill.

Once it is established that an agency is authorized to fill a position at a given pay level, active recruitment may begin. Most governments do not aggressively recruit, but assume qualified applicants will find the agency at the right time. The most common forms of advertisement are personnel bulletin boards (most likely to be seen by current employees or jobseekers who know where vacancies are posted), newspapers, and some specialty publications (whose readers are members of the desired profession). Some government agencies, such as school districts, work from waiting lists of qualified applicants who must periodically reaffirm their availability. Positions covered by civil service systems (see Chapter 6) recruit from a register of tested applicants. The clearest rule about recruitment is that different forms of government do it differently. The important fact is that the methods employed attract qualified applicants. The simplest test of their effectiveness is the reaction of application reviewers and the managers for whom recently hired employees work.

Once applications are accepted, the choice among candidates must be made. Most governments employ tests to rank employees, although there are strong doubts about the effectiveness of tests. The purpose of any selection procedure is to discriminate between the higher- and lower-qualified employees. Many tests also discriminate on the basis of prohibited classifications, such as race or sex. Requirements that police officers be at least 5 feet 8 inches tall, for instance, will discriminate against many applicants of Oriental and Hispanic ancestry, since a greater proportion of those groups are under the standard than is the case for whites. General intelligence tests tend to rank blacks lower than whites, but the tests do not predict job performance. Mathematics tests tend to rank women lower than men, even when both are able to perform particular jobs. Technical discussions of test validity are available in many sources.[4] The overall finding is that tests are improving in ability to select the best-performing applicants, but that perfect selection is unattainable. The highest test validity scores indicate that guessing errors (mistakes made in selecting who the best employees will be) are cut in half compared to a fairly random method of selection; but many errors are still made. The errors should not deny public employment to blacks, women, Hispanics, and other groups. The fact is that minorities and women are not as successful as white males in securing public jobs. Later in the chapter we will discuss some interpretations of why this may be so.

The statutes and court decisions concerning selection methods are discussed below, in the section on equal employment opportunity and affirmative action, but the bottom line can be simply stated here: If a selection procedure has an adverse impact on a protected class (race, sex), it is assumed to discriminate illegally, unless the procedure is clearly job-related.

A popular way to avoid illegal discrimination in tests is to use tests only to cull the lowest-qualified employees and then employ human judgment in interviews and assessment centers. In these situations, interviewing panels use a structured interview for each applicant so that comparable information is available. The panel can discuss their findings to see if initial reactions generate an acceptable pool of final candidates. If unacceptable discrimination has taken place, the cases may be reviewed to see if the choices were clearly job-related. In any case, the most common final procedure is to send the top three to five applicants to the hiring managers for final interviews. The personnel office monitors the overall record of hiring various groups of people to assess the outcomes of hiring procedures.

BOX 8.3 How Do You Get a Government Job?

This chapter summarizes government hiring procedures, but it does not give enough details to guide you in getting a government job. Moreover, governments differ in their hiring procedures, so detailed guidelines would cover many pages. To find out how to get a government job, complete this exercise.

Either interview or invite as a class guest speaker a personnel official who manages government recruitment and hiring. The person may be from any level of government (groups of students may wish to each investigate a nearby government). Ask them the following:

   Where are government jobs advertised? How can I find out about them?

   Who decides just what qualifications are required for a job? How are these checked to make sure they are job-related?

   What kinds of tests are used? Does the government maintain a register (a list of applicants for a class of positions, ranked by test scores and experience)? Do the tests really select the best employees?

   What is the process for screening job applicants? Who is involved? Who makes the final decisions?

   What percent of the jobs are filled competitively? Are exceptions granted? Why? How are these handled differently?

   How did you get your job?

   If you did this by interviews, report findings to the class.

Training and Development

All employees require some orientation to the organization and job. These functions are usually filled by employee handbooks, orientation meetings, training by the supervisor, and similar contacts. Training and development usually refer to more sophisticated activities that address inadequate skills or desired behavioral changes in continuing employees.

It is possible to focus training on individuals or the general skill level of the entire organization. The individual focus starts with the supervisor's identification of a particular employee or group of employees who need additional skills to perform their work. Someone needs to clarify the training objectives, develop the training procedures, and carry them out. It is often the case that new technologies (such as computers) and legal developments (such as prohibitions against sexual harassment) need to be delivered to large numbers of employees.

The professional literature on training and development advocates a more general and planned orientation to such activities, to be carried out by professionals in a personnel department. Some larger governments do a great deal of training in this way. The training professionals take inventories of skills of current employees, make forecasts of skills needed in the future, work with employees and supervisors to develop training methods, and deliver the training or find the right people to carry it out — very much according to the logic of human resource planning.

Training sounds like a good idea, and the professional literature is impressive,[5] but there are problems with training. The payoffs are not often as tangible or immediate as the costs of the training. When managers are faced with scarce resources, they have to make choices. A widely used rule of thumb is that costs of the problem have to be much greater than the costs of training, on the order of two to three times. Smaller governments cannot afford many expensive training programs. They rely heavily on hiring the right people, encouraging people to maintain and improve their skill levels, getting training from people who sell them equipment (such as computers), and on-the-job training.

One of the reasons training has a slightly tarnished name is that many people sell poor training packages to government. Those of you who join the American Society for Public Administration, the International City Managers Association, the Municipal Finance Officers Association, or any of a dozen other professional groups will find your mail filled with advertisements for training packages and seminars. The advertisers usually charge several hundred dollars per person for large-group seminars. Some firms and consultants sell directly to the top executive officers of local and state governments. Here are some important rules of thumb for dealing with entrepreneurial training: (1) Be sure of your training needs before you buy (you do not need motivation seminars if your employees are motivated, or are unmotivated because of concrete problems on the job). (2) Be sure to get and call references of all consultants and trainers;

find out specifically whether the objectives you have in mind are fulfilled by the sessions. (3) Establish a way to evaluate the outcome of training. Are the employees really better off several months down the road? A little checking can guard against wasted resources.

Training and development can play a key role in organizational change. Where managers and employees need to think and act in new ways, where organizations face new challenges such as budget cutbacks, and where long-term commitments to change are possible, training programs can be devised which help to build and carry out plans for organizational change.

Compensation

Although there are many factors at work in the relationship between organizations and employees, most revolve around the cash nexus. Employees get the money to buy life's necessities and a bit of fun, but they also get status, and some motivation to perform.

Employees receive financial compensation in several forms. The monthly or bimonthly paycheck is cash to be spent immediately. Benefits not included in the paycheck may include health insurance, transportation and parking, vacation and other compensated leave time, and other items the employee may consume (although it is common that the employee pays for part of these through payroll deductions). Finally, employees receive deferred income in the form of pension benefits. It is possible to design a flexible pay plan that fits the package of financial benefits to an individual employee. For instance, a young mother may be most interested in straight cash, with day care, health insurance, and leave time in the benefit package. An older childless male worker may be most concerned with health insurance and pension benefits.

Pay plans must follow legal and political requirements in particular jurisdictions. Among such requirements are[6]: collective bargaining policies, minimum wage laws, prevailing wage laws, minimum benefits laws, maximum pay policies, equal pay and antidiscrimination statutes, laws governing the timing and form of payment, merit pay policies, cost-of-living adjustments, comparable worth policies, public opinion, and elected officials' responses to pay trends. Pay is clearly not simply a matter of running checks through a computer.

Performance Evaluations

It is generally accepted that employee performance needs to be evaluated. There are disagreements on how closely productivity and rewards can be tied to the formal evaluation of performance. Performance appraisal is based on knowledge of what an employee should be doing. Job analysis and performance standards are relied upon to build a system of appraisal

BOX 8.4 Science and Modern Personnel Systems

Most descriptions of the techniques of personnel administration emphasize the use of systematic analytical techniques. Specialists in the social sciences, particularly psychology and organizational behavior, continually produce new developments in areas like testing and performance appraisal. It is the best science has to offer.

It is a mistake to assume that such techniques can be transferred to any government, however. Cultural and political differences between areas belie the science and expose the conflict between public administration and politics. One place to see the conflict is to see what happens when the best techniques of American bureaucracies are transferred to Native American tribal governments. The Confederated Salish and Kootenai Tribal Government (CSKT) faced problems in the late 1970s. The government was getting larger, partly in response to national government programs to offer services on reservations, and several economic operations owned by the CSKT needed better management. Bureau of Indian Affairs officials suggested that the Office of Personnel Management (OPM) might be able to help.

An OPM consultant visited the CSKT and made several suggestions. The main idea was to apply for a grant under the Intergovernmental Personnel Act (IPA), a source of funds to build the management capacity of governments. The CSKT applied for and received a grant to do the things they wanted, but there was a catch. If a government uses IPA funds or similar national government resources, the grantee must keep track of the funds and organize itself the way the OPM requires. This is usually not a problem for governments, but Indian tribal governments often do not have bureaucratic organization structures. To use the IPA money, they had to acquire them.

Traditional CSKT organization was characterized by face-to-face relations between people. They organized by consensus, not coercive hierarchy. In a government meeting people who felt capable would present their position, and at the end simply say they have spoken. Meetings would eventually develop a trend of opinions, and at some point agreement was reached. It was clear to everyone that a decision had been made, and that they understood each other.

Anthropologists refer to such behavior as a central part of a North American Indian personality, which lacks "dominance-submissive hierarchies." This is another way of saying that in family, social, and most work situations, "thou shalt not push others around." It is clearly at work in the CSKT. When someone comes into the tribal office seeking credit or some service, they are regarded first as a tribal member, someone's in-law or cousin, and so on. The discussions aim at gaining cooperation through consensus. When the same people go to the county seat or state offices for services, they are treated as a case that must meet certain eligibility criteria.

The CSKT has always had problems making bureaucracy and culture meet. The elaborate rules and coercion found in bureaucracies show that people do not share common beliefs, do not work from consensus, and are then not allowed to share in decisions, demonstrate initiative, or take on responsibilities. In practice in nearly all tribal operations, it means people have to accept things that they would never otherwise consider as worthy of attention except as a condition of employment.

The new IPA grant brought in a personnel office with separate officers for position classification and management training. Interns from a nearby university were hired to help do the work of position analysis, partly directed by an OPM consultant. The end result was that the central CSKT government did gain more control and was able to better manage the operations they were concerned with, but it came at a cost. There was more coercive power coming out of the tribal government office than before. The younger tribal members who had gone to college and learned modern management techniques did best at running the new system. They gained considerable authority that used to reside in the older members and the tribe in general. Tribal council members had to learn bureaucratic leadership skills in order to be able to direct CSKT managers.

As long as the CSKT wants the resources of the national government, it must adopt the bureaucratic methods. To many this looks like progress, like putting new ideas and education to work in tribal government. Yet, even outsiders cannot help but feel the awkward moments in tribal council meetings when the tribal spiritual leader speaks. He speaks from a quiet and deep authority, and with pain, of the forces that are hurting families and killing tribal members. The same things are happening on most Indian reservations. His comments do not easily fit into the meetings which now sound much like county council meetings everywhere. He helps us remember, for a while, that modern techniques of personnel administration do not serve all people and all purposes.

---

that is acceptable to both raters and ratees. Employees can be rated by an immediate supervisor, a group of supervisors, a group of peers, by subordinates, by clients served, by themselves. It is important to discern what is expected of performance appraisal and who is most likely to have relevant information. A mixed rater system is used in many places.

The design of a performance-rating instrument is a long and complicated process.[7] Many methods are available, but the instrument itself is not as important as the way in which it is constructed and used. Raters and ratees have to believe it can achieve the desired goals, whether those goals are to apportion pay according to performance, determine orders of promotion, improve performance, certify continued competence, or some other objective. The people who use it must have confidence that it is not "personality appraisal," a common epithet used with some justification by government employees. A technical discussion is not possible here, but some general conclusions are possible. There are many successful performance appraisal systems in use, and many employees believe it can be done well. There are many failed systems as well, probably more numerous than the successes.

There are reliable guidelines for the conduct of performance appraisal at the personal level. Before actual appraisals, supervisors and employees should discuss performance frequently. Clear performance goals should be set, and progress toward them should be periodically discussed. If possible, organizational rewards can be made clearly contingent upon performance. Both supervisors and employees have to understand how a given appraisal system works and must prepare their thoughts for an appraisal meeting. During the actual appraisal and discussion, it is important to focus on specific instances and patterns of performance, not personalities. The exercise should lead to shared goals for future improvement.

Equal Employment Opportunity and Affirmative Action (EEO/AA)

The people charged with carrying out the personnel function in government are constantly working out the tensions between public administration and politics. The techniques discussed so far focus on ways to analyze and categorize positions and people so that they may serve organizations. Government policies on equal employment opportunity and affirmative action are good examples of the ways these techniques are used to serve explicitly political goals.

The legal basis of EEO/AA has evolved over the last generation from a minor to a permanent concern of public officials.[8] Although based on legislation, EEO/AA policies have grown mainly through court rulings, executive orders, and administrative procedures. The important milestones in EEO/AA are:

1. The Equal Pay Act (EPA) of 1963 (an amendment to the Fair Labor Standards Act of 1938) prohibited discrimination in wages unless it is

the result of seniority or a system based on the quality and quantity of worker production. Courts have broadened the applicability of the EPA to cover state and local governments and such issues as comparable worth.

2. Title VII of the Civil Rights Act of 1964 prohibits an employer from discriminating on the basis of race, sex, national origin, and religion in matters of hiring, working conditions, and other matters relating to employee opportunities and status. This is still the most important piece of EEO legislation, and subsequent amendments and court cases have refined definitions of impermissible discrimination.

    The most far-reaching court interpretation of Title VII was *Griggs v. Duke Power Company* (401 U.S. 424 [1971]), which held that the results of hiring actions matter, not the motives of employers. The Duke Power Company required all employees to have a high school diploma and achieve a certain score on a general intelligence test. The U.S. Supreme Court found that neither standard was related to job performance, and that the effect of the standards was to discriminate against blacks. Further court cases have refined the idea that adverse impact is unlawful even if employers had no intention of discriminating on the basis of Title VII categories.

3. The Age Discrimination in Employment Act (ADEA) of 1967 sought to protect workers over 40 against the same types of discrimination prohibited in Title VII. Court interpretations have run into the interesting problem of having to decide what is more important, discrimination on the basis of age or on the basis of race and sex. In general, the statute and court interpretations exempt application of ADEA in governments that specifically seek to alleviate other areas of discrimination or have clear goals involving other classes, such as recruitment of young professionals.

4. Executive orders 11246 (1965) and 11375 (1967) broaden Title VII's coverage to federal contractors and subcontractors. The orders also brought about the policy of affirmative action, employment practices that seek to increase the employment of underrepresented groups. Important court cases have contested whether quota or goal-oriented programs for women and minorities constitute prohibited discrimination under Title VII ("reverse discrimination"). In general, the courts have ruled against strict quota systems, but have approved clear goals to be achieved in a specified period — in short, temporary quotas. The Reagan administration came out strongly against any type of quota and directed its appointees in the Justice Department and other agencies to contest programs that discriminate against particular individuals in the interest of protected groups.

5. The Equal Employment Opportunity Act of 1972 broadened Title VII's provisions to cover employers in state and local governments

and public and private education institutions. The Congress did not extend coverage, however, to elected officials' appointees and staff. The act also provided a statutory basis for AA and extended its coverage to include government employers.

6. The Rehabilitation Act of 1973 prohibits discrimination against handicapped individuals and requires employers to make "reasonable accommodations" for the needs of handicapped workers.
7. The Uniform Guidelines on Employee Selection Procedures is a set of administrative rules adopted in 1978 by the main national government offices that set personnel policy. The rules were made to help federal, state, and local agencies make sense of the increasing number of laws and court rulings concerning EEO/AA. The guidelines provided a test for adverse impact. (This is the famous "80 percent rule." For example, if 20 percent of white males applying for clerical jobs are offered positions, but less than 16 percent of black males who apply are offered clerical jobs, the selection method creates an adverse impact.) The guidelines also provided procedures for ensuring that any selection instrument that produced an adverse impact actually tested skills needed to perform the job.

The uniform guidelines illustrate the ongoing conflict between public administration and politics in America's governments. Policies are made in many places, often resulting in a patchwork administrative structure charged with enforcement. By the late 1970s, complaints against reverse discrimination and unpredictable EEO/AA requirements prompted the Carter administration to devise the uniform guidelines and a more coherent administrative structure for personnel. One interesting milestone in the backlash against EEO/AA policies was a suit by Sears, Roebuck and Company in 1979 (47 L.W. 2734), which charged that the company was given conflicting requirements by agencies of the national government, and that Sears had gotten into trouble by actually following government policies. A federal district court dismissed the suit, suggesting that such difficulties are political questions best addressed by the Congress and the president.

Currently, the agencies charged with enforcement of EEO/AA policies are the Equal Employment Opportunity Commission, with responsibilities for Title VII enforcement, coordination of EEO enforcement in the federal government, and equal pay and age policies; the Department of Labor, which enforces provisions for handicapped workers and affirmative action; and the Justice Department, which looks after state and local governments' EEO/AA policies.

The late 1980s are an uncertain time for EEO/AA policies, particularly in state and local governments. Almost all jurisdictions have strong policies and procedures in place dating from the early 1970s, but Reagan administration policies have emphasized both a decentralized approach and a renewed focus on individuals instead of group-based tests of discrimination. The Justice Department under Reagan has expected states and localities to work out their own policies and has even gone to court seeking to dismantle temporary quota systems constructed in the late 1970s. The Supreme Court has shown less interest in deciding personnel policies unless clear constitutional questions are at stake, and the net effect is that states and localities are now responding more to local and regional political pressures than to national government initiatives.

The most important part of EEO/AA policy is sensitivity and knowledge of the people who do the everyday work of hiring, promoting, and managing employees. The job of the personnel office is to clarify policies and procedures so that managers have clear guidelines to follow. While the people in personnel are the focus for the policies of hiring, they have to find a way to make the politics fit the needs of administration.

Other, Occasional Policy Responsibilities

When new issues emerge that involve the hiring, firing, paying, and managing of public employees, the personnel office is usually asked to perform the analytical work and build the consensus for governmental responses. This means that new duties are continually given to people in personnel, and choices have to be made about office priorities. In this sense they are just like a budget office, except that the resource they deal with is people. Box 8.5 provides examples of recent issues taken up by many personnel offices in state and local governments.

BOX 8.5 Newer Duties of Personnel Offices

Personnel offices are often asked to find administrative solutions to obdurate political problems. Among the most pressing contemporary issues are comparable worth, drug testing, and the use of polygraph tests (lie-detector machines).

The idea of comparable worth can be stated simply: Incumbents of predominantly female occupations are paid less than incumbents of predominantly male occupations, even though the two occupations are essentially alike in demands on workers and contributions to the organization. This is an injustice. The reality of comparable worth is very complicated. Most government employees are compensated with some reference to a "market" wage or salary. Job analysis techniques, widely accepted for ranking positions for other purposes, show that markets tend to underpay females in certain occupations by about 20 percent. Advocates of comparable worth battle those who would have the market guide decisions about the worth of government goods and services. At the same time, public employee unions and other interest groups put pressure on elected officials to respond to demands for comparable worth. Several cases have gone to the courts.

Another recent issue is the public realization of the extent and costs of drug use in America. A movement is underway to have members of certain occupations, such as military service and professional sports, undergo regular drug testing. In early 1986 a presidential commission on drug abuse suggested that all national government employees be subject to drug tests as a condition of continued employment. Advocates acknowledge that tests are less than perfect (under ideal conditions they are 95 percent accurate), but stress that provisions for retesting will eliminate all but a few errors and stop the alleged abuse problem in the federal service. Opponents of drug testing are led by public employee unions and civil rights organizations. They point out that the program is an intrusive, mandatory search of a person following a presumption of guilt.

A similar issue concerns the use of polygraph tests to stop "security leaks" in the national government. Policy advisers in the Reagan White House suggest that all government employees be required, when requested, to take polygraph tests in order to find out who may have leaked information or sold secrets to foreign spies. Some members of intelligence agencies have worked under such requirements for many years. Opponents of the practice are not convinced. Some government employees who turned out to be spying for decades passed polygraph tests with flying colors. The leaks that most frequently raise the ire of the White House are politically embarrassing rather than threats to national security; and professionals in government regard the idea as a slap in the face. Secretary of State Schultz threatened to resign if one of his employees were asked to take the test.

These are all difficult political issues, yet personnel offices are asked to find ways of administering solutions. The work should not be thought of as dull routine.

Cheating on the Nuts and Bolts

We started this chapter by focusing on the services that personnel offices provide to managers. The discussion of the nuts and bolts of personnel administration showed that the personnel function must serve many constituencies, and that technical means are created that aim to satisfy all of them. In a pure sense, this is an impossible task. The political sources of the disagreements remain.

This leaves public administrators in a difficult position. They are the ones under pressure to deliver results in public programs, but the tools available to them are geared to do many other things as well. It is not surprising that enterprising managers cheat a little in personnel management. The cheating is not really violating a public trust, not at all like stealing a typewriter. Rather, the cheating is done to recruit employees quickly, reward the excellence of subordinates when few official forms of recognition are available, to recognize heavy responsibilities when the position classifiers are more concerned with cost control. This helps to explain, for instance, why in 1985 only 20 percent of federal civil service jobs were filled competitively (and some of that 20 percent included "wired" jobs, where the people doing the hiring knew who was going to get the job beforehand). Maybe "fudging" or "finessing the system" are more polite ways to describe the behavior, but the fact is it goes on. Box 8.6 shows how the tension may result in problems in position classification systems.

The cheating at times is probably cause for admiration. It reminds us that organization systems cannot control everything, particularly when their ultimate purpose is to achieve some complicated and ambitious public goal. Serious problems occur when the cheating results in adverse impact on minorities and women, or when other arbitrary, personal, and illegal purposes are injected into government personnel work. Yet the creative energies of people are needed to apply the tools of government in an intelligent manner. That is really what the cheating is about — the people who perform the work of government trying to do it in a way that rules cannot clearly guide.

SUMMARY

We began this chapter on personnel administration with a description of the work of personnel offices. These offices are made to fill a staff function, that is, to provide a service; yet personnel offices serve several masters. They serve the line agencies by helping to recruit, train, pay, ap-

BOX 8.6 Cheating — How to Destory a Classification System

The people who implement position classification systems do not always share the goals of the system. The presentation below takes a practical view of such goal displacement and presents a guide on how to destroy a classification system. The list on the left is taken from a U.S. Office of Personnel Management description of the functions of classification systems. The list on the right, the advice for saboteurs, is adapted from Jay Shafritz et al., *Personnel Management in Government* (New York: Dekker, 1976).

What a Classification System Is Supposed to Do	*How to Sabotage It*
Determine classifications of positions and relations between classes.	Make career lines restrictive; make it hard to qualify for anything other than next step up in your line of work.
Determine job knowledge and skill requirements	Put too much job description into class specifications; use the terminology of factor, but actually describe specific activities.
Set like pay for like positions.	Use the classification system to get raises for particular employees (this is easier than changing the entire system).
Recruit qualified applicants	Be unrealistic about job qualifications.
Establish valid performance evaluations for each classificaiton.	Don't review positions to keep up with changes brought about by time and personal differences.
Comply with required recordkeeping.	Fail to keep the system up to date, let it serve your particular needs and the general objective of cost control.

praise, and discipline employees. They serve political officials by helping to watch budget limits on personnel matters, such as the number of positions in an agency or the management of a pension plan. They may be involved in intergovernmental services, such as when a local government's personnel office is in charge of ensuring compliance with federal antidiscrimination laws.

Personnel officials find it difficult to serve their many masters. The crucial link in their contribution to an organization's effectiveness is the relationship between the personnel office and the line managers. A spirit of cooperation comes from a commitment by both parties to achieve the organization's goals and to follow applicable laws and regulations. This is an example of where leadership in an organization makes an important difference.

We then described the nuts and bolts of personnel administration. Human resource planning is a way to marshal resources to meet the many, and often conflicting, goals facing the personnel function. The plans are not highly technical but instead reflect the ability of a personnel office to foster cooperation in an organization. Position classification is the basic technique of personnel administration, since it serves as a basis for paying employees, establishing qualifications for hiring, training new employees, evaluating performance of individuals, and controlling personnel budgets.

Next we described the legal framework and procedures for equal employment opportunity and affirmative action (EEO/AA). This is an area where politics and administration are highly intertwined. Government employment is an important community resource, and there are special requirements to ensure that citizens are treated fairly, particularly in regard to their sex, race, religion, creed, or recognized handicap. Arguments over the definition of fairness and the methods of achieving it are sure to continue in the coming decades.

We closed the chapter with an unsettling irony. The many goals of personnel systems often make it difficult for personnel offices to clearly serve line managers. Even people with good intentions often cheat the system to achieve their goals, but this means that overall control of personnel goals suffers. The fact remains that trying to marshal the best efforts of employees in a bureaucratic system is tremendously difficult.

NOTES

1. Robert Townsend, *Up the Organizati* (New York: Fawcett, 1971), p. 126.

2. Useful sources on human resources planning include Albert C. Hyde and Torrey Whitman, "Workforce Planning: The State of the Art," in Jay M. Shafritz, ed., *The Public Personnel World* (Chicago: International City Managers Association, 1978), pp. 65–73; and U.S. Civil Service Commission, *Planning Your Staffing Needs* (Washington, D.C.: 1977).
3. Forecasting techniques applied to human resources planning are discussed in many places, among them James W. Walker, *Human Resources Planning* (New York: McGraw-Hill, 1980). More detailed discussions of forecasting techniques are available in Steven C. Wheelwright and Spyros Makridakis, *Forecasting Methods for Management*, 2d ed. (New York: Wiley, 1977); and William G. Sullivan and W. Wayne Claycombe, *Fundamentals of Forecasting* (Reston, Va.: Reston Publishing, 1977).
4. See Wayne Cascio, *Applied Psychology in Personnel Management*, 2d ed. (Reston, Va.: Reston Publishing, 1982).
5. See R. L. Craig, ed., *Training and Development Handbook*, 2d ed. (New York: McGraw-Hill, 1976); and Jack Rabin et al., *Handbook on Public Personnel Administration and Labor Relations* (New York: Dekker, 1983).
6. See Rabin et al., op. cit.
7. A detailed discussion of available techniques is found in Cascio, op. cit.
8. Discussions of EEO/AA policy and procedures can be found in Rabin et al., op. cit.; Francine S. Hall and Maryann H. Albrecht, *The Management of Affirmative Action* (Santa Monica, Calif.: Goodyear Publishing, 1979).

CHAPTER NINE

Managing Public Agencies

Develop a much greater number of capable administrators in the public service, and prepare them for promotion to any bureau or department in the government where their services may be most effectively used.

Enforce the accountability of administrators by a much broader pattern of controls, so that the statutes and regulations which govern administrative practices will encourage, rather than destroy, initiative and enterprise.

Permit the operating departments and agencies to administer for themselves a larger share of the routine administrative services, under strict supervision and in conformity with high standards.

Only by taking these steps can the operations of the executive branch be managed effectively, responsibly, and economically.

—*from* The Hoover Commission Report

Do you mean you actually train people to be bureaucrats?

—*A citizen's reaction to a description of a university's public administration program*

The most visible activities of government revolve around high politics and scandal. Congressional struggles over the budget deficit are news. Tax reform is news. The drunk driving arrest of an administrator awaiting trial for malfeasance of office is news. Competent management of a government agency is not news. Citizens expect government agencies to be run well, government employees to do their jobs, and services to be delivered at a reasonable cost. Most of the time this is what happens. It happens when government employees with adequate skills can assemble the talents within a bureaucracy into effective operations.

This chapter is about the internal workings of public organizations, the management of our public administration. Although it is not headlines, the underlying themes are central to how we understand ourselves. Efficiency comes at a cost. In an extreme case, under the fascists, the Italian trains were made to run on time. Certainly we want efficiency and productivity from our government, but not at the expense of democracy.

What Do Managers Do?

Managers are people whose responsibilities include the organization and direction of other people and organizational resources (such as budgets and equipment). Managers are found at many levels of organizations, generally below leaders (when there are leaders to follow — see the discussion in Chapter 7) and above supervisors, who are delegated the responsibility to direct and check subordinates' work.

A simple way to look at management is to find out how managers spend their time. The first thing such observations show is that the way managers spend their time depends on their responsibilities in the organization. Employees with no supervisory responsibilities spend their time on assigned tasks. Their main concerns seem to be fulfilling such assignments, achieving some acceptance among fellow workers, and receiving adequate compensation and promotional opportunities. The person who delivers your mail, issues a license, or collects your garbage is such a worker. Employees with supervisory responsibilities spend a great deal of time giving directions, checking the work of subordinates, and solving problems encountered in delivering the organization's services. The shift supervisor at your local post office is such a worker. Top managers spend most of their time working on problems arising from the need to plan, coordinating various units of the organization, and responding to forces and people outside of the organization. The heads of postal service regional distribution centers have such responsibilities.

In a study of federal bureau chiefs, among the top managers in the national government, dealings with people outside the bureau were found to occupy about 25 to 30 percent of their time; the act of motivating the work force, about 10 to 20 percent of their time; and receiving and reviewing information for decision making, motivating the work forces, and for steps to avoid embarrassment and appraise the organization's performance, about 55 to 60 percent.[1] A study of supervisors (middle and lower management) reported that 25 percent of time is spent on directly supervising subordinates; 28 percent is spent on interpersonal relations on the job site; 22 percent is occupied by the equipment and materials of the workplace; about 5 percent is spent planning; and 20 percent of time is spent in meetings.[2] One interesting finding of most such studies is that management is mainly a verbal activity. Much of the time is spent interacting with other people, either in meetings, face-to-face conversations, or on the telephone. Managers typically spend little time just thinking, but spend a great deal of time finding out what others think.[3]

Henry Mintzberg describes the work of managers by debunking widely held myths about managing. According to him,

1. *Folklore:* The manager is a reflective, systematic planner....
   Fact: Study after study has shown that managers work at an unrelenting pace, that their activities are characterized by brevity, variety, and discontinuity, and that they are strongly oriented to action and dislike reflective activities....
2. *Folklore:* The effective manager has no regular duties to perform....
   Fact: In addition to handling exceptions, managerial work involves performing a number of regular duties, including ritual and ceremony, negotiations, and processing of soft information that links the organization with its environment....
3. *Folklore:* The senior manager needs aggregated information, which a formal management information system best provides....
   Fact: Managers strongly favor the verbal media — namely, telephone calls and meetings....
4. *Folklore:* Management is, or at least is quickly becoming, a science and a profession....
   Fact: The managers' programs — to schedule time, process information, make decisions, and so on — remain locked deep inside their brains....[4]

New Perspectives on Management

A more complicated way to consider agency management is to picture the environment of an agency and the ways people must respond to that environment. The problem is especially acute in the federal service, as reported by Lynn.

> The executives of those government agencies we depend on to conduct the public's business, especially those two hundred or so officials appointed to head the cabinet-level departments, and key subordinate and independent agencies, have been given responsibilities of immense importance, complexity, and difficulty by Congress, the president, and the courts. Each year, moreover, hundreds of new legislative enactments, executive orders, and court decisions expand and diversify these responsibilities. At the same time, the political and judicial processes that create these responsibilities generate centrifugal forces that tear away at executive authority and force the manager to share control. The result is that top executive jobs, of great importance in principle, are very hard to perform with distinction.[5]

The "centrifugal forces" are a prominent focus in the literature of Public Administration.[6] Figure 9.1 represents two things: the multiple functions public managers must fulfill, and the outside forces and actors that share authority in the exercise of those functions. The problems of governmental management thus percolate into every level of bureaucracy. As public administrative systems, their barriers are quite permeable. Public managers must serve many masters.

Managers have several tools at their service to effect operations in government agencies. Figure 9.2 lists these tools for each of the functions and accompanying centrifugal forces. This figure represents an approach to management that focuses on the following skills and abilities:[7]

1. An awareness of leadership, to be able to pursue the organization's core mission.
2. An awareness of the extended managerial system in the organization.
3. An understanding of relationships with other actors in the system.
4. The development of diagnostic skills.
5. The ability to make consistent and constructive decisions.

A similar perspective on management is used by the U.S. Office of Personnel Management in its "management excellence inventory" (MEI), developed to help federal agencies develop their managers. The MEI is based on the idea that leaders, managers, and supervisors perform similar functions, but differ in which functions are most important. Leaders are most concerned with providing a broad perspective and a strategic view for the organization. Managers are most concerned with actual results, an action orientation, and the details of program resources. Supervisors are most concerned with interpersonal sensitivity and technical competence. This diagnostic tool emphasizes that management skills must be adapted to particular organizations and situations, and that management is the application of human judgment, yet in definable and trainable areas. The MEI is expected to show where such training is most needed in an organization.[8]

A recent suggestion on enhancing management skills suggests where the field is moving for the remainder of the century.[9] Basically, the argument ties types of brain power to kinds of organizational skills. The human brain is divided into two hemispheres, the left and the right. The left side is the place where deductive and quantitative reasoning take place, whereas inductive and holistic thinking take place on the right. Integrative brain skills, where both sides are in use simultaneously, are of course the best at seeing the big picture of an organization and how particular pieces fit. It is now possible to broadly classify the brain skills of individuals. The next steps will be to enhance those skills and find the best location in the organization for people to use this brain power. Those with left-dominant brains should do "planning, management science, financial management,

FIGURE 9.1 Functions and Forces in the Environment of Public Managers

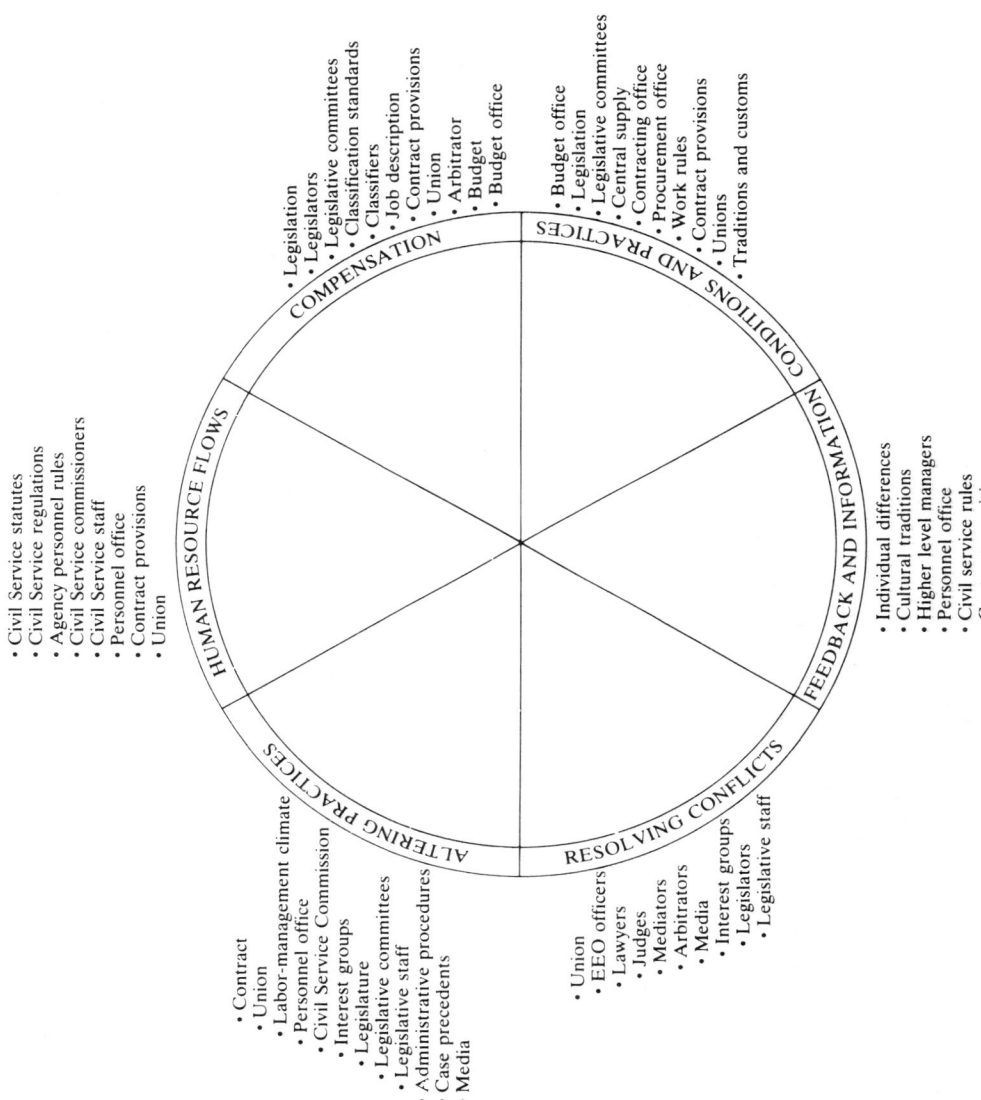

(*Source:* Adapted from Jonathan Brock, *Managing People in Public Agencies: Personnel and Labor Relations,* p. 31. Copyright © 1984 by Jonathan Brock. Reprinted by permission of Little, Brown and Company.)

FIGURE 9.2 The Tools and Masters of Public Managers

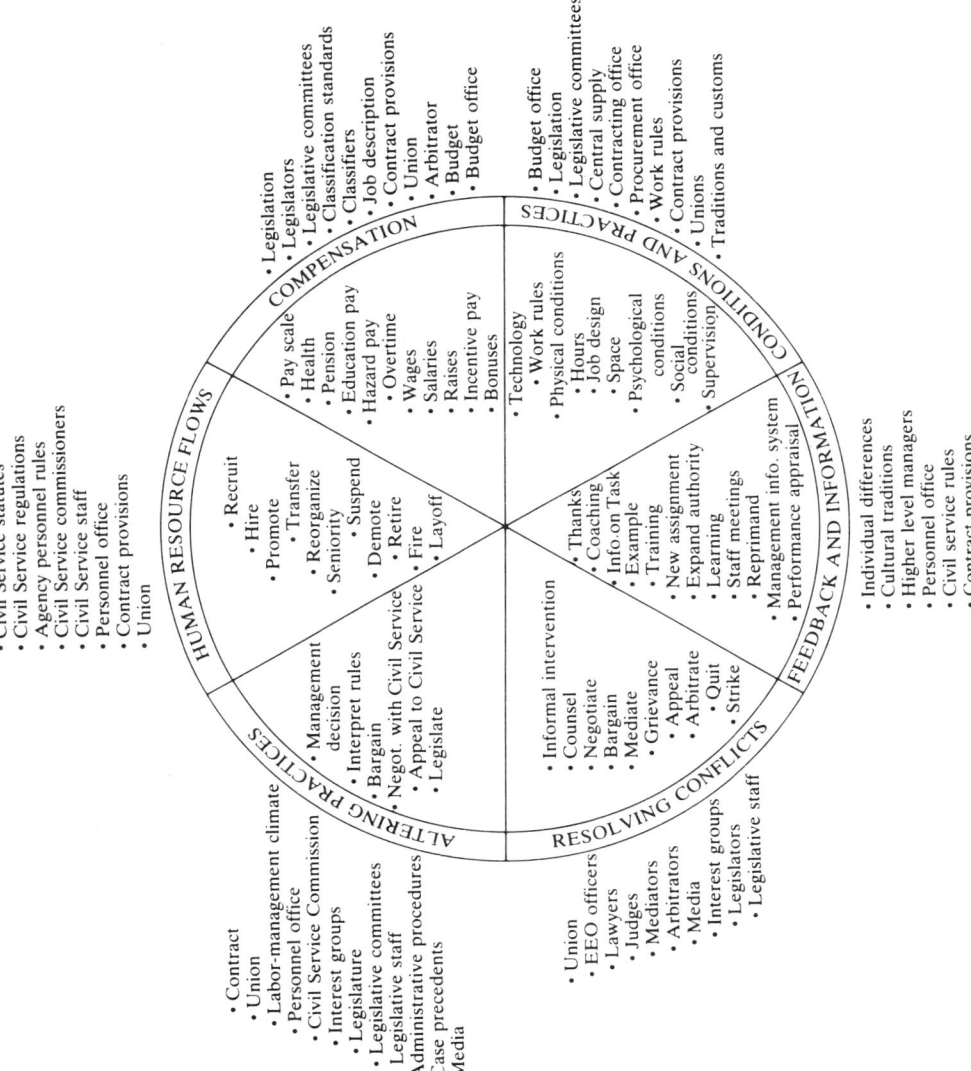

(*Source:* Adapted from Jonathan Brock, *Managing People in Public Agencies: Personnel and Labor Relations,* pp. 26 and 31. Copyright © 1984 by Jonathan Brock. Reprinted by permission of Little, Brown and Company.)

law enforcement and the military" functions; those with right-dominant brains will be assigned to the "personnel, counseling, health, and organizational development" functions; those with integrative brain skills get the "top policy and management, general administration, and intelligence" functions.[10] Put like this, the idea of matching brains and jobs seems to make a lot of sense.

There are several important ideas embodied in these descriptions of management and methods of improving the skills of managers. First, management is a separate kind of work. It includes things we call organizing, coordinating, and controlling, and perhaps a bit of planning. But the activities that fulfill such functions are not simple, perhaps not even definable. Management skills are to be "honed," not directly taught. This is because management skills are difficult to define at the individual level. Managers are supposed to be flexible, action-oriented, and have a focus on results. These are overly broad categories. The organization needs certain functions fulfilled, but as Mintzberg indicated earlier, the programs managers use for doing this remain locked deep in their brains. There are many personal styles for dealing with matters in organizations. Although some people claim to have developed a science of matching people to organization slots, a hard-and-fast classification system that selects the "right" people for particular jobs eludes us.

Second, as discussed in Chapters 3 and 4, management and organization theory relies heavily on the idea of hierarchy and vertical division of labor. The public emphasis sought by Mary Parker Follett virtually eliminates hierarchy from organization, but modern organization theory will have none of that. There are recognizable benefits from a more flexible and fluid structure, but control and authority are not left to chance. Newer techniques may seek to deemphasize hierarchy, but the elemental need for authority and clear division of vertical responsibilities is ever present. To push techniques further and claim that top positions are available only to those with certain brain patterns smacks of the most ominous science fiction.

The Modern Manager

There are dissenting voices in the management literature, and they need to be listened to. The dissent shows important criticisms managers need to understand in order to comprehend just what it is they are trying to do. Some historians of the workplace find that job ladders, modern hierarchies, and definitions of management emerged from a conflict over the control of new technologies and, most importantly, who was to benefit from these technologies.[11] One of the key foundations of management as a separate type of work is the deliberate segregation and control of skill levels in various jobs so as to bring them more under the control of the owners and top officials of organizations. This legacy of the industrial revolution lives on in public organizations.

The story goes like this: Modern management did not exist at the onset of modern industrial technology. Many industries were still organized on guild or gang principles. In the former, skilled workers exercised a great deal of control over the cost, timing, and quality of production. In the latter, a foreman would contract with a company to produce a given amount and quality of goods, and then assemble a gang to complete the work. Control over the work force was in the hands of the foremen, not the owners and top managers of the company. An important change occurred, however. Engineers sold an idea to company owners. Engineers seized upon the technological possibilities that substituted owner for worker control of the productive process, and through discipline achieved what new machines could not.

The main new ideas of discipline were the introduction of interchangeable parts, work scheduling, time-and-motion studies, and the assembly line. The work of Frederick Taylor is most famous from this era, but even before him important principles became accepted by the engineering profession. Some of the thinking that went into the change was discussed in the journals of the machine tool industry, and they still make interesting reading. The criteria for machine design stand out. The most profitable machines, and thus the ones that would sell the best, were the ones that employed labor of "moderate skill." The engineer, or the employer, would receive the rewards of increased output, and a relatively unskilled operator would tend the machine for a low wage. By embodying the skill in the machine and redesigning jobs so that individual workers had less authority at the job site, industrial output would soar and social harmony would reign. Progress would result from greater output, the increasing amount of knowledge embedded in machines, and such things as the moral influence of better-lighted factories and trade school education.

It is important to see these changes as social and political, not merely technical. Workers and owners saw the control over the benefits of new technologies to be a class conflict. New technologies introduced by owners created an obedient work force that acceded to the needs of capital. One result was a violent period of management-labor relations. From the early 1880s into the turn of this century, many people were killed or badly injured, and many more lost their jobs and property in the conflict. The owners' strategy worked because there were benefits to obedience. For workers and union leaders who kept jobs and accepted the new arrangements, higher pay and a promise of progress and social harmony were appealing. The Ford Motor Company, for instance, offered work at twice the wages of any other company, but there was a catch: workers would live where Ford instructed, be stable family men, attend church, and be obedient workers. Ford managers claimed the investments in the new job structures and benefits were the most productive ever made.

This became the pattern of modern management. Intelligence, skill, ingenuity, and inventiveness, the main elements in the improvement of production, were placed in the hands of managers and machine designers. The worker docility required to implement such a program was achieved by inculcating an acceptance of managerial control and obedient liberal social harmony in the workforce. The classic studies of management that found their way into the lexicon of public administration are straight from this tradition. POSDCORB sounds logical to us only if we ignore its political history. Ralph Hummel reminds us that control relationships remain paramount.[12] The division of labor does allow the growth of expertise through specialization, but it also divides work to make people dependent on managerial control. He writes,

> If you want to survive as a bureaucrat, you will never forget that the prime relationship you engage in is that between you and your manager. not between you and your client. And that functionary-manager relationship is a control relationship. The successful manager never forgets this.[13]

Given general acceptance of Wilson's division between politics and administration, an obedient public work force is a widely held tenet of public management. But, remember the history. It did not have to be that way, and a long and violent conflict made it that way.

What Is Public about Public Management?

Public administration is caught in a special spot between the citizens it serves and the elected officials who often have important powers over it. In this section, we will begin to get a sense of how citizens and elected officials affect the workings of public management.

It is not at all unusual for public managers to draw media attention to their actions. Consider the following three cases:

1. Brook manages the emergency medical system for a city fire department. In this particular city the fire department makes the first response to emergency calls, and a private ambulance transports people to hospitals. The first year of the system required the selection of a private ambulance company to provide the transport service. Brook solicited bids, had a committee evaluate whether bidding companies could do the job, and then selected the lowest bid from among those judged competent. The company happened to be a local "mom and pop" outfit. That was only the beginning of his troubles. The company that submitted the second-lowest bid, a much larger company

owned by a national corporation, charged that the bidding was rigged. Before a city council meeting, Brook was virtually accused of accepting bribes. A swimming pool in his backyard was referred to as the "Don G. (the owner of the low-bidding company) memorial pool." An investigation showed that Brook and the decision process were entirely honest and in compliance with city regulations. But, the following year Brook made sure the recommendation to the city council came from a blue-ribbon panel of experts.

2. Don manages a substance abuse treatment center for a large city. His organization treats the patients who want, but cannot afford, private medical treatment for alcohol and drug abuse. Six months after taking the job, he submitted a budget to the city council. The budget was based on previous years' levels and costs of treatment, and a reorganization study produced about the time he took the job. Three weeks later, during budget hearings before the city council, a state audit found that for two years money earmarked for drug abuse was spent for alcohol abuse. Don's agency was required to reimburse the state for the amount, approximately 12 percent of his budget. This problem was not uncovered in the reorganization study, and it should have been. Don told reporters and the city council that he relied on the report, but that he had not produced it. The previous incumbent of Don's job made the same claim. Don faced the prospect of having to rebuild his reputation and that of the agency from scratch.

3. Jill is director of a city-county health department. Her subordinates have a number of public health responsibilities, among them interviewing and counseling citizens with sexually transmitted diseases and other afflictions that may be embarrassing to discuss in public. Because the health department offices are small and individual stations are separated only by low partitions, Jill allows public health workers to do some of this work, including phone calls, from their homes. As long as they cope with the work load in a professional manner, such flexibility keeps the workers happy and lowers office costs. Jill's troubles arose in a strange way. A woman suspected her unemployed husband of having an affair with the wife of one of Jill's public health workers, who lived next door. The neighbor kept watch on the house and noted that a well-paid public employee spent many hours at home. Angry to begin with, she decided to report this apparent abuse. She called her city council member and the town newspaper and insisted that something had to be done about the problem. After verifying (with the help of checks by deputy sheriffs!) that the public health workers indeed spent many working hours at home, the city council member raised the charges at a city council meeting. The press made it a front-page story, Jill spent the better part of two weeks coping with the charges, and the health department workers returned to the office, a bit demoralized.

In these stories, all true, managers had to run their agencies from the front pages of newspapers. Many of their operational choices were subject to public scrutiny, often very ignorant scrutiny. Public managers must operate "in the sunshine" because they are accountable to the citizenry and elected officials, but the cases show that public scrutiny imposes difficulties. The constitutional and statutory bases for governmental agencies provide for more "watchers" than are found in the business world.

The legal foundations of public decision making and management are discussed at length in Chapter 13, but several items should be mentioned here. First, legislatures exercise oversight over public agencies. Legislators do not agree whether they should simply review past agency performance at budget time or attempt to control present and future performance as well. Legislators tend to make decisions on the basis of exceptions, such as problems for which they hold an agency responsible. The noble effort to make sure a problem does not again occur leads to new rules and guidelines for agency managers.

Second, there are many provisions for public participation in administrative decisions, particularly in regulatory agencies. When agency actions affect the public, hearings are often required. Notice-and-comment periods are required before many actions are taken. Interest groups, including employee unions, have regular opportunities to press suggestions and demands on legislators, agency leaders, and sometimes program managers. Budget hearings are generally open to the public. These suggest why a great deal of public managers' time is spent dealing with forces and actors outside of the organization.

American public management practices stand in fairly stark contrast to other industrial democracies. Except at the local level, public servants in the other industrial democracies are much less exposed to the scrutiny of legislators and the media. Canada, for example, initially borrowed many of its administrative forms and practices from the British, but followed many American developments such as the scientific management movement, reform and classification periods early in this century, and budget reforms following the Second World War. Yet, Canadian civil servants are comparatively insulated from close scrutiny of their operational decisions. Department ministers, who are elected members of the Parliament, are expected to stand for sometimes stinging denunciations and questions before Parliament, but the rank-and-file civil servants follow a tradition of competently and anonymously serving different parties with equal dedication and expecting delegated responsibilities. The 1960s and 1970s trends toward more openness affected Canadian administration as well (for instance, a civil servant may now be a designated department spokesperson and speak to the media) but to a lesser degree than in the United States.

Management Systems

The management functions depicted in Figures 9.1 and 9.2 are fulfilled only by planning and implementing fairly detailed operational guidelines. Most agencies have some system to provide these guidelines. We will discuss one here, a management by objectives (MBO) system, to illustrate the design and uses of management systems.[14]

The central purpose of MBO is to help managers set and review performance goals. There are many variants of MBO, and many purposes as well. It can be used to evaluate the performance of employees, to motivate them, to set job expectations and enhance job satisfaction, and to enhance understanding at different levels of the organization.[15] Newland describes the steps of MBO:[16]

1. Setting goals, objectives, and priorities in terms of results to be accomplished.
2. Developing plans to accomplish the results.
3. Allocating resources.
4. Involving people in implementation of plans, with emphasis on communications for responsiveness.
5. Tracking or monitoring of progress toward goals and objectives, with specific intermediate milestones.
6. Evaluating results.
7. Generating and implementing improvements in objectives and results.

MBO is based on research findings in four areas.[17] First, people tend to set their goals at levels somewhat higher than their previous performance. Second, people who receive feedback on their performance tend to perform better than people who do not. Third, if employees respect supervisors, the latters' confidence and high expectations tend to elicit higher performance. Fourth, people who help determine their own work objectives tend to set higher objectives than would others, and they tend to accept the objectives more readily. All other things being even, MBO can be a powerful psychological motivator.

MBO requires a major training effort to enable managers to understand and support the system. It is a long-term commitment to a management approach, and an appropriate investment must be made. In practice, top managers of many organizations decide to bypass the extensive training required and, in effect, use MBO as a way to impose objectives on subordinates. Setting goals and objectives is the same thing as program planning, discussed in Chapter 13. The special contribution of MBO is an emphasis on the results to be achieved, instead of processes within the agency. The development of MBO plans is often done in great detail. Fig-

FIGURE 9.3 MBO Action Plan

City Comptroller Implementation Planning

Projects	July	Aug	Sept
1. CFMS system backup training	X		
2. CFMS desk procedures manual	X		
3. Banking & investment procedures	X		
4. Affirmative Action program	X		
5. CFMS Comptroller Dept. training	X	X	X
6. Position descriptions	X		
7. Develop performance criteria		X	X
8. Implement performance appraisals			
9. Pay & classification study			
10. Certify CFMS account balances		X	X
11. State Auditor's findings — work program			X
12. MFOA Certificate of Conformance			
13. City Clerk Div. reorganization	X		
14. Audit div. reorganization		X	
15. Accounting Div. reorganization			X
16. CFMS quality control standards			
17. CFMS user survey			
18. User requirements analysis			
19. Physical inventory procedures	X	X	
20. Fixed asset work program	X	X	

ure 9.3 is an example of an MBO action plan. Descriptions of the numbered items in the left-hand column are written to enable managers and subordinates to understand the need for each item and its place in the overall objectives of the organization. Figure 9.3, for example, represents several months work by a team of four that conducted a performance audit of the agency's operations. The individual items in the action plan must be put in a practical sequence so that early building blocks come together at the right time to produce achievement of goals. The action plan serves as a set of milestones that can be used to check progress at specific dates.

At the same time the details of the action plan are established, estimates of required resources are made to ensure that the goals are ambi-

Oct	Nov	Dec	Jan	Feb	Mar	Apr	May	June
			X					
X	X	X	X					
X	X		X				X	
X	X	X	X	X	X	X	X	X
X	prepare for FYE closing statements					respond to audit findings		
X					X			
X								
X	X		X					
X	X		X					
			X	X		X	X	
				X	X	X	X	
				X	X	X	X	X

(*Source:* Adapted from City of Seattle, Comptroller's Office, Internal Documents.)

tious yet reasonable given agency personnel and other resources; then the implementation of the plan begins. If the training and planning of MBO have been done well enough, implementation mainly involves informal communications among workers, both horizontally and vertically, to share ideas and check progress toward milestones. A crucial element of MBO is that most supervisory checks are embodied in the plan. The work of supervisors should consist of helping others when requested, and otherwise leaving subordinates to do their work. Progress toward milestones can be checked without heavy-handed supervision. The best plans will have operational problems, and individuals may not perform as expected. A sign that MBO is working is that such problems occur as, and are regarded as, exceptions that do not override the general injunction to leave employees to accomplish their work.

The last steps in MBO are evaluating results and attempting to improve subsequent plans. Here the management of the agency is likely to come under the watchful eye of outside controllers. Promises made at budget time are kept or broken, and unforeseen events are considered to explain discrepancies between plans and achievements. Overall, agencies with clear MBO plans have an advantage in contacts with outside controllers. Changes imposed from above can be evaluated rather clearly, since impacts on operations and results achieved can be discussed with reference to the action plan. The discussion of cutback management later in this chapter pursues this issue further.

Supervision and Motivation

Remember that relationships between managers and subordinates are control relationships. Control is an odd word, however, implying coercion in its raw forms. Although some observers claim that worker anxiety is the main everyday motivator on the job,[16] the more frequent picture is of a symbiotic power relationship. Effective control of subordinates is achieved with their permission. Managers in search of a service orientation and achieving desired program performance will have to understand how to secure that permission.

Chester Barnard offered a useful concept for understanding control relationships. Employees of an organization have a "zone of acceptance" or indifference, a range of actions that they agree the organization may legitimately take. A person hired as a confidential secretary will expect that many tasks will be confidential, and accept supervisors' requests along those lines. There are actions that the employee will regard as outside the legitimate actions of the organization. Murder and theft are likely to be outside the zone, and perhaps racial discrimination, organization corruption, and political infighting may be there as well. The point is that there is a psychological bond between the organization and the employee, and that employees generally expect to be directed. The supervisor must manage the limits of the zone of acceptance in order to establish effective control relationships.

As suggested in Figure 9.2, there are tools available to supervisors, and constraints upon them, that impinge upon such control relationships. To summarize some of the key variables that structure supervisory relationships:

1. The extent of professional guidelines for subordinates. Engineers and accountants belong to strong professional associations that establish many standards for members. Such workers have an allegiance to the profession that may actually transcend that to their employer. For the

less-professionalized workers, unions may partly fulfill this function. In the absence of such outside standards, employees are constrained only by the often weak moral standards of their communities. In American society such standards do not probe deeply into manager-subordinate relationships, as we suggested in the earlier discussion of the history of managerial control.
2. Work rules imposed by outside controllers or through negotiations. Civil service regulations have the reputation of tying the hands of supervisors who wish to reward and to discipline subordinates. Legislatures occasionally pass detailed reorganization plans or substantive rules. Both are often the subject of collective bargaining. Managers usually find themselves in a complicated situation over which they have little control, but they are responsible for the details of supervision.
3. Procedures for budget approval and expenditure, personnel recruitment, selection, and appraisal. These are often jointly controlled by the employing organization and staff organizations within a government. The budget and personnel offices are most prominent here, and many governments have additional offices and commissions that must be consulted on everything from purchasing supplies to hiring new employees.
4. The skills of individual supervisors. Supervision is not an innate talent of our species. Enormous variability is found in the temperament and judgment of individuals, and these show up in the workplace. Supervisors typically are promoted from within an organization, often from a technical specialization, and receive little formal training in the nature of supervisory work. Since supervision is used by the organization as a distinct type of work, it needs to be done as competently, and with the same attention to maintaining skills, as other specializations.

The key tools available to supervisors to manage employees' zones of acceptance are:[19]

1. Recruiting and staffing decisions. Supervisors can affect job descriptions and other documents that support the recruitment and hiring processes to encourage the selection of workers who best fit the immediate supervisory situation.
2. Training both new and continuing employees. Employees schooled in work methods and expectations will be better able to work without close supervision. To the extent supervisors' expectations can be part of the training, employees may independently monitor and correct work much in the way the supervisor would.
3. Planning the work. Supervisors with a clear sense of who does what are able to give better directions to subordinates. Time will likely be

> **BOX 9.1** The Best of Supervisors, the Worst of Supervisors
>
> Supervisory skills are not in great supply or evenly distributed among the working population. To acquire a better understanding of what makes a good supervisor, talk to people about the best and worst supervisors they have had. Using the functions and tools described in Figure 9.2, ask people with several years of work experience to describe their best and worst supervisors. Allow them to tell stories in their own words, and use the items in Figure 9.2 to guide follow-up questions and to clarify points they make. Work in teams of two to three students, and take notes on your interviews. Write up concise descriptions of best and worst supervisors to share with the rest of the class.

better spent, tasks can be pursued to completion, and more consistent supervision can be maintained. The discussion of MBO showed one approach to work planning.

4. Communicating effectively. Our earlier reports on the time spent by managers showed that verbal and written communications occupy the majority of their time. Yet communications are often handled very poorly in public organizations. Some of the problem is due to the sheer volume of information. Information flows between levels of organizations always require some selection and condensation of material. Individuals find ways to make such selections and condensations, and the result is sometimes destructive to the organization and its employees. Whose preferences will guide the choices? If expectations about work are not widely shared among levels of the organization, the flow of information will be distorted. The main purpose of organizational communications is to support the production of services by conveying instructions and making people aware of problems perceived by individual members. Yet, communication takes place within the context of organizational missions and management. If management is not done well, communication will suffer.

5. Monitoring and appraising performance. This is discussed in more detail in Chapter 8. Supervisors can reinforce plans and training through a continuing discussion of individual performance.

6. The administration of discipline and rewards. Here the power embodied in management-subordinate relationships becomes most apparent to the individual. There is usually a set of expectations, often written, about appropriate behavior and the penalties for inappropriate behavior. The relationship of work expectations, discipline,

and rewards is a complicated one that follows no set theory. In general, people in each organization create and learn to live with a set of procedures. Whether these contribute to motivation is the subject of the next section.

Motivation Theory and Practice

So far, the discussion of supervision has concentrated on the organization forms and tools available to the supervisor — in other words, things that are external to the worker. But what motivates people? Many theories differ on the subject, but there is consensus on one point: individuals decide whether to be motivated. The supervisor and organization can influence the decision, but not invariably determine it.

Motivation theories can be divided into content and process theories. Content theories posit certain human needs that can be filled (the "content"). These usually build upon Maslow's theory of the hierarchy of needs, discussed in Chapter 5. Briefly, the idea is that humans first worry about their fundamental needs, such as food, shelter, and clothing, and once these are satisfied, we begin to focus on more social needs. Once social relationships are basically satisfying, a person can focus on greater self-development. Content theories (none of which have been empirically proved) suggest that workers' needs be identified and addressed, and motivation can then take place. This is something supervisors and the organization can control.

Process theories focus on the thought process leading to the decision to be motivated. Since they refer to something that goes on in a person's head, it is difficult to test process theories of motivation. Still, it is useful to consider both approaches to motivation. They fit closely together in a general understanding of motivation, depicted in Figure 9.4.

The combination of the two types of theories implies several things about motivation. First, a management style has to be consistent with the understandings of employees. If attitudes stress flexibility and responsiveness to constructive criticism, the management style must reflect this. Second, jobs have to be structured consistently with motivation ideas. People should have skills necessary to do a job, and jobs should require the respected skills and discretion workers expect. Third, selection and training practices must be consistent with a respective management style. The skill levels of employees, their attitudes, and their expectations will not automatically be consistent with the aims of the organization. Fourth, the benefits and incentives, performance evaluations, and setting of standards must be consistent within a management style. If motivation is based upon an individual's concept of self plus an understanding of the entire organization, virtually all acts of management have something to do with mo-

FIGURE 9.4 Will Motivation Take Place?

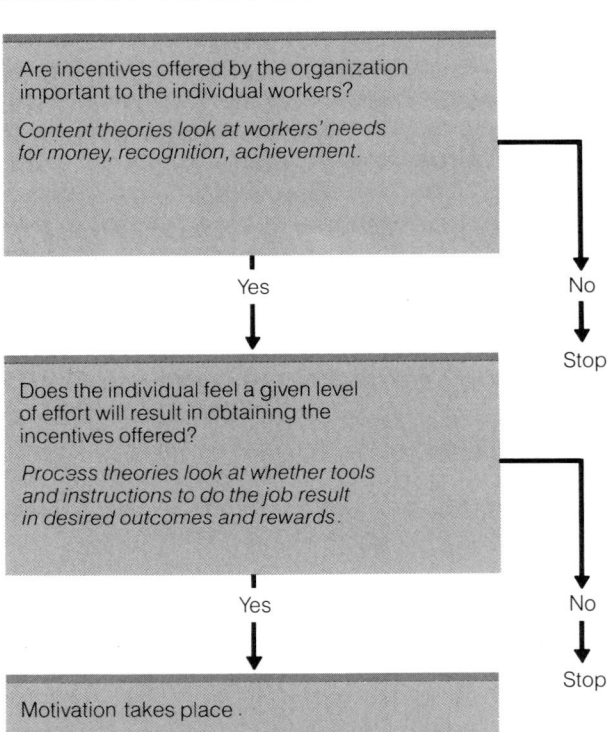

tivation. If motivation is so important to management, we should expect a great deal from motivation theories. If the theories are useful, they will guide managers in their behavior toward subordinates. What follows is a look at the advice offered by motivation theories.[20]

A Closer Look at the Theories

First we will discuss the content theories. The most popular is Frederick Herzberg's "two-factor theory." Many private businesses and public agencies have found his theory persuasive. His method promises managers the ability to distinguish the factors that individual workers will respond to. Herzberg distinguishes between "dissatisfiers" or hygiene factors on the one hand, and "satisfiers" or motivation factors on the other. The hygiene factors are things like salary, job security, working conditions, status, quality of technical supervision, the quality of communications, and so on.

These lie in the context of the job, but exclude the work itself. Herzberg claims that when not present, these factors result in dissatisfaction. Their presence will prevent dissatisfaction but will not necessarily result in motivation.

The satisfiers or motivation factors are those intrinsic qualities of the job that result in good job performance. These are things like achievement, responsibility, recognition for achievement, and personal growth and development. If these are not present, the worker will not necessarily be dissatisfied, but they are crucial to motivation or top performance.

Evidence on Herzberg's theory is mixed. Sometimes pay seems to cause satisfaction, sometimes not; in some industries well-paid workers are highly dissatisfied. Herzberg's theory does not offer clear guides to diagnosing the needs of individual workers in a way that allows distribution of rewards and opportunities for achievement that will motivate the entire work force. So, the advice to managers is somewhat vague and difficult to apply. Managers may find Herzberg consistent with their actions, but the theory is short on operational guidelines.

Process theories are more specific about individual proclivities toward motivation, but they may have exceeded the ability of research tools to test propositions. The most popular process theory is called *expectancy theory*, first proposed by Victor Vroom. Briefly, here are its ideas:

1. Individual workers will evaluate various strategies of work, such as working hard mornings only or working hard three days per week, and choose the strategy they believe will lead to the rewards they value.
2. Individual calculations to be motivated are done in two stages. The first deals with the relation between perceived effort needed to reach a performance level. Workers will assess this relation. The second deals with the perceived relationship between levels of performance and probable rewards. These second-level outcomes, such as money, promotion, accomplishments on the job, job security, and recognition, thus do not directly motivate people. Motivation is rather a result of the strength with which workers value the findings of their two stages of calculations, and the degree of agreement between the calculations.

No studies of expectancy theory have tested all variables at the same time. The literature is highly suggestive, but social science research tools are unreliable about how people think and why they act.

If we accept the logic of expectancy theory, there are several implications for managers. It is important to know that workers will place certain values on work-related rewards and make conscious estimates of relationships between effort, performance, and rewards. The manager has many tools to clarify and influence these relationships. The most important implication is that managers should clearly state what performance expectations are and how these are tied to rewards. Considerable effort is also needed to ensure that employee attitudes are similar to management assumptions. In most organizations this is not done. If the employee initiates a discussion, it is often awkward for everyone involved. There is no guarantee that such a talk will be successful.

The reality of motivation is something more complicated than the theories, of course, and the theories may not add much to some rather old rules of thumb about simple consideration for other people. A clear, polite presentation of expectations, coupled with a frank discussion of individual preferences and beliefs, goes a long way toward establishing clear and effective relationships in the workplace.

Self-Management

The motivation theories just reviewed, and most management ideas in the United States, accept as a basic premise a traditional hierarchy of authority. An alternative view is possible. The idea of workers' self-management has found a great deal of acceptance and economic success in the private sector. Some of its characteristics are described in the left-hand column of Figure 9.5. The private sector successes may not be easily repeated in the public sector. The right-hand column of Figure 9.5 compares conditions for an application of workers' self-management to the public sector. The barriers are formidable, but the point is direct: our central assumptions about managing organizations leave many questions unanswered. Serious scrutiny of organizational forms may lead to radical reassessment of accepted management practices. For example, if it is a good idea to let workers participate in setting objectives, is it also a good idea to let them decide to choose a new mission for the organization?

Less radical forms of employee participation have been attempted. Quality circles consist of groups of employees who volunteer to meet and discuss issues about service and production quality. Their organization supports them by providing training where needed, management information, and the facilities to meet on company time. The quality circles generally choose their own topics, devise ways of improving quality and implementing their solutions. Some organization development techniques, such as an emphasis on team building, talk about employee participation. The reality is often quite different. (See the discussion in Chapter 5.)

Cutback Management

A central theme of this book has been the need to recognize the increasingly stringent finances of governments. The pressures on state and local governments are especially acute. In response to this problem, a new area has arisen in the literature of public administration, usually called "cut-

FIGURE 9.5 Workers' Self-Management

Minimal Conditions for a System of Workers' Self-Management (WSM) in the Private Sector

The Conditions Adjusted for Application to the Public Sector

1. Regular participation in decision making by employees at all levels of the organization.
2. Frequent feedback of economic results of actions and distribution of surplus above regular wages, benefits, investments.
3. Sharing of management expertise and information.
4. Guaranteed individual rights. Personnel decisions cannot be made by fiat.
5. An independent board of appeals, composed of peers, to settle disputes.
6. A set of values compatible with WSM, including willingness to initiate action, flexibility, and a refusal to shun responsibility.

1. Same, except workers do not strictly control the organization; meanings and actions negotiated.
2. Performance-based rewards; economic surplus not measurable, dispensable.
3. Same, yet need to negotiate the need for such information to solve conflicts.
4. Same.
5. Since political leaders can cancel WSM experiments, a board of appeals must only mediate disputes, not as a decisive court.
6. Same. Extra care needed through permanent negotiating body to pay attention to the processes of reaching goals, managing tensions between levels of the organization, conflicts between decision rules, and conflicts between individual responsibility and political accountability.

Source: Adapted from Dick W. Olufs, "Workers' Self-Management in the Public Service," in David H. Rosenbloom, ed., *Public Personnel Policy: The Politics of Civil Service* (Port Washington, N.Y.: Associated Faculty Press, 1985).

back management." Is there a set of tools and concepts specially tailored to coping with fiscal stress?

Charles Levine writes that the first issue encountered when dealing with fiscal stress is that there is a great deal of uncertainty and ambiguity about what can be done to cope with it. He lists eleven questions to help unravel the ambiguity:[21]

1. What activities are required by law and must be performed?
2. Which activities are discretionary and can be terminated?
3. What additional revenues can be raised?
4. Which activities can be farmed out to others?
5. What things can be done more effectively?
6. Where can low-cost or no-cost labor be used?
7. Where can capital investments be substituted for labor expenses?
8. Where can information-gathering methods be improved to enhance forecasts and assess services?
9. Where can demand for services be reduced (e.g., through fees) and services rationed?
10. What policies can help strengthen the economic base and promote economic development?
11. What arrangements can be made to identify and strengthen the leadership of this process?

A government that begins to answer this set of questions is on the road to managing fiscal stress and devising strategies for cutback management.

For managers, cutbacks mean that they must deal with greater conflict, must begin to be more innovative, and must make difficult decisions. Managing government programs during times of growth is a relatively simple matter. Incremental growth does not present as many problems as either rapid growth or cutbacks, simply because the established routines usually serve the new budget levels. Rapid change or even small cutbacks strain the routines of government as managers and employees are asked to behave in new ways, under greater political pressure, and with less confidence about their own skills and tenure in their organization.

It is difficult to cut back incrementally. Organizational characteristics such as span of control (average number of subordinates per supervisor), case loads, proportion of budget devoted to human resources, frequency of training, and countless other variables evolve slowly and represent accumulated experience rather than a rational plan. Cutbacks are likely to have large unforeseen consequences as the poorly understood aspects of organizations are disrupted by cutbacks.

Government organizations usually attempt to cut back incrementally for several reasons. Across-the-board cuts seem fair to most organization members and clients, and so are easier to implement. Such cuts do not invite the political scrutiny that often accompanies program comparisons and deletions. Across-the-board cuts can be controlled from the top of the organization, at the same time pushing the pressures for coping with the cuts downward. Across-the-board cuts implicitly make the assumption that cuts are temporary, and so short-term solutions are acceptable. Except in emergency situations, governments do not cut budgets 20 percent by having workers stay home on Fridays.

Across-the-board cuts have serious drawbacks. We mentioned the organizational consequences. Not all programs are equally valuable or equally well managed, nor do they have equal "slack" in their resources. Some of the most effective programs may be operating at 100 percent of their capacity. To cut workers would harm program outputs. Other programs may be producing far less than they are capable of and are able to absorb cuts without changing outputs. From a management point of view, across-the-board cuts do not make sense, yet programmatic cuts may not make political sense.

Figure 9.6 offers a partial catalogue of Levine's cutback management tactics. Depending upon the source of the fiscal stress, different strategies are called for. The tactics are for the most part nothing new, but rather a closer look at some things an agency was doing, or should have been doing, during times of fiscal growth or stability. There is no "secret handshake" to cutback management, and like supervisory skills, the successful

---

BOX 9.2 Cutback Management in Idaho

In fiscal year 1982, the state of Idaho ran a general fund budget of $420 million. The late 1970s and early 1980s had been difficult for state officials, because the state's lumber and tourist industries sagged and state coffers contained fewer revenues than predicted. As the 1982 recession hit the state even harder, trouble struck. In early May, just seven weeks short of the close of the fiscal year, the state budget office revealed to the governor that revenues were dramatically below predicted levels. There was no way to raise additional revenues during that time, and the state's constitution prohibits a budget deficit.

The governor, John V. Evans, found that he must cut $12.1 million, about 3 percent of the state's annual general fund budget, in those last seven weeks of the fiscal year. Although a small proportion of the total year's expenditure, the amount represented about 20 percent of the remaining fiscal year budget. Few states have ever had to cut a budget that drastically. The governor's problem was complicated by the fact that much of the budget is not subject to his control. Some expenditures are required by law, others are matched with federal funds, so that a cut would cause even deeper pain.

With the cooperation of the legislature, the governor cut almost $5 million by eliminating various programs; sent half of the state's 13,000 employees home without pay on Fridays, saving almost $2 million; purchasing was frozen; and some expenditures were delayed until the next fiscal year. The budget was balanced, but state officials and employees were in shock.

FIGURE 9.6 Cutback Management Tactics

Source of Fiscal Stress	Tactics to Resist Decline	Tactics to Smooth Decline
Internal Politics	1. Issue symbolic responses like forming study commissions. 2. Develop a siege mentality to retain esprit de corps. 3. Strengthen expertise.	1. Change leadership at each stage in the decline process. 2. Reorganize at each stage. 3. Cut programs run by weak subunits. 4. Shift programs to another agency. 5. Get temporary exemptions from personnel & budget regulations which limit discretion.
Organizational Atrophy	1. Increase hierarchical control. 2. Improve productivity. 3. Experiment with less costly service delivery systems. 4. Automate. 5. Stockpile and ration resources.	1. Renegotiate long-term contracts to regain flexibility. 2. Install rational choice techniques like zero-base budgeting & evaluation research. 3. Defer maintenance and downscale personnel quality. 4. Ask employees to make voluntary sacrifices like early retirement & deferred raises. 5. Improve forecasting capacity. 6. Reassign surplus facilities to other users. 7. Sell surplus property, lease back when needed. 8. Exploit the exploitable.

FIGURE 9.6 continued

Source of Fiscal Stress	Tactics to Resist Decline	Tactics to Smooth Decline
External Politics	1. Diversify programs, clients, and support. 2. Improve legislative liaison. 3. Educate the public about agency mission. 4. Mobilize dependent clients. 5. Become "captured" by a powerful interest group or legislator. 6. Threaten to cut vital or popular programs. 7. Cut a visible and widespread service to demonstrate client dependence.	1. Make peace with competing agencies. 2. Cut low-prestige programs. 3. Cut programs to politically weak clients. 4. Sell and lend expertise to other agencies. 5. Share problems with other agencies.
Weak and Changing Economy	1. Find a wider and richer revenue base. 2. Create incentives to stop disinvestment. 3. Seek foundation support. 4. Lure new public and private sector investment. 5. Adopt user charges for services where possible.	1. Improve targeting on problems. 2. Plan with preservative goals. 3. Cut losses by distinguishing between capital investments, sunk costs. 4. Yield concessions to taxpayers and employers to retain them.

Source: Charles H. Levine, "Organizational Decline and Cutback Management," in Charles H. Levine, *Managing Fiscal Stress* (Chatham, N.J.: Chatham House, 1980) pp. 21–22. From an article in *Public Administration Review,* 1978.

programs for decision making are firmly hidden in the brains of successful managers. The basics of management are required in order to cope with cutbacks.

What is important to remember is that cutbacks are really a political decision. As carried out by the Reagan administration, cutbacks are a part of a political philosophy about what a "good" government should *not* be doing. To look at the budget, one gets the notion that a good government should provide for the national defense, but not necessarily for public higher education. (Budget trends and figures are presented in Chapter 12.) Cutbacks, at least during the 1980s, are more the result of political philosophy than of economic necessity.

Productivity

Most discussions of public sector cutbacks look for a solution in the idea of productivity. The logic goes like this: If we can find a way to deliver the services, keep our jobs, satisfy the public, and not raise taxes, our problems are solved without painful decisions. We will manage the problem rather than turn it over to the unpredictable whims of legislatures and the citizenry. The contemporary concern with productivity is a stark example of the way we look for administrative solutions to political problems.

Businesses have long been concerned with productivity. There the relationships are clear. If a given amount of output is secured with fewer inputs than before, we are doing better. The concept can be expressed by a simple ratio:

$$\text{Productivity} = \frac{\text{Output}}{\text{Input}}$$

The important concept is productivity *increases*. An organization that becomes more productive will probably make more money, and that is doing better. But the attraction does not end there. Stevenson describes the general preoccupation with business productivity:

> The interest in productivity is not merely academic; productivity increases are largely responsible for the high standards of living enjoyed by industrial nations. Moreover, wage and price increases not supported by productivity increases create inflationary pressures on the economy.[22]

Leaders in government and industry are concerned that if America does not improve its rate of productivity increases, our economy will lose many jobs to foreign competitors. Living standards and economic growth are the central concerns of leaders in a liberal democracy. When they are imperiled, the pressures on government increase dramatically.

The contemporary concern with productivity is remarkably similar to the national preoccupation with efficiency in the first decades of this century. The discussion of Frederick Taylor in Chapter 3 pointed out that the concern with industrial efficiency was tied to promises of diminishing class conflict and securing national and world peace. The work of Taylor and others did not stop at factories, however. Reformers in both the private and public sectors called for a mechanical and technological criterion of efficiency to solve a large array of problems. The closing of the western frontier, a series of financial panics followed by short but severe depressions, labor and management violence, corruption in government — all could be solved through the application of proper techniques.

The promised benefits of efficiency were the same as those claimed for productivity in our time. The interests of employers and employees are ultimately the same, if only a source of additional wealth can be found. Conflict between classes is wasteful and can be solved if additional wealth can be found and distributed to disaffected groups. A moral clean-up of the country would restore our sense of national purpose and solidify our position in the world. And, the answer to all was improvement through greater efficiency.[23] In government, this efficiency took the form of nonpartisanship, a strong executive, and the separation of politics from administration. Such reforms rested on the belief that the right people to run society were those who knew the most about efficient management.

It turns out that the periodic concerns with productivity, efficiency, and similar concepts are part of our reliance on a frontier to solve political problems. The tough choices of how wealth is generated and distributed are avoided by opening new sources of wealth. Cheap land, gold rushes, and industrial improvements have been the ways America has purchased relief from political conflicts. Only once, in our Civil War, did the strategy really fail. But in the twentieth century the sources of wealth have changed. The management of technology and people in organizations has taken the place of the western lands. While the search for productivity is not a public, politically open method for dealing with problems, it does seem to be one of the fundamental ways Americans cope with social and economic troubles. At times, wars have helped in the same way, as has much personal effort at self-improvement.

Contemporary concerns with government productivity emphasize both the quantity and quality of services. Efficiency, the familiar ratio of outputs divided by inputs, refers to the quantity, while effectiveness refers to the quality of services. Delivering a large amount of poor-quality services or delivering too few of the right services results in poor productivity. It is possible to construct productivity indexes that refer to both the quality and quantity of services. Counting the number of potholes filled and cubic yards of asphalt laid only refers to the quantity of activity by a pothole-patching crew. Counting the number of good patches and dividing by the total potholes patched is a start to calculating both quantity and quality. It is possible to factor in the costs of fixing defective patches as well. Adequate productivity indexes are not likely to be single numbers, but rather a set of numbers that refers to the overall performance of particular services.

Productivity measurement must be regarded strictly as operational data, not as abstract indicators of the relative worth of government services. Productivity numbers from a pothole-patching crew are just not comparable to productivity indicators of police services or primary schools. Their use lies in assessing how particular services are delivered over time. Thus, the pothole-patching crew will have productivity figures for several years running. Trends in their productivity will indicate whether a given level of efficiency is maintained. It is difficult to arrive at objective optimal levels of productivity for services aside from looking at past figures, studying the operations to find possible methods of improvement, and then trying to do better each year. As new technologies become available, including better training, machines that substitute capital for labor, better organization of the work, and redefined services, productivity may improve.

Governmental productivity programs have produced mixed successes at best. Highly touted programs are simply abandoned after a short time.[24] Reports in respected journals are sometimes suspect, being written by the consultant and manager in charge of the program.[25] Careful analyses of "state-of-the-art" programs often find the results are minimal and that benefits to taxpayers, managers, and workers are not worth the extra effort.[26] There are success stories, but much of the literature on productivity is advocacy or reports on projects in progress. Guidelines have emerged from the successes:[27]

1. Skills are necessary to improve productivity. Needed skills must be identified and used. In most governments few people know about work measurement techniques, although they do employ mechanics, supervisors, budget analysts, and so on, who know the processes of work and can be trained to do job and work-flow analysis. Outside consultants may be needed for initial training and direction, but the emphasis should be on developing skills within the organization.

2. The key to successful productivity programs will be commitment by political officials. They must have a role in initiating and sustaining the programs.

3. Most successful productivity programs have taken place in growing organizations that can afford to make the following provision: Workers are assured that no one will lose their jobs because of productivity programs. People who are displaced should be trained for other jobs. Such provisions are probably necessary to secure the full support and efforts of employees. Because of this, productivity may have to be seen as a long-term program that can control growth, *not* as a means to cut expenditures.

4. The productivity director or analyst should have that one responsibility. Productivity programs are less urgent than many other concerns and are likely to suffer because of it. On the one hand, organizations with less than 200 or so people will not be able to afford a full-time productivity analyst and so will have to rely upon supervisors and management to ensure proper work planning and control procedures are followed. On the other hand, small organizations usually place severe demands on highly skilled employees. Since productivity is a long-term commitment rather than a pressing day-to-day concern, momentum is difficult to sustain.

5. The major cost savings will result from streamlining work processes, not work measurement per se.

What Is the Difference Between Good and Poor Management?

Earlier in the chapter we emphasized that lists of management functions do not really describe what managers do. Watching what managers do will not really show how to be one, since the decisions made by managers do not follow recognizable patterns. Our perspective emphasizes the skills of managers, but these skills are difficult to describe and develop in operational terms. In Chapter 13 we will go through various models of decision making, but for now one conclusion is warranted: the programs managers use for making choices are hidden in their heads. Clear guides on how to manage are not available.

It is not at all clear that management skills can be taught. Curricula in Master of Public Administration and Master of Business Administration programs reflect the current consensus among academics on what managers need to know, but that is not the same as teaching people to be managers (see Box 9.3). Most schools adopt the case method of teaching, an acknowledgement that the way to learn to make decisions and to manage is by making decisions and managing. Peter Drucker emphasizes this experiential side of management skills and argues that this is precisely the purpose of hierarchy in organizations. It provides a way of testing whether individuals can adequately handle a given level of responsibility. Those that demonstrate competence, he says, can be promoted to higher levels. So we can describe what managers must accomplish, but we cannot tell them how to do it. We can describe the skills managers need, but perhaps do not know how to teach them reliably. On-the-job training, coupled with an awareness of organizing concepts and vicarious experiences from cases, may teach management, and those who learn may be promoted to higher management positions.

It is perhaps going too far to assume that managerial competence is so readily promoted. Earlier sections of the chapter emphasized the difficulties of recognizing outstanding management abilities and suggested that the public aspects of management impart special problems as compared to private-sector management. The history of management shows a number of fights over propositions that later become widely shared assumptions about who should control organizations. Management orthodoxies practiced in governments are based on traditions of what managers are supposed to do — and the tradition may be suspect.

In the immediate future, efforts to improve the operations of government will focus upon the development of management skills and management systems. To the extent that government agencies are responsive to the public, management there will remain demanding.

BOX 9.3 What Should Public Administration Students Know?

The National Association of Schools of Public Affairs and Administration (NASPAA) establishes standards for degree programs in public administration. Undergraduate programs should be staffed by at least four to five faculty, at least half of which should hold doctorates. The curriculum they offer should consist of (a) political, social, economic and legal environment of public affairs and public administration (pa/pa) (15 to 25 percent of course work); (b) analytical tools, both quantitative and nonquantitative (20 to 25 percent); (c) individual, group and organizational dynamics (10–15 percent); (d) policy analysis (5 to 10 percent); (e) administrative and management processes (10 to 20 percent); and (f) an arts and science general education foundation, in addition to (a), (b), and (c) (15 to 25 percent).

Graduate programs, usually offering the Master of Public Administration degree, should be staffed by no fewer than five full-time faculty members, of which at least 75 percent should hold doctorates. Practitioners should be an integral part of the program. The curriculum should consist of a large required core that gives each student an understanding of the environment of public policy and the ability to deal with:

- Political and legal institutions and processes
- Economic and social institutions and processes
- Organization and management concepts, including human resource administration
- Concepts and techniques of financial administration
- Techniques of analysis, including quantitative, economic, and statistical methods.

No percentage distribution of the various core areas is suggested. The core areas are to be supplemented by additional work in these areas or other course work and internships to enable students to:

Define and diagnose decision situations, collect relevant data, perform logical analyses, develop alternatives, implement an effective and ethical course of action, and evaluate results

Organize and communicate information clearly to a variety of audiences through formats including oral presentations, written memoranda and technical reports, and statistical charts, graphs, and tables.

Sources: "Standards for Professional Master's Degree Programs in Public Affairs and Administration," effective September 1, 1986; and "Guidelines and Standards for Baccalaureate Degree Programs in Public Affairs/Public Administration," both from National Association of Schools of Public Affairs and Administration, 1120 G. Street NW, Suite 520, Washington, D.C., 20005.

SUMMARY

Management involves the organization and direction of employees and organization resources. We began our discussion by looking at how managers do this, both in the use of their time and in the way they deal with the "centrifugal forces" in organizations. These forces are really the effects of politics on the details of managing organizations. A look at politics reminds us that different visions of organizations are possible, and that the dissenting theories in management theory and practice deserve a careful reading.

What is public about public management? In general, little that goes on in public organizations is unaffected by politics and requirements to serve citizens. Citizens present many demands to public organizations, and are unlikely to be fully satisfied. This helps to explain why people who have managed in both the public and private sectors commonly report that public management is much more difficult.

Our discussion of management systems, supervision, and motivation of employees showed that there are fairly straightforward guidelines to the practice of management. The success of management, however, depends on very human qualities. The techniques only provide a framework for relationships among employees of an organization. Their best efforts are combined when they can agree on the goals of the organization and on the means of reaching them.

We closed the chapter with two recent topics that have dramatically changed the face of public management. The fiscal stress faced by many governments has forced managers to get by with fewer resources and to practice cutback management. This has spurred interest in government productivity, the relationship between resources, and the quality and quantity of goods and services produced by governments. Managing under conditions of heightened scarcity is a political reality of the coming decade.

NOTES

1. Herbert Kaufman, *The Administrative Behavior of Federal Bureau Chiefs* (Washington, D.C.: Brookings Institution, 1981), p. 87.
2. John H. Jackson and Timothy J. Keaveny, *Successful Supervision* (Englewood Cliffs, N.J.: Prentice-Hall, 1980), p. 9.
3. Lyman W. Porter and John Van Maanen, "Task Accomplishment and the Management of Time," in James L. Perry and Kenneth L. Kraemer, eds., *Public Management: Public and Private Perspectives* (Palo Alto, Calif.: Mayfield Publishing, 1983), p. 213.
4. Henry Mintzberg, "The Manager's Job: Folklore and Fact," *Harvard Business Review* (July/August 1975), pp. 49–51.
5. Laurence E. Lynn, Jr., *Managing the Public's Business* (New York: Basic Books, 1981), p. 4.
6. See John Gaus, "The Ecology of Administration," in *Reflections on Public Administration* (University, Al.: University of Alabama Press, 1947), reprinted in Richard J. Stillman II, *Public Administration: Concepts and Cases* (Boston: Houghton Mifflin Co., 1983); William G. Scott and David K. Hart, *Organizational America* (Boston: Houghton Mifflin Co., 1979); David Schuman, *The Ideology of Form* (Lexington, Mass.: Lexington Books, 1978); Harold Seidman, *Politics, Position, and Power*, 3d ed. (New York: Oxford University Press, 1980); and Francis E. Rourke, *Bureaucracy, Politics, and Public Policy*, 3d ed. (Boston: Little, Brown, 1984).
7. Adapted from Jonathan Brock, *Managing People in Public Agencies* (Boston: Little, Brown, 1984), p. 41.

8. See Loretta R. Flanders and Dennis Utterback, "The Management Excellence Inventory: A Tool for Management Development," *Public Administration Review* 45, no. 3 (May/June 1985), pp. 403–410.
9. Weston H. Agor, "Managing Brain Skills to Increase Productivity," *Public Administration Review* 45, no. 6 (November/December 1985), pp. 864–868.
10. Ibid., p. 865.
11. Several sources are available on the development of American technology and work organizations. See David Noble, *America by Design* (New York: Alfred Knopf, 1976); Stephen A. Marglin, "What Do Bosses Do?" and Katherine Stone, "Origins of Job Structures in the Steel Industry," both in *The Review of Radical Political Economics* 6, no. 2 (Summer 1974); Charles Babbage, *On the Economy of Manufactures*, 4th ed. (London: Charles Knight, 1835); and Donald Nelson, *Managers and Workers* (Madison: University of Wisconsin Press, 1975).
12. Ralph Hummel, *The Bureaucratic Experience*, 2d ed. (New York: St. Martin's, 1982), p. 29.
13. Ibid.
14. On MBO see George L. Morrisey, *Management by Objectives and Results in the Public Sector* (Reading, Mass.: Addison-Wesley, 1976); and Peter Drucker, *Management* (New York: Harper & Row, 1974).
15. Douglas Fox, *Managing the Public's Business* (New York: Random House, 1979), p. 107.
16. Chester A. Newland, "Policy/Program Objectives and Federal Management: The Search for Government Effectiveness," *Public Administration Review* 36, no. 1 (January/February 1976), p. 26.
17. Jackson and Keaveny, op. cit., pp. 241–242.
18. Ralph Hummel, op. cit., p. 119.
19. Jackson and Keaveny, op. cit.
20. This section is based on John M. Ivancevich, Andrew D. Szilagyi, Jr., and Marc J. Wallace, Jr., *Organizational Behavior and Performance* (Santa Monica, Calif.: Goodyear, 1977), pp. 103–132; and Wayne F. Cascio, *Applied Psychology in Personnel Management*, 2d ed. (Reston, Va.: Reston Publishing, 1982), pp. 280–289.
21. Charles H. Levine, ed., *Managing Fiscal Stress: The Crisis in the Public Sector* (Chatham, N.J.: Chatham House, 1980), pp. 6–7.
22. William J. Stevenson, *Production/Operations Management* (Homewood, Ill.: Richard D. Irwin, 1982), p. 13.
23. See Samuel Haber, *Efficiency and Uplift* (Chicago: University of Chicago Press, 1964).

24. For a description of a model program that disappeared by the time it appeared in the productivity literature, see Nancy S. Hayward, "The Productivity Challenge," in Charles H. Levine, op. cit.
25. For example, see Ronald Contino and Robert M. Lorusso, "Theory Z Turnaround of a Public Agency," *Public Administration Review* 42, no. 1 (January/February 1982), pp. 66–71.
26. See National Commission on Productivity, "Improving Municipal Productivity: The Detroit Refuse Collection Incentive Plan" (Washington, D.C., 1974). See also Marc Holzer and Stuart S. Nagel, *Productivity and Public Policy* (Beverly Hills: Sage Publications, 1984).
27. See "Tried and Tested: Case Studies in Municipal Innovation," *International City Management Association*; and Harry Hatry et al., *How Effective Are Your Municipal Services?* (Washington, D.C.: The Urban Institute, 1979).

CHAPTER TEN

Labor-Management Relations

> The Congress finds that (1) experience in both private and public employment indicates that the statutory protection of the right of employees to organize, bargain collectively, and participate through labor organizations of their own choosing in decisions which affect them — (A) safeguards the public interest, (B) contributes to the effecive conduct of public business, and (C) facilitates and encourages the amicable settlements of disputes between employees and their employers involving conditions of employment; and (2) the public interest demands the highest standards of employee performance and the continued development and implementation of modern and progressive work practices to facilitate and improve employee performance and the efficient accomplishment of the operations of the federal government. Therefore, labor organizations and collective bargaining in the civil service are in the public interest.
>
> —*from the Civil Service Reform Act of 1978*
> *(PL No. 454, 95th Cg., October 13, 1978, sec. 7101)*

To read the above section of the Civil Service Reform Act of 1978 is to realize that the relationship between management and labor in the public sector is more complicated than the same relationship in the private sector. The private sector is regulated, but in the end profits are the bottom line. In public administration, where do we draw the line between the public good and the rights of the worker? Will collective bargaining that strengthens the union also strengthen the public good? Should *all* public employees be able to engage in collective bargaining? Should strikes be allowed? Can you imagine, for example, the Army going on strike for higher wages? Why not?

It is unrealistic to think that everyone in the public service has the same sense of what is right. What we will see is that the relationship between public employers and public employees has never been defined clearly. We will also see that in the public sector, the labor-management disputes are really a three-sided affair, with elected officials periodically playing an important role.

The source of the ambiguity was captured by Donald Devine, the director of the U.S. Office of Personnel Management for the first five years of the Reagan administration. Devine stated that he supports the obligation of government to consult or negotiate with employee organizations, but he made it clear that the

> Civil Service Reform Act did not establish the private sector system of collective bargaining for the federal service. . . . The law contains a strong management rights clause, and the major economic issues of pay, pensions, and hours of work are not negotiable. The federal service is an open shop, and the strike is prohibited.[1]

What separates the public- from the private-sector system of collective bargaining is that strong concerted actions, such as the strike, constitute "a political weapon against the government." Devine goes on to say, "Collective bargaining is a process for dealing with disputes over conditions of employment, not governmental policy." He cites the experience of Great Britain, where labor unions have not limited demands to workplace issues, but have extended the collective bargaining process to include government policies such as ownership and regulation of transport industries. With the exception of the recent conservative government, labor unions have been the decisive political force in Great Britain. There will always be political differences between government employees and elected officials. "This disagreement, of course, is an energizer of Western culture, as long as it is in a political forum."[2] And to Devine, collective bargaining is not a political forum.

Devine's argument is fairly common in regard to public-sector bargaining. A clear line is drawn between private and public sectors. Bargaining in the private sector is an economic, not a political affair. The underlying model involves conflict over the division of economic returns. It is difficult to isolate just what bargaining is in the public sector. Although it is economic, it is also very much a part of public policy. We know that it is not simply politics, yet often, bargaining is decided politically. When labor unions lobby a legislature, that is clearly political and acceptable, but a strike muddles the political and administrative realms. With a few exceptions, American law treats public sector collective bargaining as an administrative relationship. The underlying model is unclear, although most descriptions emphasize cooperation to enhance the effectiveness of government operations.

This is an area where it is important to remember the context and history of American politics and administration. Without the background, current practices do not make much sense.

Conflict in the Workplace

Private-sector collective bargaining was born of politics and conflict. Labor unions were not generally regarded as legitimate in the nineteenth century, and the fight for legitimacy, as well as the definition of union roles, was violent. The Molly McGuires of the 1870s, the great railroad strike of 1877, the Haymarket affair of 1886, the Homestead strike of 1892, the Pullman strike of 1894, the extensive violence in the western mines, the rise and fall of the Industrial Workers of the World ("Wobblies"), just to name a few, were not simple fights over wages. The labor strife of the time was raising questions of the rights of factory owners versus the rights of workers, of a capitalist versus a socialist or anarchist organization of the economy, of whether unions were to pursue political or solely economic goals. Class politics was at the core of the Knights of Labor, the Wobblies, and several Congress of Industrial Organization (CIO) unions during the 1930s.[3] The rise of modern management, discussed in Chapter 9, is a clear response to the class politics of the labor movement in America.

American unions took a conservative turn with the rise of the American Federation of Labor, under the leadership of Samuel Gompers. Gompers is often portrayed as the tough, cigar-chewing union boss willing to strike and fight for workers, but he represents much more. His basic insight was that for unions to succeed, they had to accept the American business system. Unions, to be acceptable and effective, had to concentrate on getting a share of the rewards of business and lobby for major political changes in the traditional ways. Although unions have become a significant political force in the United States, they operate like any other interest group. Unions helped conserve the way the country does business, and compared to unions in other industrial democracies, they are essentially conservative and relatively apolitical.

Clashing Purposes

It is interesting that even the relatively mild stance of American labor looks too political for the public sector. As we discussed in Chapter 2, Americans rely on government, but often have profound feelings of dislike for government. At times attitudes are supportive of government growth and greater scope for public unions, such as in the 1960s and 1970s. At other times attitudes emphasize a static or diminished role for government, and at such times the scope of public-sector unions generally shrinks. Again, Devine's view expresses the relationship:

> A lean federal government, doing work which it understands and can accomplish, is key to solving the problems of federal employment. Public approval of government and its programs will lead to public acceptance of federal employees. It is hard to ask the country to be considerate of the economic needs of federal em-

ployees when taxes and inflation, largely the result of government policies, are so inconsiderate of the economic needs of the country.[4]

Although public-sector labor-management relations are generally peaceful, a consensus on this issue is lacking. The natural tensions between workers and their bosses are bound to come up. Unions are organized to meet specific needs of workers, to organize concerted actions of employees, and to deal with conflicts in the workplace, The needs of administration emphasize the desirability of a controlled, predictable work force at an affordable cost. These purposes will clash.

The Legal Framework of Collective Bargaining

For the most part public-sector labor-management relations parallel private-sector developments, although lagging about 40 years. Figure 10.1 lists the major legal developments in private- and public-sector legal recognition of collective bargaining.[5] Some important differences should be noted. First, in the public sector the management side is fragmented but is able to set the rules of bargaining. Unions are bargaining with the state, and the state is made up of several actors. The negotiators may work in a personnel office. State policy toward labor is usually set at the top of the executive branch, but legislatures have a lot to say about the conduct of bargaining. Most public-sector collective bargaining agreements must be ratified by legislatures before money can be spent. This means the management side may sometimes find it difficult to present a coherent front to labor, as illustrated in Box 10.2. Although labor-management relations in the private sector can be called "bilateral" (a relation between two equal sides), public-sector relations are more properly thought of as "multilateral," involving officials from different branches of government, as well as the public. Most significantly, legislatures lay down the rules under which bargaining will take place and define bargainable issues (called the "scope" of bargaining). For example, some states allow unions to bargain on wages, others do not. Some states allow full bargaining between labor and management, whereas some still only require that management "meet and confer" with labor, but not negotiate issues.

The economics of public- and private-sector bargaining are quite different. In the private sector both sides are alleged to be constrained by a market. If steelworkers ask for too high a raise, their companies would not be able to operate at a profit, and jobs would be lost to competitors or to the company moving operations overseas. In the matter of strikes, union members and company owners lose money, thus each feels pressure to come to an agreement. In the public sector these forces do not operate the same way, since taxes, not consumer choices, underwrite government activities. A government is not likely to go out of business because a neigh-

BOX 10.1 A Tale of Two Cities

The variety found in the role and conduct of public employee unions reflects the diversity of American politics. That variety also reflects the uneasy truce between political and administrative values in management-labor relations. The experience of school districts in Seattle, Washington, and Missoula, Montana, illustrate the issue.

The Seattle school district is the state's largest, employing nearly 2500 teachers. The district has a history of last-minute negotiations and threatened strikes, but the last major strike was in the early 1970s. In 1985, the main bargaining issues were pay, class size, and methods of assigning teachers to different schools. The class size and pay issues remained the main obstacles to agreement, and four days into the school year the teachers went out on strike.

Public employee strikes are illegal in the state of Washington, but school district officials were reluctant to ask the courts to enforce this legal prohibition out of fear of the political backlash from voters. The teachers were claiming to defend the quality of education, and public attitudes were mixed on which side was at fault. Eventually, union officials called the governor to help mediate the strike (no one called the superintendent of public instruction, who is supposed to intercede in bargaining impasses), and through his encouragement the two sides reached a compromise. The teachers went back to the classroom. Since state law requires that students attend 177 days of school each year, the schools were in session until the July 4 holiday. Teachers received their full year's pay since they worked all 177 days.

The Missoula school district is one-fifteenth the size of Seattle's, but labor-management conflicts were just as intense. The district had a good record on labor negotiations, with one minor strike in the early 1970s. Strikes are permitted in Montana. The 1981 contract negotiations were stuck on the same issues found in Seattle. Many school board members were just recently elected and felt they needed to match the negotiating skills of the union. The school board decided to hire an out-of-state negotiating consultant, paying him $65,000. His attitudes turned out to be somewhat rigid, but the school board liked his approach. It became apparent at the start that the district was willing to take a strike with a few weeks of the school year remaining, rather than give in on expensive pay demands of the union.

At the inception of the strike, the district announced schools would remain open by hiring substitute teachers. Even at $100 per day, the district had trouble finding teachers to cross the picket lines. After two weeks, the district announced that striking teachers would be replaced permanently if the matter was not solved immediately.

Only twenty teachers returned to the classrooms. The strike, as well as charges and countercharges hurled from the two sides, filled the news. Pressure from citizens and local business groups eventually wore down the two sides, and a settlement was reached — one that closely resembled the district's prestrike offer. The most important outcome of the strike was political: During the next school board election, four union-endorsed candidates were chosen by voters, and negotiations have since been much more positive — without outside consultants.

FIGURE 10.1   Milestones in Union Recognition

Development	Private Sector	Public Sector
First union	1820s, 1830s trade unions	1890, National Association of Letter Carriers
Early recognition	1926 Labor Railway Act (Recognized right of some employees to organize unions)	1912 Lloyd-LaFollette Act (Federal employees may join nonstriking unions and petition the Congress)
	1936 Norris-LaGuardia Act (Prohibited courts from issuing injunctions in most labor disputes)	1962 Executive Order 10988 (Federal employees may join unions, meet, and confer with agency management)
		1959 Wisconsin first state to recognize right of all employees to organize and bargain
		1969 Executive Order 11491 (Established Federal Labor Relations Council, still part of management, to decide labor-management policy issues, set uniform rules for federal collective bargaining
		1970 Postal Reorganization Act (Allowed bargaining on wages and working conditions; mainly private sector model except strikes prohibited

FIGURE 10.1 continued

Development	Private Sector	Public Sector
Full recognition	1935 National Labor Relations Act (The Wagner Act recognized the rights of most workers to organize and bargain; established procedures for union recognition; defined employer unfair labor practices; National Labor Relations Board, a neutral body, sets policy and hears complaints)	1978 Civil Service Reform Act (Federal Labor Relations Authority set up on NLRB model as neutral body, statutory recognition of all federal employees' right to organize and bargain; no bargaining on pay, hiring, and firing decisions, no strikes
	1947 Labor Management Relations Act (The Taft-Hartley Act counterbalanced union strength by defining employee unfair labor practices)	1986: 27 states have comprehensive collective bargaining laws recognizing rights of all employees; 14 states have coverage for some employees; 9 have no collective bargaining laws. Of states with laws, 9 are "meet and confer" laws, not full bargaining statutes. 12 states allow some form of strike

BOX 10.2 Organizing for Bargaining

How are legislatures involved in the negotiating process? States employ a number of devices to present a clear and united front at the negotiating table. Some states solve the problem by prohibiting bargaining on matters legislatures prefer to decide. Washington and Wisconsin, for instance, have prohibited bargaining on economic issues. The unions instead engage in direct political lobbying on economic issues. The Wisconsin legislation did not like the direct pressure and changed the process to allow full bargaining. In Washington unions concentrate bargaining efforts on working conditions and have won perhaps the most widespread participation by employees and unions in the authority to manage programs of any state in the union. Washington unions also used lawsuits and lobbying to push the state toward negotiations that resulted in a landmark comparable worth agreement.

Other states establish a legislative committee that is to act as a consultant to the state's bargaining team. Wisconsin's newer arrangements and Montana's policy fall into this category. Montana came to accept this idea after years of indecision. In 1979 a strike occurred while the legislature was in session. Legislative leaders resented the pressure and strongly suggested that the executive branch should complete negotiations prior to the session. Yet when this request was complied with, legislators then complained of being a "rubber stamp" to matters decided within the executive branch. Similar to this category, Minnesota has a commission composed of legislators who may tentatively approve bargaining agreements if the legislature is not in session, but final approval rests with the full legislature.

In still another model, the Alaska and Oregon legislatures exercise final approval of contracts with no prior organized contact with bargaining parties. Alaska is one of the few states where labor is truly the dominant political force. The unions are very effective at negotiations. They are also effective in lobbying the governor and legislature, each of which may put additional pressure on the bargaining team. In Oregon the parties bargain to final legislative approval of working conditions and economic items. If the agreements are not completed while the legislature is in session, a fund is established to be drawn upon as contracts are completed.

Michigan is unique in placing authority to review and approve negotiated agreements in an independent, constitutionally established commission. The commission receives a percentage of bargained wage packages to cover its operating costs and has full authority to regulate collective bargaining, including the economic components of agreements. The commission's decisions may be overturned by a two-thirds vote in both houses of the state legislature. Michigan clearly has sought an administrative solution to the political difficulties of collective bargaining.

In a final model, the legislature appropriates money for the executive branch in a lump sum, and then lets the governor worry about divisions of money among programs and wages. Pennsylvania, which follows this model, excludes executive authority to negotiate only on pensions.

Politics and administration literally meet face to face at the bargaining table. The diversity of state bargaining models points to the difficulty of constructing a public administration.

boring jurisdiction offers lower taxes or pays lower wages. A popular business management argument in the 1980s says that wage concessions are needed so that the company can remain competitive; unless concessions are given, the union members may be out of a job. Similar forces operate on public sector unions. Unions have dramatically reigned in bargaining demands, and the most celebrated "breaking" of a union occurred in the public sector. (See Box 10.3.)

BOX 10.3 The PATCO Strike

In early 1981, the Professional Air Traffic Controllers Organization (PATCO) was negotiating a new contract and not making much progress at the bargaining table. The workers complained of overwork, fatigue, and inadequate recognition of the responsibilities they shoulder. They wanted a large salary hike and a cut in the number of hours per week. Actuarial data for PATCO members showed the job killed them, and they asked for generous early retirement provisions. They charged that new, safer air control technology was available that would improve their working conditions, technology the Federal Aviation Administration chose to ignore (see Box 13.4). Government negotiators would not agree to what they regarded as major and costly changes in the civilian air traffic control system, and the negotiations were at impasse.

In July virtually all of the 13,000 PATCO members voted to strike. They felt their demands were reasonable and that the government negotiations would not seriously consider them. And they believed the government could not operate without them. They believed a strike at the height of the tourist season, in addition to the distress caused to business, would cause the government to give in to their demands.

The Reagan administration would not give in. They wanted to set an example for other government unions (six months before they had acquiesced to postal union demands in the face of a likely strike), and felt public opinion would be on their side. Some PATCO members made over $55,000 per year, and the government offered to raise average salaries to $38,000. With median household income running at about $25,000, most citizens felt the PATCO members had high-paying jobs.

The Transportation Department operated the air traffic control system during the strike. Airport control towers were operated by supervisors, former controllers brought out of retirement, and military controllers. Some scheduled flights were cut back. The striking air controllers argued it was unsafe to fly; the administration said things were under control. There were several near misses. Finally, President Reagan appeared on television to explain his actions to the public. He said that the strike was illegal; that each PATCO member had signed a promise not to strike as a condition of employment, and if they did not return to the job in 48 hours they were fired.

Although about 1000 workers reported back to work after the president's speech, the union leadership and most members did not believe the threat would work. Letters of dismissal were sent out, PATCO's assets were frozen by court order, and its leaders were taken to jail. No other major unions would support PATCO's strike, and it collapsed. The union's activities were found to be illegal, and PATCO was decertified.

The PATCO episode set the tone for labor relations during the Reagan administration. Unions did not work together out of fear of losing their own small pieces of political support (PATCO had supported Reagan in the 1980 elections). Reagan appointed several antiunion people to the National Labor Relations Board, and its enforcement division was headed by an official from the National Right to Work Legal Defense Foundation, perhaps the most antiunion interest group in the United States. The message was clear to both public and private employers — the national government is on the side of management.

Small stories about PATCO members appeared in the papers for another few years. For example, one controller who had made more than $50,000 per year was found living on a steam grate on a Washington, D.C., street, less than a half mile from the White House. Controllers who replaced the PATCO workers formed a union and were complaining of overwork, fatigue, and the need for more generous pay and retirement benefits. But, the big story was that a union had broken the rules, and the union was in turn broken.

The Public-Sector Model

Despite the differences between the public and private sectors, a model of public-sector bargaining has emerged that is largely based on the private-sector model. Most comprehensive bargaining laws in the states, and the federal law governing collective bargaining, adhere to the model. It consists of:[6]

1. Recognition of employee rights to organize and bargain collectively, or to refrain from joining labor organizations.

2. Recognition of employer rights in a "management rights clause" and, compared to private sector, a limited scope of bargaining.
3. Inclusion of an administrative agency (the NLRB in the private sector, the FLRA in the federal system, or state employee relations boards) to oversee the process and make rulings on unit determination (deciding who is and who is not represented by the union), negotiability of issues, and unfair labor practices.
4. Standards for bargaining unit determination.
5. Procedures for recognizing unions as exclusive bargaining agents.
6. Impasse resolution procedures.
7. Provisions for union security arrangements.
8. A statement of unfair labor practices, often including strikes.

Each of these items needs further explanation.

As we noted, the public-sector recognition of employee organizations lagged behind the private sector by about a generation. Employee organizations in the public sector are more than a generation behind their private-sector counterparts in some respects. Public employees can strike in only a dozen states and are limited to bargaining about economic issues in most places, as depicted in Box 10.2. The worker is caught in conflicting roles: That of public employee and of citizen and wage earner. Citizens like taxes to be as low as possible; wage earners like wages to be as high as possible. The right of unions to bargain creates another conflict between private rights and the public good that can only be decided by political means. Union members, as individuals, have a right to a wage that will support them; as workers they have a loyalty to their union; as citizens, they want lower taxes. These rights and loyalties are, almost naturally, in conflict.

Management rights clauses are one recognition of this political difficulty. The private-sector experience shows that the management rights of one decade are the bargainable subjects of the next, but most public officials want a firm and predictable line beyond which union demands will not reach. Usually management rights clauses will include such things as determining the size, structure, and most work rules of organizations. Yet it is impossible to draw a precise line between the interests. In the case of school teachers, for instance, their salary is related to rank and workload. Workload is related to class size and teaching effectiveness. Both size and effectiveness are related to the range of class offerings and general curricular policy. What should management determine and what should be negotiable? The question defies objective resolution, so legislatures draw lines according to political alignments of the time.

An independent administrative agency is the hallmark of the private-sector model. The National Labor Relations Board (NLRB) was intended to be the government referee that would promote the peaceful settlement of management-labor conflicts. It has fulfilled that expectation; management-labor violence decreased dramatically once the NLRB was operating. Although the legal framework in the public sector is more limited the Federal Labor Relations Authority (FLRA) seeks to build a similar body of case law and guidelines that the NLRB has used to settle disputes in the private sector.

There are also problems concerning which workers are included in a union (called *unit determination*) and which unions the employer must work with (exclusive bargaining agents). Some employers desire to consolidate as many unions as possible. To deal with one or two unions is simpler than dealing with twenty-five. Other employers pursue a more ambitious strategy of preferring several unions, playing them off against each other by bargaining "pacesetter" agreements with the weakest unions. Whether employees are better off with one or many unions is a matter of current politics; if unions in a particular area have strong traditions to band together on strikes, for instance, it may be better strategy to form many organizations. Where unions are fragmented politically, it is probably better to have one large union, especially when striking. What we find is a mix of unit determination and recognition of exclusive bargaining agents that has been decided by political compromise, based on the labor management history and political preferences in each jurisdiction.[7]

The Problem of Impasses

It is important that collective bargaining statutes clearly outline procedures for resolving impasses. Bargaining is based upon a model of underlying conflict, and it is the consequences of unsettled action that drive the parties to seek solutions. When negotiations can go no further toward resolving differences, the negotiations are said to be "at impasse." In most governments the impasse procedures are as follows:

- Mediation is the first step, where a third party enters the bargaining arena and encourages the two sides to restart negotiations. The mediator has no concessions to offer either side, just the skills of defusing issues and enlisting trust.
- Fact-finding, so called because an independent party collects information about the nature of the impasse, is a more serious step than mediation. The fact finder, chosen from a list provided by a state or federal mediation board, works under a deadline. The report of the fact finder remains secret until the deadline, and then is released only if issues are not settled. The danger to the bargaining parties is that they may lose public support and confidence if an independent party places the blame on one or the other. This step is designed to raise the costs of delay.

- Arbitration is, literally, to let someone else decide. In the private sector both binding and nonbinding arbitration are found, but in the public sector binding arbitration is usually only allowed when both sides agree to it, if then. Legislatures, not surprisingly, are not fond of letting unelected officials determine the state wage bill. Nonbinding arbitration is similar to fact-finding in that it puts additional pressure on one or both sides to come to agreement. One example of an interesting public sector experiment with arbitration is "last-best-offer" arbitration. Each side begins the process of negotiations by submitting one or two sealed contracts, which are put away for safekeeping. If the two sides cannot come to agreement by a specified date, an arbitrator takes the sealed offers and decides which one to accept. This places a great deal of pressure on the bargainers to be fair, since the costs of obstinacy can be disastrous. This is an attempt to design a strikelike mechanism into the bargaining process to encourage the parties to come to agreement.
- The final method of impasse resolution is, of course, concerted job action. The strike is the most overt form, but there are additional ways to pressure the other side. Employers may ultimately lock out employees, but this is rarely, if ever, used in the public sector. Employees may engage in work slowdowns (for instance, transit drivers may observe safe following distances, speed limits, wait for passengers to sit before starting, etc., and the schedules will degenerate into chaos) or catch bargaining-related occupational diseases (police get the "blue flu"). Such job actions and strikes mark the near total breakdown of bargaining and are a sign of political failure.

Research on such areas as impasse resolution points to a lack of reliable knowledge about the entire collective bargaining process. A review of academic literature on impasse resolution techniques found that conclusions are rarely empirical and that a systematic framework is lacking.[8] Practitioners should not be chided for failing to find guidance in the literature.

Union Security

Union security arrangements are important to the conduct of bargaining. A secure union is one with a stable membership, a reliable source of income, and is recognized by the employer and the public as the legitimate bargaining agent. The federal system is a good example of progressive union security. During the early days of the executive order format, union officials had to conduct their business and collect dues off the company clock. This does not make union officials popular with the rank and file (who associate a visit from the union steward with a request for money) and it takes their time away from careful preparation of bargaining. Under statutory recognition, federal unions may have dues collected through payroll deductions (called a dues checkoff), and negotiate maintenance of dues and membership clauses into contracts (where employees, once a member of the bargaining unit, must remain so or continue to pay dues for the duration of the contract).

From the union point of view, the best union security provision is the "agency shop," where all employees are required to either belong to the union or to pay a fee that recognizes the benefits received through the union. There is a strong logic to the position: all employees in a bargaining unit benefit from union bargaining and representation, particularly during individual disciplinary matters, whether or not they belong to the union. They should therefore contribute to the maintenance of the union, which the employer and the polity recognize as the legitimate spokesperson for employee concerns.

Not all states accept this logic. The "right-to-work" states (for instance, Arizona and Arkansas) passed laws which, in effect, prohibit most forms of union security. Ostensibly passed to protect employees from pressures to join a union, they actually seek to make it difficult for unions to exist. Their main target has been the stronger union security provisions found in some private sector industries: the "union shop," where all employees must join the union upon being hired, and the "closed shop," where only previous union members may be hired. Right-to-work laws are more symbolic than effective, however. They may affect the growth of unions, since they indicate a negative state view toward unions, but since the strike is only permitted in twelve states, public sector unions are already constrained in the force of their concerted actions. Collective bargaining settlements in the right-to-work states are not significantly different from those in other states of similar size.

Finally, collective bargaining laws contain statements of unfair labor practices (ULPs), prohibited practices for each side. Many ULPs are found in laws, among them: Unions are usually prohibited from striking (and in states which permit strikes, some workers, such as nurses or police, are prohibited from striking), employers are prohibited from interfering with an employee's choice concerning participation in a union, and both sides are admonished to bargain in "good faith." If one side formally charges that the other is engaging in an unfair labor practice, the complaint is adjudicated before an independent hearing board.

The Practice of Collective Bargaining

Collective bargaining is a cyclical political process. Once the legal framework is established, unions seek recognition according to the appropriate procedures. Bargaining teams for both sides can then be selected, and the actual work of negotiation can begin. The most critical part of negotiations is the preparation for bargaining. It is important to learn what should and might come up at the bargaining table, set goals for what to achieve in bargaining, and coordinate strategies among the various components of each bargaining party. Unions can learn from grievances during the last contract (complaints that the other side is not living up to the terms of the contract; see Box 10.4), informal talks with union representatives in various offices, and from the experience of other unions in the region. They must develop a basis of support and interest before they can make demands at the bargaining table. Negotiating is thus a process of building a political coalition, and effective conduct at the bargaining table is mainly an outcome of adequate coalition building.

Similarly, employers can learn from past grievances and supervisors. Supervisors should be attuned to the needs of employees, and in this sense the employers should be able to anticipate much of what the union wants and needs. They too need to develop a basis of support and interest, but this is difficult to do in the public sector. Public support for most mundane political and administrative matters is quite diffuse. It is only when the citizen feels a direct impact of bargaining that such support becomes overt and clear. In San Francisco, for instance, little public support for management was available during tense negotiations in 1980. The mayor needed additional political support for her bargaining team, and took a chance. She called for a public referendum on the level of settlement to make with the union. Faced with a direct choice concerning their pocketbooks, the public gave management overwhelming support.

The main concern is that neither side should go to the bargaining table unprepared. Issue papers should be prepared, with each side assessing the likely positions of the other. Issues, goals, and alternative language acceptable in a contract should all be reviewed before negotiations begin. Yet, on many occasions, the bargaining table is where one side finds out it miscalculated the desires of the other side. Bargaining itself consists of proposals and counterproposals. Usually, the union begins, and issues are broken down into various categories to facilitate discussion. Those items that increase direct costs are of greatest interest to both sides, while the noncost items can usually be worked out quickly. The essence of bargaining, until an entire package is assembled, is tentativeness. Sign-offs on early issues are almost always contingent on the whole package, and it is hard work for both sides to bargain the substance of issues while minimizing threats to egos and political support.

Bargaining in Good Faith

The central but subtle requirement for effective labor-management relations is that both sides bargain in good faith. This simply means that each side regards the other as the representative of legitimate interests,

FIGURE 10.2 The Collective Bargaining Process

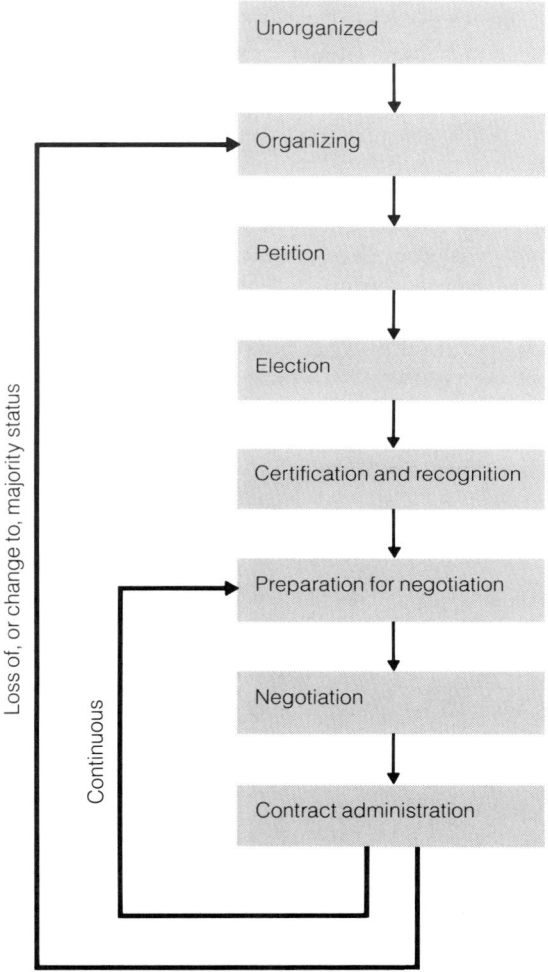

Source: U.S. Office of Personnel Management

that proposals are taken seriously and given a response, and that bargaining is part of a larger working relationship that will continue indefinitely. These simple rules are difficult to put into practice in the heat of bargaining, however.

The preeminent guide to the conduct of negotiations is Roger Fisher and William Ury's *Getting to Yes*.[9] They describe a method called *principled negotiation* or *negotiation on the merits*, which consists of four points:

1. Separate the people from the problem.
2. Focus on interests, not positions.
3. Generate a variety of possibilities before deciding what to do.
4. Insist that the result be based on some objective standard.

The method is not simple to follow, particularly for those without experience in negotiations and in a politically charged atmosphere.

The final stage to negotiating the contract is ratification. The union usually accepts a contract by a majority vote, while in most jurisdictions the legislative branch must approve agreements for management.

Once a contract is ratified, the collective bargaining cycle continues with contract administration, or implementation of the agreement. It is not enough that both sides bargain in good faith at the table. Administrators, supervisors, union officials, and employees must work to live by the agreed-upon rules. This is not always easy, as depicted in Box 10.4. Contract administration goes on throughout the year, and the cycle comes full circle as experience under the contract forms the basic wants and needs of the two sides for the next bargaining round.

BOX 10.4   The Arbitration Case

This is an actual case used to train supervisors in contract administration. People's names have been changed, but the events actually happened.

This is a complete record of the grievance filed by an assistant professor, Ms. Janet Vernon. Please do not create any additional information or surmise anything that is not found in the case.

Answer the following five questions, remembering that you are at the last step preceding arbitration. Depending upon what you decide, the case will or will not go to arbitration. Notice that questions 4 and 5 ask you to answer from the points of view of different roles, those of the dean (management) or the union representative.

1. Was this grievance properly filed?
2. Identify the nature of the grievance and the remedy sought.
3. What should be management's response at this level?
4. What offers, if any, are you willing to make (a) if you are on the union side, and (b) if you are on the management side?
5. Will you go to arbitration (a) if you are union, (b) if you are management?

Date of Occurrence	Facts of the Situation
Wednesday, January 6, 1988	Assistant Professor, Ms. Janet Vernon, files personal leave request form with her chairperson. She requests a personal leave day on Friday, January 15, 1988, stating that the leave is for important personal business, not of a recreational nature, that cannot be conducted on a nonduty day.
Friday, January 8, 1988	Chairperson, Dr. Harvey Stewart, overhears a conversation in the lunchroom regarding Ms. Vernon attending a wedding. He later casually asks Ms. Vernon about the wedding and she tells him that she is going to attend her son's wedding in California; the wedding is on Friday night and she will depart on Thursday night to arrive in time for all the festivities.
Monday, January 11, 1988	Dr. Stewart calls Ms. Vernon into his office and states that it has come to his attention that it is her *stepson* and not her son who is being married. She confirms this to be the relationship. He advises her that this relationship does not qualify as a reason for a personal leave day. He also states that this is a bad time of year for an assistant professor to be absent because the quarter ends on Friday, January 22. He informs her that her request is denied. Ms. Vernon states that she intends to go anyway. Mr. Stewart remarks that she may regret it.
Friday, January 15, 1988	Ms. Vernon is absent from school.
Monday, January 18, 1988	Ms. Vernon returns to school.
Friday, January 22, 1988	Ms. Vernon receives her paycheck from which has been deducted one day's wages. With the paycheck she also receives a letter of reprimand. (Attached.)

Monday, January 25, 1988	Ms. Vernon consults her grievance representative. They recall that at least two other faculty members in the college had taken personal leave days during the current quarter. Upon checking with them, the following is learned:

DICK BROWN, PROFESSOR
Absent on Friday, September 25, 1988. Attended wedding of former roommate. Submitted request for personal leave day on Friday, September 18. Never was asked reason for the request.

MARY ARNOLD, ASSOCIATE PROFESSOR
Absent on Monday, October 12, 1988. Attended funeral of her uncle. Submitted request for personal leave day on Friday, October 9. Explained that her request was for funeral in her family. Chairperson never asked the relationship of the deceased.

Tuesday, January 26, 1988	Ms. Vernon and the grievance representative go together to discuss the matter with the chairperson. He reiterates his position that the wedding of a stepson is not sufficient reason for a personal leave day at the end of a quarter and, furthermore, the request had not been submitted 10 days in advance as required.

He refuses to retract the letter of reprimand stating that it was warranted.

CSU
Central State University

January 21, 1988

Dear Ms. Vernon,

This notice is given as an official reprimand for your absence without authorization on Friday, January 15, 1988.

Not only did you absent yourself in direct defiance of my directions, you also failed to make appropriate arrangements for your classes to be covered by another faculty member.

A copy of this letter will be placed in your personnel file.

Very truly yours,

Harvey Stewart

Harvey Stewart
Chairperson

GRIEVANCE REPORT FORM

Assignment: Assistant Professor   Name of Grievant: Janet Vernon   Date Filed: 1-26-88

Type of Grievance   X A. Non-Economic
                     X B. Economic

LEVEL I

Date Cause of Grievance Occurred: 1-22-88

Statement of Grievance: I received my paycheck on 1-22-88 and found it one day short; also there was a letter of reprimand.

Relief Sought: I feel that personal leave should be granted me for 1-15-88. Also the letter of 1-21-88 should be removed from my file.

Signature: Janet Vernon   Date: 1-26-88

Disposition by Chairperson: Grievance denied, see my letter dated 1-21-88

Signature: Harvey Stewart   Date: 2-1-88

Position of Grievant: Request level II

Signature: Janet Vernon   Date: 2-7-88

LEVEL II

Date Received by Dean or Designee _____

Disposition of Dean or Designee _____

Signature _____   Date _____

(from the contract)
13.000 GRIEVANCE PROCEDURE

An allegation by a faculty member or the Association that there has been a violation, misinterpretation or misapplication of any provision of this Contract may be processed as a grievance as hereinafter provided.

Level I.

a. *Informal Discussion of Grievance.*
   In the event that a faculty member believes there is a basis for a grievance, he shall first discuss the alleged grievance with his chairperson either personally or accompanied by his Association representative.

b. *Filing of Grievance with Chairperson.*
   If, after the informal discussion with the chairperson, a grievance still exists, the faculty member may invoke the formal grievance procedure through the Association on the form prepared for this purpose, signed by the grievant and representative of the Association, which form shall be available from the Association grievance representative. A copy of the grievance form shall be delivered to the chairperson within twenty-eight (28) calendar days after the event giving rise to the alleged grievance occurred. If the grievance involves more than one chairperson, it may be filed with the Dean or a representative designated by him.

c. *Decision of Chairperson.*
   Within seven (7) calendar days of receipt of the grievance, the chairperson shall meet with the Association in an effort to resolve the grievance. The chairperson shall indicate his disposition of the grievance, in writing within seven (7) calendar days of such meeting, and shall furnish a copy thereof to the Association.

Level II: Dean's Level

If the Association is not satisfied with the disposition of the grievance, or if no disposition has been made within seven (7) calendar days of such meeting (or fourteen (14) calendar days from the date of filing, whichever shall be later) the grievance shall be transmitted to the Dean. Within seven (7) calendar days the Dean or his designee shall meet with the Association on the grievance and shall indicate his disposition of the grievance in writing within seven (7) calendar days of such meeting, and shall furnish a copy thereof to the Association.

Level III: Vice President of Academic Affairs' Level

If the Association is not satisfied with the disposition of the grievance by the Dean or his designee, or if no disposition has been made within seven (7) calendar days of such meeting (or fourteen (14) calendar days from the date of filing, whichever shall be later) the grievance shall be transmitted to the Vice President of Academic Affairs by filing a written copy thereof with the Secretary or other designee of the Vice President of Academic Affairs. The Vice President of Academic Affairs, no later than two (2) calendar weeks, shall meet with the Association on the grievance. Disposition of the grievance in writing by the Vice President of Academic Affairs shall be made no later than fourteen (14) calendar days thereafter. A copy of such disposition shall be furnished to the Association.

Level IV: Arbitration Level

If the Association is not satisfied with the disposition of the grievance by the Vice President of Academic Affairs, or if no disposition has been made within the period above provided, the grievance may be submitted to arbitration before an impartial arbitrator within twenty-one (21) calendar days after the Vice President of Academic Affairs' decision. If the parties cannot agree as to the arbitrator within fourteen (14) calendar days from the notification date that arbitration will be pursued, he shall be selected by the American Arbitration Association in accord with its rules which shall likewise govern the arbitration proceeding. The Vice President of Academic Affairs and the Association shall not be permitted to assert in such arbitration proceeding any ground or to rely on any evidence not previously disclosed to the other party. The arbitrator shall have no power to alter, add to or subtract from the terms of this contract. Both parties agree to be bound by the award of the arbitrator and agree that judgment thereon may be entered in any court of competent jurisdiction.

The fees and expenses of the arbitrator shall be shared equally by the parties.

If any probationary faculty member for whom a grievance is sustained shall be found to have been unjustly discharged, he shall be reinstated with full reimbursement of all professional compensation or advantage, the same or its equivalent in money shall be paid.

The time limits provided in this Article shall be strictly observed but may be extended by written agreement of the parties. In the event a grievance is filed after May 15, of any year and strict adherence to the time limits may result in hardship to any party, the Vice President for Academic Affairs shall use his best efforts to process such grievance prior to the end of the academic year or as soon thereafter as possible.

Not withstanding the expiration of this Contract, any claim or grievance arising thereunder may be processed through the grievance procedure until resolution.

No reprisals of any kind will be taken by the Vice President of Academic Affairs or the Dean against any faculty member because of his participation in this grievance procedure.

8.000 PERSONAL LEAVE

Two personal leave days shall be granted each year for incidents involving special obligations or emergencies which cannot be scheduled on nonduty days and are not authorized under other leave provisions. Such days shall be granted according to the following guidelines:

1. Guidelines for Granting Personal Leave:

a. The administration reserves the right to require a satisfactory explanation and prior approval in individual cases of requests for personal leave days to be taken immediately before or after a holiday, weekend or vacation period, and reasonable restrictions may be imposed on personal leaves on such days.

b. Personal leave days taken at other times shall require no explanation. The faculty members shall, however, state in writing that the leave is to be taken for important personal business, not of a recreational nature, that cannot be conducted on a nonduty day.

c. In emergency situations, written requests for personal leave may be submitted after the fact. It is understood that the faculty member will assume the responsibility in such an emergency of notifying the chairperson at the earliest possible time of the absence.

d. Personal leave will only be authorized in those incidents involving special obligation or emergencies which are impossible to schedule on nonduty days and cannot be performed by someone else or which are not authorized under other leave provisions.

e. Examples of legitimate claims for personal leave:
 —Urgent legal matters
 —Religious observances
 —Special examinations in connection with degree programs
 —Weddings in immediate family

f. Examples of situations which will not be approved for personal leave:
 —Personal recreation activities
 —Convention attendance with spouse
 —Social activities

2. Requests:

Requests for personal leave shall be initiated on the form provided, Personal Leave Request Form, and submitted to the chairperson at least ten (10) days prior to the anticipated date. The chariperson should take whatever action is necessary to satisfy himself/herself that the requests are consistent with the guidelines established.

The Future of Collective Bargaining in the Public Sector

Public employee union growth has been stagnant since the middle 1970s. Prior to that time many observers were predicting continued and strong growth until virtually all public sector employees were union members. Considerations of the determinants of union growth, however, cut both ways and suggest that the overall trends are highly political. The strongest determinant of union growth is state policy toward unions. States that recognize the full bargaining rights of all employees, and particularly those allowing strikes, send a clear message of encouragement. There seems to be some regional catching up, as in the case of southern sanitation workers, but for the most part the south is the least conducive to unionization. The northeast is most favorable, followed by the Pacific coast and the Rocky Mountain and Plains states. Other factors have weak or mixed power in explaining public sector union growth.[10]

The PATCO experience has heralded an era of setbacks for unions in the private sector. Although the period up to the mid-1970s saw public employee unions following the lead in the private sector, government policy toward its unions may now be strongly influencing private sector developments. The politics of these times, along with the fiscal problems at every level of government, add new problems for labor-management relations. That President Reagan would actually break a public employee's union was a sign of the times. The federal government, deep in debt as we write this book, is trying to find ways to cut expenses. Salaried workers are one area in which cuts take place — 75,000 federal employees were laid off between 1981 and 1987. There is a ripple effect; as state and local governments get less money (because of cuts in federal grants, aid programs, and training programs) there are corresponding layoffs in the lower-level governments. Unions, which once lobbied for higher wages and benefits, must now bargain for greater job security and to save jobs.

The politics of retrenchment will not end soon, and labor unions will be at the center of many political issues. For example, retrenchment pits labor unions against groups that support affirmative action. In a case that reached the Supreme Court in 1986, *Wygant v. Jackson Board of Education*, union seniority rules came into conflict with an affirmative action plan approved by the same union. Wendy Wygant was one of several white teachers who lost their jobs to budget cuts, while less senior black teachers kept theirs. The Jackson, Mississippi, school board was attempting to maintain the percentage of minorities targeted in the affirmative action plan. The Supreme Court had earlier ruled that preferential hiring is acceptable to correct the "lingering effects" of discrimination. But in Wygant, the court said that while it is acceptable to burden whites in order to meet minority hiring goals, it is going too far to deny whites existing jobs. The type of injury is simply too great.

The Wygant case suggests the theme of collective bargaining in an era of retrenchment. Job security is the dominant concern of the unions, while employers search for ways to save money. Some goals, such as affirmative action, are put under greater pressure in the search for solutions acceptable to citizens and wage earners. How will labor and management meet the challenges of retrenchment? Our discussion of the history and practice of collective bargaining shows that the current legal framework and bargaining procedures are the product of a long and often painful process. Government in the United States is intended to be responsive to particular organized interests. Parties on both sides of the bargaining table are likely to draw upon those same sources to find agreements they can live with.

SUMMARY

We began our discussion of labor-management issues by noting that such relations are inherently political. The many actors involved differ not only on particular issues, such as the size of wage increases or concessions, but also over what constitute labor or management prerogatives. This means that the field of labor-management relations is not clearly defined, and the range of issues as well as particular outcomes are the product of contemporary political conflict. This situation is a continuation of a long history of conflict between labor and management.

Students of labor-management relations need to pay attention to the legal framework of bargaining. The crucial difference between private- and public-sector collective bargaining is that in the public sector unions bargain with the state, and so the rights of employees become intertwined with the rights of individual citizens and the interests of the state. Labor-management relations vary tremendously among governments, and the model we presented that describes public sector relations is quite general.

Given governmental acceptance of unions under a legal framework, the process of collective bargaining normally works best when the parties are adequately prepared and committed to an agreement that each side can live with. However, when resources are tight, conflicts heighten. Bargaining in good faith becomes more difficult when each side sees itself losing ground. Political relationships are especially important in setting the tone for bargaining relationships. During the Reagan administration, for instance, it quickly became apparent that the president and his appointees came out strongly on the side of management, and that unions would have to accept their terms. This political stance helped set the tone for labor-management relations in the states and in the private sector during the 1980s. The PATCO and Wygant examples show that public-sector collective bargaining will remain a challenging area for some time.

NOTES

1. Donald J. Devine, "The Challenge to Federal Employees Today," *Labor Law Journal* 32, no. 7 (July 1981), p. 391.
2. Ibid.
3. Useful histories of labor-management relations are J. David Greenstone, *Labor in American Politics* (New York: Alfred Knopf, 1969); Stanley Aronowitz, *False Promises* (New York: McGraw-Hill, 1973); for a public sector emphasis see Jack Stieber, *Public Employee Unionism* (Washington, D.C.: Brookings Institution, 1973); and Richard Kearney, *Labor Relations in the Public Sector* (New York: Marcel Dekker, 1984).
4. Donald J. Devine, op. cit., p. 389.
5. Public sector labor law is described in David H. Rosenbloom and Jay M. Shafritz, *Essentials of Labor Relations* (Reston, Va.: Reston Publishing, 1985); and Hugh D. Jascourt, ed., *Government Labor Relations* (Oak Park, Ill.: Moore Publishing, 1979).
6. Jay Shafritz et al., *Personnel Management in Government,* 3d ed. (New York: Marcel Dekker, 1986), p. 295.
7. Ibid., p. 304.
8. See Michael D. Nash and Nolan J. Argyle, "Old Mother Hubbard Revisited: Comments on the Reliability of the Collective Bargaining Literature," *Review of Public Personnel Administration* 4, no. 2 (Spring 1984), pp. 1–12.
9. Roger Fisher and William Ury, *Getting to Yes* (New York: Houghton Mifflin, 1981), p. 11.
10. Jim Seroka, "The Determinants of Public Employee Union Growth," *Review of Public Personnel Administration* 5, no. 2 (Spring 1985), pp. 5–20.
11. This possibility was discussed by George Sulzner, "Public Sector Labor Relations: Agent of Change in American Industrial Relations?" *Review of Public Personnel Administration* 5, no. 2 (Spring 1985), pp. 70–78.

CHAPTER ELEVEN

Public Budgeting

> Whenever there are great strains or changes in the economic system, it tends to generate crackpot theories, which then find their way into the legislative channels.
>
> — *David Stockman, former director of the Office of Management and Budget*

In her book *The Human Condition*,[1] Hannah Arendt makes the following argument. She writes that we have lost a real sense of politics. Although citizens rarely participate in any meaningful way in the important decisions of the government, the government itself has become more and more powerful. Arendt demonstrates this dynamic in a convincing manner. She concludes that it is accurate to think of our state as a big family, and that it has become the responsibility of the state to take care of family needs. The state, to put it a little differently, has become the surrogate parent of us all.

The budget, then, becomes the method by which the parent manages the financial affairs of the family. The budget becomes the central focus in much of our material well-being. Which family members contribute what — and get what — are the stakes of the budget. Power in the budgetary process is power indeed. Not only that, we will see that *how* the budget is made is worth fighting about. One important part of this chapter is to see the biases behind particular budget-making schemes.

Thinking about Budgeting

In order to systematically study the budgetary process, the study must be based on some theory of what budgeting is about.[2] Budgeting might be considered as any one of the following six categories:

1. *Budgeting is a way to manage the economy.* The fiscal policy of a government is the use of taxing and spending to influence the economy. The overall goals of fiscal policy are healthy economic growth, low un-

employment, and low inflation. We will discuss fiscal policy later in the chapter, but you should know that in all the years of trying to actively manage these measures of the economy, the national government has hit its targets only twice.

2. *Budgeting is a way to choose among priorities.* How do we decide to divide the money between farmers and the cities, defense and social welfare, space and medical care, and the like? In most families explicit trade-offs among food and clothes, rent and travel, insurance and education are not continually made. In government the problem is compounded by sheer size and amazing diversity in the people served. We will see that government keeps trying new budget systems that are expected to help choose among these priorities.

3. *Budgeting is a way to produce the right mix of programs in order to balance the public and private sectors so that our economy is productive and individuals are provided for.* Our capitalist economy is productive, but many human needs go unmet. Government usually provides most of the "infrastructure" of the economy, which includes transportation networks and other basic services as well as setting the rules of the economic game. Government also provides direct services to individuals who do not prosper under capitalism — in the 1980s these are collectively referred to as the "social safety net."

4. *Budgeting is a way to review and control agencies.* Agencies are reviewed at budget-making time, and budgets are monitored by offices in both executive and legislative branches. Budget review and control is discussed in Chapter 12.

5. *Budgeting is a form of accounting.* The government's budget is a comprehensive statement of what the government did the previous year and what it proposes to do the following year. The various budget formats discussed below have each attempted, with mixed success, to improve on the categories of keeping track of government budgets.

6. *Budgeting is a power struggle.* Winning is a value in itself, because the results of the budgeting process reflect the individuals, agencies, and parties involved. The national budget exceeded $1 trillion ($1,000,000,000,000) in 1987; that adds up to a great many people winning and losing a great many conflicts.

It makes sense to think of budgeting as a combination of these six functions. Although some functions may be more compelling than others, the budget-making process has come to be one of the — if not the — most important things the government does.

The Evolution of Budgets

Governments have used a number of methods of budgeting. These are now called *budget systems*. Looking at the evolution of budget systems tells us a great deal about what is at stake in government budgeting. Most systems are concerned with the executive budget — the budget submitted by the executive to the legislature. Reform in budgeting usually means a strengthening of executive administration.

Line-Item Budgeting

Before 1900, the federal government was relatively small and the budget-making process was quite simple. Except in exceptional times, such as the Civil War, there were no great worries about the size of budgets, the size of deficits, and establishing detailed priorities. Each department in the government prepared its budget request and submitted it directly to the appropriation committees of Congress. The Congress did its work and sent the budget to the president. This was the earliest point in the process that the executive branch became involved.

Governments at all levels were in need of reform at the turn of the century. (See the discussion of civil service reform in Chapter 6.) The budget process was a way in which reform could come about. In the spirit of that reform, the National Municipal League drafted a model budget in 1899. By 1907 the Department of Health of New York City presented the first comprehensive budget. It was a line-item budget.

In essence, a line-item budget is based on those things that the government purchases: services, salaries, materials, travel, and so on. The line-item budget increased accountability of departments and allowed management to control how much was spent on what. By 1912 the federal government began seriously to consider changing its budgeting process. President Taft appointed a commission to make recommendations about how government could be run more efficiently. The commission recommended that the executive prepare the budget, that the budget be line-item, and that the executive also prepare a revenue estimate.

With the Budget and Accounting Act of 1921, the United States government began what we would recognize now as the budget process. The act established two new bureaus: the Bureau of the Budget (BOB, later to become the Office of Management and Budget, or OMB) to help the president prepare the budget, and the General Accounting Office (GAO) to oversee government accounts and to report to the Congress. The act also set up a new budgetary process. The budget is prepared by the executive and then sent to the Congress for its authorization. It is later executed by the executive branch and is finally audited by the GAO. Within that general structure there has been an ongoing debate about how best to make a budget.

BOX 11.1 A Page from a Line-Item Budget

CITY OF SHELBY ANNUAL BUDGET - FISCAL YEAR 1988 - 89 EXPENDITURES

Code: 4340   Fund General   Department Fire   Page No. 16

		1986-87	1987-88		1988-89	
	Number	Expended	Budget	Estimated	Recommended	Approved
Salaries and Wages	.120	419,472	473,200	470,000	520,120	
Longevity Pay	.130	-0-	-0-	-0-	6,000	
FICA Expense	.210	-0-	-0-	-0-	66,500	
Retirement Expense	.220	-0-	-0-	-0-	35,000	
Group Insurance	.240	-0-	-0-	-0-	12,320	
Workmen's Compensation	.250	-0-	-0-	-0-	12,800	
Unemployment Compensation	.260	-0-	-0-	-0-	-0-	
Professional Services	.310	-0-	2,000	3,300	2,000	
Utilities	.320	13,966	16,000	17,000	18,000	
Travel, Meetings, Schools	.340	10,433	7,000	7,000	7,500	
Telephone	.351	4,014	4,200	4,200	4,500	
Building Repairs	.381	663	1,200	900	3,000	
Equipment Repairs	.382	7,722	10,000	9,000	12,000	
Equip. Maint. Contracts	.383	-0-	-0-	-0-	500	
Land & Water Area Main.	.384	409	1,000	400	-0-	
Printing & Publishing	.386	898	1,500	1,500	1,500	
Laundry and Dry Cleaning	.387	517	800	500	800	
Dept. Supplies & Expense	.410	4,180	3,400	3,000	3,400	
Janitorial Supplies	.420	1,434	2,000	2,100	2,400	
Auto Supplies	.430	6,335	9,800	9,000	10,000	
Uniforms & Accessories	.440	9,525	10,500	10,000	12,500	
Small Tools	.450	191	900	700	800	
Dues & Subscriptions	.530	1,020	1,000	1,000	1,000	
Insurance & Bonds	.540	-0-	-0-	-0-	15,400	
Capital Outlay - Other Imp.	.603	11,268	5,000	4,500	4,000	
Capital Outlay - Equipment	.604	9,797	10,970	11,000	21,000	
Capital Outlay - Vehicles	.605	6,584	24,475	24,400	-0-	
Transfer to Debt Service	.983	-0-	-0-	-0-	21,917	
Contributions - Other Agencies	-	1,500	1,500	1,500	-0-	
TOTALS		509,978	586,445	581,000	794,957	

PERSONNEL   35 plus 13 P.T.   35 plus 20 P.T.

Source: Girard Miller, *Effective Budgetary Presentations: The Cutting Edge* (Chicago: Municipal Finance Officers Association, 1982), p. 93.

Performance Budgeting

The early budgets were line item and were a big change from the days when departments simply submitted requests to Congress. But, there is at least one major weakness in a line-item budget: Although a person looking at the budget can tell where the money is being spent, it is impossible to get a sense either of programs involved or the performance of those programs. Line-item budgets do not reveal much about what government agencies *do*.

By the mid-1940s there was a need to use the budget for several things. There was the need to be able to monitor programs more closely, to centralize power and management in order to control a much bigger government, and to make programs more effective.[4] The Hoover Commission Report, whose recommendations were repeated in the Budget and Accounting Procedures Act of 1950, recommended the government adopt a performance budget.

A performance budget focuses upon the efficiency of the work being done and helps decision makers calculate the cost per unit of output in government agencies. The logic behind a performance budget is straightforward: it helps to plan and keep track of the business of administration. Yet, as we have pointed out several times in the book, that is a narrow way to envision the work of government agencies. It leaves out a concern for meeting the objectives of programs. More importantly, it leaves out the question of whether the objectives are appropriate. A wider sense of accountability, political accountability, was needed to be seen from budgets. People who produced these budgets were asking questions that were different from the ones they asked while putting the budget together. Although parts of performance budgets are more popular than ever, performance budgeting alone is simply too narrow a focus for public organizations.

Planning-Programming-Budgeting System (PPBS)

The different kinds of budgets discussed up to here have a ring of history to them. With PPBS we get closer to the heart of contemporary budget debate. Although something like PPBS has been around a long time, it became prominent relatively recently. It came into its own in a dramatic way and represents a powerful method of thinking about budgeting ... and how to think about public administration. PPBS is an effort to see and solve problems whole. What follows are the key terms used to help us to see the politics of PPBS:

PROGRAMS. A program is a collection of all efforts toward a common objective. To achieve this objective means that a program will be coordinated by a single head. Programs will tend toward centralization. It is a way to draw together as many resources as possible, to assess an overall

BOX 11.2 A Page from a Performance Budget

ANNUAL BUDGET

CITY OF ABILENE
ACTIVITY PERFORMANCE INDICATORS

Department		Division		Activity		Fund	
PUBLIC WORKS	400	STREET SERVICES	4040	ASPHALT & CONCRETE REPAIR	0434	GENERAL	100

Activity Description: Patches and restores cut or damaged pavement in asphalt and concrete streets and alleys.

OBJECTIVES

1. To reduce the cost of repairs to asphalt streets and alleys by 2.5% using a Porta-Patcher pug mill asphalt re-cycling machine.
2. To reduce citizen complaints by 10% through decreased repair response time.

INDICATORS OF PERFORMANCE

	MEASUREMENT	Last FY	current FY	next FY
DEMAND	Linear miles of paved streets	425	440	445
	Linear miles of paved alleys	80	85	86
	Square yds. of concrete paving	246,400	246,400	246,400
	Number of calls for service	–	120	120
WORKLOAD	Tons of asphalt cold patch used	1,000	1,000	1,000
	Tons of hot mix asphalt used	4,000	4,000	4,000
	Cubic yds. of concrete used	200	500	500
	Cubic yds. of base material used	45,000	45,000	46,000
	Number of pavement patches required	–	24,000	23,400
	Number of valid calls for service	–	120	108
PRODUCTIVITY	Annual cost to maintain 1 mile of asphalt street	$486	$539	$622
	Annual cost to maintain 1 mile of asphalt alley	$1,290	$1,396	$1,612
	Annual cost to maintain 1 cu. yd. of concrete paving	$1.68	$1.93	$2.28
	Annual cost of patching and restoration	–	$104,000	$120,000
	(See remarks)			
EFFECTIVENESS	Number of complaints – paved streets	–	84	76
	Number of complaints – paved alleys	–	36	32

REMARKS: Productivity indicators are based upon projected inflation rate of 18% annually for construction and maintenance (APWA Study).

Source: Girard Miller, *Effective Budgetary Presentations: The Cutting Edge* (Chicago: Municipal Finance Officers Association, 1982), p. 137.

approach and costs, and to compare these with the efforts of other agencies.

PROGRAM ALTERNATIVES. The PPBS budget calls for a series of choices for reaching objectives so that management can choose the best alternative.

PLANNING ORIENTATION. The preferred alternatives for reaching objectives are projected for several years, typically five, rather than just for one year in previous budget systems.

PROGRESS MEASUREMENT. Program fulfillment means that (1) the output that was planned materialized and (2) the output distribution intended was completed. Process measurement simply has to do with how these two conditions are being met.

BOX 11.3   PPBS: Planning-Programming-Budgeting Systems

The PPBS system is built upon three types of documents: (a) Program Memoranda (PM) which are drafted each year for each program category and present . . . recommendations . . . within a framework of agency objectives, identify the alternatives considered, and support the decisions taken; . . . (b) A comprehensive multi-year Program and Financial Plan (PFP) which annually presents in tabular form a complete . . . summary of agency programs . . . in terms of their outputs and costs; and (c) Special Studies (SS) which are started and finished as appropriate and provide the analytic groundwork reported in the Program Memoranda. Costs in the PFP are defined in a more limited sense than the costs which may — and usually should — be utilized in the Program Memoranda or in Special Studies. The analysis of a program should include economic opportunity costs, marginal costs, and systems costs. . . . Special studies will . . . review in terms of costs and benefits . . . prior efforts, compare alternative mixes of programs, balance increments in costs against increments in effectiveness . . . and assess the incidence of benefits as well as their totals.

Source: U.S. Bureau of the Budget, Bulletin no. 68–2, July 18, 1967; reported in Leonard Merewitz and Stephen H. Sosnick, *The Budget's New Clothes* (Chicago: Markham Publishing, 1971), p. 2.

SYSTEM ANALYSIS. System analysis is the "S" in PPBS. It is, basically, the application of benefit-cost analysis techniques to programs. Put more directly, it is "an application of the scientific method;" it is "quantitative common sense."[5]

The effort behind PPBS was to centralize and rationalize the budgetary process. In order to do that, it was necessary to institute goals for which administrators could be held accountable. It was the task of every agency to be able to state what needs were to be served, what services were to be provided, and to be able to compute their costs and benefits. The business of government was to become much more businesslike.

The list of PPBS advantages is impressive. It employs "the method of science," which is "an open, explicit, verifiable, self-correcting process." The "scientific method is objective." By using the scientific method, "each hypothesis is tested and verified by methods appropriate to the hypothesis in question; and "where a quantitative matter is discussed, the greatest clarity of thought is achieved by using numbers instead of avoiding them, even when uncertainties are present." The value of applying the scientific method to budgeting was summed up by one writer who claimed that it was a way to gain "great control over uncertainty."[6]

The first PPBS budget was prepared for the Department of Defense in 1961. Robert McNamara was the secretary of defense, and John Kennedy was president at the time. By 1964, PPBS was well ingrained at the Defense Department (it still is), and in 1965 President Johnson asked all budget makers in the federal government to practice PPBS. For fiscal year 1967, the budget given to Congress by Johnson reflected a significant shift to PPBS.

PPBS failed. In the end, almost nothing went right.[7] Agencies at the bottom of the system did not like it. Instead of giving superiors the power they wanted, most agencies regarded the forms as bothersome paperwork. In addition, the power of agencies was threatened because PPBS focused on coordinated programs instead of strengthening agencies. The BOB did not like it, mainly because the system was imposed by a different part of the executive branch. All they were to do is oversee the system. Congress did not like it, for somehow the executive branch forgot that the Congress used a different way of considering budgets. Congress was never included. But there was much more to it than these reasons indicate.

The effort to quantify, to be analytic, to be comprehensive and "scientific" knew no limits in PPBS. It embodied the triumph of the administrative over the public. But that was the point. To know the names, the dates, and what was going on in the country during PPBS gives an important message about the limitations of systems analysis in the public sector.

To read the names and dates is to remember that the Defense Department PPBSed its way through the war in Vietnam. The real battle for what was at stake for the Vietnamese — and for Americans — could never

BOX 11.4 A Page from a Program Budget

PUBLIC PROTECTION	FIRE PROTECTION

Program FIRE EMERGENCY RESPONSE	Department FIRE

Program Description

To respond to emergency calls, extinguish fires, perform rescues, and salvage property; to maintain equipment, stations, and grounds, provide pre-hospital emergency care; and promote fire prevention education.

PROGRAM OPERATING EXPENSE				
Resource Requirements	1986-87 Actual	1987-88 Budget	1987-88 Estimated	1988-89 Recommended
Personnel/Personal Services	94.2/$2,308,902	90/$2,457,848	89.1/$2,564,586	88.8/$2,675,969
Operating & Main. Supplies	115,931	106,752	63,607	100,280
Charges & Services	827,930	539,235	657,789	684,890
Capital Outlay	80,564	65,350	67,550	28,936
Work Order Credits				
TOTAL	$3,333,327	$3,169,185	$3,353,532	$3,490,075

PROGRAM RESOURCES				
General Fund	$3,333,327	$3,169,185	$3,353,532	$3,490,075
TOTAL	$3,333,327	$3,169,185	$3,353,532	$3,490,075

PROGRAM BUDGET HIGHLIGHTS

Fire Emergency Response increase of 20% is due to an increase in personal services of 25% (due to salary contingency). Other than that, program costs all remaining fairly static. Fire emergency calls are expected to remain constant as are 2.5 minute response times. The encouraging aspect to the 1987-88 budget year is that fire loss was reduced by 69%.

Source: Girard Miller, *Effective Budgetary Presentations: The Cutting Edge* (Chicago: Municipal Finance Officers Association, 1982), p. 113.

be quantified. Although we were able to calculate how cost efficient it was to kill a Vietnamese, that never gave us a hint about why we were there and if we were winning.

This flaw in PPBS was central to its failure. There is no built-in way to assess whether the objectives of a program are appropriate or not. Although it may be a fine method to judge if a program is economically efficient or effective, the whole question of political accountability cannot be asked. Making government budgets is a political process. There are political questions to be answered and political choices that need to be defended. Any process that takes the focus too far from politics will find few political supporters.

In 1971, Richard Nixon formally abandoned PPBS. Although it still lingers, in changed form, there is little question that it is inappropriate for public institutions.

Management By Objectives (MBO)

The idea of MBO has been around (and popular in the private sector) since the mid-1950s.[8] Richard Nixon used it and changed budgeting from the policy-planning of PPBS to a management orientation.

Basically, MBO is a process by which policymakers and managers work together to influence the future. They gather together and define the goals of the organization and the goals of each subunit. They establish objectives that can be identified, obtained, and verified. Plans are then developed, and within these plans there are identifiable milestones from which to measure progress and monitor responsible individuals. There is regular monitoring of the progress of the program, and each individual monitors his or her own programs.

In 1973, Nixon put MBO into practice in twenty-one agencies. The results were mixed. Those who used it found that MBO demanded an extraordinary amount of time for the managers and generated an enormous amount of paperwork. Those in the middle-level jobs did not seem affected by it. There were also those who did not use it at all.

The reasons for the problems are quite similar to the PPBS experience. Agency and even OMB people regarded MBO as an effort to exert more control from above, even though one goal of MBO is to decentralize decisions. There was some question of how sincere Nixon was in his willingness to decentralize.[9] In the end MBO had little support from the bottom, whereas at the top, the president and his advisers were preoccupied with reelection, burglaries, and obstruction of justice — the Watergate affair.

In 1974 Nixon resigned. President Ford appointed new budget people and, although he supported MBO, executive leadership seemed at loose ends during that period. In 1977, President Carter introduced the zero-base budget (ZBB) system. Before we go any further, let's think about what we have so far. Since 1920 the federal government has grown and budgeting has become more important. The history has been for presidents to seek more centralized power through the budgetary process. In various names (efficiency, economy, science, effectiveness, management) we have seen almost frantic attempts to rationalize the process, and at the same time add to the power of the president. As we shall see, ZBB is simply the next logical step.

Zero-Based Budgeting (ZBB)

ZBB has been around in public agencies since the early 1960s. While governor of Georgia, Jimmy Carter instituted ZBB; when he became president of the United States, he brought ZBB with him.

There are four basic steps to ZBB. First, managers determine the objectives of each program and define standards of performance as well as establish the services and/or products each program will provide. Second, within each program, managers are given areas for which they will prepare budgets. Each of these areas is called a *decision unit*. Third, the decision unit manager works out a variety of ways to accomplish the job and figures out different levels of performance and spending. Finally, the decision unit manager prepares budget plans, called *decision packages*, for at least two spending levels (say, 100 percent of last year's budget and 105 percent of last year's budget.).

In theory, ZBB requires that every year every agency start at zero and justify every dollar spent. One need not go beyond common sense to understand this is not necessary and is just not possible. We really do not need to wrestle with the question each and every year of whether we shall have a navy. And the time and effort needed to reinvent the federal budget every year is truly beyond calculation.

Bending to reality, ZBB is actually 80 percent–base budgeting, or 90 percent–base budgeting. Of course, the main question for budgets is who gets to decide which 80 percent is considered the "base," and which 20 percent gets closely scrutinized. In the federal government, decision unit managers made those decisions. It is not surprising that federal budget spending patterns changed less under ZBB than they did under the earlier budget systems.[10]

Changes under Reagan

Unlike all elected presidents of the previous 20 years, Ronald Reagan did not institute a new budget "system." He did not claim to be guided by science, or efficiency, or cost-effectiveness (although he wanted those things as well). He came into office on a deliberately political agenda — a promise to spend more on defense, cut taxes, stop rampant inflation, re-

FIGURE 11.1 Some Differences among Budgetary Concepts

Feature	Line-Item	Performance	PPB	MBO	ZBB
Basic orientation	Control	Management	Planning	Management	Decision making
Scope	Inputs	Inputs and outputs	Inputs, outputs, effects, alternatives	Inputs, outputs, effects	Inputs, outputs, effects, alternatives
Personnel skills	Accounting	Management	Economics, planning	Management, planning	Management, planning
Critical information	Objects of expenditure	Activities of agency	Purposes of agency	Purpose of program or agency	Purpose of program or agency
Policy-making style	Incremental	Incremental	Systemic	Flexible	Marginal analysis
Planning responsibility	Largely absent	Dispersed	Central	Central	Decentralized
Role of the budget agency	Fiscal propriety	Efficiency	Policy	Policy, management	Policy prioritization

Source: From Nicholas L. Henry, *Public Administration and Public Affairs*, 3d ed., © 1986, p. 184. Reprinted by permission of Prentice-Hall, Inc., Englewood Cliffs, N.J.

BOX 11.5 Formulation of Executive Budget

Approximate Timing ▶	Agency	Office of Management and Budget	The President
Budget Policy Development			
March (earlier in some agencies)		Develops economic assumptions. Obtains forecasts of international situations. Prepares fiscal projections.	Discusses budgetary outlook and policies with the Director of the Office of Management and Budget, and with the Cabinet as appropriate.
April	Reviews current operations, program objectives, issues, and future plans in relation to upcoming annual budget. Submits projections of requirements that reflect current operations and future plans; program memoranda and related special analytic studies which identify major issues, alternatives for resolving issues, and comparisons of costs and effectiveness.	Issues instructions and policy guidance on material to be developed for Spring planning review.	
		Discusses program developments and management issues, and resulting budgetary effects, with agency heads.	
May		Compiles total outlay estimates for comparison with revenue estimates. Develops recommendations for President on fiscal policy, program issues, and budget levels.	
June	Issues internal instructions on preparation of annual budget estimates.	Issues technical instructions for preparation of annual budget estimates.	Discusses with the Director of the Office of Management and Budget and others as necessary, general budget policy, major program issues, budgetary ceilings, and projections. Establishes general guidelines and agency budgetary ceilings for annual budget.
Compilation and Submission of Agency Estimates		Conveys President's decisions to agency heads on Government-wide policies and assumptions and the application of policies and budgetary ceilings to individual agencies.	

The Evolution of Budgets

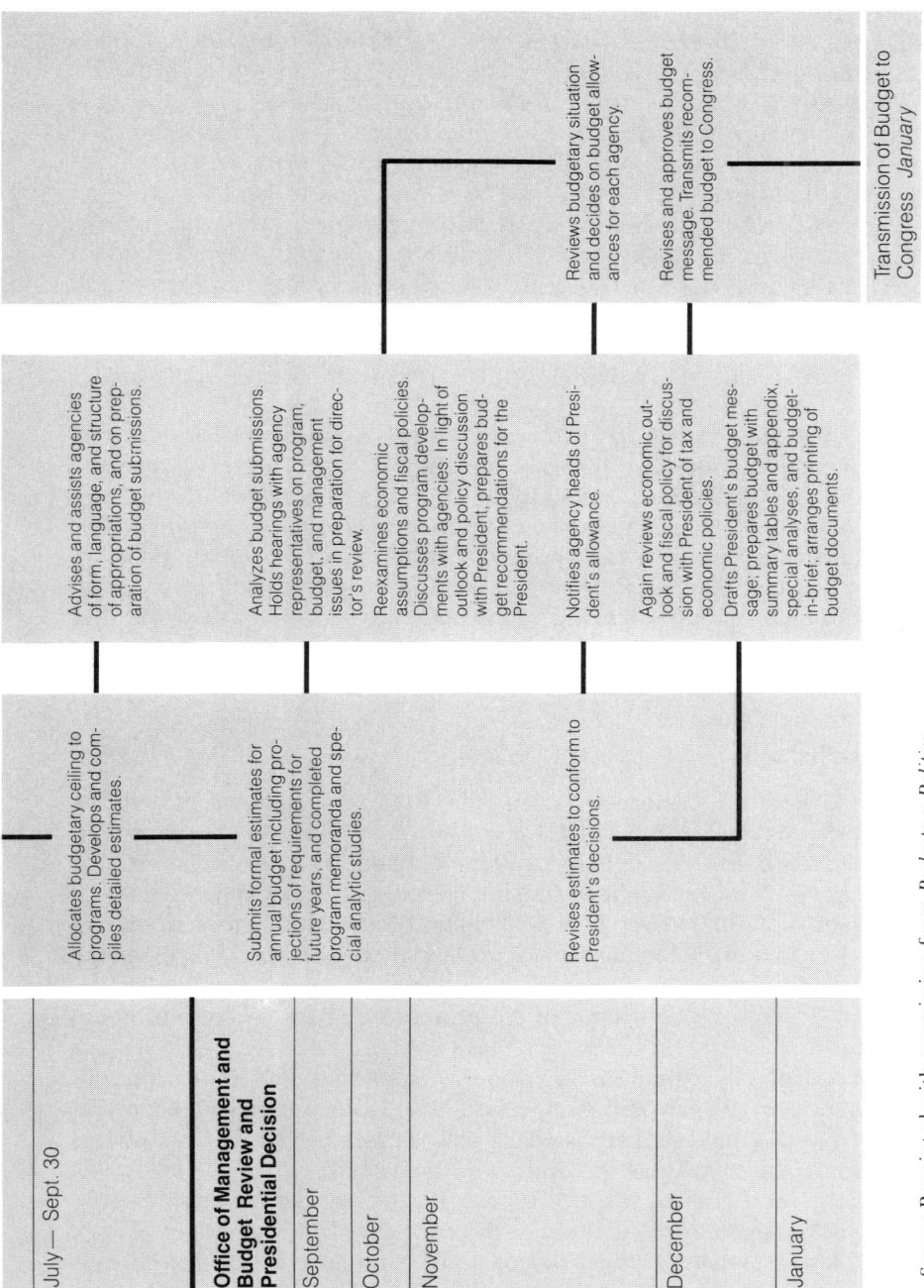

Source: Reprinted with permission from *Budgetary Politics,* by Lance T. Leloup, 3d ed. (King's Court Communications, Brunswick, Ohio, 1986).

tain social programs only for the "truly needy," and balance the budget — and used openly political tactics to get his way in budget decisions.[11]

Earlier, in Chapter 6, we discussed the Reagan administration's ideological view of government employees. The same approach was applied to the budget process. He and his advisers were determined to use his election to rule the government, and that meant filling important positions only with people who firmly believed in the political agenda of the president. In this way a political agenda came out looking very much like the budget systems of earlier presidents — imposed from above, resisted by the rank and file within agencies, and not shared with the Congress. Yet by acting quickly his first year, before his appointees started to adopt some of the views of their respective agencies and before Congress could establish its own agenda on the budget, Reagan was able to enact more changes in the budget than any postwar president. (Some of these specific changes are discussed in Chapter 12.) For at least the first year, his budget nonsystem worked.

In subsequent years, Reagan was not much more successful than previous presidents in getting his way with the budget. Congress reasserted its role in making budgets, and many of Reagan's appointees adopted values from their agencies, rather than imposing his from the top down. The experience is instructive. His approach, although more openly political, was not more public. Subsequent presidents are sure to learn the lesson of how to enact changes quickly, but no one has seriously asked whether a more political and more public method of budgeting might be a more democratic way to run a government.

Gramm-Rudman-Hollings

In late 1985, the Congress passed and President Reagan signed the Gramm-Rudman-Hollings bill. The bill was a response to the pattern of unprecedented budget deficits under Reagan. The government was spending much more than it was taking in. Indeed, the government spent an average of $200,000,000,000 ($200 billion) more than it took in during five of the first six Reagan years. The Congress was unwilling to make large spending cuts, the president kept asking for more money for defense, and neither was willing to raise taxes in order to get additional revenue.

By cutting taxes, maintaining domestic spending, and increasing military spending, Reagan and Congress doubled our national debt in five years. In 1986, the debt surpassed $2 trillion. Gramm-Rudman-Hollings called for a way to balance the budget in five years.

The central part of the law is this: If, by August, it is clear to the Office of Management and Budget (the executive branch budget office), and the Congressional Budget Office that taxing and spending decisions would not yield a prescribed lower deficit, then the Comptroller General (head of the General Accounting Office) would certify a plan to cut spending "across the board." In effect, the budget cuts would be made by neither the president nor the Congress. An impartial, nonelected third party would make what would be clearly unpopular spending cuts. It would take much of the politics out of the budgetary process and make it impossible for the voting public to assign responsibility for any cuts they thought were wrong.

The Gramm-Rudman-Hollings law never got through an August intact. The heart of the law, the automatic cuts by the Comptroller General, were declared unconstitutional by the Supreme Court. The court ruled that the Constitution placed the responsibility for the budget in Congress and the president. If hard decisions are to be made, they must be made by elected officials.

We can appreciate the reasoning of the Supreme Court. Yet, reformers on the other side of the question have their point. During the first two years of the Gramm-Rudman-Hollings budget process, Congress and the president each "fudged" the numbers in their budgets to avoid making tough cuts themselves. For example, Conrail, the government-organized railroad, was to be sold. Money from the sale, which was not completed in either fiscal year, was counted in both budgets. The idea of professional independence is appealing to people fed up with such political games. The idea, however, is a flight from politics and an embrace of technocracy.

Approaches to Budgeting — A Summary

It is likely that, at least for a time, we have seen the end of budget "systems" that promise to deliver efficiency, effectiveness, and rationality.[12] The evolution of systems offers important lessons for what is at stake in budgeting and how people have tried to control administration through the budget process.

We began the chapter with a summary of the many functions a budget fulfills. To put it simply, budgets are the vehicle for deciding what is most important to us, and how we shall live, but in an administrative way. Through budgets, officials try to gain control of administration, and thereby gain control of what is important to us and how we shall live. The formal budget systems do this in the name of rationality. The more explicit political approach to control does this in the name of electoral "mandates." Both methods have an administrative sense of what government is about. Both operate to have administration do a little more, and the public a little less.

It is not at all difficult to observe directly this administrative dominance of budgeting in governments. Attendance at budget hearings and budget ordinance meetings of city and county councils illustrates the same trends. For instance, if the government uses a line-item budget, discussions of the budgets concentrate on defining what each of the line items contains and why they differ from previous years. For governments using performance budgets, the discussions tend to focus on why the cost per units have changed. For governments using program budgets, comparisons of amounts used to complete packages of objectives tend to dominate the conversations.

The budget formats are administrative devices, yet they truly dominate the consideration of public purposes. A look at the complexities of budget behavior may help us understand why.

Budget Behavior

The prevailing understanding of budget behavior helps us understand why rational systems seldom work and why a deliberate application of political power does seem to work. That understanding is what Aaron Wildavsky calls *incrementalism*.[13] In the fights over which is the best way to make a budget in the United States, it is always incrementalism versus every other method.

The following are the traits of a budget made incrementally. The emphasis is on congressional behavior, and each term is defined from that perspective.

> Budgeting is *specialized* (or *fragmented*). Basically, that means that the congressional committees are specialized in order to handle particular parts of the budget. A congressional subcommittee will know more about one item in the budget than any other subcommittee. They will be protective of their interests.
>
> Budgeting is *historical*. Those on appropriation committees serve on them for long periods of time. They become identified with and attached to the various programs they fund. Every budget is full of this history.
>
> Budgeting is treated *as if it were nonprogrammatic*. This does not mean that people in Congress are not interested in programs. Indeed, they are. But, most budgets most of the time are budgets of ongoing programs. The large majority of budget work is done on the margins, the differences from what was done the previous year, and is made in terms of adjustments of needs, politics, and power. This is what causes so much distress to the PPBSers and the ZBBers.
>
> Budgeting is *repetitive*. According to Wildavsky, problems in budgets are never solved, they are merely settled for a fiscal year only to return the following year. The problems are treated in this way each year until they are worn down or eclipsed by other, more pressing, problems. Over the years, budgets seem to look alike.

Budgeting is *sequential*. All this means is that those in Congress can only try to deal with a limited number of problems in any one budget, meaning that there is intensive review of a handful of programs and the other programs are simply carried on for another fiscal year. Congress, like people in other organizations, only has so much time, brain power, and energy to consider things.

There is something appealing about incrementalism. It appeals to one's notion of what is possible and how human beings really act. There is a certain foolishness in dismissing all of the work of previous budgets and beginning anew every year. That amount taken mostly for granted becomes the "base" for the next year's consideration. Individuals are often able to do their best work when considering a small portion of something that they know well. This translates into some predictable strategies on the part of people involved in the budget process (see Box 11.6). Also, incrementalism appeals to those who are interested in how the public gets heard in the political system. If nothing else, incrementalism is a statement of the deals, bargains, adjustments, and incoherence that characterize our political system. Although that may not be efficient management, it at least represents the public in public administration.

That is not to say that incrementalism is without problems. Indeed, incrementalism focuses too much on the Congress and not enough on the president; too much on the politics of the increment and not enough on the base; and finally, too much on the informal and not enough on the formal methods of coordination. There can be, and indeed there are, studies that try to solve some of the problems in incrementalism. But it should be noted that they do not disprove incrementalism as much as fill out the reality of the budgetary process.[14]

It is, for example, possible to ask meaningful, nonincremental questions about any budget. Any student, citizen, or public official can do so. As an exercise, look at any part of a budget from your city or county and ask these questions:

1. Where is the money coming from?
2. Where is the money going to (where is it spent)?
3. What results will be achieved there?
4. How will we know if the results have been achieved?
5. Is there a way to determine how well results have been achieved (the productivity question)?

A budget that is properly prepared should offer clear answers to these questions, but that does not mean this logic drives the creation of budgets. On any item in the budget, find out the politics of its funding. There you are likely to see incrementalism at work.

> **BOX 11.6** Incremental Budget Games
>
> | *Strategies Used by Spenders* | *Strategies Used by Cutters* |
> |---|---|
> | Pad, always ask for more, yet don't be outlandish. | Always cut something. |
> | Spend it or lose it. | New or expanded activities are prime targets. |
> | Structure presentations to emphasize best and minimize worse aspects. | If possible, delay so that some savings can be achieved this year. |
> | Round to nearest large figure (best if upward). | Challenge workload data, soundness of other program data. |
> | Use different categories than last year. | Put responsibilities for cutting on requesters by specifying items that may not be cut. |
> | Shift money among funds. | |
> | Emphasize work backlogs that can be eased through more money; refer to national standards of similar programs. | Concentrate on apparent frills to judge familiarity of requester with entire budget. |
> | Make new activities look like old activities. | Argue that a small amount is available for new ideas; spark competition among agencies. |
> | Offer popular programs to cutters; in any event put responsibility for cutting benefits to groups squarely on them. | |
>
> *Source:* Adapted from Aaron Wildavsky, *The Politics of the Budgetary Process*, 3d ed. (Boston: Little, Brown, 1980).

Congressional Budgeting

Although most of the news we read and hear about budgeting centers on presidential proposals and congressional reactions, there is a congressional process that is more than merely receiving and reacting to an executive budget.[15]

The history of the change began in 1972 and 1973. In those two years, President Nixon refused to spend all of the funds that Congress authorized him to spend. He impounded congressional appropriations in order to act on his own spending priorities. At that point, it was also clear that the budget process was not set up to relate spending to fiscal policy and that much of what Congress did was simply reaffirm long-term commitments. The Congress was also angry at Nixon over Watergate and decided it had to exert more influence in the important matter of the budget.

In 1974, Congress passed, and Nixon signed, the Congressional Budget and Impoundment Control Act. The act established the House and Senate Budget Committees, and the Congressional Budget Office (CBO). By looking at the CBO, we can see what kind of questions the Congress wanted answered about the budgetary process. The CBO was created to provide Congress with information comparing enacted legislation and the executive budget. It also projected the impact of taxing and spending bills, five-year projections on the impact of authorization bills, alternative budgets, and various analyses of federal policies. The timing of such reports coincides with the presentation of the budget by the president.

What is clear is that as the budget became more central to all that the government does, it was necessary for the Congress to do more than just react. The budget committees of each house of Congress are important, because they can provide a much more comprehensive sense of the budget than any single committee or subcommittee. They are not supposed to be as specialized, fragmented, nonprogrammatic, repetitive, or sequential, to use the terms introduced earlier.

Yet the effects of these reforms have been mixed. Although the Congress does have a better picture of how the last budget passed is doing and is better able to recognize new spending proposals, the public and many members of Congress find the whole process confusing. As Louis Fisher writes, "the risks are high when an inherently decentralized Congress tries to imitate the president by producing a budget."[16] The things Congress is supposed to do — to deliberate problems and policies — are displaced by administrative procedures that aim at competing with the administrative arm of the presidency. So far, more administration has not produced better budgets.

Before leaving the process of budget making, there is one more overriding fact that needs to be remembered. The key people in the making and passing of the budget are members of political parties, and their continued participation in the process depends on their party (or themselves) being elected. That means that party politics, and ideology, runs through all phases of the process. No matter which method of budgeting is used, the bottom line is political preference and political survival. To read the news is to read about presidential, House, Senate, Republican, and Democratic budget proposals.

BOX 11.7 The Congressional Budget Process (as revised by Balanced Budget and Emergency Deficit Control Act of 1985)

Approximate Timing ▼		
January	President submits budget (first Monday after January 3)	
February	CBO Report to Budget Committees (February 15)	Committees submit views and estimates (February 25)
Adoption of Budget Resolution		
March	Budget Committees hold hearings, begin markup of budget resolution	
April	Senate Budget Committee reports resolution (April 1)	House and Senate consider first budget resolution
	Congress completes action on budget resolution (April 15) — Deficits may not exceed specified levels	Conference action and adoption of conference report
		Conference report joint explanatory statement allocates total levels of budget authority and outlays among committees
May	All committees must promptly make allocations to subcommittees	
Reconciliation		
June	Congress completes action on reconciliation bill instructing committees to alter authorizations and appropriations (June 10)	House completes action on appropriations bills (June 30)

Approval of Spending Bills	
July	Congress may not recess for Independence Day unless action completed on all spending bills and reconciliation
Mandatory Deficit Reduction — if Necessary	
August	CBO and OMB issue "snapshot" of economic indicators, revenue, and spending projections to determine if automatic cuts are needed (August 15)
	OMB and CBO report to GAO on content of sequestering order (August 20)
September	President issues sequestering order based on GAO report (September 1)
Sequestering Order Takes Effect	
October *Fiscal year begins (October 1)*	CBO and OMB issue revised reports reflecting additional congressional action (October 5)
	Congress must approve sequestered cuts
	GAO issues revised sequester report to president (October 10)
	Final sequestering order takes effect (October 15)
November	GAO monitors compliance with sequestering order and issues report (November 15)

Source: Reprinted with permission from *Budgetary Politics*, by Lance T. Leloup, 3d ed. (King's Court Communications, Brunswick, Ohio, 1986).

Big Money

In 1987, the United States government spent more than $1 trillion: $1,088,000,000,000. Of course, they took in about $200 billion less than that. In the same year, the states spent over $230,000,000,000, while local governments spent almost twice that amount. Put in a different way, governments in the United States, in 1987, spent about $57,000 each second, or a bit under $3.5 million each minute. It is fair to say that it is probably impossible to relate to budgets on a human level. The numbers have nothing in common with ordinary experience.

It is also reasonable to say that what the government does is so wide-ranging that simple lists cannot do it justice. From tracking tropical storms to funding research for space laser rays to providing medical care for veterans to building the roads to get to the care, all levels of government provide services. All of these services are packaged in one or another budget. The fight for those budget lines takes a remarkable amount of time on the part of managers, and a great deal of time and money on the part of groups who want their share.

This process of administrators, pressure groups, and politicians fighting over funding is the ongoing activity of our governmental system. It is the intrusion of the public on the public administration. It is the fight of experts who hold different expert opinions; it is the struggle of administrators to gain and then to keep power; it is the life blood of the politician who wants to provide for his or her constituents.

The stakes are big for those involved, and the absolute stakes in terms of money and the financial well-being of the nation are even larger. During the past several years one gets the feeling that something is out of control. President Reagan has submitted eight budgets. As a columnist wrote, the Congress has approved every balanced budget the president has submitted, the joke being that Reagan has submitted budgets with deficits which range from $45 billion to over $200 billion.

To make up for those deficits, adding to a national debt of over $2.5 trillion as we enter 1988, we must borrow money. The interest on the money borrowed is a serious amount of the nation's expenditure, approaching 15 percent of annual expenditures. Foreign countries — especially Japan — are loaning us billions of dollars. There are several distinct ways of understanding how to get out of this economic mess. Each way is related to how the budget gets made.

Economic Theories

There are three economic theories that we will review. These reviews are not complete, but they will give a sense of the policies that would be encouraged in any particular budget. The theories are (1) monetarism, (2) conventional economics developed by John Maynard Keynes, and (3) supply-side economics. The monetarists and the supply-siders are first cousins; Reaganomics is something of a mix of the two. Democrats are generally Keynesians, in one form or another.

Monetarism

Monetarists believe that economic demand is determined, in large part, by the supply of money. It follows that the regulation of money is the key ingredient in maintaining a healthy economy. The monetarists argue that the current problems of the economy have been caused by too much government activity.

The activity of the government — receiving and spending all those billions of dollars a year — distorts the activities of the free market. It is the monetarists' contention that any government policy is *always* reactive; it always lags behind what is actually gong on in the economy. Because of this lag, the fiscal policy of the government, the taxing and spending embodied in budgets, simply serves to accentuate the boom and bust cycle of the American economy.

The monetarists have several strong recommendations. They want the government to reduce its participation in the economy drastically. The job of the government would be to concentrate on reducing inflation, which is caused by the too rapid growth in the money supply. The Federal Reserve Board (see the discussion in Chapter 1) is the government agency whose job is to regulate the money supply.

The ideal monetary policy would be to maintain a steady growth of the money supply that individuals and businesses could count on — and that means making it automatic instead of having it controlled by a government agency. The idea is that economic growth would be keyed to increased productivity instead of an increased money supply. The monetarists have a great faith in the free workings of the economy.

Keynesianism

The *Keynesians* have no such faith in the free workings of the economy; nor do they have much faith in the singular power of monetary policy. The Keynesians believe that a healthy economy revolves around the demand for goods and services, and the demand for goods and services depends on how much money people have to spend. If too much is spent on a given supply of goods, there will be inflation. If too much money is saved, there will be reduced demand and recession.

The job of government, then, is to have a fiscal policy that will ensure a high level of demand to keep people working and consuming, and a low interest rate which will keep people from saving too much. The government can do these things by increasing spending, increasing public works, decreasing taxes, setting interest rates low, and the like. As you can see, these attitudes get translated directly into budget lines at all levels of government.

The Keynesians believe that if left to itself, the free workings of the economy will lead to profound periods of boom and bust and will eventually lead to monopoly capitalism. Indeed, the cycles of booms and busts were the economic rule until the 1930s. During the thirties, the government began to become more and more involved in economic matters.

One should remember that the government has *always* been involved in the economy. Ours has never been an economy totally free of government policy and actions, but it was not until the 1930s that government policies were meant to make a major difference in the economic life of the country. The most important element for the Keynesians is that the economy remain healthy — if the price is an unbalanced budget, then that is the price to be paid.

Supply-Side Economics

The *supply-siders* are the newest of the theorists, and Reagan is really the first supply-side president. Like the monetarists, the supply-siders believe in market principles; that is, if left alone the free market will work just fine. It has been Reagan's constant theme that if government taxing and spending are cut, and if government regulation of the economy is reduced, then prosperity *must* follow. The long version of this belief system can be found in *Wealth and Poverty*, by George Gilder.[17]

One element of supply-side belief is the Laffer curve, depicted in our discussion of taxation in Chapter 12. The curve is an explanation of the relationship between economic activity and taxing. Economist Arthur Laffer claims that there is a point at which taxing is so high that economic incentives are diminished. What the government must do is cut taxes to fund only the most essential governmental activities. As taxes decrease, economic incentives increase (thus supplies become more plentiful, hence the name "supply-siders"), the economy becomes stronger, and everyone is more prosperous.

During his first years, Reagan did make supply-side arguments, and he did cut taxes and the economy did improve. Yet, during those same years we have had the biggest deficits in our history. Cutting taxes meant cutting revenues; it did not seem to translate into balanced budgets.

Economists disagree with just what the Laffer curve proves. While critics grant the truism that a 100 percent tax will leave no incentives for anyone to work, they argue that it proves nothing more than that. There is no magic point at which people will work more if taxes are cut. Other critics of supply-siders say that the tax breaks of the Reagan programs were just so many examples of Republicans serving their traditional interests. The biggest tax breaks were for businesses (although this changed somewhat in the tax law which took effect in 1987), under the theory that if businesses were profitable then all individuals would be better off. The result of the tax breaks is that the rich increased their wealth and the poor stayed poor.

The trickle-down theory of wealth did not operate during the first half of the 1980s. Also, the president's budget was not wholly a supply-side document. Although it is true that he has cut much from education and the social services (which is what supply-siders should do), he has increased the budget for the defense department each year. The increase in defense was so un-supply-side-like, that OMB chief David Stockman constantly opposed it. Like most of us, Reagan really wants it both ways: He wants to economize (cut spending on programs he does not support) while being progressive (increase spending on programs he does like). In

---

BOX 11.8 Supply-Siders and the Politics of Getting Elected

Too few people appreciate the political brilliance of the supply-side budget theory. To understand it, we have to go back to the traditional fights over the use of fiscal and monetary policies.

Since World War II the Republicans and the Democrats have accepted the categories of Keynes — that demand is the primary influence on the health of the economy. That left the parties in a politically unpopular deadlock: The Democrats were more willing to increase demand through government spending, and thereby increase inflation, in order to fight unemployment. The Republicans were more willing to limit demand, and thereby increase unemployment, in order to fight inflation. The prevailing theory left citizens in the role of choosing between two evils.

The supply-side argument freed Republicans from the deadlock. They can make the following claim: Our theory allows us to cut your taxes, cut government spending, and we will thereby stimulate the economy. Inflation is mostly a monetary phenomenon (which means it is not our fault when it happens).

With these claims, Reagan won election — twice — by claiming that he would cut taxes, cut government spending, balance the budget, and improve our defenses. Republicans in the Congress, and in state and local governments, experienced a resurgence on the strength of the claims.

budgetary terms, the difference between a Reagan and a Carter is that each likes different things.

As we have seen, it is difficult to make radical changes in the budget. Yet, during his term in office, Reagan has incrementally changed some spending priorities. With enough incremental budget changes, programs eventually are changed beyond recognition. Although Reagan set out to eliminate the Department of Education, he was unable to do it, but he was able to reduce how much the department was able to spend.

In an earlier chapter, we discussed the effect of presidential beliefs on the personnel working in the public administration. It was shown that President Reagan, who is antigovernmental action in many areas, appointed people to high-level positions who did not believe in the work of the agencies in which they were working. With the budget, we can see another example of the power of belief on government. The budget is being used to support certain parts of the economy and to pull back support from certain groups of citizens.

Budget Making in Two Contexts

To present different theories about how budgets are or should be made, and then to leave it at that, is of little service to the reader. There are at least two levels of understanding that should be mentioned in order to think in some intelligent way about budget making.

The first has to do with economics. Each of the budget theories is based on a broader sense of economics and the state. Some believe in the free play of the market, others believe that we act "rationally" and we therefore need a rational budget-making process.

It is important to remember that human beings are unpredictable. Or, to put it in an even more accurate way, although most human beings act rationally, their beliefs often begin at different places and often seek different ends. Economic theories are sophisticated statements of belief in how most people will act most of the time. So, when great claims are made for certain budget choices based on economic theory, remember that what you are hearing is not truth so much as faith.

The second context has to do with politics in the United States. When the government of the United States (or any state, or town, or city) makes a budget, it does so for a plural society. There are hundreds of millions of Americans, and those budgets affect each of us. The case can be made that the more we have to say about the process, the better off we will be as a society.

But, this statement runs contrary to the fact that we want our public organizations to operate under the principles of efficiency, effectiveness, and professionalism. Those public administrators *should* know more about running the agencies of the country than we do. If that is so — and we know it is — then why should not administrators be in charge of budget making? Why should not the principles of business be applied to the business of public administration?

Budgets, and the budgetary process, give us a good look into one aspect of the public-administrative split. Budgets seem to give us a clear way to measure efficiency — money. We can see how much is being spent on what, how the spending compares with other agency spending, and what is achieved for what is spent. In the recent past there have been budgetary processes (PPBS and ZBB) that have tried to focus on that kind of efficiency.

But budgets are also the most political of documents. They represent how we spend our money. They give a sense of what priorities we have; of what we think is important enough to encourage and support. In no small way they represent the degree of power held by the president and influential members of Congress.

We have, then, two different ideas of efficiency when we discuss the budget and the process of producing one. One idea is administrative; it is a businesslike kind of efficiency in which money is the bottom line. The other kind of efficiency is about the wants of citizens and making certain that they are taken care of. The *cost* of integration or of making buildings accessible to the handicapped are not central issues. The fact is that these two things are critical to the health of the body politic and must be done. By understanding the budgetary process, we can better understand the split between public and administration.

SUMMARY

In this chapter, we discussed the different roles the budgetary process plays in government, and the various ways in which budgets are made.

Basically, we can look at the budget in terms of at least six different functions. (1) It is a way to manage the economy. (2) It is a way to choose priorities. (3) It is a way to produce a mix of programs to help balance the needs of the public and private sectors. (4) It is a way to review and control what agencies do. (5) It is a form of accounting. (6) It is a yearly struggle for power. In many ways, budgeting is at the heart of the business of government, and everyone in government is concerned with the budgetary process.

In earlier times, when government was small, the first reform was line-item budgeting, then came performance budgeting. As we moved into more current times — and much bigger budgets — we got Planning-Programming-Budgeting System. PPBS was an attempt to rationalize the budgeting process. It was tried extensively during the 1960s, and essentially failed.

Richard Nixon tried management by objectives (MBO), which was an effort to have policymakers and managers work together to define goals and make budgets. This effort also failed. Jimmy Carter brought the Zero-Base Budget system (ZBB) to Washington from his home state of Georgia. In theory, every year every agency would have to begin at zero and justify every dollar spent. This system, too, failed.

What we found was that no matter how much rationality was proposed, it seemed as if budgets were made incrementally. Incrementalism, basically, describes a method of budget making which goes on over time, is sequential, fragmented, repetitive, and nonprogrammatic. Budgeting at the national level is not, nor has it ever been, rational.

There are various economic theories which underlie the reasons for budgetary decisions. Monetarists believe that economic demand is determined in large part by the supply of money. They are in favor of less government activity. The Keynesians believe that it is the job of government to have a fiscal policy which will ensure a high level of consumer demand, and a low interest rate which will keep people from saving too much. The Keynesians believe in an active government. The supply-siders believe in market principles; that, if left alone, the free market will work just fine. Naturally, they believe in less government activity.

Given the debates on both the basic grounds on which the budget should be made, and the very process of budget making, it is no surprise that the budget is often at the center of our administrative and political fighting. It seems to center on questions of economic faith as well as on the equally important questions of business efficiency versus political efficiency. To understand the budgetary process is to understand better the split between public and administration.

NOTES

1. Hannah Arendt, *The Human Condition* (Garden City, N.Y.: Doubleday, 1959).

2. Joseph White, "Much Ado about Everything: Making Sense of Federal Budgeting," *Public Administration Review* 45, no. 5 (September/October 1985), pp. 623–630.

3. An excellent brief history of federal budgeting is contained in Louis Fischer, *Presidential Spending Power* (Princeton, N.J.: Princeton University Press, 1975).

4. C. David Billings, "Highlights of American Budgeting: The Evolutionary Synthesis of Fiscal Management," in Robert Golembiewski

and Frank Gibson, eds., *Readings in Public Administration,* 4th ed. (Boston: Houghton Mifflin Co., 1983), p. 178.

5. Alain C. Enthoven, "The Systems-Analysis Approach," in Louis C. Gawthrop, ed., *The Administrative Process and Democratic Theory* (Boston: Houghton Mifflin Co., 1970), pp. 277–279. An excellent summary of the history and procedures of PPBS is in Fremont J. Lyden and Ernest G. Miller, eds., *Planning Programming Budgeting: A Systems Approach to Management* (Chicago: Markham Publishing, 1968). For a critique of PPBS, see Leonard Merewitz and Stephen H. Sosnick, *The Budget's New Clothes* (Chicago: Markham Publishing, 1971).

6. Gawthrop, op. cit., p. 302.

7. See Alan Schick, "A Death in the Bureaucracy: The Demise of Federal PBB," *Public Administration Review* 33, no. 2 (March/April 1973), pp. 146–156.

8. See Peter Drucker, *Management* (New York: Harper & Row, 1974).

9. See the symposium on MBO in *Public Administration Review* 36, no. 1 (January/February 1976), pp. 1–45. See also Richard Rose, "Implementation and Evaporation: The Record of MBO," *Public Administration Review* 37, no. 1 (January/February 1977), pp. 64–71.

10. The Office of Management and Budget description of ZBB is evaluated and reproduced in *Budget Formulation: Many Approaches Work but Some Improvements Are Needed,* U.S. General Accounting Office PAD-80-31 (974500). See also Alan Schick, "The Road from ZBB," *Public Administration Review* 38, no. 3 (March/April 1978), pp. 177–180; and Robert N. Anthony, "Zero-Base Budgeting Is a Fraud," *Wall Street Journal,* April 27, 1977, p. 1.

11. An unusually candid assessment of those days, must reading for students of the budgetary process and public administration, is William Grieder, "The Education of David Stockman," *Atlantic Monthly,* December 1981, pp. 27–54. See also Gregory B. Mills and John L. Palmer, *Federal Budget Policy in the 1980s* (Washington, D.C.: The Urban Institute Press, 1984).

12. There are, of course, attempts to develop and sell new systems. See Michael Babunakis, *Budget Reform for Government: A Comprehensive Allocation and Management System* (Westport, Conn.: Quorum Books, 1982); and the review of Babunakis's book by Dick W. Olufs, *Public Budgeting and Finance* 4, no. 4 (Winter 1984), pp. 100–102.

13. Incrementalism in budgeting is best described by Aaron Wildavsky, *The Politics of the Budgetary Process,* 4th ed. (Boston: Little, Brown, 1984).

14. See Mark S. Kamlet and David C. Mowery, "The Budgetary Base in Federal Resource Allocation," *American Journal of Political Science* 24, no. 4 (November 1980).

15. See Allan Schick, *Congress and Money* (Washington, D.C.: Urban Institute Press, 1980); and Louis Fischer, "Ten Years of the Budget Act: Still Searching for Controls," *Public Budgeting and Finance* 5, no. 3 (Autumn 1985), pp. 3–28.
16. Fischer, op. cit., p. 25.
17. George Gilder, *Wealth and Poverty* (New York: Basic Books, 1981). The book deserves serious attention, particularly its description of the society that underlies supply-side theory.

CHAPTER TWELVE

Fiscal Administration

> Several of the offices of a state, if not all, handle large amounts of public money. There must accordingly be a separate office for finance ... which receives and audits the accounts of other offices, and is only concerned with this one function.
>
> — *Aristotle,* Politics *(ca.* B.C. *328)*

A classic definition of politics defines it in terms of resources; i.e., *politics* is the way we determine who gets what, when, and why. Although certainly not the only and maybe not even the best way to understand politics, this definition helps to focus our attention; but for students of public administration, the definition stops about where it should start. Many of the real problems of administration begin *after* the budgets are made, the resources tapped, and the money allocated. The public's attention stops with the passage of the budget; the public administrator's job begins at that point. This chapter is about fiscal administration; that is, about what happens in public organizations when they acquire and spend money.

Revenues: The Other Half of the Budget

Governments collect a great deal of money from citizens. In fiscal year 1986, per capita taxes were $3340 at the national level, $973 at the state level, and $1473 at the local level. Table 12.1 lists the amounts of various taxes paid over the last decade. The numbers are large and growing larger. As large as the numbers may be, they are not large enough. We spend more than we get. The national government has run a deficit in the neighborhood of $200,000,000,000 ($200 billion) for several years. In spite of antideficiency laws (legal prohibitions against deficits), states and local governments ran a collective deficit of almost $4 billion in fiscal year 1986.[1]

These numbers suggest there are several problems, and several decisions to make, about the revenue side of budgets. The critical questions are these: (1) How much tax revenue should be collected? (2) Who should pay the taxes? (3) What forms of taxation are appropriate? (4) What are the other, nontax sources of revenue? Each of these will be discussed here.

TABLE 12.1 What the Taxpayers Paid, 1975–1985 (all figures in current $billions)

STATE AND LOCAL TAXES

Year	Income	Sales	Property	Total*
1985	73.6	128.9	104.1	575.5
1984	67.7	120.0	98.5	539.8
1983	58.3	106.6	91.9	487.7
1982	51.8	95.5	85.1	439.1
1981	47.9	90.4	75.1	418.1
1980	44.9	82.9	67.5	384.0
1979	38.8	76.9	64.4	351.2
1978	35.5	71.3	63.2	331.0
1977	30.9	63.9	62.4	298.8
1976	26.8	57.3	57.6	264.7
1975	22.8	51.4	52.3	235.7

FEDERAL TAXES

Year	Income	Payroll	Total*
1985	343.7	309.9	785.4
1984	304.9	283.6	725.1
1983	288.6	252.2	658.1
1982	296.7	217.9	617.4
1981	291.4	204.5	627.0
1980	251.0	172.2	540.8
1979	225.7	159.0	494.4
1978	189.4	137.0	432.1
1977	162.3	118.9	375.4
1976	141.6	105.7	332.3
1975	120.6	94.2	286.9

Source: Survey of Current Business, U.S. Department of Commerce, various years.

*Totals include other taxes not listed, such as excise, corporate, and estate taxes.

How Much Tax Revenue Should Be Collected?

One of the jobs of each government is to judge how much money will be spent in a particular fiscal year. A great many variables go into the calculation. Governments must factor in any surplus on hand or any deficit; they must also calculate the amount of revenue available from taxes, fees, intergovernmental transfers, and the like. This involves guessing what the economy will be like, the effects of various possible crises, and the needs of the citizens. We will return to some of the problems of forecasting later in the chapter.

Who Should Pay the Taxes?

Although most people will agree that a tax system should be fair and equitable, they will strongly disagree on what that means. Several principles can guide choices about who should pay taxes, called "tax incidence."[2]

BENEFITS. Should people pay based on the benefits received from government services? This idea adapts the logic of markets to governmental finance. What could be more fair, the argument goes, than to have each pay in proportion to their benefits from government? The relationship between citizen and government takes on a clear, contractual basis. Yet the practical details of taxing according to benefits received are exceedingly complex, and so such taxes are extremely rare. Most governmental services are in some degree collective goods. In the case of national defense, it is not possible to divide the costs and benefits accrued to different citizens, and one person's "consumption" of national defense does not subtract from the share available to others. In many local government services that are not pure collective goods, such as police services and primary education, there are considerable "neighborhood effects" that all citizens can enjoy. Moreover, what would we do with all the various welfare programs that exist *because* a person or a family has no money?

Attempts to measure the distribution of governmental benefits falter over assumptions about the distribution of collective benefits.[3] Benefits from national defense, for instance, could be assigned according to different assumptions: (a) on the basis of the number of households protected, or (b) on the basis of the amount of wealth protected. The former assumption would show the poorer people in society reap most of the benefits; the latter would show the rich reap most of the benefits. Beyond these problems, it is difficult to allocate taxes according to benefits received because of democracy. Lacking some automatic mechanism for assigning the costs of government services, we must rely on the decisions of people working in democratic institutions. Equity and justice are political terms over which reasonable people disagree. The outcomes of political compromise usually involve shifting money from one group of citizens to another and do not at all resemble the outcomes of market transactions.

ABILITY TO PAY. Should people pay according to their ability to bear the burden? If we accept income as a measure of economic capacity, it becomes possible to tax on that basis. Ability to pay lends itself to considerations of equity as well. It is possible to distinguish two forms of equity. Horizontal equity consists of treating those with similar income similarly. All persons earning $50,000 per year should pay the same in taxes under a scheme ensuring horizontal equity. Vertical equity refers to assigning different tax burdens to persons of different incomes. A progressive tax takes a higher proportion of higher incomes and is consistent with the idea of vertical equity. A regressive tax takes a higher proportion of lower incomes. One problem with using ability to pay as the criterion for tax payments is that people disagree on what constitutes ability to pay. In addition to income, it is possible to tax consumption or wealth. Differences between types of taxes are discussed below.

How well does the U.S. tax system follow the ability-to-pay criterion? Table 12.2 shows tax incidence by population tenths and the lowest fifth. The numbers show that, overall, the tax system is neither progressive nor regressive. The mildly progressive federal income tax is countered by regressive payroll and consumption taxes. It is difficult to argue that the U.S. tax system follows any clear principle of equity.

In recent battles over taxation, reformers claimed that U.S. citizens are overtaxed and that we have approached some limit of permissible taxation. Have we exceeded our ability to pay taxes? Table 12.2 shows the approximate percentage of income going to all levels of government. How does this compare with other industrial democracies?[4] With the exception of Japan, our main trading partners all meet or exceed the U.S. figures for percentage of national product going to government. The northern European countries, including Scandinavia, often exceed the U.S. proportion by 10 percent or more. The point is there is no objective sense of "overload" or limit on ability to pay. The limit is rather a function of political traditions, colored heavily by contemporary political issues.

ADMINISTRATIVE EFFICIENCY. Should taxes be assessed on the basis of the costs of collection? Income taxes are generally the most progressive, but they are costly to collect. Each citizen must keep track of his or her income and eligible deductions and file a report at the end of the year; each employer must keep similar records, withhold taxes each payroll, and transmit the withheld taxes to government; the government must keep track of withholding transactions, review all reports of citizens and employers, and adjust individual accounts for refunds and taxes due. In addition, income taxes are highly visible to citizens. Each year they are pointedly reminded of just how much government costs.

Sales taxes, by comparison, are much simpler to collect. Retail outlets already have to keep track of their total sales, so it is a simple matter for them to add a percentage to each sale and mail the proceeds to govern-

TABLE 12.2 Tax Incidence in the United States (percentage of personal income going to taxes*)

POPULATION DECILES	ALL FEDERAL TAXES	FEDERAL INCOME TAX	FEDERAL PAYROLL TAX	ALL STATE & LOCAL TAXES	SALES & EXCISE TAXES	TOTAL ALL TAXES
1 & 2	19.2	2.8	8.8	12.1	5.6	31.5
3	20.8	5.1	8.8	10.0	4.4	30.8
4	20.8	7.1	9.3	9.7	3.6	30.5
5	23.3	8.1	10.0	11.0	3.5	34.3
6	25.8	10.9	10.1	11.8	3.4	37.6
7	25.1	11.0	9.5	12.7	3.4	37.8
8	23.7	11.3	8.4	11.7	3.0	35.4
9	23.1	11.7	7.3	12.1	3.0	35.2
10	22.9	13.0	4.4	11.2	2.1	34.1
All	23.3	10.7	7.5	11.5	3.0	34.8

Source: R. A. Musgrave and P. B. Musgrave, *Public Finance in Theory and Practice*, 4th ed., © 1984, pp. 257, 267. Reprinted by permission of McGraw-Hill Book Company.

*All figures are percentages of total personal income, using definitions employed by U.S. Commerce Department *Consumer Expenditure Survey*, 1978, Bulletin 1992.

ment on a quarterly basis. The smart money managers in business will recoup some of their administrative costs through interest on deposits held until payment is due. By using sales taxes, the government has a much smaller and simpler tax collection operation, and citizens pay out taxes in a large number of small transactions. From the standpoint of easing the pain of taxation, consumption takes rank high.

Another side of administrative efficiency with regard to taxation is the stability of various taxes.[5] The income tax tends to produce a predictable amount of revenue regardless of economic fluctuation, while consumption taxes are notoriously unstable. Box 12.1 describes one state's problem with sales tax revenue during a regional depression. A final efficiency consideration concerns the way a particular tax affects citizen perceptions of government. For example, in the 1980s the Reagan administration consistently argued that corporations do not really pay taxes, since corporate taxes are passed along to consumers in the form of higher prices. Raising corporate taxes, they claimed, only raised prices. In several speeches, Reagan complained that corporate earnings were "double-taxed," that is, taxed once when earned by the corporation and taxed again when paid to the stockholder. Reagan administration tax proposals would have virtually abolished corporate income taxes. But, most citizens did not share this benign view of corporations. The popular view of corporations is that they are rich, powerful, and privileged forces in the economy. To absolve corporations from taxes would seriously undermine citizen confidence in the fairness of government. National tax reform in 1986 included substantial increases in business taxes, while the tax rates of the highest income earners were cut dramatically.

ECONOMIC EFFECTS. Taxes change peoples' economic behavior. Governments often propose to do this in desirable ways through taxation. "Sin" taxes, for instance, have commonly been seen as politically palatable as well as useful for discouraging smoking, drinking, and gambling. The largest recent taxation proposal to consider economic effects is that of the supply-siders in the Reagan administration. Stated simply, the claim is that high tax rates discourage individuals from working hard to earn more money. Since individuals will earn less than their potential, high tax rates actually reduce tax revenues. Lower rates encourage people to earn more, and so more income can be taxed. This relationship between tax rates and revenues is illustrated in the "Laffer curve," named for its creator, economist Arthur Laffer. (See Figure 12.1.) If the tax rate is 0 percent, obviously no tax revenue will be collected. Similarly, if the tax rate is 100 percent, no tax revenue will be collected. There is simply no incentive to earn money, and so people will stay home. There is some rate between these extremes, point R_o in Figure 12.1, where tax revenue is optimized. Supply-siders claim that tax rates are now too high, say at rate R_n. Lowering the rate from R_n to R_o will cause tax revenues to rise from T_n to T_o. An added

BOX 12.1   Financial Instability

Most governments have a diverse tax base. Income, wealth (and its various forms in real estate, personal property, inheritances, etc.), consumption, various business activities, and more are relied upon for revenues. The tax sources respond differently to economic growth and recession, however, and this makes financial forecasting difficult.

Washington state relies on a retail sales tax for approximately 35 percent of its general fund revenues. The general fund accounts for about two-thirds of all state revenues, including intergovernmental transfers. Revenue from the sales tax is a function of the total value of taxable items sold in the state. If fewer tourists come to the state, less will be purchased and fewer taxes will be collected. In a recession, citizens decide to hold off on buying automobiles, videocassette recorders, washing machines, and televisions. They may also decide to purchase these items in neighboring Oregon, which does not have a general sales tax. Some citizens even resort to more intensive gardening, bartering for goods and services, and other behavior that does not get counted in the sales tax collection system. This happened in unprecedented fashion in 1982.

Throughout the 1960s, Washingtonians spent about 67 percent of their incomes on taxable items. After a drop in the middle 1970s, the percentage of income spent on taxable items rose to an all-time high of 71 percent. Forecasters assumed citizens would continue this level of spending, yet something unusual happened in the 1981–82 recession. Suddenly, the percentage dropped to 57, and near the end of the fiscal year, a full 10 percent of the annual budget's revenues did not materialize.

The state resorted to a variety of measures to cope with the crisis. The largest state agencies, including the Department of Social and Health Services and the state university system, took the largest cuts. A hiring freeze was instituted, and state employee salary raises were cut. The state's leadership received strong praise for its actions during the crisis, but the overall picture was still one of confusion and disarray. Political observers in the state blamed the failed reelection bid of the governor in 1984 on the financial crisis, and it was not his fault.

More recently, we have seen recessions in oil-producing states. These states (Alaska, Louisiana, New Mexico, Oklahoma, and Texas) tax all of the oil and natural gas produced. The taxes are tied to the price of oil and gas. During the 1970s these states often did not know what to do with all of the money they collected. Alaska gave each of its citizens a large check at the end of every year. But by the end of 1985, the price of oil and gas dropped. Production on many small wells stopped, and state revenues were drastically cut. All of these states are considering new forms of taxation.

FIGURE 12.1 The Laffer Curve

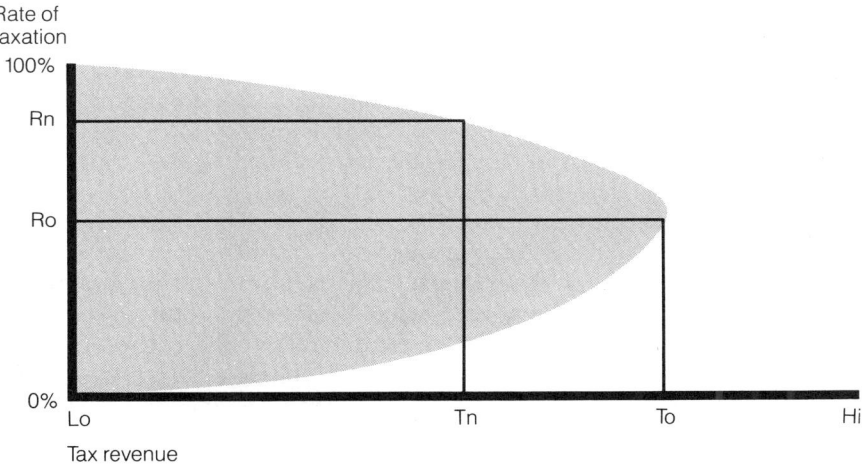

benefit is that from the standpoint of economic growth, some people are better at spending money than others. Supply-siders claim a tax break for the poor leads to a bit more consumption of noodles and shoes. A tax break for the rich leads to more factories being built.

There is no evidence that supply-side tax cuts have the effects claimed by proponents in the Reagan administration. Still, the idea is intuitively appealing, particularly to the wealthy: You can help other people best by paying fewer taxes. As we discussed in Chapter 11, the supply-siders may not have a wonderful economic theory, but it is politically brilliant.

What Forms of Taxation Are Appropriate?

Several forms of taxation are currently in use:[6]

INCOME TAXES, BOTH ON PERSONAL AND CORPORATE INCOME. Together they account for over 60 percent of federal taxes, with personal income taxes about one-half of the total. Income taxes provide approximately 28 percent of state taxes and 4 percent of local taxes. Figure 12.2 is a facsimile of the federal income tax Form 1040EZ. If you have not filled out federal tax forms before, you should work through Figure 12.2 to see the kinds of information asked of citizens.

There are many different state income tax systems. Of the forty-one states using the income tax, most use the federal definition of adjusted gross income (see line 3 of Figure 12.2), and a few assess taxes as a percentage of federal tax owed. The typical rate structure is progressive, taking between 2 and 8 percent of income. Local governments make little use of income taxes, although some localities in the northeastern United States use it for a substantial part of their revenues.

CONSUMPTION TAXES, INCLUDING SALES, EXCISE, AND VALUE-ADDED TAXES (VAT). Prior to use of the income tax, the federal government received almost half of its tax revenue from consumption taxes, mainly excise taxes. Since then, the percentage has declined to about 4 percent. Consumption taxes account for about 43 percent of state taxes and 13 percent of local government taxes. The general sales tax is used by all but five states, although all exclude various items from the tax. Housing expenditures are seldom taxed, and most grant exclusions for medical items, food for home consumption, and other basic expenditure categories. Often there is a provision for local governments to charge 1 to 3 percent sales tax "piggybacked" on the state system.

Selective sales taxes are usually called "excise" taxes in the United States. (In several English-speaking countries excise refers to any tax.) Excise taxes are charged on such items as liquor, cigarettes, gasoline, and rubber (in automobile tires). Excise taxes are often "sin" taxes used to discourage particular behavior and to raise money by politically popular means. A multimillion dollar plan to clean Puget Sound in Washington state, for instance, is financed by a special tax on tobacco.

Many European countries use a sales tax assessed in a different way, on the incremental value added in the production of consumer goods. Under a value-added tax (VAT), one firm may buy raw animal hides, then split and tan them, thus adding to their value. A second firm may buy the tanned hides, then cut and sew them onto shoe welts, thus adding to their value. Each firm would be taxed by the amount of value added to the material. The consumer sees only a shoe at a given price, but pays the taxes in the form of higher prices.

A major problem with consumption taxes is they tend to be regressive. Poorer people consume all of their income. Wealthier people place more of their money in tax-free retirement accounts, stocks and bonds, and spend more on certain nontaxed luxuries, such as foreign travel.

The major practical problem with consumption taxes is their unpredictability. If consumers buy less, tax revenue declines. Consumer behavior is notoriously fickle and surprising, as earlier illustrated in Box 12.1.

FIGURE 12.2 Federal Income Tax Form 1040EZ

| Form **1040EZ** | Department of the Treasury - Internal Revenue Service **Income Tax Return for Single filers with no dependents** (0) **1986** | OMB No. 1545-0675 |

Name & address

Use the IRS mailing label. If you don't have one, please print. If your address is different from the one shown on your 1985 return, check here ☐.

▶ Print your name above (first, initial, last)

Present home address (number and street). (If you have a P.O. box, see instructions.)

City, town, or post office, state, and ZIP code

Please print your numbers like this.

1 2 3 4 5 6 7 8 9 0

Your social security number

Presidential Election Campaign Fund
Do you want $1 of your tax to go to this fund? ▶

Yes No

Dollars   Cents

Report your income

1 Total wages, salaries, and tips. This should be shown in Box 10 of your W-2 form(s). (Attach your W-2 form(s).) 1

2 Interest income of $400 or less. If the total is more than $400, you cannot use Form 1040EZ. 2

Attach Copy B of Form(s) W-2 here

3 Add line 1 and line 2. This is your **adjusted gross income**. 3

4 Enter your cash charitable contributions. See the instructions for line 4 on the back of this form. 4

5 Subtract line 4 from line 3. 5

6 Amount of your personal exemption. 6   **1,080.00**

7 Subtract line 6 from line 5. If line 6 is larger than line 5, enter 0 on line 7. This is your **taxable income**. 7

Figure your tax

8 Enter your Federal income tax withheld. This should be shown in Box 9 of your W-2 form(s). 8

9 Use the **single** column in the tax table on pages 31-36 of the Form 1040A instruction booklet to find the **tax** on your taxable income on line 7. Enter the amount of tax. 9

Refund or amount you owe

10 If line 8 is larger than line 9, subtract line 9 from line 8. Enter the **amount of your refund**. 10

11 If line 9 is larger than line 8, subtract line 8 from line 9. Enter the **amount you owe**. Attach check or money order for the full amount, payable to "Internal Revenue Service." 11

Attach tax payment here

Sign your return

I have read this return. Under penalties of perjury, I declare that to the best of my knowledge and belief, the return is true, correct, and complete.

Your signature   Date

For Privacy Act and Paperwork Reduction Act Notice, see page 41.   Form **1040EZ** (1986)

> **BOX 12.2   Free Market Capitalism and Drugs**
>
> For the last ten years or so, we have had a curious relationship between "sin" and the "free" market in the United States. We know, medically, that the two biggest killers in this country are alcohol and cigarettes. These are, of course, legal. Other very bad habits, which are illegal, are various kinds of smokes, cocaine, and heroin. Together, these illegal drugs do not kill as many people as the legal ones. However, the majority of the people in our prisons are there because of drug-related crimes. Millions of Americans break the drug laws every day, while others take drugs, only legally. Why are some bad habits criminal, and similar bad habits legal? There can be no reasonable answer.
>
> What free market economists argue is that we should legalize *all* drugs. After all, if there is a demand there should be a supply. They also argue that, with uncontrolled supplies, no one could make money selling bad drugs, so pushers would not try to get kids hooked. They are not worried much about advertisers encouraging use, since free market economists believe individual choice is wiser than government restraints, and because advertisers have shown some sensitivity by aiming ads at current users and adults. The sense is irresistible: The products would be "clean," industry could make a taxable profit off those who still wanted the drugs, we could collect a "sin" tax, and we would save a great deal of money not having so many people in jail.
>
> A friend of ours suggests that it is time to make the name "drug store" really mean something.

PROPERTY TAXES, ACTUALLY A TAX ON WEALTH HELD IN REAL ESTATE.   State and local governments derive about 18 percent of revenues from property taxes. Although declining in overall importance, many local governments and school districts rely heavily on property taxes. The tax is assessed as a function of the value of property. Administration of the tax is anything but simple, however. First, a value must be assigned to all parcels to be taxed. Physical inspection of parcels is necessary for an accurate assessment, but inspections take time. No governments inspect each parcel each year, although many attempt to do so on a regular basis, such as every three years. Residential and commercial property is valued at a proportion of market value. The total amount of property taxes needed by the government is divided by the total taxable value of property, which yields the necessary tax rate.

Second, valuation must take account of the factors that lead to change of property values over time. Inflation, the owner's improvements on the property, and changes in development patterns may all dramatically affect the value of a parcel. Third, governments set policies concerning how certain types of property are treated. Veterans, elderly people, the handicapped, and certain types of businesses may be granted exemptions. These add to the problems of calculating the tax base.

These factors combined to produce the "tax revolt" in several states, largely directed at property taxes. In California, voters passed an initiative that limited property taxes to 1 percent of market value of a parcel and limited growth to a 2 percent annual increase of assessed value from the 1975–76 base year. In Massachusetts, proposition 2½ required a 15 percent reduction in property taxes each year until they reach 2½ percent of market value, which remains as a ceiling on tax rates. Movement backers in both states complained of government as inefficient, but citizens were generally satisfied with the level of services. Most citizens voted for the measures because of increases in tax bills during years when property values soared as a result of inflation and because of exemptions granted to other types of property. Perhaps not surprisingly, corporations with large holdings in land were in the best position to benefit from property tax reductions.

Since 1978, the tax revolt has lost momentum. For example, in the 1986 elections California voters approved $2.1 billion in bond issues (which require a two-thirds majority), most county requests for increases in sales taxes, and a ballot measure that allows voters to approve an increase in the Proposition 13 property tax lid, although they did require that all use-taxes be approved by popular vote. Citizens in Montana turned down a measure that would have eliminated property taxes and required that voters approve all increases in sales and income taxes, although they did approve freezing property taxes at 1986 levels. Oregon voters turned down all tax measures on their ballot, some of which would have increased taxes, and some of which would have limited taxes in a manner similar to Proposition 13. Colorado voters rejected a measure that would have required voter approval of all tax increases. Massachusetts voters tied tax increases to growth in general wages. Voters in Washington and New Mexico approved a variety of new taxes. Highly visible taxes like the property tax will continue to keep the attention of voters, and simplistic views of voter preferences should be avoided.

OTHER TAXES, INCLUDING THE "VOLUNTARY" TAX OF STATE LOTTERIES AND INNOVATIVE FORMS OF TAXING CITIZENS. Lotteries are now run by twenty-seven states and the District of Columbia, and regional lotteries have been instituted. In the lottery states, annual betting averages over $90 per person, of which about $37.50 goes to the state. Although voluntary, the $4.6 billion in net revenues (about 40 percent of the $11.5 billion in ticket sales) is becoming an important source of funds.

An interesting example of innovative taxation is provided by the city of Escondido, California. The city's sewage treatment system was operating near capacity, and voters turned down a bond proposal to expand the plant. There was simply no money to expand the sewage system. The city had to place a moratorium on new sewer connections, in effect halting new construction, even for projects which had already received building permits. Builders sued the city for $200 million, claiming breach of contract. One possible source of money was the sewer connection rights sold by the city, but the problem was how to sell enough of them to generate the $25 million needed to expand the sewer system. The city came upon the idea of selling sewer connection "futures." The connection fee was dropped from $2100 to $1500 for a period of three months. A schedule of permits was published (a new single-family home needed one certificate, a carwash needed several), buyers were freed from future connection fee increases, and the sale was on. The city sold $33 million of the connection futures and was able to upgrade the system.

Tax systems are as numerous as governments, and we have only touched the top of the iceberg in this discussion. Box 12.3 includes instructions for investigating the tax system where you live.

BOX 12.3   What is Taxed Where You Live?

Descriptions of state and local tax systems are full of generalities because of the enormous variety of tax systems. To find out specifically what is taxed in your community, you need to do some investigating. The first place to start is with the budget. Budgets should include a detailed section on the sources of various types of revenues. Remember you live in a number of jurisdictions: a state, a county, probably a city or town, a school district, perhaps a fire district, a recreation district, a public port district, and so on. Consult budgets from the general government entities and the local school districts to find out where their money comes from.

Next make a trip to your county assessor or treasurer's office. Call to find out who keeps lists of tax rates paid in various towns and school districts. The office should have a list of all separate taxes collected within the county, except sales and income taxes. A finance office probably keeps records on these sources, but call to find out who the responsible officials are. You will probably find that a county assessor will gladly arrange a tour for a number of students. Organize one and find out how the office operates and what issues are most pressing on their responsibilities.

What Are the Other, Nontax Sources of Government Revenue?

Governments operate many fee-for-service programs, particularly in jurisdictions which have recreation programs, community colleges, power-generating facilities, and similar services. One of the most important and politically divisive sources of revenue is intergovernmental transfers, the subject of this section.

In Chapter 2, we discussed federalism. The idea of multiple jurisdictions in an area gives rise to conflicts among government powers. The intended result of federalism was protection of democratic and local political controls, but the reality is not stable or simple. Several stages of federalism under the current constitution should be noted:

THE IMPASSE, 1789–1860. Prior to the Civil War, basic questions of the extent of states' rights and national supremacy were not settled; 780,000 Americans were killed or wounded in four years of war fought over these issues. The war should remind us that federalism clearly matters.

DUAL FEDERALISM, 1865–1933. After the war roles of the state and national governments were relatively stable and separate. The national government was in the business of giving away newly won lands of the west, and taxing and controlling customs. Although important instances of economic regulation occurred during this period (the Sherman Anti-Trust Act passed in 1890, following legislation in several states; the Federal Reserve Board was created in 1913), the state and national governments went their separate ways. It was also during this period that "Dillon's rule" was pronounced by the Federal courts. Dillon's rule states that local governments are the creatures of state governments and may have only those powers expressly granted by the state. Since the early days of federalism, local governments have been last in line.

COOPERATIVE FEDERALISM, 1933–1961. Responding to the depression of the 1930s, the national government enacted legislation to help people where they lived — which happened to be in states and localities. Housing, unemployment, and income assistance programs were commonly administered by state agencies supported by federal funds.

INTERGOVERNMENTAL RELATIONS (IGR), 1961–PRESENT. During the 1960s, the types and amounts of federal aid to states and localities expanded dramatically. The dominant form of aid during the Johnson administration (1963–1968) was the categorical grant, or giving money for specific purposes. The number of such grants increased from under 50 to over 400, and at the same time total federal aid to states and localities nearly doubled. This means that national purposes guided more of the state and local spending policies than ever before. A new dependency was established. The categorical grants were created by policy area, so that federalism became less a relationship between separate levels of government as one between politicians and policy professionals in related national, state, and local bureaucracies. Figure 12.3 diagrams this relationship. In each policy area officials in each level of government do part of the work. In education, for instance, federal officials in the Department of Education, state officials in a Superintendent of Public Instruction's office, and local officials in school districts work together to carry out the work in this one policy area. Although the intergovernmental relationships are vertical, each policy area, and the people working in it, is separate from the others. National officials working in Washington, D.C. and ten federal regional centers around the country interpret legislation by making regulations that define where aid will be placed. State officials must comply with the regulations, continually keep in touch on rule changes, and report on how the funds are used. Usually, states play more than a "pass-through" role and make regulations of their own on how local governments are to use the money. Local officials must comply with applicable federal and state regulations (again continually keeping in touch on rule changes), report on how funds are used, and often make rules about selecting contractors to do some or all of the work supported by the aid.

These new intergovernmental relationships have amounted to important political changes in states and localities. A larger federal presence, usually very specific about permissible state and local government behavior, was a direct consequence of the remarkable increase in categorical grants. When the specialists in policy areas wield authority, the generalist politicians lose some of their power. Indeed, such bypassing of local politicians was an important goal of members of Congress who wanted less discretion on the part of officials in Chicago and Little Rock. It is no coincidence that the changes took place while the Democratic party occupied the presidency and large majorities in both houses of Congress.

Some changes accompanied a new Republican president in 1968. Richard Nixon proposed, and eventually passed in altered form, the General Revenue Sharing (GRS) program.[7] The main purpose of GRS was to put fewer strings on federal aid and to allow greater political autonomy in the states and localities. The Congress remained thoroughly Democratic and transferred little categorical grant money over to GRS. But the thought was there: an alternative to federal control was state and local control financed with federal dollars. The idea was attractive to government officials who liked to talk about grassroots democracy but who had grown used to doing things on a big, centralized scale.

GRS became another source of federal aid to states and localities, one which recipients did not want cut, but its larger purposes went unfulfilled. To the Republicans who believed in decentralization, GRS was to be an "end run" around the Washington bureaucracies. But, most federal aid

FIGURE 12.3 The Structure of Federalism

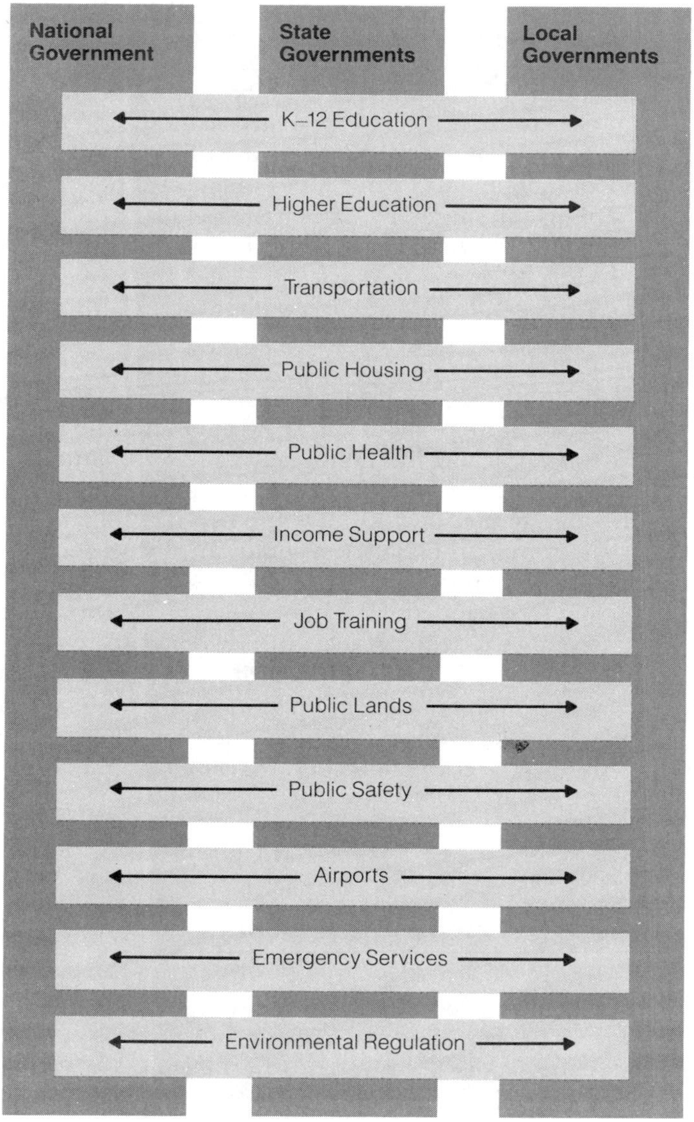

National Government	State Governments	Local Governments
←————————	K–12 Education	————————→
←————————	Higher Education	————————→
←————————	Transportation	————————→
←————————	Public Housing	————————→
←————————	Public Health	————————→
←————————	Income Support	————————→
←————————	Job Training	————————→
←————————	Public Lands	————————→
←————————	Public Safety	————————→
←————————	Airports	————————→
←————————	Emergency Services	————————→
←————————	Environmental Regulation	————————→

Source: Adapted from Deil S. Wright, *Understanding Intergovernmental Relations,* 2d ed. (Monterey, Calif.: Brooks-Cole, 1982).

continued to involve the Washington agencies. To the Democrats who believed in doing a few more things through government, the money devoted to GRS started off small and got smaller in real terms. To get such a program through the Congress required that a little something be given to everyone, with the result that amounts given to particular jurisdictions had little to do with need. To the state and local officials who wanted aid and autonomy, GRS never appeared as a convincing shift in federal priorities. It is not wise to become dependent on a temporary source of funds. Most cities put the money into paint for courthouses, police equipment, and similar ongoing commitments, rather than embark on new ventures and responsibilities. Administrative reforms intended to accompany GRS are described in Box 12.4.

Under the Reagan administration, another attempt to alter the substance of intergovernmental relations has met with more success.[8] Reagan was able to cut the amounts going to entitlement programs administered by states (welfare and food stamps) and virtually eliminated GRS on the grounds that states had more money to spend than did the national government. Between 1981 and the end of 1985, federal aid to states and localities declined over 23 percent in real terms (and this in low-inflation years), and the elimination of GRS in 1987 cut aid still further.[9] Many categorical grants were consolidated into block grants, which give more administrative and spending flexibility to states. While lacking an overall design for new intergovernmental relationships, the Reagan era has promoted a trend to reduce federal presence where politically possible — and that means overall conclusions are difficult to make. Less is being spent, and that is the main message received by state and local government officials with budget responsibilities. Box 12.5 describes how you can find out the effects of intergovernmental aid flows on governments where you live.

Predicting Revenues

Governmental budgets are estimates of the revenues and expenditures in a particular year. The estimates are made long before the taxes are collected and the money spent on programs. In the case of states with biennial budgets, the lag between initial revenue forecasts and the end of the fiscal year may be as long as three years. Yet, adequate forecasting is a requirement for government budgeters. Such a forecast will give elected officials the parameters within which they must operate. Forecasts are usually the basis for decisions on the type and amount of tax increases. Although technical in origin, they are infused with political conflict and meaning.

BOX 12.4 The Administration of Intergovernmental Relations

The politics of intergovernmental relations obviously involves the amounts and forms of grants, but the administrative details have much to do with who controls the money.* The expansion of categorical grants during the Kennedy-Johnson years (1961–68) was accompanied by administrative changes that allowed newly formed local agencies to bypass general-purpose governments in applying for federal aid. The Congress believed state and local officials had been unresponsive to the poor and minorities, and the administrative changes favored these groups.

General revenue sharing (GRS) was partially an attempt to reverse this new pattern of aid, and administrative reforms were established to give control of intergovernmental flows back to general-purpose governments. The Office of Management and Budget under President Nixon (1969–74) issued its circulars A-85, A-95, and A-98 to give governors and mayors a role in the planning, application for, and implementation of federal grant programs. State and local elected officials were to meet with national officials in the planning of grant programs; all requests for aid in a region were to pass through regional clearinghouses so that leaders of general-purpose governments were notified before organizations in their areas applied for federal grants; and federal agencies were to keep the clearinghouses informed of grants approved in their areas. These regular contacts and flows of information were aimed at building an intergovernmental administrative network that would put more influence in the hands of state and local officials.

During the Reagan administration, the Nixon IGR administrative structure was formally abolished, and responsibility for regional grant oversight was given to state officials. This complemented the Reagan block grant strategy to give states more discretion and control over federal dollars, and to diminish national influence in state affairs. Reagan thought it important to decrease state dependence on federal aid, but the more important objective was to have state officials controlling the flow of aid into American communities.

*See R. P. Nathan and F. C. Doolittle, "The Untold Story of Reagan's 'New Federalism'," *The Public Interest* 51 (Fall 1984); P. A. Russo Jr., "In Search of Intergovernmental Coordination: The A-95 Project Notification and Review System," *Publius* 13 (Fall 1983); R. W. Gage, "Federal Regional Councils; Networking Organizations for Policy Management in the Intergovernmental System," *Public Administration Review* 44, no. 2 (March/April 1984); and Janet A. Weiss et al., "Reflections on Value: Policy Makers Evaluate Federal Information Systems," *Public Administration Review* 46 (November 1986), special issue on public management information systems, pp. 497–505.

> **BOX 12.5** Local Governments and Intergovernmental Aid
>
> Your own local governments will have some means of managing and keeping track of intergovernmental relations. At least one person is usually assigned to follow national and state legislative and administrative changes that may affect the local government and to coordinate local responses. Smaller governments may not have the personnel to devote full-time attention to intergovernmental issues, but advice is available through such organizations as the International City Management Association. Find out who is assigned such responsibilities in your local government. How do they handle the job? Are regular meetings scheduled with similar officials in other local governments? With state legislators or their staff? Are all intergovernmental grant applications reviewed? At what stage in the application process? Is an inventory of all active grants available to legislators and the executive? How are other, overlapping policies (e.g., civil rights enforcement, historic preservation) coordinated in the local government?
>
> A simple way to detect local reliance on intergovernmental aid is to compare budgets over time. Dramatic changes should be detectable over the past 25 years, but significant changes should be seen over the last decade as well. How much money is received from all state and federal sources? Have the purposes and divisions of such aid changed? Has the local government changed its expenditure patterns in response to intergovernmental changes?
>
> A few students can work as a team to collect this information and report the results to the class.

A great many variables must be understood to make accurate forecasts. The tax base is a function of the types of taxes used, the number of people in a jurisdiction, their income, their spending habits, business activity, the numbers of tourists, and so on. Other forms of revenue include federal aid, fees from licenses and fines, and other sources outside the control of the taxing government.[10] Box 12.1 described the volatility of one such forecasting variable.

Although it is difficult to predict revenues at any level of government, the problems multiply for state and local governments. The entire U.S. economy fluctuates a great deal, but the federal tax base is very stable compared to that of some states and localities. The U.S. economy may experience strong growth, while at the same time Michigan's economy may contract from cutbacks in domestic auto production, and the state of Washington's economy may be stagnant as a result of lower demand for finished wood products. Variability in international trade, housing markets, the tastes of tourists, and the weather all hit the state and local governments more directly than the federal level.

The political side of revenue forecasts only complicates the technical problems. State-of-the-art forecasting can usually deliver revenue projections to within 5 percent of the actual amounts, although unforeseen circumstances not included in forecasting assumptions (oil embargoes, volcanic eruptions, etc.) will utterly destroy budget plans. Forecasters and politicians understand the tentative nature of forecasts, but only the most responsible, a small group, use forecasts conservatively. Given the uncertainty of forecasts, prudent financial management requires a planned budget surplus of approximately 5 percent. Yet the tendency is to lean the other way. Imagine yourself in this situation: You are a governor, up for election in seven months, and it is time to submit a budget proposal to the legislature. Your forecasters tell you their best guess is that the economy will slow down, and to maintain current services a 7 percent tax hike is required. You ask them about their economic assumptions, and you find uncertainty. The most likely scenario is a deep recession, although it is possible growing trade and a weakening dollar will spur the economy, in which case a small budget surplus will result. Given the choice between proposing a tax hike and fudging some numbers just a bit, what will you do?

Some states have amassed surpluses or set aside special funds to promote future economic development. Montana's coal severance tax set aside half of state coal revenues for the future. Alaskans required that large proportions of oil revenues go to capital projects that provide lasting value. Most states with such boom and bust resources, such as the oil-rich states of the southwest, have not used this approach.

It is likely that the technical side of forecasting will not improve very much. This is a comment less on the forecasters than on human beings. To our great credit, we are simply not predictable, which means the burden of reality belongs to the politicians. It seems natural for those in public life to see the best of all possible worlds when looking at economic forecasts. We also want to hear those things from our public figures. Regrettably, the best of all possible worlds does not happen very often.

You can judge forecasting practices where you live. The finance office of your county, city, or state will have forecasts that accompanied past budget preparation documents and executive budgets. Compare them to later documents to judge the accuracy of key assumptions about revenue and expenditures. Do you find systematic errors?

The Political Economy of Tax Revenues

The late 1980s are a time of fiscal stress for governments at all levels. It is a rare government that is not now concerned with levels of taxation and expenditure, or engaging in ways to cope more with fewer resources. The tax revolt of the late 1970s has dissipated, yet there is still pressure on the national level. The emerging trend is for a small or nearly flat rate of growth for the revenues of most states and localities. They can expect little financial relief from the national government.[11]

As mentioned earlier, citizens put this pressure on their governments not out of a general dissatisfaction with services, but from a sense that governments are somehow less efficient than they should be. Claims that government should get out of our lives are often heard, but they have yet to grab the interest of the citizenry. This vague sense of trouble, the idea that somehow there must be a way to do better, stems from two sources. The first we have touched on before; as we argued in the early chapters, Americans have never decided on a clear sense of what we want from government. Because we have never arrived at a clear sense of public administration, it remains the poor relation of business administration and suspicions abound. The second reason is a problem shared by governments throughout the industrialized world: a financial crunch that will not go away soon.

A look at the largest industrial market and mixed economies of the world reveals similar economic and budget problems to those faced in the United States. Looking at nations belonging to the Organization for Economic Cooperation and Development (OECD), virtually all ran into deficit trouble in the late 1970s and early 1980s, but, like the United States, began to show some progress toward reducing them by 1985. Deficits as percentages of gross national product (GNP) showed that the United States was not the greatest sinner; for 1985, the United States was at 2.7 percent; France, 3.2 percent; Britain 3.6 percent; Canada 4.7 percent; Italy, 13.1 percent; Japan, 1.1 percent; and West Germany, 0.9 percent.[12] The similarities are all the more striking when we consider that nearly every industrial country, no matter what "burden" government places on the economy, has problems with deficits.

Over the same period the OECD, countries ran into trade deficits similar to those in the United States.[13] Overall, businesses were just not as profitable as before.[14] Economists are not sure why these trends are occurring.[15] Much of this is because western economies are moving from manufacturing, which used to pay workers well and make large profits, to services, which pay workers poorly and have lower rates of profits.[16]

The trade deficit garners attention in the media, but is seldom included in discussions of budget deficits. It should be. A trade deficit is partly a by-product of a budget deficit, a sign of an underlying problem

BOX 12.6 State and Local Governments Brace for Hard Times in the Late 1980s

State and local governments feel the fiscal pressure brought on by sluggish economic growth, changes in intergovernmental aid, and citizen demands. Officials' attitudes range from guarded optimism in the more prosperous areas to a desperate search for solutions in the hard-pressed regions. Fiscal problems of state and local governments vary by region of the country and over time. In the late 1970s and early 1980s, the northeast was referred to as the "rust belt," with huge infrastructure repair bills, soaring energy costs, and sluggish economic growth. In the late 1980s the prospects are bright as New York is able to cut taxes, Connecticut has a large budget surplus, and Massachusetts shows the rest of the nation how to cut welfare costs and limit state revenue burdens on citizens. The midwest was riding an oil boom to prosperity in the late 1970s and early 1980s, but their fortunes dramatically reversed in the mid-1980s. Oklahoma sent some state workers home for several days to save money, Texas faces its largest deficits ever, and Iowa, Mississippi, Montana, Nebraska, and Utah all had to cut budgets dramatically.

Many local governments are in a better position than the states. States rely heavily on sales and income taxes, which are sensitive to economic slumps. Most local governments rely more on property taxes, which are less sensitive to the economy and are revalued only every few years. The counties in particular are in a good position. Suburbs tend to be where new service and manufacturing industries locate.

Unions are particularly worried about these financial troubles. Several midwest states are proposing wage and benefit concessions at the bargaining table, and privatizing government services is appealing to more state and local governments. In Wisconsin, for instance, state nursing homes are under pressure to spend less, and the state is considering closing some centers. Government nursing home workers make almost twice as much as their private sector counterparts. There is even serious talk of letting industry take over penal institutions.

Overall, the outlook is for flat or modest growth for state and local governments in the aggregate. The longer-range prospects are not better. As Middle East tensions mount and the Arab states settle their differences, oil prices will once again rise, bringing inflation and another cycle of boom and bust to various regions of the U.S. economy.

in the economy. Industry and labor have lost a former advantage and are not generating enough products for sale at desirable prices in the world economy. This sharply diminished ability to compete in world markets means a decreased ability to increase incomes in the United States, although it does help increase the incomes of countries with more positive balances of trade.

Here is the general picture for the last two decades: The sources of wealth for industrialized countries have become generally more sparse. The comparative advantage in terms of trade has become much weaker. The proportion of GNP devoted to public purposes has become much larger. Over time the result of such changes is inevitable. Budgets become tighter and old thinking about "full employment" budgets and budget deficits becomes outmoded.

Richard Rose[17] developed a simple model to explain the problem. An economy generates only so much income. If governments take a larger share than before, there cannot be the increase in personal wealth that citizens have come to expect. When an economy actually shrinks, the process is very painful. Budget deficits — the act of spending money that government does not have — are a way to cushion the loss of income. This understanding of deficits is not a clear guide to action for policymakers, but it can be helpful in several ways. First, it helps to direct research toward factors largely ignored in most studies of the causes and possible responses to deficits. Second, it helps us get our bearings in a largely unknown terrain of political economy; it helps to focus attention on the major roadblocks to goals and alerts us to red herrings in the search for causes and responses. Third, it connects the issue of budget deficits to other policy areas — trade, industrial policy, foreign economic policies, as well as the trade-offs within the budget of the United States.

Income and Wealth

Since the Second World War, the budget of the United States has been expanded to support many new, enlarged, and expensive programs. Budget lines in veterans' affairs, education, aid to state and local governments, public assistance, and social security have all dramatically increased over the long term. While defense spending decreased from the levels of World War Two, the global military role assumed by the United States called for much larger post- than prewar defense budgets.

The dramatic expansion was affordable. Although the United States ran budget deficits for many of the first twenty-five postwar years, the deficits did not create concern comparable to that of today. Table 12.3 indicates strong growth in U.S. budgets coupled with healthy increases in national income, at least until 1973. Increases in revenues and outlays generally outstrip those of income, particularly after 1973. The long trend is also evident in the steady increase of government share of gross national product, rising from under 16 percent in 1950 to 24 percent in the early 1980s.

Most of this was accomplished at a time when living standards and personal incomes dramatically increased. In constant dollars, median family income increased 57 percent during the 1950s and 1960s. For the middle class the growth was dramatic, 63 percent during the 1950s and 49 percent during the 1960s. Although the poorest 20 percent of households earned roughly the same small share of total income during this period, public assistance of various types lifted virtually all of this group above the official poverty line.[18]

The picture over the last 15 years is quite different. Median family income, measured in constant dollars, has dropped from its 1973 high, while total income has increased. Although much has been made of income inequalities during the Reagan years (the average real income for the wealthiest 20 percent rose, whereas that of all other quintiles dropped), the trend of modest growth for the wealthy with real loss of income for the rest predates Reagan by almost a decade.

The trends in income and spending show that for more than a decade additional income has gone to government growth, and even then considerable amounts were borrowed from the future. This pattern holds for almost all of the OECD countries. Expansion in the industrial economies slowed, and governments borrowed to make up the difference.

One way to look at government's role is to consider how much government spends where. Important changes are evident, as depicted in Table 12.4. The changes show a couple of things. First, recent changes, including those during the Reagan administration, are not larger than earlier ones. Second, the total spent by government has increased over time, during which period the economy has failed to increase incomes as before. These trends have worried a great many people, even though there is not much agreement on why expenditures are increasing much faster than incomes. There is agreement that the biggest worry is on the income side. A popular argument is that forces outside our economy are to blame and that we need to readjust to fit the new environment. The recent popularity of the "national industrial policy" concept, described in Box 12.7, illustrates just how worried people are.

To summarize, growth rates have declined for virtually all industrial market economies. Profitability is down, productivity is constant or declining, and terms of trade have worsened. Government expenditures, although restrained the last several years, continue to grow at a faster rate than incomes. Incomes have become imperiled by the twin forces of decreased productivity and increased government presence in the economy. Governments have borrowed heavily from the future in order to lessen pressure on incomes. In the United States, political pressures to address the size of deficits continue. The fiscal environment of today's governments is indeed turbulent.

TABLE 12.3 National Income, Budgets, and Deficits in Constant (1985) Dollars

YEAR	NATIONAL INCOME*	% GREATER THAN†	TAX REVENUE*	% GREATER THAN†	GOVERNMENT OUTLAYS*	% GREATER THAN†	DEFICITS*
1985	3042.8	0.95	736.9	1.42	959.1	4.51	222.2
1984	3046.1		685.9		876.6		190.7
1983	2816.6		636.6		860.8		221.3
1982	2689.7		679.1		819.7		140.6
1981	2757.9		699.2		791.3		92.1
1980	2725.5		665.9		760.9		95.0
1979	2874.9	2.81	677.2	3.60	736.0	4.85	58.8
1978	2862.7		650.0		746.0		96.0
1977	2714.9		622.7		716.5		98.9
1976	2570.7		555.6‡		693.0‡		137.4‡
1975	2443.6		550.3		655.2		104.9
1974	2502.6	2.37	567.5	0.96	580.9	1.80	13.2
1973	2593.6		551.1		586.7		35.6
1972	2444.7		525.9		585.2		59.4
1971	2283.2		490.2		550.7		60.3
1970	2215.0		526.8		534.4		7.7
1969	2225.6	4.38	541.0	7.03	531.4	5.56	8.1
1968	2203.4		466.6		543.2		76.9
1967	2104.2		472.8		500.5		27.3
1966	2053.3		427.6		439.7		12.1
1965	1924.7		392.7		397.4		4.7

Year							
1964	1795.8	4.57	385.2	6.30	405.4	4.20	20.2
1963	1692.7		369.4		385.7		16.6
1962	1620.5		349.7		374.6		24.9
1961	1521.1		334.9		347.3		11.7
1960	1489.4		331.4		330.3		–.8
1959	1436.0	3.85	283.8	0.62	330.0	3.35	45.9
1958	1346.4		292.1		302.4		10.3
1957	1374.5		301.1		288.3		–12.8
1956	1364.3		291.3		275.7		–15.2
1955	1309.4		259.5		271.0		11.9
1954	1188.7	3.22	275.2	12.19	279.9	10.51	4.7
1953	1198.8		276.2		302.0		25.8
1952	1150.7		264.6		270.6		6.0
1951	1119.7		210.8		185.9		24.9
1950	1047.2		173.7		187.7		13.7

Sources: Calculated from *Statistical Abstract of the United States* and *Budget of the U.S.*, various years.

*Constant Dollars (1985)

†Annual growth (APR) for previous 5 yrs., 6 yrs in case of 1985

‡Transition quarter omitted; revenues = $152.3; outlays = $176.1.

TABLE 12.4 Federal Transactions in the National Income and Product Accounts Selected Categories as Percentages of GNP, Federal Fiscal Years 1950–1986

| | PURCHASES | | TRANSFER PAYMENTS | | Aid to State and | |
Year	Defense	Nondefense	Persons	Foreign	Local Govt.	Total
1950	4.9	2.5	4.2	1.6	.9	16.1
1951	7.0	1.3	2.6	1.0	.8	14.3
1952	12.3	1.6	2.5	.8	.7	19.4
1953	13.5	2.1	2.5	.6	.8	20.9
1954	12.5	2.2	2.8	.5	.8	20.2
1955	10.1	1.5	3.1	.6	.8	17.5
1956	9.5	1.5	3.1	.4	.8	16.9
1957	9.7	1.3	3.3	.4	.8	17.4
1958	10.1	1.4	4.0	.4	1.0	18.5
1959	9.7	1.8	4.1	.4	1.3	19.2
1960	8.9	1.6	4.1	.4	1.4	18.1
1961	9.1	1.8	4.6	.4	1.3	19.1
1962	9.1	2.0	4.5	.4	1.4	19.3
1963	8.7	2.3	4.5	.4	1.4	19.2
1964	8.2	2.5	4.4	.4	1.6	18.8
1965	7.3	2.4	4.2	.3	1.6	17.8
1966	7.5	2.5	4.3	.3	1.7	18.1
1967	8.7	2.4	4.7	.3	1.9	19.8
1968	9.0	2.3	5.0	.3	2.1	20.5
1969	8.4	2.3	5.3	.3	2.1	20.1
1970	7.9	2.2	5.6	.2	2.3	20.1
1971	7.2	2.1	6.4	.2	2.5	20.5
1972	6.6	2.4	6.6	.3	2.8	20.6
1973	6.0	2.2	6.8	.2	3.1	20.3
1974	5.6	2.2	7.2	.2	2.9	20.0
1975	5.7	2.5	8.7	.2	3.2	22.0
1976	5.4	2.4	9.1	.2	3.4	22.3
1977	5.1	2.5	8.6	.2	3.4	21.7
1978	4.9	2.4	8.2	.2	3.4	21.2
1979	4.8	2.3	8.1	.2	3.2	20.7
1980	5.1	2.4	8.8	.2	3.2	22.1
1981	5.4	2.4	9.2	.2	3.0	22.9

TABLE 12.4 continued

	PURCHASES		TRANSFER PAYMENTS		Aid to State and Local Govt.	Total
Year	Defense	Nondefense	Persons	Foreign		
1982	6.0	2.5	9.7	.2	2.7	24.1
1983	6.4	2.3	10.2	.2	2.6	25.1
1984	6.2	1.9	9.3	.3	2.5	23.7
1985	6.5	2.2	9.1	.3	2.5	24.5
1986*	6.4	2.1	9.0	.4	2.4	24.2

Source: Office of Management and Budget, *Historical Tables: Budget of the United States Government, Fiscal Year 1987,* adapted from Table 15.2.
*Estimated.

After the Budget Passes

When the legislature and the head of the executive branch finish with the high politics of budgeting, the overall taxing and spending questions, it is time to spend money. Elaborate procedures are used during the budget execution phase to accomplish several goals:

1. To fix and monitor spending authority. Except in special areas such as spying, spending authority is given to specific positions in agencies. The people in these positions are responsible for spending money in the intended categories, and antideficiency acts prohibit overspending. There is general agreement on this point: Budgets are plans that frequently go awry, which is why governments have procedures for changing their spending plans during any fiscal year.

2. To establish an audit trail. Spending authority must be documented by vouchers (a record that a financial transaction has taken place) that are summarized in an agency's accounts. In a recent case the General Accounting Office (GAO) was asked to investigate previous use of U.S. aid to the Contras in Nicaragua (a rebel army supported by the United States). The information was to help the Congress decide whether an additional $100 million in aid would be spent as intended. The GAO found that expenditures were spent in ways that destroyed the audit trail. The money would be given to a Contra supplier in

> **BOX 12.7** National Economic Policy and Fiscal Stress
>
> Government officials understand that the state of their finances depends on the health of the economy. Their main problem is that available policy tools are clumsy or ineffective in promoting and controlling economic growth. The strongest tools are in the hands of federal officials, although state and local officials fiercely compete to encourage new industries and tourists to come to their areas.
>
> A recent focus of some national officials is the idea of a national industrial policy. Instead of government providing subsidies to failing industries, they say, we should plan which industries provide the best chance for future economic growth and channel resources into them. If successful, such a policy would promote growth, enhance international competitiveness, and enhance the global leadership position of the U.S. economy. The robust economic growth would help governmental finances as well.
>
> The promises are appealing, but several issues are unsolved. The governments who have attempted such policies have not been good at picking the best growth companies. The Japanese, for instance, did not want Honda to enter the automobile business. Further problems involve the role of government, labor, and business leaders in a capitalist society. Will such a "syndicalist" approach to economic policy further concentrate government power in the hands of the leaders of our largest economic organizations? Will the administrative organs of such planning institutions be given powers that now lie in the Congress? It is not at all clear that a national industrial policy can be effective and at the same time democratic.

Florida, who would in turn transfer the money to bank accounts that included money from other sources. It was also found that blank vouchers were issued by the ultimate suppliers of goods in Central America, so that the Florida merchant could fill in whatever amount they wanted. It was impossible to say just how much money had actually been spent the way Congress intended. We should note that these management issues are usually lost in the wider politics of the program. The audits had little effect on funding for the Contras.

3. To monitor performance of government agencies. In addition to spending money in the right place, it is important to keep track of what is achieved by an agency. Performance monitoring relates the amounts spent to the work performed by an agency — the number of clients served, the numbers of checks processed, the number of passenger-miles logged, and so on. This allows decision makers to

assess requests for budget amendments and requests for next year's funds.

Smaller governments may keep a single set of books to keep track of financial flows. In such entities appropriation acts may be specific enough to keep adequate track of expenditures. Governments with more than a few hundred employees find the need for more elaborate procedures. Appropriation acts for these governments are likely to include many different types of activities in line items or program categories. The line item budget of the U.S. government, for example, includes many line items of several hundred million dollars. The budget office constructs a financial plan to control such spending and fulfill the budgetary goals.

The large line items are first divided into manageable categories by agency, program, or more specific line items. Next, a spending plan of quarterly or month-by-month expenditures is constructed to monitor the rate of expenditures. Many public expenditures are a function of need or in some cases cooperation from other governments. Welfare expenditures may increase as a result of a downturn in the economy, and budget controllers may want to limit expenditures to ensure that enough will be left for the last weeks of the fiscal year. Federal matching grants may be uncertain, and an allotment plan may be conditional upon receipt of the matching funds. The allotments allow a budget office to watch the progress of expenditures according to the financial plan.

The financial plan relies on several other tools for control of expenditures. There are, for example, two obvious ways to control expenditures. Because the largest single expense is for personnel, the number of positions can be cut. The second way is to be more efficient in purchasing or to cut out some buying altogether. Most importantly, a regular system is devised to watch over spending by particular agencies. Figure 12.4 depicts the financial controls in the federal government.

Financial controls rely heavily on the responsible conduct of managers. It is physically impossible, and surely undesirable, to install detailed watchers on all managers. The essence of management is to diagnose, judge, and adjust to situations in a way that fulfills organizational goals. This necessary discretion is the source of many budget problems, however. Often government managers are promoted from within an organization because of achievements in technical aspects of work, and little time is devoted for management training. An unfortunate result is that many of the people assigned to manage agency budgets do not have the necessary skills.

Budget management skills are particularly crucial for managers in agencies with a variety of intergovernmental funds. A typical local government agency receives funds from several sources. A public library, for instance, may receive federal funds for services to the handicapped, state funds from education trust funds, local funds for operating expenses, private bequests and donations, and many proprietary funds (such as pro-

FIGURE 12.4 Execution of Enacted Budget

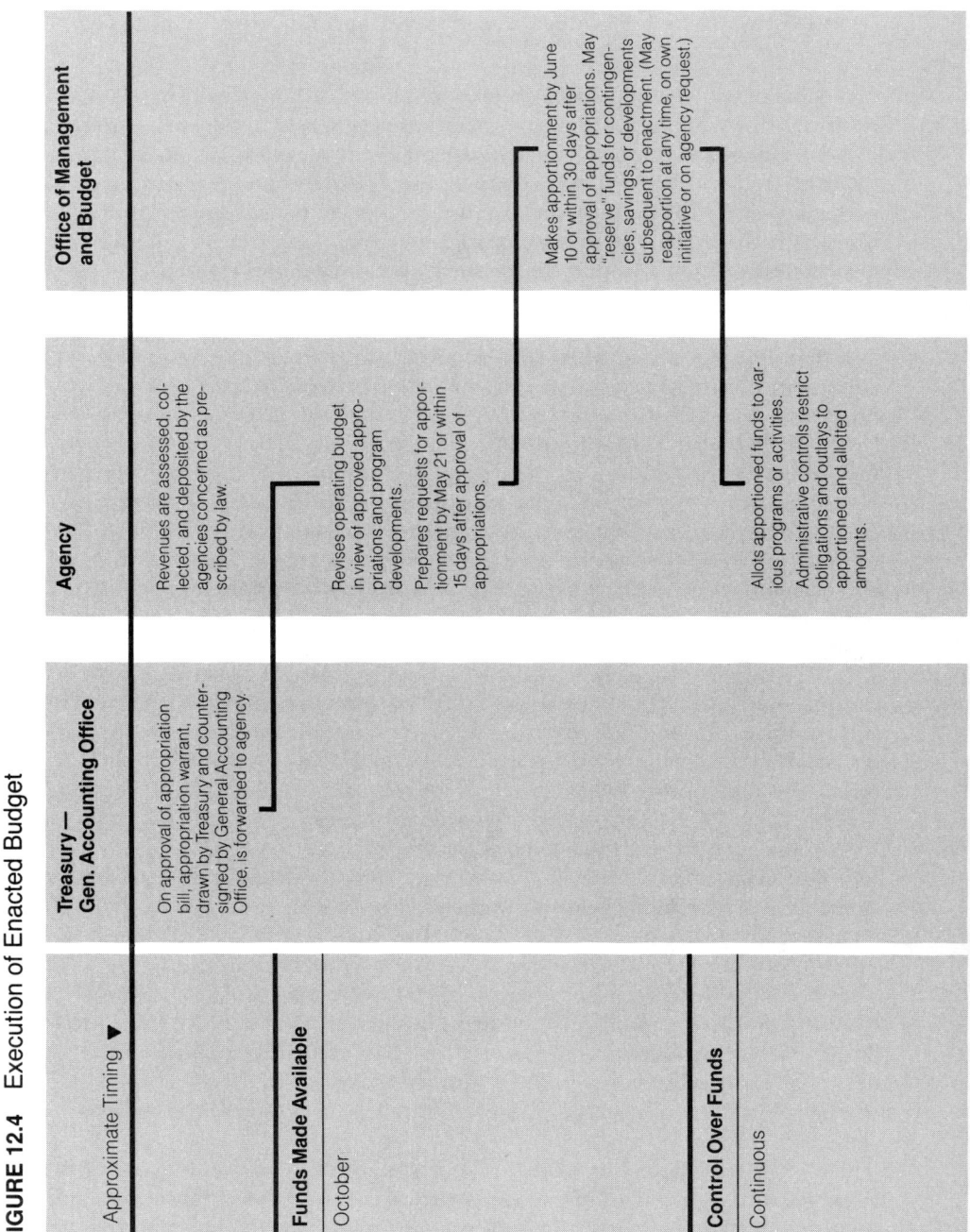

After the Budget Passes 353

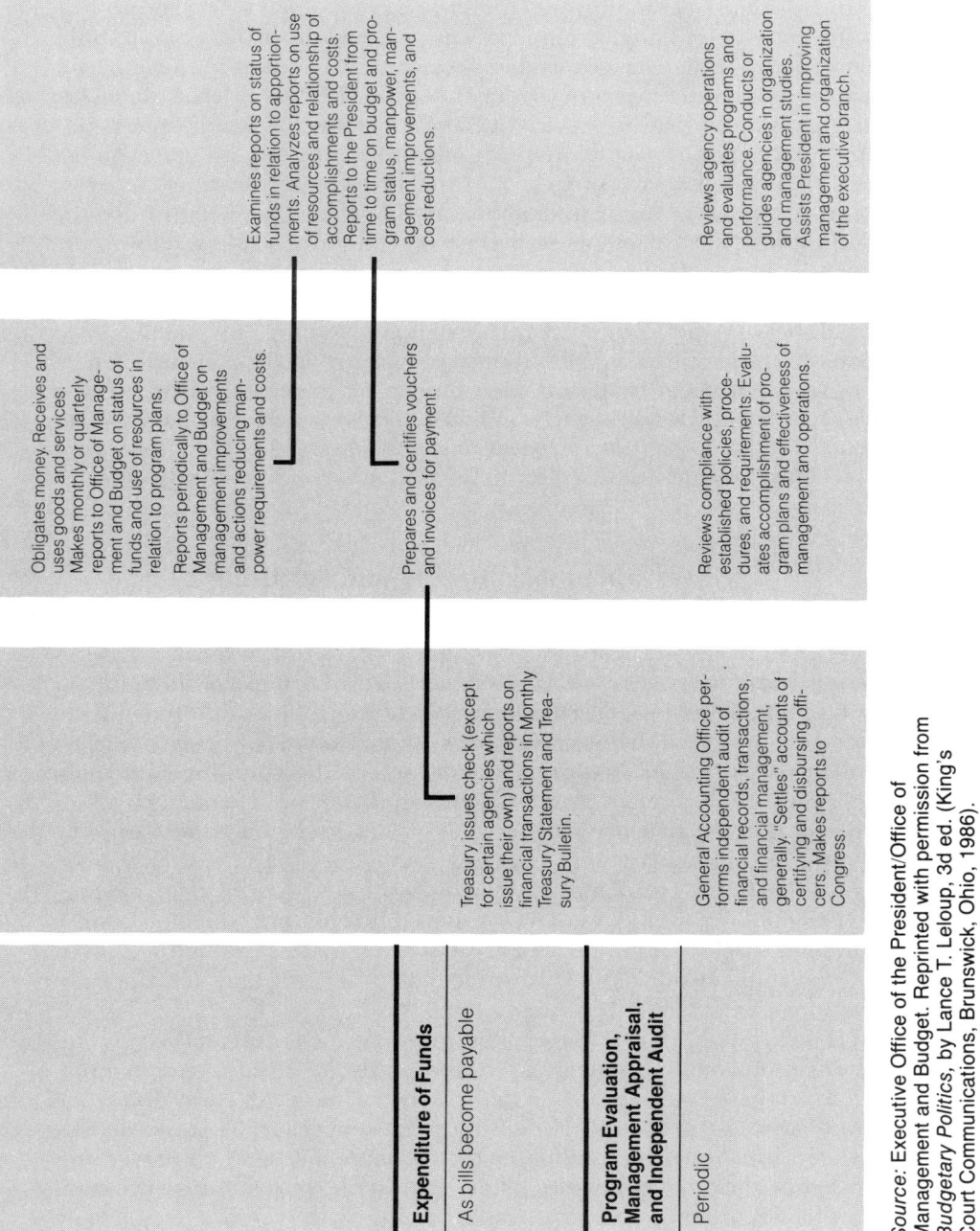

Expenditure of Funds

As bills become payable

Obligates money. Receives and uses goods and services. Makes monthly or quarterly reports to Office of Management and Budget on status of funds and use of resources in relation to program plans.

Reports periodically to Office of Management and Budget on management improvements and actions reducing manpower requirements and costs.

Treasury issues check (except for certain agencies which issue their own) and reports on financial transactions in Monthly Treasury Statement and Treasury Bulletin.

Prepares and certifies vouchers and invoices for payment.

Examines reports on status of funds in relation to apportionments. Analyzes reports on use of resources and relationship of accomplishments and costs. Reports to the President from time to time on budget and program status, manpower, management improvements, and cost reductions.

Program Evaluation, Management Appraisal, and Independent Audit

Periodic

General Accounting Office performs independent audit of financial records, transactions, and financial management, generally. "Settles" accounts of certifying and disbursing officers. Makes reports to Congress.

Reviews compliance with established policies, procedures, and requirements. Evaluates accomplishment of program plans and effectiveness of management and operations.

Reviews agency operations and evaluates programs and performance. Conducts or guides agencies in organization and management studies. Assists President in improving management and organization of the executive branch.

Source: Executive Office of the President/Office of Management and Budget. Reprinted with permission from *Budgetary Politics*, by Lance T. Leloup, 3d ed. (King's Court Communications, Brunswick, Ohio, 1986).

ceeds from the operation of research offices, copy machines, and so on). At the extreme of budget complexity are the not-for-profit organizations that contract to deliver government services. It is not at all unusual for such agencies to receive funds from as many as fifteen different agencies. An organization that acts as trainer and advocate for handicapped persons, for example, may receive funds from the federal government through the following sources: Health and Human Services, separate grants for building funds to demonstrate innovative architecture for the handicapped, a TTY telephone system (a typing translator to allow mute people to use a telephone), a position for a sign-language translator, and for a lift-equipped van; state funds from its Department of Social and Health Services for vocational rehabilitation, assistance for handicapped people applying for income support programs, and for an office telephone system; local funds for some operating expenses, planning of a city's handicapped awareness month; United Way and other nongovernmental funds for a variety of programs, and so on. The many sources of funds must be kept informed of the ways in which the money is spent.

Government Accounting and Auditing

The details of budget management impose heavy demands on a government accounting system. Because of the political context of government taxing and spending, governmental accounting follows different procedures than found in the business sector. Organizations of professional accountants have established the generally accepted accounting principles, or GAAP. The principles contain broad guidelines for keeping track of and reporting financial transactions, as well as numerous practices to be followed by accountants and financial managers. The GAAP have been adapted to the governmental context by *Governmental Accounting, Auditing, and Financial Reporting*, or GAAFR (often referred to as "the blue book"), published by the Municipal Finance Officer's Association and endorsed by the National Council on Governmental Accounting and the American Institute of Certified Public Accountants.[19]

The main differences between business and governmental accounting are direct outcomes of politics. Elected officials are given a great temptation to adopt financial practices that enhance chances of reelection while hiding financial problems. For officials who expect to be succeeded by members of another political party, the temptation is to adopt procedures that saddle the other party with blame. This is one reason for special standards of accounting and financial reporting in the public sector. The professionals who keep track of public dollars must have some standards of comparison, and a measure of political independence, to give public officials and citizens an accurate picture of government finances.

Governments employ "fund accounting" or segregation of revenues and expenditures into categories that reflect limitations on the funds. For instance, trust funds include money for pensions and other functions that government holds as a trustee for others. General and special revenues need to be segregated since the latter are by law earmarked for a specific purpose. A fire department may receive a special tax levy to purchase equipment for paramedic emergency responses, and this must be accounted for separately from general expenses of the department. Government businesses have a special legal status that requires separation of revenues from general government funds. In all, the GAAFR lists eight types of funds, and a single government typically will have at least twenty separate funds in its accounting system. Some governments carry the earmarking of funds to extremes and have over a hundred funds. The GAAFR is intended to simplify and clarify government financial practices and requires competent judgment of individuals to fulfill its promise.

Accounting guidelines are not terribly specific, however. Considerable discretion in accounting system design is left to the financial authorities in particular governments, often in individual agencies. A GAO survey of federal government accounting procedures found 258 separate designs for accounting systems, a clear sign of the human hand at work. The main basis for different designs lies in determination of who needs what information, and because this differs by the type of agency and its operations, so will the accounting systems differ.

Managers do not need to be accountants, but they have to understand the purposes and reports of governmental accounting systems. The type of knowledge required will vary by level of the organization. First-level supervisors, for instance, must be aware of purchasing and reimbursement procedures, work-load reporting requirements, and the form the data takes on reports used by higher decision makers. Program managers need to know how much of the budget is already encumbered or spoken for, so that new purchases can be embarked upon without violating existing financial plans or antideficiency acts. Agency heads must be aware of the slack in program finances so that calls for cuts can be responded to with minimal damage to agency performance. The accounting system must provide each of these people with different types of information, the information they need to do their jobs.

Elected officials and citizens need to understand government financial practices, yet the size and complexity of government operations is beyond the scope of amateur oversight. At the national level the GAO is charged to undertake periodic and special audits of government programs. Periodic audits are done to make sure each agency is checked; the special audits are requested by Congress or prompted by complaints of waste or malfeasance. About half of GAO audits focus on fiduciary audits (Was the money spent responsibly?). The more controversial audits focus on program outcomes (Is this program effective?). All states and most local governments have a special office to audit programs. Local governments are commonly audited by a special state office.

The mass media often contain reports of government waste and poor financial management. Rarely are officials guilty of theft or other deliberate abuse, although such crimes do occur. The most frequent reason for poor financial management is simply neglect. GAO reports often tell the same story about new agencies: Accountant positions left unfilled, errors reported by auditors left uncorrected, deadlines not met, lack of proper vouchers for transactions, and so on.[20] The mistakes are most frequent where managers are promoted from specialized work without receiving adequate training for their new responsibilities.

There are two things that seem to be at the core of fiscal management. Each provides an interesting counterpoint to many of the best-laid plans. First, although it is possible to make changes, major improvements (and there have been improvements) take the better part of a generation. This suggests that changes are made not because of new ideas, but because people are replaced by others who believe in different work methods. The second point is a monument to politics. The political and professional traditions of our public organizations probably have more to do with financial practices than do the technical designs of financial management procedures. Money, in the end, is a strong bond between politics and administration.

BOX 12.8 Budget Control: The Case of Defense

Many well-publicized stories of wasteful procurement practices have put heat on the Department of Defense. Among the worst examples were the Navy's $436 hammer, available in most hardware stores for $9; a piece of wire worth several hundred dollars to the Air Force, wire that can be had at any Radio Shack for under a dime; millions of dollars for entertainment expenses billed by General Dynamics, including chili cookouts and boarding of animals to allow owners to attend a retreat. In one story, two defense contractors, McDonnell-Douglas and Northrup, were suing each other over which would get a lucrative defense contract. Together, they billed the government for $47 million in legal fees.

There are plausible administrative explanations for all of these items. The cost-control systems that watch over the big items tend to miss some of the small ones. Many employees of defense contractors used to work for the Department of Defense, and their work, their travel, and their weekend conversations all seem to be work-related. For companies that do nearly all of their business with the government, perhaps overhead, such as legal fees, is an appropriate expense. These are plausible administrative explanations, but the public is not buying them.

Congress is used to cost overruns in programs. It is a common practice for companies to bid on government contracts that, for many reasons, end up costing twice as much as original estimates. But the complaints about defense management came at the same time the Reagan administration was maligning social programs for waste and abuse, while increasing defense budgets.

Congress has responded with harsh words about defense management, and not coincidently defense budget requests now come under increased scrutiny. Partly to allay concerns and partly to improve management, the Department of Defense announced several steps to stem the embarrassing tide:

*Defense Secretary Weinberger suspended overhead payments to several contractors who were under investigation.
*Contractors are now required to swear under penalty of perjury that billed items contain nothing unrelated to contract performance.
*Navy Secretary Lehman got back the money billed for legal fees. No one in Congress liked the idea of the government paying for corporations to sue over government contracts.
*Officials from two defense contractors lost their jobs when the Department of Defense found they had billed the government for work their companies never performed. Other companies had to return several hundred million dollars of "excess profits" from the sale of spare parts.

It seems that the management of defense budgets got out of hand because, for years, the Congress had not paid serious attention. If experience is a guide to the future, the flurry of attention will eliminate many excesses for a time. But defense is large, and new problems will arise.

SUMMARY

We began the discussion of fiscal administration by looking at taxation. Governments collect a great deal of taxes and must decide *how* to tax (choosing among income, property, sales, and other taxes), *whom* to tax (choosing among income earners, consumers, property holders, businesses, and so on), and *how much* to tax. A major problem for governments lies in the budgeting of tax revenues. Typically, budget estimates of revenues and expenditures are made eighteen months or more before the end of a fiscal year, and techniques for fiscal forecasting are not precise. There are technical reasons for this, such as the inherent unpredictability of consumer spending. Perhaps more important are the political forces that affect budget forecasts. Governments find it hard to predict a recession, and include such estimates in their budget figures. The large federal budget deficits in the 1980s are a clear sign that politics dominate the technical concerns.

Our discussion of other industrialized countries' experiences shows that we are not alone in our financial difficulties. In general, citizen expectation exceeds the outputs of the western economies, and as a result government budgets get squeezed. OECD countries share the problems of slow economic growth, greater demands on the state, and budget deficits.

We then turned to the other side of fiscal administration: the spending and keeping track of money after a budget passes. Budget execution requires an elaborate system of controls and plans to see that money is spent according to law, and that it is spent productively. Managers do not have to be accountants, but some knowledge of budget control and accounting procedures is necessary for every student of administration.

NOTES

1. Joseph M. Winski, "States Revenues Lag Expenditures by $3.6 Billion," *City and State* 3, no. 5 (May 1986), p. 13.
2. For a thorough discussion of tax concepts, see R. A. Musgrave and P. B. Musgrave, *Public Finance in Theory and Practice*, 4th ed. (New York: McGraw-Hill, 1984).
3. Ibid., p. 262.
4. For comparative analysis of government finances and programs, see Richard Rose, *Understanding Big Government: The Programme Approach* (Beverly Hills: Sage Publications, 1984).
5. See John Mikesell, "The Cyclical Sensitivity of State and Local Taxes," *Public Budgeting and Finance* 4 (Spring 1984), pp. 32–39.
6. On the various tax types, see Musgrave and Musgrave, op. cit., Part 4.
7. See Richard Nathan, *The Plot that Failed* (New York: Wiley, 1975), and the "Revenue Sharing Watch" series from the Brookings Institution, also authored by Nathan.

8. See David R. Beam, "New Federalism, Old Realities: The Reagan Administration and Intergovernmental Reform," in Lester M. Salamon and Michael S. Lund, *The Reagan Presidency and the Governing of America* (Washington, D.C.: The Urban Institute Press, 1985).
9. Rodd Zolkos, "Budget Cuts Transform Federal-Local Relationship," *City and State* 3, no. 5 (May 1986), pp. 1, 61.
10. For examples of variables involved in financial forecasting, see Carole W. Lewis and A. Grayson Walker III, *Casebook in Public Budgeting and Financial Management* (Englewood Cliffs, N.J.: Prentice-Hall, 1984), Chap. 9.
11. A discussion of recent trends is included in Roy Bahl, *Financing State and Local Government in the 1980's* (New York: Oxford University Press, 1984).
12. The Organization for Economic Cooperation and Development (OECD) includes the largest twenty-five market-oriented industrial economies of the world. See OECD, *Historical Statistics* (Paris, 1984); and various issues of their journals, *Economic Outlook* and *OECD Observer*. In this chapter we compare only the OECD countries because their financial problems are most similar to ours. Budgeting in third world countries shows many of the same tendencies, yet raises a host of other issues beyond the scope of this book. For illustrative literature, see Naomi J. Caiden, "Comparing Budget Systems: Budgeting in ASEAN Countries," *Public Budgeting and Finance* 5, no. 4 (Winter 1985), pp. 23–38; and discussions of India, Malaysia, and Mexico in *Public Budgeting and Finance* 4, no. 1 (Spring 1984).
13. OECD, *Economic Outlook*, various issues, Table R5.
14. OECD, *Economic Outlook*, 37 (1984), pp. 63–70.
15. Charles R. Hjulten and Robert M. Schwab, "Regional Productivity Growth in U.S. Manufacturing: 1951–78," in *The American Economic Review*, 74, no. 1, pp. 152–162; and Peter K. Clark, "Productivity and Profits in the 1980's: Are They Really Improving?" in William Brainard and George Perry, eds., *Brookings Papers on Economic Activity*, no. 1 (Washington, D.C.: Brookings Institute, 1984).
16. OECD, *Historical Statistics* (Paris, 1984), pp. 45–46.
17. Richard Rose, op. cit., pp. 218–220.
18. See Frank S. Levy and Richard C. Michel, report on American living standards to the Joint Economic Committee, United States Congress, 1986; also John E. Schwarz, *America's Hidden Success* (New York: W. W. Norton, 1983).
19. *Governmental Accounting, Auditing, and Financial Reporting* (Chicago: Municipal Finance Officers Association of the United States and Canada, 1980).

20. To check on the most recent findings of problems in federal government financial practices, consult the *General Accounting Office Index,* located in government document repository libraries. Reports will be listed under "financial management," "accounting," and "budgeting" headings. GAO reports are sent free to any citizen.

CHAPTER THIRTEEN

Decision Making

> Modern man prides himself for living in the "rational" society. In the rational society, the connections between means and ends are no longer shrouded in tradition or faith but are purported to be open and aboveboard. Bureaucracy — all of modern organization — is alleged to be the carrier of such rationality in the rational society.
>
> *— Ralph P. Hummel*

Laws are full of ambiguities. Compromise is at the heart of our political process, and that compromise leads to ambiguous laws. For legislation to be sent to the president, a majority of the members of key committees — and a majority of voting members of Congress — must vote for it. Given the range of interests represented in Congress, it makes sense that compromise is the glue of most working coalitions. Specifically, those compromises often show up as ambiguities in our laws. The Congress avoids problems by letting various public agencies establish rules and procedures for translating abstract laws into governmental action. Even ongoing public programs must continually readjust to new budgets and to legal challenges that require different rules and procedures. This kind of choice making is a fact of administrative life. Administrators must make decisions.

At an abstract level, a decision is a choice among alternative ways to achieve some goal. In academic Public Administration, people often study various parts of the process of making decisions. Consider, for instance, the way government defines goals. Elected officials are in charge here, but the process of compromise will often produce ambiguous, multiple, or conflicting goals that government wishes to achieve. Moreover, conflicting goals are often the responsibility of a single agency. Given a set of goals, an agency still has difficult choices to make about ways to achieve them. Choices begin with ambiguity and take place in a political setting.

In order to make the discussion of decision making easier to understand, some distinctions need to be made, mostly in the way we conceptualize things. The first distinction is between decisions made by people and decisions made by organizations. Reason tells us that we cannot really make this separation, because it is people who fill the roles in organizations. Organizations, in other words, cannot "make" decisions. People in organizations make those decisions. But, there are different ways to study decision making.

The psychology of individual decision making is quite complex. Yet, because all of us are forced to decide things, we all have some sense of what is involved. We are able to compare our backgrounds, pressures, training, attitudes, and the like, with those of any public decision maker, and see if we would make different decisions. We feel capable of judging their decisions by our standards. This focus is closely related to studies of leadership discussed in Chapter 7. Understanding the way organizations make decisions is much more abstract. The heart of this focus is the idea that the dynamic of the whole is greater, and different, than the sum of all the interactions of the individuals involved. We will discuss several models that attempt to bring order to these haphazard-seeming events. It also makes sense to distinguish the level of organization occupied by various people contributing to decisions. A governor obviously has a different picture of public welfare programs than a caseworker. Each makes choices, but not of the same types. The differences between these roles must be considered in a thorough understanding of governmental decision making.

Finally, it is important to distinguish decisions at different stages in the development of a program. Important decisions are made in the planning of a program — lines of authority and communication, methods employed, political relationships, size and use of budgets, and so on. The decisions made in the implementation of a program tend to be more incremental in nature, more responsive to particular political needs, and have a short time frame compared to planning decisions. Decisions made during program evaluation can be distinguished from the earlier stages by the focus on the goals of the evaluators, which are often handed to the organization from legislative controllers, budget office officials, and questions that reflect public perceptions of an agency and its work. These distinctions about decisions — people and organizations, level of organization, and stages of program — help to unpack some of the complexities of the politics of decision making in public administration. We will use these distinctions in subsequent sections of this chapter.

Decisions are not simple to observe or describe. There are many serious controversies in Political Science and Public Administration over the proper methods for observing decisions, how particular decisions are actually made, and what guidelines are best to follow in making decisions.[1] For example, when has a decision taken place? The final act of choice may be recorded with responsible signatures attached, but prior to that stage many subchoices structured the decision in important ways. Were some alternatives left out? What criteria guided the choice of alternatives? Did analytical methods produce systematic bias in consideration of alternatives? The example could be extended for some time: The point is that

FIGURE 13.1 The Context of Decisions

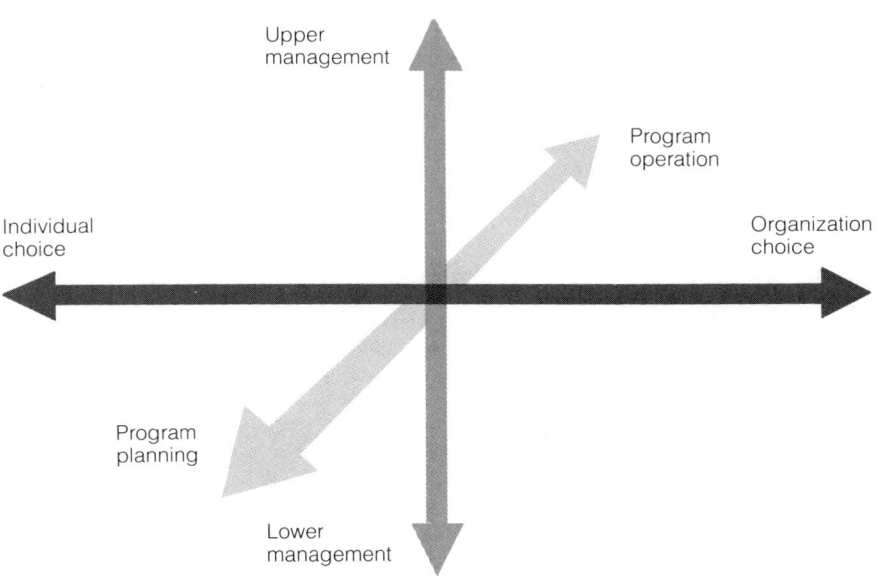

BOX 13.1 Decisions Are Seldom Simple

Public administrators have a difficult time understanding and managing many public problems. The problems are usually complicated, require many decisions rather than one, and are difficult to assess once action is taken. Consider the experience of Wilson Goode, mayor of Philadelphia in the mid-1980s. In one of the city's neighborhoods a group called MOVE had created a "back to nature" commune. MOVE members did not believe in bathing or using such city services as garbage and sewage removal. They did want to share their ideas with the surrounding neighborhood, and installed loudspeakers from which they would harangue people on the street, often at all hours of the night. They just did not fit in, and the neighbors complained to the city.

The police and the health department each tried to order MOVE members to obey city laws, but to no avail. MOVE members armed themselves and erected barricades around their building. A local minister often served as a mediator between MOVE and the city. The city's approach to new incidents was usually to call in the minister and negotiate, trying to defuse tempers on both sides. The mayor was soundly criticized for what the neighborhood saw as a lack of real action. This situation went on for several years.

Finally, an incident got out of hand. Shots were fired in the neighborhood, and the police surrounded MOVE. The mayor decided he had had enough, and instructed the police to order MOVE members to give up their arms. MOVE refused, and an armed standoff ensued. The police chief, believing he had the mayor's permission, and reacting to years of simmering tensions, ordered his officers to take the MOVE building from the roof. In an attempt to breach a bunker built on top of the building, the police dropped a large percussion grenade from a helicopter. The building caught fire. The fire department was slow to respond to the fire, out of fear of being shot, and the fire got out of hand. More than sixty households were burned to the ground before the fire was contained, and the MOVE members, including the children, were burned to death.

The mayor was heavily criticized for "bombing" a city building and using "Rambo" tactics. Neighborhood residents who had complained of inaction before, but who had now lost homes, did not support the mayor. Goode guaranteed that the homes would be rebuilt — yet they were completed more than a year later than planned, and at twice the estimated cost. One neighborhood resident said that "had they given me that much money, I could have bought a house in [one of the city's affluent suburbs]." Now the mayor was accused of abetting racial segregation in the city.

In retrospect, many people say the mayor should have acted differently, made different decisions. The fact is that the situation defied understanding and effective action. It was difficult to say just what all was involved, difficult to see the consequences of actions, and next to impossible to make the decisions that would satisfy all of the people involved.

reasonable people will disagree over basic questions in the study of decision making. In a sense, preliminary concerns about analytical frameworks are critical for what we are able to see and describe. Recall that this book has two central themes: first, that public administration represents an uncomfortable marriage between contending values of politics and administration; and second, this is an era of postprosperity where there is less slack in government resources, and so more critical decisions are being made in state and local governments. These themes also will guide our consideration of decisions in public administration.

Theories of Decision Making

Most descriptions of decision making can be grouped into several broad categories. In this section the major decision-making models under consideration will be: (1) rational models, where the decision problem is approached as if it were the choice of a single, logical decision maker; (2) legal models, where a formal institutional process considers alternative claims on the public interest; (3) political models, which emphasize the limited rationality of individuals and the interplay of organized interests in devising courses of action; and (4) social-psychological models, which focus on the individual decision maker but emphasize the way choices are framed by the perceptions and actions of others. There are several variants to each category, and other categorizations are possible.[2]

Rational Models

Discussions of decision making usually employ a very specific definition of "rationality." The common meaning of the term refers simply to the use of reason in accordance with accepted standards. In Chapter 2, we made the point that rationality is an important part of our cultural tradition and that it is no coincidence that rationality occupies a central place in our liberal and capitalist ideologies. It is important to remember that rationality takes on the meaning of its surroundings. For example, in American politics it is "rational" to compromise; however, in economic modeling the numbers "tell" us the rational thing to do. Rationality is simply one way of thinking, and not always the best way. Decision theorists shun this consensual approach in most instances and define rationality according to clear, objective standards. A decision maker is said to be rational if:[3]

1. There is a set of existing priorities
2. When applied to a decision problem, the priorities will serve to rank alternatives
3. If applied to the same decision problem twice, the priorities will serve to rank alternatives the same way each time.

Given such a decision maker, a problem is approached as follows:[4]

1. *Establishing the context.* What is the underlying problem that must be dealt with? What specific objectives are to be pursued in confronting this problem?

2. *Laying out the alternatives.* What are the alternative courses of action? What are the possibilities for gathering further information?
3. *Predicting the consequences.* What are the consequences of each of the alternative actions? What techniques are relevant for predicting these consequences? If outcomes are uncertain, what is the estimated likelihood of each?
4. *Valuing the outcomes.* By what criteria should we measure success in pursuing each objective? Recognizing that inevitably some alternatives will be superior with respect to certain objectives and inferior with respect to others, how should different combinations of valued objectives be compared with one another?
5. *Making a choice.* Drawing all aspects of the analysis together, what is the preferred course of action?

These assumptions about rationality and problem solving are somewhat relaxed when the organizational context is taken into consideration. In Anthony Down's terms, decision makers are rational if:

> they act in the most efficient manner possible given their limited capabilities and the cost of information. (They are) utility maximizers. In practical terms, this implies that whenever the cost of attaining any given goal rises in terms of time, effort, or money, they seek to attain less of that goal, other things being equal. Conversely, whenever the cost of attaining a goal falls, they seek to attain more of it.[5]

There is an important difference between the two versions of rationality. The first presents the decision problems of a single decision maker who faces no significant uncertainties.[6] When it comes to choosing analytical techniques this assumption is attractive; abstruse political and personal variables do not enter into the analysis.

The second version is much more realistic. This decision maker is trying to be rational in an organizational context. The problems are numerous. The decision maker occupies a role in an organization that is changing (expanding or contracting); the decision maker is working with other people (who have their own outlooks and approaches to their jobs); and the decision maker works in an environment of affairs over which he or she has little control. The bewildering complexity of this context drives rational decision makers to take shortcuts in the five-step process described above. We discussed some of these shortcuts in Chapter 4, while considering the ideas of Herbert Simon.

We will refer to rational models below in our discussion of techniques for informing decisions, but this needs to be said: No one sets out to be irrational. Of course, bureaucracies, representing the rule of law, must be guided by people following rationality, not irrationality. Rational models have limited application in accounting for the array of factors at work in public decisions; they are the basis for important techniques, such as benefit-cost analysis, but they do not explain the overall context of decisions as well as some of the other models considered here.

Legal Models

Many areas of public administration decision making can be understood by applying a legal model. Regulation of businesses and other government units, rule making within agencies, judicial policy-making, and adjudication processes within administrative agencies all may be usefully described according to legal models. The first attribute of such decisions is that they take place in a legal setting. A court is an obvious example. Elaborate rules and procedures direct the order of proceedings, the roles of participants, the methods of arriving at the facts of the matter, and requirements about the form and content of decisions. The specific type of legal reasoning may vary by whether the court is involved with constitutional principles, statutory interpretation, or development of common law, but the setting is easily recognized.[7]

BOX 13.2   How Rational Is Expert Judgment?

The marriage of analysis and administration seems to make sense, but is the marriage a good one? It is supposed to work because administration needs guidance, and analysis can provide the guidance. By relying on (a) the judgment of experts, (b) professional controls on groups of experts, and (c) scientific method, analysis can be put into the service of organizations. Complicated problems can be studied, interpreted, and managed.

A number of researchers have studied the reliability of expert judgments.* Their findings are not encouraging. Experts, just like regular people, have a limited ability to understand and manage complicated problems. Professions and groups do not overcome the limitations of individual experts. And the scientific method, understood as a set of procedures that will detect error, does not keep the experts from making these mistakes. Consider the following examples. A group of physicians was given detailed case histories of 100 patients, including laboratory reports, and were asked to diagnose the patients' illnesses. Correlations between the physicians' diagnoses and what patients actually had were *negative*. That means the physicians were wrong more often than we would expect a random guesser to be. In a study involving clinical psychologists, again given detailed case histories of patients, the experts were not able to predict important behaviors any better than would a random method of prediction, like flipping a coin. Many similar studies, looking at experts in many professions, show the same outcome.

Experts have the bad habits of their fellow human beings. They accept results based on small numbers of cases. They use strategies to prove their hypotheses, rather than disprove them. They judge based on the most recent or simplest information.

Experts tend to ignore base rates. For instance, a drug-testing program may be 95 percent accurate, but when applied to a large population, such as 2 million civil servants, about 100,000 mistaken tests will result. If civil servants use drugs as frequently as the general population, 90,000, or 9 out of 10 of the mistakes, will result in a false accusation against an innocent civil servant. Because of the low "base rate" of drug users, the apparently small amount of errors creates a major problem for nonusers.

The researchers found that experts make many mistakes and that while making these mistakes, the experts believed they are being scientific. In the words of one researcher, the study of human judgment is "a profoundly humbling experience." Perhaps we rely too much on experts, and too little on politics.

*The examples are from David Faust, *The Limits of Scientific Reasoning* (Minneapolis: University of Minnesota Press, 1984).

Administrative agencies must follow particular procedures in establishing the rules by which they operate and implement policies. This too is a legal setting and will be discussed in more detail later in the chapter. The rules are used for such activities as the regulation of business and evaluation of requests for particular services from government, such as public assistance and social security benefits. In the example of regulating businesses, an agency such as the Environmental Protection Agency will set procedures for how inspectors select which businesses to inspect, their course of action when they encounter a violation of law and rules, and what action the agency may ultimately take. The proceedings generally work on an adversary basis, so that businesses charged with a violation are entitled to notification of an alleged violation, time to prepare a response, a hearing or set of hearings to determine the facts of the case, and opportunities for appeal.

In the case of social security benefits, the Social Security Administration establishes rules for dealing with applications, such as one for survivor's benefits. Once they receive the application they analyze the case to determine if the applicant is eligible by looking at such things as whether the minimum time and earnings were accumulated, the number of dependents to receive benefits in the case, and the required division of benefits according to the age of dependent children. If the applicant disagrees with the agency finding, there is an opportunity for appeal before an impartial hearing board, and the case may ultimately wind up in federal courts.

In each of these cases the emphasis is on elaborate procedures that find the facts of a case, apply relevant criteria for decisions (meeting eligibility standards, balance the interests of contesting parties) and, most importantly, protect the rights of individuals involved in the process. Due process, the opportunity for an individual to have an impartial hearing, is the right that protects all other individual rights before the power of the state.

The purpose of the legal setting, elaborate and adversary procedures, facts, rules, precedents, and emphasis on individual rights is an attempt to separate politics from decisions on individual cases. As we know from the work of Max Weber, one of the great benefits of a legal-rational bureaucratic system is that, at least in principle, every citizen is treated equally. Although politics permeate the entire process of decision making, the selection of judges and "impartial" boards, the bottom line of our administrative system is that all laws should apply equally to all citizens.

Yet we know this is not exactly true. Studies of legal proceedings[8] show that laws are not applied equally to individuals. In the criminal justice system, for example, whether a defendant receives a sentence, and the length of the sentence, depends a great deal on personal characteristics of the defendant, which judge does the sentencing, and just a little on the quality of the evidence. Moreover, the patterns of what influences sentences vary remarkably across different cities.

Political Models

According to rational models, decisions reflect fairly exhaustive calculations of means-end relationships in the pursuit of objectives. The means that deliver the best mix of ends are chosen according to preselected criteria. In the legal model the stress on objectivity is relaxed a bit since the process recognizes competing interests and the need for balance among adversaries. Yet the overall formal setting provides clear rules by which solutions are reached. Political models of decision making revolve around different considerations. The main criterion for arriving at decisions has less to do with the content of choice than with political consensus on a choice. The search is for a means-end combination that can *win*, and the process for reaching this is fluid. Usually the combination that meets the test of consensus is not very different from earlier policies — change comes in increments, and so the model is often referred to as "incremental" decision making.

This is not to say that political decisions are irrational. Political models assume that the rationality of each individual actor is limited, and that it is the interaction of many such actors that produces results acceptable to most parties. The results may meet some individual tests of rationality, but it is the overall process of reaching consensus, and not calculation and analysis, that renders a decision. This is often called "political rationality."

Individuals may "muddle through" following a political model. In an original description of the model, Charles Lindblom described a process of "successive limited comparisons," or "incrementalism" (discussed in Chapter 11):[9]

1. Selection of value goals and empirical analysis of the needed action are not distinct from one another but are closely intertwined.
2. Since means and ends are not distinct, means-end analysis is often inappropriate or limited.
3. The test of a "good" policy is typically that various analysts find themselves directly agreeing on a policy (without their agreeing that it is the most appropriate means to an agreed objective).
4. Analysis is drastically limited; important outcomes are neglected; important alternative potential policies are neglected; and important affected values are neglected.
5. A succession of comparisons greatly reduces or eliminates reliance on theory.

Graham Allison describes the dynamics of incrementalism in a bureaucratic context.[10] Organizations are collections of offices, each with its own operating procedures, its own biases and desires, and its own political skills. Organizations only act when a number of people in these different offices act. Politics is an integral part of what bureaucracy does. Allison summarizes the tension:

> Men share power. Men differ concerning what must be done. The differences matter. This milieu necessitates that policy be resolved by politics. What the nation does is sometimes the result of the triumph of one group over others. More often, however, different groups pulling in different directions yield a result distinct from what anyone intended. What moves the chess pieces is not simply the reasons which support a course of action, nor the routines of organizations which enact an alternative, but the power and skill of proponents and opponents of the action in question.

Within the political or incremental model, there is room for a good deal of individual rationality. Amitai Etzioni suggests that a kind of modified incrementalism called "mixed scanning" is a good description of government policy-making.[11] Typically, says Etzioni, the search for alternatives goes on at two levels. The first level is a general "scan" to ensure that the most relevant variables are considered; the second level is a detailed consideration in those areas where calculation seems possible and desirable. For example, a fundamental decision may be made on the choice of means to explore space, and incremental decisions may be made over several years on the budget levels for the space shuttle.

Something important happened to "rationality" in the political models of decision making. We are presented with a picture of people with active wants and desires who try to make reasonable decisions in political organizations. Rationality looks very different when several people try to achieve it. What disappears are the connotations of truth and efficiency. What remains is the bureaucratic context.

BOX 13.3 Decisions in the Cuban Missile Crisis

An important study in decision making describes the people and organizations involved in the Cuban missile crisis.* In that crisis we came close to nuclear war (President John Kennedy described the odds as "between 1 out of 3 and even"). The decision makers involved are often thought of as doing the right thing, and being tough enough, to find a good solution and to avoid war. A close look at the crisis shows a different picture.

The crisis took place in the context of congressional elections. Each side was trying to look "tough" on communism, to show they would not tolerate Soviet military forces, or missiles, in Cuba. Yet to avoid a confrontation that might make him look weak, the president stopped sending spy planes over much of Cuba, so he found out too late that missiles were indeed there. Politically, the president could not afford to ignore the missiles, or to deal with the problem through diplomacy. That was never really considered.

For a time it seemed a "surgical" air strike was the best idea — but because of technical definitions of the targets and Air Force operating procedures, the success of the air strikes could not be guaranteed. Almost by default, a naval blockade became the preferred solution. The naval blockade was filled with similar confusing decisions. The head of naval operations had a manual describing how blockades were done. The head of the Department of Defense wanted it done a different way. The head of naval operations did it his way without telling the Secretary of Defense.

While this was going on in Washington, in Moscow the Soviet leaders complained they were just being fair. They pointed to our missiles in Turkey, a short distance from their major cities. President Kennedy had ordered the missiles removed the previous year, but they were still there. In retrospect, not much worked the way it was supposed to. The analyses were unsure. The decision makers were worried about elections and how they appeared to the public. The command and control of public organizations was less than complete. We did not get war, because we got lucky.

*This is based on Graham T. Allison, "Conceptual Models and the Cuban Missile Crisis," *American Political Science Review* 63, no. 3 (September 1969), pp. 689–718.

Social-Psychological Models

Social-psychological models emphasize the effect of a role on individual behavior. A role, in an organization, is constructed to play a particular part in the overall decision-making process. The roles change from organization to organization. For example, the water department head in one government may be expected to consider many political factors, whereas in another government the water department head may simply be a technician. Similarly, whole organizations may conceptualize their environments in different ways. Two organizations may perceive the same environment as quite different and make very different types of decisions in response to these perceptions. Karl Weik[12] argues that decision makers do not just react to their environment — they enact it.

How managers come to see a situation as simple or complex depends upon a number of factors. Janis[13] points out that in some situations a premium is placed on loyalty to the group and that this overrides the need to improve contacts with the environment. The feelings of loyalty are usually directed at those in power, and dissenting voices that may seriously question current policies are ignored. People in governments sometimes have a siege mentality and trust only those around them. Others may want to make a place for themselves in history and go well beyond the boundaries of good sense to defend themselves and the people with whom they work. Several memoirs by White House and other officials in the Johnson, Nixon, and Reagan administrations testify to the effect of such loyalties on criticism.[14]

Another factor affecting perceptions is a trained incapacity resulting from a field of specialization or cultural beliefs. Engineers may define an airport siting problem as essentially technical, where city planners may see it as a social and political issue. The concept of representative bureaucracy is based on concern over the cultural and ethnic composition of administrative agencies. The idea is that a citizenry as diverse as ours will have a difficult time making adequate decisions. The conflicts are even more acute in third world countries where the administrative class differs from much of the population in education, ethnic loyalties, and visions of the future.[15]

Social-psychological models and political models share certain assumptions about individuals, most notably those dealing with rationality. In both models, there is a belief that any particular person will not be "rational." In Simon's formulation:

> People are endowed with very large long-term memories, but with very narrow capacities for simultaneous attention to different pieces of information. At any given moment, only a little information, drawn from the senses and from long-term memory, can be held in the focus of attention. This information is not static; it is continuously being processed and transformed, with one item being replaced by another as new aspects of a stimulus are sensed, new inferences drawn, or new bits of information retrieved from long-term memory. Nevertheless, of all the things we know, or can see or hear around us, only a tiny fraction influences our behavior over any short interval of time.[16]

In social-psychological models, our limited cognitive capacity allows social, organizational, group, and interpersonal factors to influence decisions a great deal.

Social-psychological models have not figured as prominently as the others in the literature of public administration. The main reason has to do with the difficulties of conducting research in the field. Roles may be counted and compared, case studies may be compiled, but the core questions of the perspective are difficult to investigate. For instance, we do not know how to get at those things that influence the perceptions of a decision maker in a particular role. Most studies on managerial perceptions are done on private sector executives, and although they find correlations between middle and senior managers, between perceptions and decisions, and so on, we do not know for certain where the attitudes come from (parents, family, growing up, aging, economic status, the news that morning, bad karma, etc.). As we said in Chapter 8, the rules by which managers make choices are firmly locked inside their brains and defy close scrutiny.

The Limits of Models

The search for the "best" description of decision making in public administration will not end. Accuracy depends on the place a model is used, the issues under investigation, and the purposes of the investigator. No model will serve all purposes.

The reality of decision making is highly complex. In a sense government is like the river one cannot step in twice — the second time a new flow is underway, banks shift, and so on. The Marines are always the Marines — but they are never the same Marines. In public organizations there is a continuity to previous decisions, policies in force, and budgets already invested in an area (sunk costs represent an obstacle to doing things differently). Information is voluminous, but high-quality information that will help the decision makers make sense of a situation is probably costly and takes time to compile. The techniques used to inform decisions may be inherently rational, yet the context may defy clear understanding. Subsequent sections will discuss some of the more distinct areas of decision making — administrative law and program analysis.

Administrative Law and Decision Making

When the state makes decisions, practical questions of political theory come to the fore. Citizens are concerned with effective government, but more so with adequate controls on state power. American theories of the limits on government power have never been precise. Most revolutionary period and constitutional commentary emphasizes the fear of tyranny and combined powers, and the safeguards found in the separation of powers and an emphasis on limited government. Yet questions of "how separate?" and "how limited?" find only short-term answers.

One central ambiguity revolves around the respective roles of state and market. Although American political parties are ideologically close when compared to their European and Canadian counterparts, important differences remain. In most Democratic administrations the powers of the state expand. In most Republican administrations the powers of the state are roundly criticized, and occasionally altered significantly. This means that over a relatively short period the standards of assessment for administrative agencies may dramatically change. Effectiveness is always problematic, subject to shifting criteria in the minds of elected officials and citizens. Some years we want more regulation of the environment, others we want much less regulation, irrespective of the performance of administrative agencies. During Lyndon Johnson's presidency, we had a time of more government; with Ronald Reagan we had less. Each was effective according to different measures.

The lesson, in part, is that administrative agencies must do more than contribute their expertise to the governing of the country. We have always felt the tension between the claims to do good and the expertise to carry out those claims. Expertise is the chief resource of our administration; but, in a nation with a democratic spirit, that expertise will always be questioned.[17]

As we noted in Chapter 2, the separation of powers is popularly understood to require rigid separation between the three branches of gov-

> **BOX 13.4** Deciding How to Make Air Travel Safe
>
> The Federal Aviation Administration (FAA) is responsible for designing and administering air safety systems. The current system is one developed within the FAA and relies on many ground-based radar installations and air traffic controllers. These are the same controllers that were represented by PATCO (see Box 10.3). One of the top FAA priorities is to develop a collision avoidance system. The FAA is building its own system, one that relies on the ground-based controllers. The decision to build that system, however, may have been made for the wrong reasons.
>
> James Pope worked for the FAA for 16 years and was head of their industry-government liaison division. He told members of Congress that the FAA turned down a more reliable and cheaper collision avoidance system because there would not be a need for so many FAA traffic controllers. Pope was sent to a do-nothing job, and two years later was fired in what the FAA called a reorganization. Pope is suing the FAA for $60 million for taking what he alleges is punitive action.
>
> The system the FAA turned down was made by Honeywell. It was ready for installation in the early 1980s at a cost of about $14,000 per commerical plane, and about $1000 for private planes. Private planes make up about 98 percent of the total numbers flying. (The FAA system, when operational in the 1990s, will cost about $100,000 per commercial plane and $6,000 for private planes.) The FAA's tests showed the Honeywell system was better at preventing collisions and near misses than their own system. The Honeywell system works in clouds and poor weather, which present problems for the FAA system. Why didn't Honeywell press its case? The vice-president in charge of their system said the company did not want to jeopardize other government contracts.
>
> *Source:* James R. Carroll, "FAA Rejected Low-Cost 'Outside' Anti-Collision System," in *Seattle Times/Post-Intelligencer*, November 16, 1986, pp. 10–11.

ernment. State and local arrangements commonly follow the same pattern, although council-manager local governments have come down on the side of expertise and express less concern over abuses of state power. Yet the fact is that administrative agencies represent combinations of the various powers. They often possess both quasi-judicial (they consider cases, conduct hearings, pronounce judgments, but are not courts) and quasi-legislative powers (they consider policy, propose and pass rules of conduct for citizens, but are not legislatures). We fear combined powers, yet even the framers of the Constitution recognized the need for combination in many areas of state action. The blending of powers, at all levels, seems to be a necessary fact of political life. This very blending, however, often leaves the legitimacy of administrative actions in doubt. Administrations seek and thrive on clear-cut distinctions.

When administrative agencies apply rules to individual situations, we expect the application of judicial norms. Yet there are departures from these norms, and deliberately so. The application of rules to individual cases (as in the example of an individual applying for social security disability benefits) is generally a matter of routine. But, in particular times, it may reflect shifting emphases of a newly elected administration. Many administrative hearings are legislative in nature (as in the example of private utility rate setting). In both types of cases the function of the agency is not that of a court.

Political controls on administrative agencies are another source of ambiguity. How tight should controls be? How independent should agencies be? We need control to make sure power is not abused, yet we need independence where judicial powers are exercised. The controls are contained in the power of legislatures to change jurisdictions and the powers of agencies, conduct oversight investigations, and confirm officials, and in the power of executives to appoint officials and through them set policies. Together, these controls dramatically affect the conduct of administrative agencies, but the controls have generally failed to seize the popular imagination. As we have seen, a whole list of biases, from individualism to a distrust of big government, inform many peoples' view of public organizations.

One final reason for the ambiguity about the legitimacy of administrative agencies is the absence of a clear doctrine of delegation. Many legislatures delegate law-making powers to administrative agencies. Legislatures clearly have the responsibility to set broad purposes and policies of government, yet they sometimes sidestep these responsibilities and ask agencies to make important choices. Unless courts choose to police acts of legislatures that lack specific standards, the ambiguity will remain.

The net effect of these sources of ambiguity concerning the powers of administrative agencies is that they have a tenuous hold on public support. It is the job of the administrative process to perform required activities and at the same time elicit the support the modern state needs to operate effectively. For government decision makers, this is a challenge of the first order.

Administrative Law and the Administrative Procedures Act

Figure 13.2 presents a model of the administrative justice system for the United States government, the rules and procedures by which administrative agencies operate. Most state systems follow the national model. Figure

FIGURE 13.2 A Model of the Administrative Justice System*

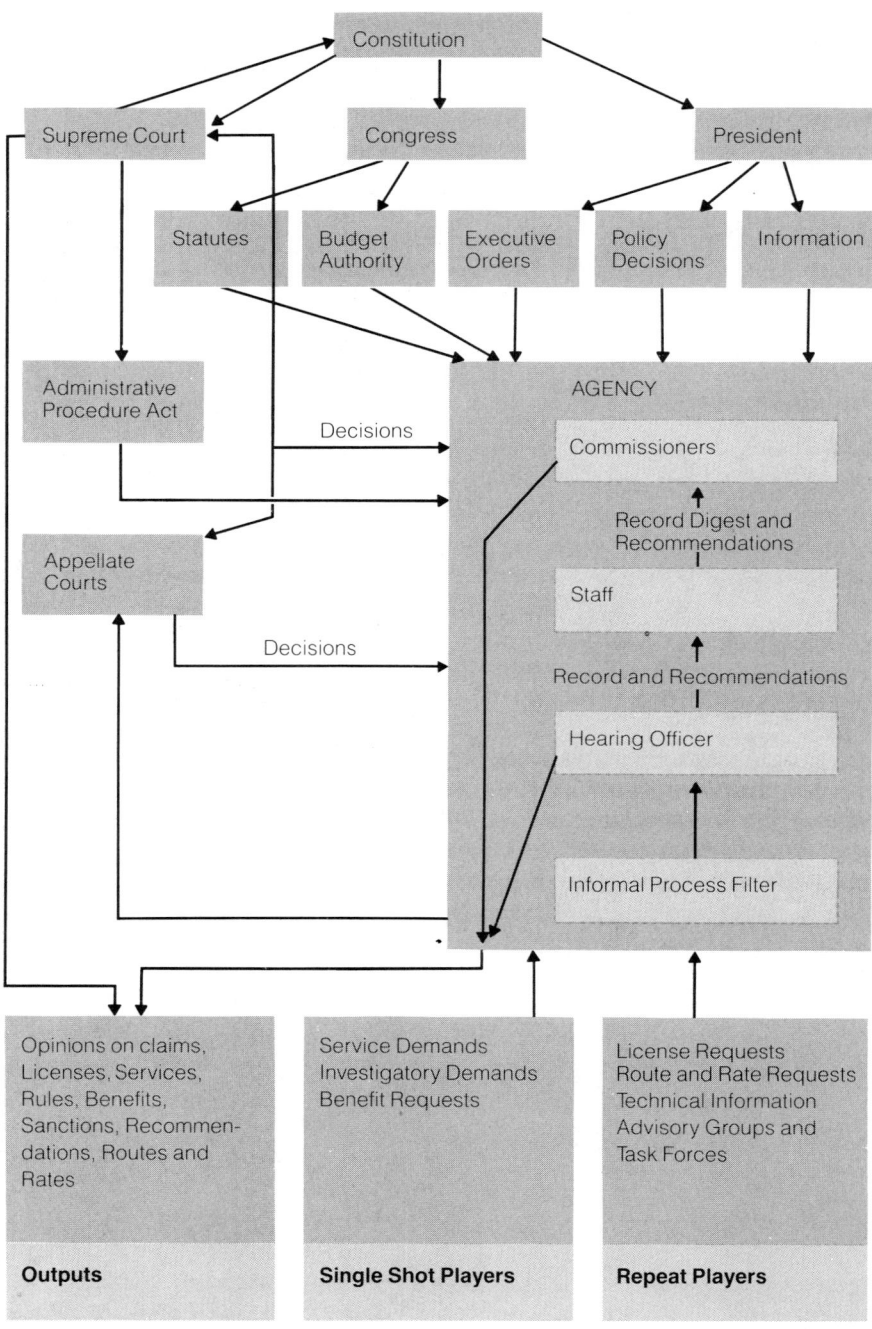

Source: Phillip J. Cooper, *Public Law and Public Administration* (Palo Alto, Calif.: Mayfield Publishing, 1983), p. 12.

13.2 emphasizes the constitutional authority exercised by the three branches of government and shows how this results in outputs of the administrative process. Congress has a good deal of control over federal agencies. Congress gives an agency its statutory authority, provides it with a budget, and makes periodic reviews of activities of the agency. The executive branch provides guidance through policy decisions, sometimes in the form of executive orders, and information that seeks to guide administrative choices. Courts hear appeals of cases and provide guidance through decisions. The overarching guide to agency conduct is the Administrative Procedures Act (APA), which tells agencies how to make rules and decisions.

The outputs of administrative agencies as depicted in Figure 13.2 are generated from two sources. Administrative agencies may initiate actions in response to legislative or executive policy, such as the pursuit of civil rights cases or regulation of shoreline uses. Administrative agencies also respond to citizens ("players") who make demands of the government. Single-shot players generally have one request; they might want welfare or social security benefits, an investigation of an apparent violation of the law, or a service they believe is due from the government. Repeat players are citizens or businesses who have regular contact with the agency. Generally, they do something that is regulated by the government or are interested in policies administered by an agency.

Within the agency, there are options on how to handle each case. According to one estimate, over 80 percent of federal administrative agency work is done informally, and similar practices exist in the states. In informal procedures, administrative agencies are the focus of negotiations and discussions among involved parties. Consider the example of an agency in charge of ensuring that toys are safe enough for infants. A new type of toy is created that does not clearly fit under existing regulations. The agency has a choice of how to proceed. It may, for example, decide to initiate formal procedures of making rules and applying rules to the manufacturers in question. There are possibly lengthy delays in conducting hearings, passing rules, and possible litigation. Another choice is to have more informal procedures. The informal procedures may take the form of discussions with the manufacturer. The agency may encourage discussions among manufacturers through trade associations or at an agency-sponsored trades practices conference. If an agency believes the toy is in violation of existing rules, it may go to court. The problem with that, of course, is that the case may be lengthy and costly, and could be lost. An agency may choose to arrive at a settlement with the manufacturer. Such settlements are called "consent decrees." The manufacturer does not admit to any wrongful practice, but agrees to stop it; the agency agrees not to pursue punitive actions against the manufacturer. These and similar practices reduce the time and cost of administrative procedures and establish less of an adversary relationship between government and affected citizens. Such informal processes often offend citizen beliefs about punishment due guilty parties, openness in government, and what is an apparently cozy relationship between regulated industries and the agency. Many informal procedures are authorized in APAs.

The formal administrative processes are given detailed guidance in the APA. The various sections include:

1. Definitions of agencies and rules. The definitions are particularly important since they establish which units of government are to follow APA provisions and what agency actions are covered.
2. The national act contains the Freedom of Information Act and the Privacy Act of 1974, which establish policies about the availability of government information and protections for citizens about whom the government has collected information.
3. Rule-making provisions describe the procedures an agency must follow in making rules. The rules must be within the power granted by the legislature. An agency must publish the intent to make a rule and allow the public time to comment on proposed rules, give opportunities for a hearing to allow parties to contest agency plans, and give advance warnings of when the rule will take effect.
4. Due process is guaranteed to individuals who have a case adjudicated by the government. They are to be given notice of actions, opportunities for comment or hearings, and decisions by impartial hearing examiners. Additional sections describe protections for the independence of hearing examiners.
5. Agency actions are subject to judicial review.

Taken together, the various parts of APAs allow citizens ample warning of and opportunity to challenge or comment upon agency actions. These safeguards are not sufficient to overcome doubts by citizens about the legitimacy of administrative actions, however. We seem to have very mixed feelings about our administrative state. During the nuclear accident at the Three Mile Island reactor, we certainly wanted more rather than less administration. Yet, when we read the stories of bureaucratic waste, we immediately want less. The people who deliver our mail are wanted; those who audit our taxes are not. As people who are raised on individualism, the whole idea of an administrative state is distasteful. As people who like our comforts and want to feel protected, we like governmental efficiency.

Our attitudes about our administration have yet to catch up with the reality of all the things we expect from it. The APA was barely a beginning for any real changes in attitude.

The Politics of Administrative Rule Making

Agencies make decisions in a political context. Consider the following sets of decisions made under the Reagan administration:

1. The Occupational Safety and Health Administration (OSHA) was a target of Reagan election promises.[18] Businesses were too closely regulated, it was argued, and changes were needed. The New OSHA administrator guided the agency to a fairly passive rule-making role, shunned new regulatory initiatives, and changed enforcement procedures. OSHA exempted from inspection industries that had fewer lost workdays and lower injury rates than the national average, exempting three-fourths of businesses from inspection (these businesses account for only one-fourth of worker injuries). The inspection process was changed to emphasize consultations rather than confrontation. The number of inspectors was cut by over one-fourth. Inspectors were told that too many contested violations would result in lower performance ratings. The Reagan administration pressed for further reforms that would result in industry self-inspections for most types of safety concerns. Evaluators differ on the effectiveness of OSHA, but this much is certain: the politics changed, and the administrative conduct of the independent executive agency changed in response.

2. The Food Safety and Inspection Service (FSIS) of USDA inspects the slaughter and processing of meat and meat products. The FSIS engages in continuous inspection, so that meat-packing plants have inspectors watching the production lines at all times. Again, the Reagan administration officials charged that regulations and inspections were too costly to business, and changes were made. The number of inspectors was cut to the point where the average chicken carcass moves twice as fast past inspectors as before. The FSIS even proposed to furlough inspectors for several weeks in response to a federal budget crisis in 1986, leaving meat factories without inspection, but inspector unions and consumer groups protested and no action was taken on the proposal. Similar to the OSHA initiatives, Reagan officials pressed (with greater success) for a shift to industry self-inspection rather than a government "watchdog" model to ensure food safety. Several outbreaks of salmonella poisoning and a hemorrhagic strain of *E. coli* bacteria that contaminates beef doubled the number of cases of food poisoning in the Reagan years, but officials disputed whether the outbreaks were due to changes in inspection practices. Again, evaluators disagree on the actual outcomes of government regulation, but it is clear that the politics changed, and the independent inspection agency changed its procedures.

3. The Office of Management and Budget (OMB) under Reagan issued a requirement that regulatory impact analyses (RIAs) be submitted by

agencies under the president's jurisdiction for each proposed regulation estimated to have an economic impact of $100 million or more. This allowed Reagan administration officials more control over the regulatory process in several ways. The OMB was to be notified 60 days prior to publication of the new regulation in the *Federal Register.* The OMB issued guidelines for conducting an RIA, and could request further information from the agencies writing regulations. Although the RIA procedure did not give direct formal authority to rewrite or cancel regulations, it did make OMB oversight activities more direct and, by implication, result in agency changes. Over the first four years of the regulation, OMB officials claimed $20 billion in savings for business costs of complying with regulations.

Making Decisions about Programs

Earlier, we noted that decisions vary by the stage of the program and whether the decision concerns planning, implementation, or evaluation. There are also problems that may affect decision making at any stage. The most basic problem underlying analysis for making decisions is the ideological biases of the analytical techniques.[19] All techniques have biases; but these biases are not always obvious. There are all kinds of questions about the techniques: Who uses them, what are the technical criteria they depend on, what is the mix of values that are considered, and so on. Generally, these problems emerge in three ways.

The first source of distortion is simply ignoring certain facts. A decision maker may accept a path of lesser resistance and choose in a way deemed acceptable to higher officials or influential interests. Examples of such analysis and decisions during the Vietnam war are a central subject of Halberstam's *The Best and the Brightest.*[20]

The second source of distortion comes from inadequate conceptual frameworks of analysts. These frameworks simply may not include important values. Jane Jacobs's *Death and Life of Great American Cities*[21] altered the field of urban planning by calling attention to the linkages between community values and the physical state of a city. Prior to her pioneering work, planners simply left those considerations out of their decisions. Many government policies involve subjects studied by sociologists, psychologists, geographers, political scientists, and other social scientists whose theories include large blind spots — and whose application has often produced much unintended harm.[22]

A third cause of distortion, perhaps the most fundamental, is the ideological bias decision makers may bring to viewing and defining problems.

For example, a popular model used to evaluate many policy areas comes from neoclassical microeconomics. Versions of the model include a set of assumptions about citizens and decision makers that allows for calculations about the outcomes of policy changes. Yet as Box 13.5 indicates, the application of the model to actual policy questions usually involves important assumptions that add biases to the calculations. The result is that the analysis is not "rational," as promised. The likelihood is that decision makers fail to recognize implicit biases, for instance, toward more government intervention or less government intervention included in analytical techniques.

BOX 13.5 Problems in Objectivity

Economic models are often presented as an example of objective analytical techniques. Among the criteria such models use to rank alternatives is the idea of economic efficiency. The key idea is that one solution is the most efficient overall use of resources as judged by consumer preferences. It is called *Pareto efficiency.* The basic rule of Pareto optimality is this: Situation A is better (more efficient) than situation B if at least one person is better off and no one is worse off. An unequivocal improvement would exist under those conditions. The rule is open-ended in the sense that many people can be better off, and if it is still the case that no one is worse off, then a Pareto improvement has taken place. Decision makers could follow the Pareto criterion in pursuing better policies.

In the real world of public administration, these conditions can never be met. Public policy issues are never so clear-cut that improvements can be made without making someone worse off. But that does not stop analysts from using Pareto efficiency. They make the following adjustments to the original idea:

1. It is OK to have losers. Not every one has to be better off.
2. We don't know what all makes a person "better off," so we will just measure income and things that can be bought and sold.
3. We really only care that winners win more than losers lose.

What started out as a precise idea, a concept used to describe a marketlike sense of efficiency, turns out to have enormous political significance.

Analytical Techniques

There are many analytical techniques employed in program and policy analysis, and we can only present an overview here. The most common and influential techniques are benefit-cost analysis, decision analysis, and operations research.[23] Benefit-cost analysis is a technique used to compare alternative means for reaching goals. For instance, assume you are giving advice to a city council on how to dispose of solid wastes in the city. Your technicians find three options that can achieve the city's goals. Option 1 costs $6 million, takes two years to build, and will generate annual operating profits of $60,000 through its effective life of eight years. Option 2 costs $3.5 million, takes eighteen months to build, and costs $400,000 annually to operate over its fifteen-year effective life. Option 3 costs $800,000, can be operational in nine months, and will cost $770,000 annually to operate over its five-year effective life. Option 1 exceeds all state and federal standards; option 2 exceeds most state and federal standards, minimally meeting others; option 3 barely meets state and federal standards. Which should be built?

This simplified example shows the strengths of benefit-cost analysis. All factors of comparison are converted to monetary terms, usually dollars. It allows comparison of alternatives that have different cost and benefit streams (the amounts and timing of costs and benefits) and reduces the various factors into a set of comparable numbers. It does this by discounting, a method of decreasing the value of future costs and benefits to reflect the idea that the future is worth less than the present. (You know this intuitively: If you are offered $100 in cash today or in cash one year from now, which will you choose?) The discounted cost and benefit streams can be compared in terms of their net benefits (benefit-costs), their benefit-cost ratios, or total benefits subject to a budget constraint.

Although benefit-cost analysis looks objective, it is subject to many judgments that affect its results. First, it does not add to the facts available to decision makers; it combines them in new ways in order to make comparisons. Remember, it is not a magic technique for generating facts. Second, there are few solid standards for making key analytical judgments. For instance, how much less is the future worth? This can be thought of as the same problem you have when putting money into a bank. What rate of interest makes it worth your while? This is, in effect, a judgment of how much you need to be compensated to allow someone else to use your money for a while. 5 percent? 7 percent? 12 percent? Should this discount rate include simply the value of time, or should it also include a factor for possible inflation? Is the discount rate constant in the future, or does it get smaller after, say, ten years?

A good example of the controversy surfaced early in the Reagan administration. The Secretary of the Interior announced that all federal environmental projects must now be subjected to benefit-cost analysis. Moreover, agencies are to use OMB guidelines, which specify that discount rates shall be calculated at 10 percent. Environmentalists announced their outrage at the decision for reasons that are obvious enough. The value of a $1 million resource left dormant for 25 years, discounted at 10 percent per year, is a little over $92,000 in present dollars, and this does not take inflation into account. Environmentalists saw that this method of benefit-cost analysis did not have much regard for the next generation. The main result of the regulations was many fewer initiatives to protect the environment.

One of the chief abuses of benefit-cost analysis involves its application to single alternatives. A benefit-cost analysis simply does not provide reliable information about the future. Although it does a good job of comparing, it also has some potentially fatal flaws. For example, it assumes that the prediction errors for each alternative will be the same. Yet we know that we are consistently wrong about the future. Applying the technique to single-project use dramatically increases the likelihood of large and undetected errors.

Decision analysis as used in public administration is really a collection of techniques that help clarify the result of policy choices. Most decision problems do not involve just one goal, but rather involve several often conflicting objectives. By clarifying expectations of program performance, agreeing upon methods of measurement and analysis, and the uses to which analysis can be put, it is possible to clarify the conflicts among a number of interested parties. Relatively simple techniques of decision analysis clarify the consequences of choice for single decision makers.

Operations research is another collection of techniques, mainly involving mathematical models of decision problems. These techniques allow decision makers to calculate trade-offs among alternatives. They are designed to enable decision makers to frame problems and to deal with vast amounts of information in making choices, often with the aid of computerized calculations and summaries of data. Analysis is no simple process. Control and influence over information are delegated to analysts; a technique may include inherent biases that distort results; the application of techniques involves human judgment at every turn, and each of them is a source of error. Again, analytical techniques seldom enhance our ability to predict the future. They organize information into other forms, forms that we hope will enhance the quality of decisions.

The State of Government Decision Making

Most of the modern decision-making techniques now used in the private sector originated in government. The defense department, for instance, has been the world leader in planning and budgeting techniques, mathematical modeling of decision problems, and program evaluation. There is much innovation and vitality in public sector decision making. There is another side to public sector decisions, however. The pursuit of rational decision support techniques has not resulted in greater public confidence in government, or in demonstrably effective programs. Often the results have been precisely the opposite intended.

It seems almost impossible to get ongoing "good" decisions out of government administration. The differences between the needs of organizations and the demands of the political environment are seemingly too great to find suitable solutions. It is clear that we have enough techniques for making decisions in organizations. It is not at all clear how citizens may come to understand, accept, or find a greater voice in government decision making.

SUMMARY

Our discussion of decision making showed that laws require public administrators to make decisions. But how do they decide? What preserves democratic accountability for officials that are not elected or closely watched by elected officials? One problem with understanding decisions is that they are not simple to describe. The context of decision making is enormously complex. Decisions have a political context, occur in an organization or among organizations, concern programs, and involve human behavior. Most approaches to the study of decision making acknowledge this complexity and focus on how administrators can approximate "good" decision-making practices (though they can never be achieved fully).

Descriptions of decision making can be grouped into several types of theory. Rational models emphasize the connections between goals and the means used to achieve them, but have a difficult time incorporating insights about politics. Legal models focus on the process of decision making and stress accountability and implementation of legislation. Political models emphasize the role of force and power in reaching agreement and achieving obedience, yet downplay the role of reason and rationality. Social-psychological models emphasize how roles and group behavior affect decisions, but also have trouble incorporating legal and political insights. No one model offers a complete description, although attention to more than one model allows the student of decision making to grasp the complexity of large organizations.

Specific attention to decisions requires an understanding of administrative law, the norms and procedures at work when administration decisions have the force of law. The Administrative Procedures Act empowers agencies to make rules and adjudicate cases, and contains protections of the rights of citizens.

We closed our treatment of decision making by looking at decisions about programs. How can a government decide whether a new program is a good idea, or whether an ongoing program is still a good idea? The political context is paramount, yet analytical techniques (such as benefit-cost analysis) often inform and shape decisions at critical stages. While the technical side of decision making is highly developed, the main problems are still citizen understanding, acceptance, and participation in government decisions.

NOTES

1. David Ricci, *Community Power and Democratic Theory* (New York: Random House, 1971); see also Michael Murray, *Decisions: A Comparative Perspective* (Marshfield, Mass.: Pitman, 1986).
2. See Murray, ibid.
3. See the discussion of rationality in Anthony Downs, *An Economic Theory of Democracy* (New York: Harper & Row, 1957), pp. 4–11; and William Riker and Peter Ordeshook, *An Introduction to Positive Political Theory.*
4. Edith Stokey and Richard Zeckhauser, *A Primer for Policy Analysis* (New York: W.W. Norton, 1980), pp. 5–6.
5. Anthony Downs, *Inside Bureaucracy* (Boston: Little, Brown, 1964), p. 2.
6. Stokey and Zeckhauser, op. cit., p. 23.
7. See the discussion of legal reasoning in Phillip J. Cooper, *Public Administration and Public Law* (Palo Alto, Calif.: Mayfield, 1983), p. 55. See also Marshall E. Dimock, *Law and Dynamic Administration* (New York: Praeger, 1980).
8. See James Eisenstein and Herbert Jacob, *Felony Justice* (Boston: Little, Brown, 1977), Chap. 10.
9. Charles Lindblom, "The Science of Muddling Through," *Public Administration Review* 19 (1959), pp. 79–88.
10. Graham T. Allison, "Conceptual Models and the Cuban Missile Crisis," *American Political Science Review* 63, no. 3 (September 1969), p. 707.
11. Amitai Etzioni, "Mixed-Scanning: A 'Third' Approach to Decision Making," *Public Administration Review* 27, no. 5 (December 1967), pp. 385–392.
12. Karl Weick, *Social Psychology of Organizing* (Reading, Mass.: Addison-Wesley, 1969).

13. Irving Janis, *Victims of Groupthink* (Boston: Houghton Mifflin, 1972).
14. Dan Rather and Gary Paul Gates, *The Palace Guard* (New York: Harper & Row, 1974); George Reedy, *The Twilight of the Presidency* (New York: New American Library, 1970); David Stockman, *The Triumph of Politics* (New York: Harper & Row, 1986).
15. See Ferrel Heady, *Public Administration: A Comparative Perspective* (New York: Marcel Dekker, 1984), Chap. 7.
16. Herbert A. Simon, "Human Nature in Politics: The Dialogue of Psychology with Political Science," *American Political Science Review* 79, no. 2 (June 1985), p. 301.
17. See Richard Hofstadter, *Anti-Intellectualism in American Life* (New York: Vintage Books, 1963).
18. This section relies on Kenneth J. Meier, *Regulation* (New York: St. Martin's, 1985), pp. 216–224.
19. Fred Kramer, "Policy Analysis as Ideology," *Public Administration Review* 36 (September/October 1975), pp. 509–517.
20. David Halberstam, *The Best and the Brightest* (New York: Random House, 1969).
21. Jane Jacobs, *The Death and Life of Great American Cities* (New York: Vintage Books, 1961).
22. Daniel Pat Moynihan, *Maximum Feasible Misunderstanding: Community Action in the War on Poverty* (New York: Free Press, 1969).
23. Sources that describe the techniques are Stokey and Zeckhauser, op. cit.; E. S. Quade, *Analysis for Public Decisions* (New York: North-Holland, 1982); and Susan Welch and John C. Comer, *Quantitative Methods for Public Administration* (Homewood, Ill.: The Dorsey Press, 1983).

CHAPTER FOURTEEN

Policy Evaluation

> "What is evaluation?" "Why do you ask?"
> — *after Aaron Wildavsky*

While preparing to write this chapter, I had a tax audit. The IRS was interested in my tax returns for 1983. Loaded with all kinds of records and notes and books and cancelled checks (and also pretty nervous because I had never been audited before), my accountant and I went to the regional office of the Internal Revenue Service.

During the course of the almost 5-hour audit, the civil servant compared her office to an office in Texas. "Our office is much better," she said, "we get more money back per audit than the Texas office does." In the most crude sense, this is a policy evaluation. The auditor believed that the measure of effectiveness was the getting of money from, in this case, the poor taxpayer. Thankfully, her boss had a more inclusive sense of how to evaluate policy, and I am now preparing for a new audit with a different auditor.

The study of public policy, how it is made, implemented, and evaluated, has become one of the critical areas in public administration. One writer estimates that more than a half billion dollars is spent every year on evaluating public policy.[1] Attention to policy studies has emerged and come into its own during the last fifteen or twenty years. As is true for most academic enterprises, there is no general agreement about either what to study or how to study it. In this chapter, we will try to sort through the general directions of policy evaluation.

Public Policy

For clarity, it is best to begin with a definition of public policy. Austin Ranney writes that public policy is

> A *particular object or set of objects* — some designated part of the environment . . . which is intended to be affected.
>
> A *desired course of events* — a particular sequence of behavior desired in a particular object or set of objects.

A selected line of action — a particular set of actions chosen to bring about the desired course of events . . . a deliberate selection of one line of action from several possible lines.

A declaration of intent — some statement by the policy makers as to what they intend to do, how and why.

An implementation of intent — the actions usually undertaken vis-à-vis the particular set of objects in pursuance of the choices and declaration.[2]

We are most interested in the implementation of policy and how to evaluate that implementation. We can get closer to some understanding of that by reading Harold Lasswell. He writes:

> The policy sciences study the process of deciding on choosing and evaluate the relevance of available knowledge for the solution of particular problems. When policy scientists are concerned with government, law, and political mobilization, they focus on particular decisions. Policy scientists also study the choosing process of nongovernmental organizations and individuals and consider the significance of the current stock of knowledge for specific issues. Since an official decision on a private choice is a problem-solving activity, five intellectual tasks are performed at varying levels of insight and understanding: clarification of goals, description of trends; analysis of conditions; projection of future developments; and invention, evaluation, and selection of alternatives.[3]

The Ranney and Lasswell definitions make it seem as if all of public administration is simply the study of public policy.[4]

If that is true, or even mostly true, then the implementation and evaluation of policy becomes the way we judge our public organizations. It may be wise to step back a moment and get a little perspective. The dictionary gives us good leads to what we will be talking about.

> **implement** — n. [from L. *implere* to fill up], v.t. **1.** to carry into effect **2.** to give practical effect to.

> **evaluate** — [Fr. *évaluer*, to value; L. *e-*, from and *valere*, to be strong, to be worth.] **1.** to determine the worth of; to find the amount of; to appraise.

Implement is the easier of the two words to understand. To carry into effect, to give practical effect to is straightforward enough. Implementing is the doing of the program. It is the auditor sitting there and asking me if I could prove that I bought my computer. It is the people from the city

FIGURE 14.1 Phases and characteristics of the policy process

Phase	Characteristics/Uses
Initiation	Creative thinking about a problem. Definition of objectives. Innovative option design. Tentative and preliminary exploration of concepts, claims, and possibilities.
Estimation	Thorough investigation of concepts and claims. Scientific examination of impacts; e.g., of continuing to do nothing and for each considered intervention option. Normative examination of likely consequences. Development of program outlines. Establishment of expected performance criteria and indicators.
Selection	Debate of possible options. Compromises, bargains, and accommodations. Reduction of uncertainty about options. Integration of ideological and other nonrational elements of decision. Decisions among options. Assignment of executive responsibility.
Implementation	Development of rules, regulations, and guidelines to carry out decision Modification of decision to reflect operational constraints, including incentives and resources. Translation of decision into operational terms. Setting up program goals and standards, including schedule of operations.
Evaluation	Comparison of expected and actual performance levels according to established criteria. Assignment of responsibility for discovered discrepancies in performance.
Termination	Determination of costs, consequences, and benefits for reductions or closures. Amelioration as necessary and required. Specification of new problems created during termination.

Source: From Brewer and DeLeon, *Foundation of Policy Analysis* (The Dorsey Press, Chicago, IL). Copyright © 1983.

filling the pothole in the road. It is the psychologist at the Department of Mental Health making a judgment about where a patient should live. It is also the immense number of people in each of those organizations who make each act possible.

To evaluate is much different. The roots of the word revolve around value, strength, and worth. What we will see is that value and worth are quite difficult to separate when we are talking about *public* policy. All too often, the goal of a policy made by an elective body is purposely vague, or unstated, or simply impossible to measure. How, for example, does one measure the success of a city baseball league? By the number of major league players produced? By the number of friends made? By computing the "babysitting" value? The fun had? The crimes *not* committed? The point, of course, is that it is really impossible to evaluate success. We will see that value and worth are attitudes that give meaning to facts, and that makes evaluation a very difficult task.

The other root of evaluate is strength. What we would like to suggest is that strength, here, is related to power. When we discuss evaluation, we are discussing different centers of power. There is the power of the political process, of constituent groups, of the administrations, and of the general public. It is also helpful to remember that there is also the power of the evaluations and the evaluators. What we are talking about, in part, is the intersection of the purity of methodology and the politics of civil servants dealing with citizens. It is a variation of public/administration.

Implementation

In the early 1970s, Jeffery Pressman and Aaron Wildavsky wrote a book titled *Implementation*.[5] They claimed that not a great deal of work had gone on in studying how decisions were made and then implemented. They concluded that there was an inverse relationship between the number of transactions required to implement a decision and the likelihood that any effect would result. In a passage of humor — something all too rare in studies of implementation — Pressman and Wildavsky decide to give us numbers to work with. They reckon that if 95 percent of all of the people working on a particular program cooperated, the overall probability of success would be about 0.000395.

That kind of "success" rate carries a clear message for some. In *The Implementation Game: What Happens After a Bill Becomes a Law*, Eugene Bardach[6] argues that the government should stop doing so many things that liberal reformers want done. Although doing fewer things certainly cuts down the possibilities of failure, it also fails to address the more important questions asked by the people making laws: How should we meet the needs of the poor, mentally ill, abused, and so forth?

> **BOX 14.1 Can Evaluations Help Get Things Done?**
>
> Policies can only be as good as their implementation. Can analysis help? At least two approaches to analysis address this question.
>
> First, analysts must serve the needs of managers.* They can do this in four ways:
>
> 1. They help to define expected performance of the program and establish clear, outcome-oriented objectives. They have to work in conjunction with key elected officials; without their agreement, it is probably better not to continue analysis. They also have to work in conjunction with program managers. If managers' concerns are not included in the analysis, the findings will be of little assistance in program implementation.
> 2. They help assess performance, and variations in performance, in terms of specific expectations. Evaluators must produce results quickly enough so that program managers can discover and correct problems before they become too costly, or too politically resistant to change. This means that there will not always be time to use exhaustive social science methods.
> 3. They help to stimulate improvements in program performance. Evaluators can do this by staying in close touch with program managers and elected officials, with the clear understanding that problems discovered are opportunities to improve rather than reasons to cut the program.
> 4. They help managers communicate the value of the organization's activities, both within and outside the organization. It makes little political sense to do a good job and be quiet about it.
>
> A second approach to making evaluation useful at the implementation stage is to manage the political relationships.† It is possible to study the intended effects of a program, the program elements and who controls them, the groups for and against the program, and so on, and then devise strategies for coping with the likely "games" these various people and groups will play. The most important element in constructing such an "implementation scenario" is to have some source of power to "fix" the political games — to help pass new legislation, to ensure the security of budgets, and so on.
>
> Neither of these techniques for implementation analysis is foolproof, of course. Both rely on the active cooperation of powerful political officials. The point is that unless these factors are taken care

of, somewhere, by someone, analysis is not likely to affect the outcomes of programs.

*See Joseph S. Wholey et al., *Performance and Credibility: Developing Excellence in Public and Nonprofit Organizations* (Lexington, Mass.: Lexington Books, 1986).
†See Eugene Bardach, *The Implementation Game: What Happens after a Bill Becomes a Law* (Cambridge, Mass.: MIT Press, 1977).

It is our sense that the issues of implementation — what things get done, how they get done, why they get done — are best answered in the more inclusive topic of evaluation. This is not to imply that implementation is unimportant. How a policy is implemented is often at the heart of how government deals with each of us. As such, implementation needs to be fully understood. What we will see is that how a policy is produced and how it is carried out have much to do with the political process. Implementation, and how it is perceived, is in large part a product of the political process. We believe that it is only realistic to see it in a broader context. To do that, we must sort out the various aspects of policy evaluation.

Early Evaluations

Before the early 1970s boom in evaluations, there were various kinds of evaluations. There were efforts as early as the 1920s to make some judgments about where money was being spent. To that end, different kinds of budgets and auditing techniques (line-item budgeting, and the like) were made standard practices in the public sphere. These checks on money were ways to begin to evaluate the effectiveness of public spending.

By the 1950s, more systematic studies were made. They are notable both for their pioneering efforts as well as their problems. In 1955, Peter Blau published a study he had done on a public employment agency.[7] The agency was to service both people looking for jobs and employers looking for workers. Those in the agency were evaluated on the number of interviews that were conducted. Although that is a logical thing to judge, it misses the more important point of actually placing people in jobs.

In another study, Blau looked at a federal law enforcement agency. He found that each investigator had a quota of eight cases per month. Often, near the end of the month, the investigator would be doing easy cases in order to fill the quota. Cases, in other words, would be chosen based on the length of time it would take to handle them rather than their importance or their urgency.

In a review essay in 1956, these kinds of performance measurements were studied.[8] The essay warned that

> Quantitative performance measurements — whether single, multiple or composite — are seen to have undesirable consequences for overall organizational performance. The complexity of large organizations requires better knowledge of organizational behavior for managers to make best use of the personnel available to them. Even where performance measures are instituted purely for purposes of information, they are probably interpreted as definitions of the important aspects of that job or activity and hence have important implications for the motivation of behavior.

With the relatively simple early studies, we can see two major themes emerging. One is the theme of quantitative measurement. It is one that has dominated the social sciences — and with it public administration evaluation — for the last quarter of a century. The second theme is just as powerful. It is that the use of quantitative measurement is unreliable, can lead to undesirable consequences, and cannot reflect the complexity of the world that it proposes to measure.

During the late 1960s, President Lyndon Johnson proposed legislation that he called the Great Society. Basically, it was a package of social legislation designed to help the poor, the uneducated, and the needy in the United States. It was a remarkably ambitious program of education, job training, and social services that was well intended, expansive, and controversial. Also, given the war in Vietnam at the time, it never really had a chance to succeed.

Quite naturally, there was a need to know if the programs were succeeding. During this period, policy evaluations emerged as a tool of judgment. Different research methods were proposed, each with a little different cut into the reality of a program. The different methods show us much about the politics of evaluations. On the next few pages, we will use project Head Start (part of the Great Society) to help us see more clearly how policy is evaluated.

The Experimental Method

In a "research strategy" proposed by Thomas Cook and Frank Scioli, Jr., this basic question is asked: "Does a public policy achieve the desired objectives for which it was designed?"[9] In order to get through their suggestions, we must set aside the point that we made earlier: We often do not know what the true "desired objectives" are for any particular public policy.

Cook and Scioli believe that a basic systems model is the best way to do research. The basics of the system are these: there are inputs to the system, the system "works" and produces outputs, and there is feedback from the outputs that helps form new inputs. When any research is done, the researcher must be sensitive to the "multiplicity of objectives, activities, and criterion measures associated with a particular program." When judging the impact of a program, it is necessary to judge the performance, the adequacy of that performance, and the efficiency of the performance.

In order to do this, the researcher must know a great deal. There are seven components necessary to consider when doing an impact study. They are

1. There must be an unambiguous statement of the specific problem that the program is designed to solve.
2. There must be an identification of the criteria of objectives upon which the impact of program is measured.
3. There must be a determination of the impact measures that form the "analytical benchmarks for measuring both the singular and relative impacts of program action."
4. There must be a delineation of the main program components that differentiates between alternative programs directed toward common policy objectives.
5. There must be estimates of the main effects, both social and economic, of each program alternative relative to the relevant criteria measures.
6. There must be a statement of the major assumptions underlying the analysis and also an estimate of the interactive component between the assumptions and the determination of main program effects.
7. There must be a statement of the types of uncertainties that are contained in the analysis. One must estimate the extent of uncontrolled error which may be present in the analysis.

What the authors are getting at, and what certainly is clear by the last point, is that the best way to do research is by using the experimental method.[10] The critical component of the experimental method is that the researcher has control over the variables. Only by controlling the variables is it possible for the researcher to understand cause and effect with any statistical reliability.

The train of thought is this: if the problem is to find out if a policy is achieving its desired objectives, then the researcher must know what action will bring about what result. In order to do that, the researcher must

> **BOX 14.2   Evaluations and Experiments**
>
> It is difficult to experiment with government programs. In technical areas, such as developing a missile that will destroy another missile, experiments are often used. In most areas of public policy — educating children, providing aid to states, helping the poor, managing the nation's public forests — experiments are rare.
>
> One experiment happened in New Jersey. The New Jersey income maintenance experiments were set up during the late 1960s to test if giving poor people money instead of "in-kind" services (food stamps, medical support, and so on) is an effective and less expensive way to deal with poverty. Briefly, the experiments showed that the poor are quite responsible with such grants of cash. They spend it on shoes for the children, better food, medical care, and the like.
>
> The politics of the experiments were not so simple. Richard Nixon was president at the time, and he and his advisers did not believe that such a program could work (although it did influence the design of his proposed "family assistance plan" — a guaranteed, although quite low, income for the working poor). They believed people on welfare needed strong incentives to work — not cash from the government that makes the choice of indolence easier to make. Although the experiments contradicted this view of poverty, they were quickly and quietly forgotten.

be able to have control of the situation so that he or she may test different variables to see what happens. Given that kind of power, the researcher should be able to produce different programs, and the different probabilities of success. This train of thought leads policy evaluation down the track of methodological purity.

Evaluation as an Experiment

As the fight for how to do evaluation progressed, methodologists demanded more sophisticated and complex models of research. Although there was an appreciation of all that must be taken into account in an evaluation, the method still preferred was the experimental method.

The problems of evaluation cover an enormous range of activities.[11] There are certain things that are not examined if we want to use the experimental method. "Policy formulation originates with the values of the policymaker and society, and . . . these values are most immune to feedback." These values are merely the ideological biases of individuals, and

FIGURE 14.2 The circular process of program planning and program evaluation

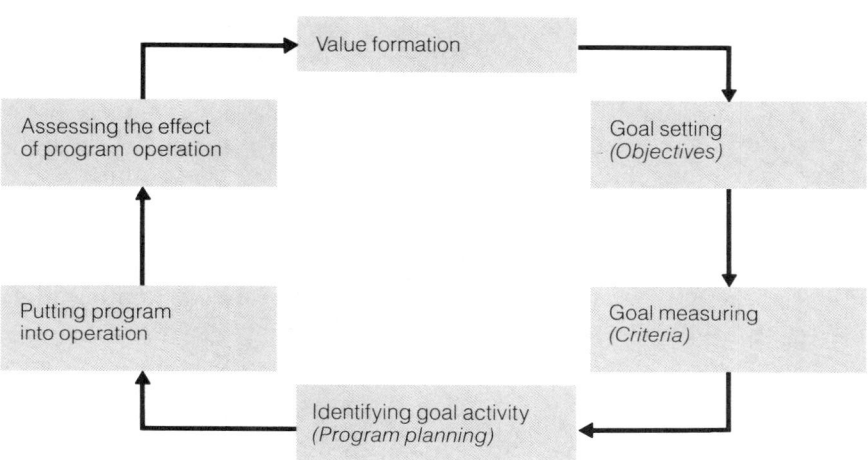

Source: From *Evaluating Research: Principles and Practice in Public Service and Social Action Programs*, by Edward A. Suchman, Ph.D. Copyright © by Russell Sage Foundation. Reprinted by permission of Basic Books, Inc., Publishers.

they in turn bias all the data that are presented. These values give meaning to program goals and cannot be measured.

For example, in various studies it has been found that pornography does not increase — and may in fact decrease — sexual crimes.[12] These findings had no effect on lawmakers who considered themselves conservatives. Or, there is evidence that alcohol can be as dangerous as cocaine; yet, one is legal and the other is not. It is foolish to treat the two substances differently, but the fact is that collectively one is "seen" as worse than the other. At this level of bias, the experimental method really does no good. To use the method, one must be ready to admit that these biases may affect how the research is evaluated, but that the research will have little effect on the biases.

In order to construct an evaluation that will yield valid results, an enormous number of criteria must be satisfied. Although it is unnecessary to review the criteria here, it is important to discuss one component of the experimental method.

To do a valid experiment, it is necessary to hold all things constant except one. As that one exception is changed, the results are changed. That way, the researcher can find out which variable "causes" what result. The easiest way to demonstrate this is to take a medical example. The way to test a drug is to take a group of people with the same illness. Give one-third of the people the experimental medication, give another third nothing, and give the final third a placebo, a pill that does nothing. If the group that was given the medication gets well, and other groups remain sick, then it follows that the medication works. Of course, even medical examples are never quite that simple, but, the way tests are constructed should be plain enough.

In order for the test to be valid, the groups must be the same, and these groups must be picked at random. In the words of the experimental method, there must be random samples. It is with random samples that methodological purity runs into problems in the public sphere.

Methodological Difficulties

The first question, which has no adequate answer, is this: How can a public agency withhold services from one segment of the population while providing it to another segment? For example, two school-aged children with the same background, motivation, and intelligence, go to school hungry every morning. In order to construct a valid test to see if a nutritious breakfast will help the student, the researcher would have to give one of the children the breakfast and let the other child go hungry. Not only that, but the test must go on over a significant period of time so that we could get a more clear idea of the long-range effect.

You may question the whole premise that it is even possible to find two people who have the same background, motivation, and intelligence. That is a fair question, and that is one of the reasons why a good experiment chooses groups randomly and tries to test as many groups as possible. The larger the group, the more likely that the groups will be statistically similar.

The search for purity is intense. There are numerous threats to the validity of a study, all stemming from the lack of randomization in constructing a test. But, the questions of randomization go beyond test validity. There is the political question of enacting legislation and providing money that will help only part of the target population. There is the moral question about withholding services from people who need them. There is the personal question of being part of a group that always gets a placebo. There is the research question about being more concerned with test validity than the human beings involved.

These questions are not new. One way out of randomization is to have people choose to be studied. The biggest validity problem with this is that the Hawthorne effect is always a possibility. People being studied act differently from people not being studied.

BOX 14.3 Using Formal Analysis to Improve Decisions

Ralph L. Keeney and Howard Raiffa are quite famous among students of analysis and decision making. They make the following points about the promises and pitfalls of using formal analysis to improve public decisions.*

Formal analysis can only be an aid to decision making. Any analysis of the future, formal or informal, tries to decipher the undecipherable, and so is subject to "uncertainty." And since public decisions usually involve some sense of equity or distribution of public resources, the values of decision makers must supplement the formal analyses of experts. They write, "Formal analysis stimulates insightful thinking about the interactions of various parts of the problem and the interrelationships between the problem and the proposed alternatives." It may lead to the search for new, creative alternatives. If experts work on different parts of the analysis, the process of producing a report can point to their different opinions, enabling them to search for the reasons behind their views. And the consumers of analysis may learn to look at problems in new ways.

There are, however, problems with formal analysis. There is no systematic procedure for isolating and defining problems. It is usually difficult to define precise objectives. Alternative courses of action defy comparison when there are many measures of an effective program. And, of course, there is no clear method for taking political preferences into account. Beyond these technical problems, there are difficulties of application. The analysts may be biased, either intentionally or unintentionally. Being human, they too have prejudices. The untrained buyers of analysis, say, members of a city council, may not be able to understand concepts in the study. Critics of a study usually dispute the more subjective parts of analysis (there is always some subjective component), and the effect is that "hard" data tend to drive out the "soft" in the course of constructing an analysis. Keeney and Raiffa write, "We are on the horns of a dilemma. The public wants more attention paid to subjective considerations, wants more honesty and openness, but is not sophisticated enough to withstand the rhetoric of those advocates who stand ready to demolish any nonobjective arguments."

On balance, Keeney and Raiffa say improvement is needed, but formal analysis for public decisions is beneficial and here to stay. The more that producers and consumers of analysis can learn about the uses and pitfalls of evaluations, the more will analysis be used. They say, "The market potential is certainly there, and the potential societal benefits are enormous."

*Taken from Ralph L. Keeney and Howard Raiffa, "A Critique of Formal Analysis in Public Decision Making," in Alvin W. Drake et al., eds., *Analysis of Public Systems* (Cambridge, Mass.: MIT Press, 1972), pp. 64–74.

Those wholly committed to the experimental method cannot allow the random sample to be tampered with. One writer argues that the random sample is "scientifically and ethically unbiased." He goes on to make the suggestion that if the "guilt-ridden experimenter" cannot make up the random sample personally, he or she should do it by lottery.

The point we would like to make is that there comes a time when methodological purity comes into sharp contrast with the realities of the real world of public administration and politics. Guilt-ridden or not, the evaluator of any public program is faced with more issues and problems and variables than he or she can ever incorporate into a study. Before looking at the messy world of evaluation, it is useful to remember the following:

> We are usually ignorant which out of innumerable possible factors may prove ultimately to be the most important.... We have usually no knowledge that one factor will exert its effects independently of all others that can be varied... *when factors are chosen for investigation, it is not because we anticipate that the laws of nature can be expressed with any particular simplicity in terms of these variables, but because they are variables which can be controlled or measured with comparative ease.*[14]

The experimental method, then, studies those things that can be controlled or measured with some ease. As we shall see, most public programs are in neither of these categories.

Evaluation Problems

It is fair to say there are some public programs that are not difficult to evaluate. If the county road commission has a policy to fix potholes in the road within 24 hours of knowing about them, then a judgment can be made if that policy is successful or not.

There are ways in which evaluations are all in the eyes of the beholder. As we mentioned earlier, political bias has a great deal to do with how we evaluate any particular program. For example, in *The Case for Bureaucracy*, Charles Goodsell writes about "reflections on the surveys."[15] Because he wants to make the case for bureaucracy, he argues that most commentators distort how the public evaluates bureaucracy.

An example from Goodsell will make the point about how to evaluate evaluations. When describing an evaluation of a social welfare agency, Goodsell complained about the negative questions asked. "Another question was 'Could you use more help than you're getting now, not just from the agency but from anywhere?' Only 37 percent answered yes, with 56 responding no." A bureaucracy advocate would argue that even given a negative question, the majority of the people had a favorable response. Another person might argue that this agency was giving satisfactory service to only a little over half the people it sees.

But the problems of evaluation are really much more serious than that. Let us go back to the Great Society, and review a program that helps to show the many ways in which evaluations reflect politics and prejudices and the society at that time.

Head Start — An Evaluation

The Head Start program began in 1964. Its purpose was to provide a range of services (educational, nutritional, health, and social) to preschool children of lower-income families. It was argued that these children were already behind middle- and upper-class children by the time they entered school, so that in order for everyone to have an equal chance it was necessary to give the needy a "head start." One of the consequences (and we do not know if it was intended or unintended) of Head Start was that it provided childcare for people who normally could not afford it. The mood of the times provided an enormous plus for the program. It was a positive social program for a class that was beginning to demand recognition.

Interestingly, the program was not understood in those terms, but was evaluated on how the Head Start children did once they got into school. The early evaluations, which were carried out by the staff of Head Start, did not produce "consistent, unambiguous" evidence; but, on the whole the results were positive.

By 1967, an evaluation division was created by the Office of Economic Opportunities, and it was decided that an outside agency should evaluate Head Start. The people at Head Start were not at all happy with the idea of outsiders coming in, and fought the evaluation. The Westinghouse Learning Corporation and Ohio University won the contract to evaluate Head Start.

The preliminary report was negative and argued that there were indications that the long-term effects of Head Start were extremely weak. The report was circulated in-house, and an effort was made to "clean it up" by consultants. There were some questions about methodological purity. (As a note, the problems had to do with randomization. We shall see later where these problems lead to ugly conclusions on the part of other social scientists.) The preliminary report was leaked to the press, which demanded that the negative results be known. The report on Head Start was finally released. It stated that Head Start children were not much different than their peers who did not have the advantages of Head Start.

The people who favored Head Start attacked the report for its questionable "methodological and conceptual validity." The program was very popular and, in spite of the report, then President Nixon asked Congress for, and got, additional funding for Head Start.

In the mid-1970s, further studies were made. These were much more positive than earlier ones. It was found that children who had been in Head Start were less likely to repeat grades or need remedial classes than other children with similar backgrounds who had not been in Head Start. It was also found that the Head Start children scored significantly better in mathematics and in reading achievement. These positive findings were published in 1979.

The fight continued when, in 1982, the director of the Office of Management and Budget, David Stockman, recommended that Head Start be phased out in four years. President Reagan announced that there would be no reduction in Head Start funding.

There are two political points that need to be brought up before we examine what this example shows us about Head Start. First, it was the contention of Head Start supporters that the original outside evaluation was an attempt by the enemies of Head Start to abolish the program. They also believed that there were people in OEO who resented the popularity of Head Start and were willing to end it.

The second political point is the leaking of the preliminary report to the press. At the time, there was speculation that the Nixon administration purposely leaked it as a trial balloon. The administration was quite prepared to end the Head Start program if it could get support. However, the negative report did not hurt the popularity of the program, so Nixon went ahead and supported it.

It may be that neither of these two political points has any basis in fact. True or false is not the issue; the issue is that evaluations are often just another part of the political process, and that must always be remembered.

Further Difficulties

There are problems with evaluations that reach far beyond the methodological difficulties we discussed earlier. Test construction and the validity of the results are important but narrow problems in the world of program evaluation. The Head Start example gives us a way to begin to see the real world environment of an evaluation.

POLITICAL CLIMATE. Any evaluation takes place in a broad social and political context. That context, like the air you breathe, has an effect on what you do. For example, in a time of economic plenty, the purchasing practices of various government agencies are simply not looked at as carefully as when there are economic hard times. What one must remember is that no matter if an evaluator approves or disapproves of the politics of the day, it is those politics that set the agenda. As in the example, the politics of the times demanded a Head Start program. Within that context, the evaluation was made and presented.

PURPOSE OF EVALUATION. With Head Start, there was some uncertainty about just why there was an evaluation. Some of those in Head Start believed that the OEO wanted the evaluation to result in the ending of the program. But an enormous number of evaluations are carried on by all segments of government. The purpose of an evaluation is often easily seen in congressional hearings. In these hearings, senators and representatives try to evaluate the worth of particular programs. The tone of the questions reveals the purpose of the investigation. When those in Congress support a program, the questions asked are easy, and are framed in a way to get the most positive picture of the program. If it is a witch-hunt, the questions will reflect it.

EVALUATION TENSIONS. If the evaluation is being made by people from outside the agency, there can often be tension between the two groups. That is understandable. First, the group being evaluated may not know the purpose of the evaluation. It is possible, for example, that the life of the agency may be at stake, and that could cause a natural lack of cooperation.

Second, to do a good job, the evaluators need to fully understand activities in the agency, which means having access to all records and spending time talking with the agency people. It is not unusual for agency personnel to feel overworked to begin with. When asked to turn over their records, as well as make time to be interviewed during an already full day, one can imagine that there might be some anger.

Third, it is only natural that the workers believe that they know all there is to know about their jobs, and that they are doing the best job possible. It is a waste of time to try to teach all of that to an evaluator. Yet, without this information the evaluation process will necessarily be incomplete.

Fourth, there has been an interesting age component to evaluation up to now. In many cases, the evaluators have been younger — and in many cases better educated — than those being judged. It is not difficult to see that the more experienced worker may resent the younger evaluator.

Fifth, there is the matter of time. As we have seen, time may be a critical variable to evaluation. For a program like Head Start, it may well be that the educational benefits are only now becoming clear. The real test may not be how Head Start kids did in high school math, but how they are doing now that they are adults. It could be that Head Start, in the end, was a place to learn personal and civic responsibility — and that would only show up years after school testing is over.

The consequences of any program of social significance simply cannot be evaluated over a short term. Any worker would rightly be bothered if an evaluator came in when the program was just getting started and made a judgment on project merits. The other side of that, and one we

FIGURE 14.3 Two views of evaluation and management

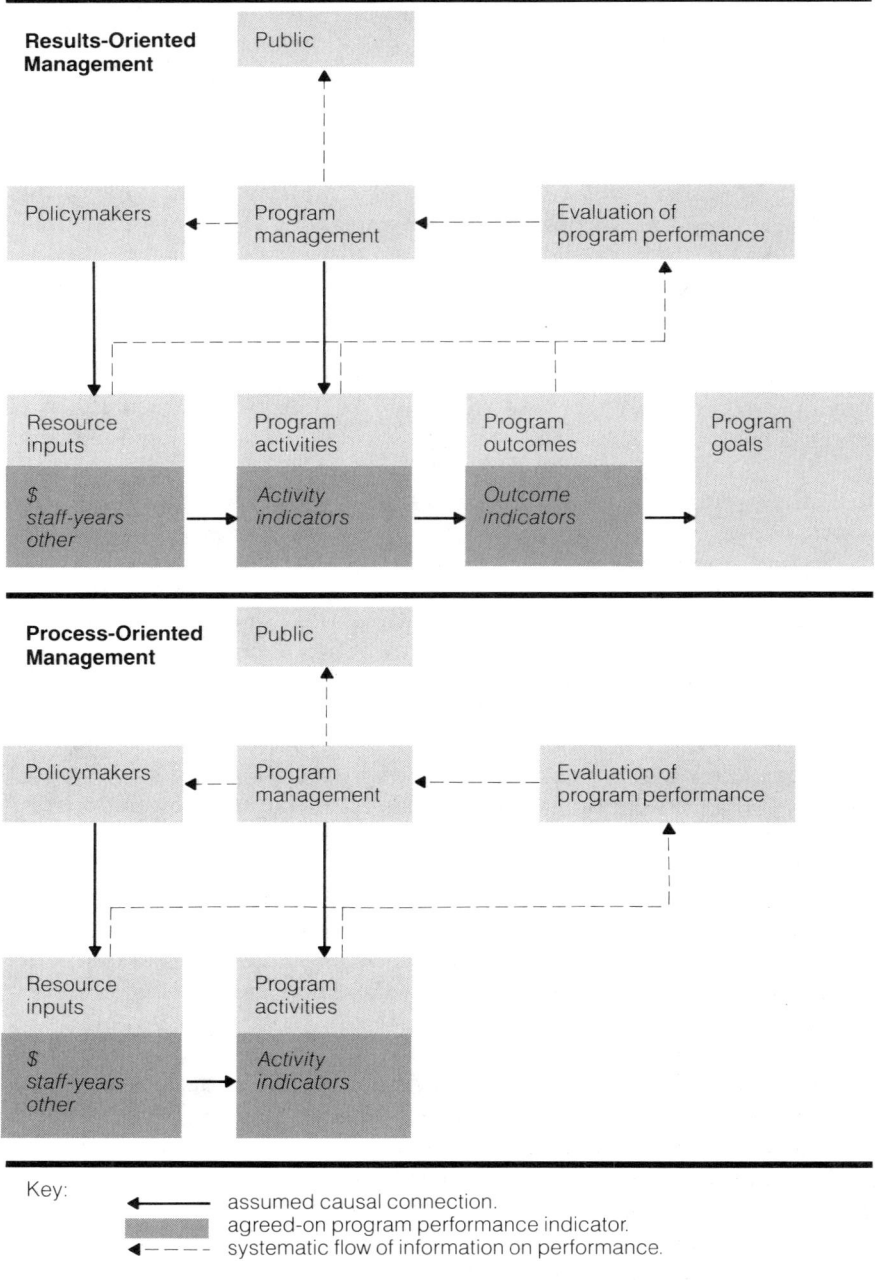

Source: From Joseph S. Wholey, *Evaluation and Effective Management*, pp. 6, 7. Copyright © 1983 by Joseph S. Wholey. Reprinted by permission of Little, Brown and Company

will mention in passing, is that it is possibly irresponsible for any government to set up a program and not evaluate it. There is no reason why any agency should have a free hand at spending the people's money. What we have is a problem without a solution: The need to evaluate a program and the guarantee that the evaluation will tell us little or nothing about the success of that program.

EVALUATION ERRORS. In the example of Head Start, we saw that there might have been some methodological problems. Although those problems did not seem to affect the funding of the program, the finding did have a negative effect. Head Start dealt mostly with blacks from the lower economic class. When the preliminary evaluation concluded that a change in environment (earlier education, better nourishment) did not make the changes sought, some social scientists came to regrettable conclusions. First, Daniel Moynihan reviewed the history of social reform dating back to the 1930s and decided that most of the reforms had been failures.[16] This certainly helped stop social reform legislation in the 1970s.

Worse still, in 1969 an article was written arguing that since the environment did not help change blacks, it must mean the problem was with the blacks themselves.[17] The article, which argued that there were inherent racial differences in IQ, was circulated in the U.S. Senate by those opposed to any further civil rights legislation. The fact is that the early Head Start evaluation was flawed, and contained "tragically misleading misanalyses."[18]

Some Reasons Why Things Don't Work

Although the list of reasons why it is difficult for evaluations to be done accurately is impressive, the list of reasons why programs do not work is equally impressive. What follows is a partial list.

Often, a program is not given enough money to do what needs to be done. To provide quality public education requires, as we continually rediscover, good teachers. One way to attract good teachers is to pay them well. Low-paid teachers in understaffed schools will never build a quality educational system.

Organizational complexity is a real problem. Pressman and Wildavsky made fun of the number of people needed to cooperate to get anything done; but, their point is a serious one. Sheer size, the basic number of transactions that need to be carried out correctly, can undermine any activity. A companion problem has to do with the workings of federalism. The coordinating of national, state, and local agencies — the number of people, the number of steps of the process, the number of regulations, and the number of personal agendas that need to be satisfied — can often be too much to overcome.

Poor planning is a common organizational problem. This is often not so much a matter of managerial stupidity as the fact that it is difficult to both invent and implement a social program. A scientist, in his or her laboratory, mixes x and y together and gets some exotic result. (This is an oversimplified statement, so take it as a metaphor and not an accurate account.) In the political and social realm, the mixing is not so easy.

Take our Head Start example. Someone came up with a good idea, Head Start, and it became law. But now the administration problems have just started. Someone must literally invent an organization to make that law work. The number of questions (where, who, why, how, how much) are quite beyond the scope of anyone's ability to answer. A first-rate administrator may be able to rough-in fairly accurate guesses; but, any early evaluation will find at least as many problems as successes.

There are two problems related to poor planning. One has to do with optimism and the other attitude. It is not unusual for a program to be "oversold." The virtues of what is being proposed often far exceed any realistic aim of the program. A War on Poverty is not a war that can be won in even one generation in this country. The systematic causes, which go back before our lifetimes, will take generations to overcome. This is not an argument against a war on poverty, it is simply a warning that to believe that poverty can be conquered in a generation guarantees that the program will be viewed as a failure.

Another problem is one of attitude.[19] Any study of the national government is in part a study of how the different branches are at odds. One of the first things that a new president finds out is that he or she is unable to fully control the bureaucracy. The fact is that programs may fail because those in the public administration want them to fail.

The last problem of implementation is timing. One of the themes we have repeated is that programs take place in a context. The political and social context of the United States is a complex and powerful one. Policies fail, quite literally, because their time has not yet come. For example, at the end of the Civil War one would have thought that segregation would have ended. There were court cases that began to make integration legal. But the context of bigotry was too powerful. It took fighting and killing before the time came for civil rights legislation to be passed and successfully implemented. Public attitude is remarkably important for the working of public programs.[20]

The Tool of Evaluation

Policy implementation and evaluation are important. Equally important is the fact that our knowledge about each of them is not impressive. What we may finally come to, after the experimental method has found its

BOX 14.4 How Creative Can Government Policies Be?

The trouble with many government policies is that they are aimed at a problem that has never been solved before. In the everyday routine matters, government bureaucracies do an efficient job. For example, the Social Security Administration writes checks more cheaply than their private sector counterparts in the insurance industry. But when governments embark upon entirely new policy areas, something often goes wrong.

Consider the swine flu affair, during the presidency of Gerald R. Ford. Government medical researchers found cases of swine flu in the population, the same strain of flu that killed thousands of people in 1917–18. The problem was that the researchers had no experience with this strain of flu. They had no way to predict the consequences of an epidemic. Faced with an uncertain situation, President Ford decided to play it safe and ordered a national vaccination program. As it turned out, the flu bug was no worse than other years, and nearly 1000 recipients of the vaccine contracted Reyes syndrome.

Or consider the example of the War on Poverty. Launched during the Johnson administration, government agencies were trying to do something no society has done before: eliminate poverty. Experts in various cabinet departments were asked for their ideas; a task force sifted the ideas and decided what could be afforded; the president approved the package and sent the proposed legislation to Congress. There was virtually no experience in how to eradicate poverty. It is popular to claim that the War on Poverty programs failed, but in fact they did lift virtually all Americans above the poverty line. They did much better than the private sector; in fact, the proportion of people living below the poverty line, exclusive of government support, has remained almost unchanged since the early 1960s. The many years of economic growth did little for the poorest people; government assistance did.

Consider also the space program. Public resources have been poured into NASA, and the shuttle program remains America's main avenue into space. The private sector simply could not afford to spend the money for research and development, waiting for an eventual payoff of commercial activities outside the atmosphere. What private sector experience there is in the area is the result of government contracts to develop components for government space systems.

Given these considerations, it is not surprising that many analyses of government programs find waste, ineffective programs, and misguided programs. What these probes usually fail to mention is that no one had ever tried to solve these problems before, and that there were reasons for trying.

proper place in research, is that the nature of implementation and evaluation is well beyond our ability to understand it. After all, this is the most public of events — the actions themselves — and human activity cannot be bound by the requirements of research methodology. Given that, let us turn to other aspects of evaluation.

One way to understand evaluation is as a tool of management. Evaluations are systematic ways in which program managers are able to understand how their programs are being run and to get advice on how to become better managers. Even here, the art of evaluation is anything but scientific. We can see this in the case of a group of "consultant/researchers" who made a recommendation to a state department of social and health services. The problems revolved around care for patients in state nursing homes. What the researchers did, basically, was go in with as few preconceived ideas as possible. They were helped by the fact that they were ignorant about nursing care and mental health services. So, they read all the documents that they could and talked with as many members of the staff as they could.

The interviews were not structured, were as unthreatening as possible, and each individual was urged to be as open as possible about what was wrong, and how to correct it. Not surprisingly, the interviews were very successful. A great number of people were happy to speak and be heard. The group found that there were three important external factors and nine problems with internal management. The external factors were (1) The nursing homes were politically vulnerable, (2) the nursing homes were fairly low in the bureaucratic hierarchy, (3) the nursing homes, given a poor record, were often picked on by the private nursing home industry, the legislature, and the public. Some of the management problems were lack of leadership, lack of clarity of goals, lack of stability, lack of support for the staff, lack of staff involvement, lack of field perspective, poor communications, and waste of resources.

After much time and hard work, the group wrote their report which, essentially, called for a better structure so that the staff and management could develop a more effective strategy. The group was especially pleased with what it believed to be the open and realistic way it went about assessing the program. By not being trapped in asking a wrong first question, and by being willing to forego "hard" data, they may well have produced a realistic evaluation of the problems the agency faced.

But that is only a part of the story. The report was produced and presented. Then, nothing happened. The report was ignored.

There is perhaps a happy ending. By sheer luck, an investigative reporter who had covered the nursing home problems got hold of the report. He thought that the report substantiated what he had been saying, so he produced a series of articles about it. Then, some memos were "leaked" to a key legislator and legislative staff members. They helped keep the nursing home problems in the public eye. Finally, a new head of the office was named and was willing to look at the report. A preliminary follow-up indicates that the suggestions of the report had been helpful.[21]

This study is useful for at least two reasons. First, it helps provide an alternative to a statistical evaluation. It shows that there may be compelling concerns that have nothing to do with methodological purity. Second, it shows that, methodology aside, public policy has a great deal to do with politics. To divide public policy evaluation from politics is a false and foolish separation.

One writer suggests that evaluators be sensitive to the following four points.[22] First, formulate the evaluation and its reports with an eye toward having an impact on policy. Second, be sensitive to the political realities of the situation. Third, be certain to release the report at the proper time on the policy-making calendar. Fourth, make suggestions and explain their implications for reform.

This is the clearest kind of political advice for an evaluator. When we discussed the meaning of evaluation earlier in the chapter, we mentioned that the evaluator had a certain kind of power. This political advice shows exactly how an evaluator can have more than his or her share of policy-making power.

BOX 14.5   How Often are Evaluations Used?

Evaluations can be done "in-house" (by people in the agency) or "contracted" (bought from consultants or analysts outside the agency). When people study how often these evaluations are used by decision makers, the in-house products come out on top — but the overall picture is dismal.

It appears that decision makers turn to formal evaluations only when all else fails. They have their usual sources of information, often political, as well as their own values and decision-making styles. Although no definitive counts are available, most experts estimate that over 90 percent of studies done to inform decisions do nothing but gather dust. Some of the reasons have been suggested before (see Box 14.2), but the challenge to analysts and decision makers is to learn from the experience and correct it.

Sources: See Nathan Caplan, "Factors Associated with Knowledge Use Among Federal Executives," *Policy Studies Journal* 4, no. 3 (1976); Joseph Woley, *Evaluation and Effective Public Management* (Boston: Little, Brown, 1983).

SUMMARY

If one were to take all of the advice from all of the pieces written on evaluations, it would be our guess that more than 99 percent of them would say that to do a good evaluation, it is necessary to know the goal of the program being evaluated. In order to run an effective program, it is necessary to have clear goals. Once the goal is known, it is just a matter of choosing the correct methodology and conducting a valid test to see if the goals are being properly implemented.

We have seen how that is often impossible. But, there is another, maybe more important, point to be made. What we lack is the freedom to fully see what is going on . . . and if what is going on is good or not. In other words, we dramatically restrict our vision when we finally become clear about our goals. The reason is this: When we use formal policy evaluation to judge a program, we substitute administration for politics. Evaluation methodology can help to avoid certain logical problems (such as making grand conclusions from small samples) and reduce complex data to understandable numbers (such as a comparison of future costs and benefits in benefit-cost analysis), but it is not the same as politics. Analysts know that many of their studies are ignored because elected officials worry more about the demands of constituents than the efficiency or effectiveness of particular problems. To be more relevant, policy analysts even include political analysis in their policy evaluations. But, to have an administrative agency consider which political groups need to be considered, and how much, and which are more important, is a dramatic substitution of administrative process for political process.

We need analysis, just as we need policies. Yet, until we have a clear sense of where the public fits into administration, policy evaluation may serve to shut citizens further out of the governance of the country.

NOTES

1. Peter Rossi, Howard Freeman, Sonia Wright, *Evaluation: A Systematic Approach* (Beverly Hills, Calif.: Sage, 1979), p. 20.
2. Ranney is quoted by Gerald Caiden, *The Dynamics of Public Administration* (New York: Holt, Rinehart and Winston, 1971), p. 75.
3. Ibid., pp. 76–77.
4. The claim is made, for example, by W. Henry Lambright, "The Minnowbrook Perspective and the Future of Public Affairs: Public Administration *Is* Public Policy Making," in Frank Marini, ed., *Toward a New Public Administration: The Minnowbrook Perspective* (San Francisco: Chandler Publishing, 1971).

5. Jeffery Pressman and Aaron Wildavsky, *Implementation* (Berkeley: University of California Press, 1973), p. 24.
6. Eugene Bardach, *The Implementation Game: What Happens after a Bill Becomes a Law* (Cambridge, Mass.: MIT Press, 1977).
7. Peter Blau, *The Dynamics of Administration* (Chicago: University of Chicago Press, 1955).
8. V. F. Ridgway, "Dysfunctional Consequences of Performance Measurements," in *Administrative Science Quarterly* 1, no. 2 (September 1956).
9. Thomas Cook and Frank Scioli, Jr., "A Research Strategy for Analyzing the Impacts of Public Policy," *Administrative Science Quarterly* (September 1972).
10. Edward Suchman, *Evaluation Research* (New York: Russell Sage Foundation, 1967).
11. Paul Wortman, "Evaluation Research: A Psychological Perspective," *American Psychologist* 30, no. 5 (May 1975).
12. B. Kutchinsky, "The Effect of Easy Availability of Pornography on the Incidence of Sex Crimes: The Danish Experience," *Journal of Social Issues* 29.
13. Wortman, op. cit.
14. R. A. Fisher, *The Design of Experiments* (London: Oliver and Boyd, 1951), emphasis added.
15. Charles Goodsell, *The Case for Bureaucracy*, 2d ed. (Chatham, N.J.: Chatham House, 1985), pp. 24–36.
16. Daniel Moynihan, *The Politics of Guaranteed Income* (New York: Random House, 1973).
17. A. R. Jenson, "How Much Can We Boost IQ and Scholastic Achievement?" *Harvard Educational Review*, vol. 39, pp. 1–123.
18. D. T. Campbell and A. Erlebacher, "How Regression Artifacts in Quasi-Experimental Evaluations Can Mistakenly Make Compensatory Education Look Harmful," in J. Hellmuth, ed., *The Disadvantaged Child*, vol. 3 (New York: Bruner/Mazel, 1970).
19. Bardach, op. cit.
20. For a more inclusive list, see Ira Sharkansky, *Public Administration: Agencies, Policies, and Politics* (New York: W.H. Freeman, 1982).
21. Betty Jane Narver and Walter Williams, "The Consultant/Researcher Role: Implications for Studying Public Management Problems," in Walter Williams, ed., *Studying Implementation: Methodological and Administrative Issues* (Chatham, N.J.: Chatham House, 1982).
22. Sharkansky, op. cit.

CHAPTER FIFTEEN

Public Administration in Post-Prosperity America

> When occasions present themselves, in which the interests of the people are at variance with their inclinations, it is the duty of the persons whom they have appointed to be the guardians of those interests, to withstand the temporary delusion, in order to give them time and opportunity for more cool and sedate reflection.
>
> — *Publius (from* The Federalist, *no. 71)*

The preceding chapters have described parts of, and directions in, public administration. Stories of remarkable achievements are mixed with attacks on public administration since the founding of the republic. Throughout the book these tensions have told the story of a large number of unsettled questions in American public administration. That we need a sense of direction is widely understood. Where to get that direction is the source of bitter conflict. As a way of figuring out where we are and where we might go, it is important to review some important themes in public administration.

Ethics

For the first six years of his presidency, Ronald Reagan was remarkably popular. In the opinion polls, he generally had a two-thirds approval rating. What is of most interest to us is that while he was personally so popular, an unusually high number of his appointees (the number is more than 100) were found guilty of criminal activity or left office in public shame. The public service, in other words, took the brunt of bad publicity for crooked and incompetent political employees. The president himself seemed untouched by these public problems.

It was only after the dealings with the terrorists, the apparent arms for hostages deal, and the possibly illegal money sent to the Contras, that Reagan's popularity dropped. The question for those interested in public administration is this: What was the quality of the appointees made by the president? What kinds of problems do these people face? Finally, should we hold the chief executive responsible for those he appoints?

Consider the possible problems for a public servant (this is a partial list):[1]

1. The public administrator may simply disregard the law. As in the case of Rita Lavelle, formerly of the Environmental Protection Agency, officials may choose to enforce some provisions of a law and ignore others. Remember that officials in the Reagan administration were selected, in part, because of their attitudes about the proper uses of government. In other words, they were chosen in the hope that they would disregard certain parts of the law.

2. The official may be dishonest. Paul Thayer, a former Deputy Secretary of Defense, was convicted of obstruction of justice after being a target of an investigation about insider stock trading.

    The former deputy White House chief of staff and one of the most influential people in Reagan's first term, Michael Deaver, was brought to trial by a special prosecutor. The charges include conflict of interest and giving false testimony before a committee of Congress. There is a law that makes it a crime for a person to lobby the government on an issue on which he or she participated substantially while at the White House.

    After Deaver left the public service, he set up a lobbying firm and had such clients as Canada and Puerto Rico. The special prosecutor is looking into charges that Deaver lobbied a part of the government that he himself had helped create while working for the government.

3. The official may have a conflict of interest. In the Senate hearings to confirm Chief Justice Rehnquist, it was shown that he had both advised the Nixon White House on an issue of wire-tapping, and then cast the tie-breaking vote when the matter came before the court. In several related matters the chief justice suffered convenient lapses in memory.

4. The official may engage in unethical behavior. Richard Allen, a national security advisor to Reagan, was forced to resign after it was revealed that he had taken a gift worth over a thousand dollars. The gift came from Japanese journalists for whom Allen had arranged an interview with the First Lady. In another case Marianne Hall was appointed chairperson of the Copyright Royalty Tribunal. She was quickly forced to resign when it was discovered that she had edited a racist tract. Hall was given her appointment on the basis of her ties with right-wing Reagan supporters whose agenda lay outside the grounds of acceptable government behavior.

5. The official may be unfair to employees. Donald J. Devine, Reagan's first director of the Office of Personnel Management, resigned when it became apparent that he could not win reconfirmation before the Senate. At a time when the Senate was routinely approving conser-

vative appointees to federal office, the substantive complaints by federal employee groups were too much for both Democratic and Republican senators.[2]

6. The Iran/Contra affair produced a remarkable cast of administrators whose ideological beliefs were stronger than their regard for the law or their desire to tell the truth.

There can be other problems, too. Administrators can be inefficient, they can cover up mistakes, they can be lazy, and so on. We want our administrators to be like Caesar's wife — above suspicion. Our schools of public administration certainly try to teach professionalism, and conferences and symposia often seek to emphasize a moral and ethical sense in the public service.[3] Yet it seems that we lack a clear sense of how ethics and public service may go together. What we seem to have verified during the Reagan administration is that ideological tests for new appointees are no guarantee of professionalism in government.

What seems equally clear is that we allow for shades of ideology in the people we elect. Many of the attitudes we found inappropriate (or illegal) in top appointees, we found justifiable in the president.

The tension between politics and professionalism influences the discussion on ethics in government. The question is: What is the best way to control public administrators? The answers typically boil down to two approaches. The first emphasizes the importance of hierarchy in directing and controlling employees. In a very direct way, the public is best involved when bureaucracy is most highly developed, and the top appointed officials think the same way as the elected officials.[4] The second answer looks for guidance in the ideas of public administrators. Given the proper set of attitudes, public administrators can extend the moral use of government power to particular cases. Ethical administrators, with the right "sense" of public needs and duty, can make more of the right decisions. This is asking a lot of administrators, and as we will see later, it leads to asking even more of them.[5] Today most elected officials seem to like the first approach; most writers in Public Administration seem to like the second.[6]

The two answers are clearly not enough. They have not been reconciled in a way that helps the reputation of public administrators, and lacking a clear basis for ethical action in public administration, the practical emphasis comes to be the reputation of public organizations and administrators. Reputation has proved to be a poor substitute for ethical action. The combination of investigative reporting and active investigative committees of Congress has tainted the reputations of many administrators.

Charles Goodsell has suggested three ways in which public organizations may improve upon their reputations.[7] First, the mass media should project a more balanced image of the public service. For example, we should hear positive things about government. Instead of just getting stories about $436 hammers, we should *also* hear stories about how the Forest Service saves lives, how people are helped in floods, and so on.

Second, Goodsell believes that there should be more direct contact between bureaucracies and the communities in which they are located. There should be tours of local government buildings, so that people will have a sense of who is serving them and what work goes on. And third, he recommends that bureaucrats develop closer ties with academic institutions. Public employees should go to classes and talk with students. If this happened more, then people would talk less about faceless bureaucracies.

There is nothing radical, or even controversial, in what Goodsell writes. It makes good sense that there be a fuller picture, and more human contact, so that we have a better idea about our public service. In this case, regrettably, good sense is merely cosmetic. The suggestions of Goodsell are, at best, middle-range proposals that do not reconcile the basic dilemmas Americans have about public administration. It may be that the dynamic of the enterprise of public administration in the United States is greater than the sum of its parts. If that is the case, and we believe it is, then these suggestions do not get to the heart of the matter.

Public organizations have made attempts to make citizens feel more comfortable and to believe that justice is being served.[8] For example, some governments create an office of the ombudsman. The ombudsman takes citizens' complaints and sees what can be done to help. The complaint is investigated, taken to the appropriate agency, and some action or response to the citizen takes place.

Another way in which government has tried to help is to put many service organizations in the same place. The mere physical location helps people do their business more quickly.[9] A third way government helps is with outreach programs. The agency goes into the community it wants to serve and opens an office in a store front. Community mental health clinics and legal aid offices are examples of this kind of outreach. Some governments have regular contact with client or citizen groups, such as neighborhood associations or parent-teacher associations.

Clearly, there are ongoing attempts to improve understanding between citizens and their government. But, as we suggested in the first chapter, there is a tension underlying these efforts. What we have discussed to this point has not gotten at the tougher problems.[10]

Silent Tensions

As you read this, it is useful to think about what changes were made in government by the Reagan administration. There have been major changes in the perception of government since he took national office. The years of anger of the sixties and the years of discouragement during the seventies are, for the most part, history. There is no question that people liked Ronald Reagan in the role of president. We need to see what has been happening to our public organizations during the time of a very popular chief administrator.

We will discuss these issues by looking at the topics with which we began the book. We suggested that American public administration can be understood by looking at three forces: The Constitution, liberalism, and politics.

The Constitution

With the Constitution, we really want to begin by focusing on federalism. Who gets to do what and to and for whom is an important theme in public administration. During the 1930s, Roosevelt redefined the role of the national government, and the roles of state and local governments changed in important ways. Since then, there has been a steady growth in what government does. The government grew under both Republican and Democratic leaders.

In the Reagan era people started out to reduce the size of government and to place more reliance on the private sector. So far, the results have been mixed. Federal spending has increased every year of Reagan's administration. State and local government spending has increased at a faster rate than the federal. Reagan promised a new partnership in federalism, but that partnership has mostly meant fewer federal dollars, with the states having to tax and spend more.

To hear governors and mayors tell it, the federal government has done less and less to help them. If there is to be a new federalism, then we will have to pay more attention to the taxing and spending at state and local levels. If this is the case, it may be that taxing and spending decisions will be made in a variety of ways. A new federalism may bring more direct taxing and spending decisions from the voters.

The private sector has also gained in strength as Reagan has set out to cut government regulation. For example, the government was able to cut in half the inspection of the national meat supply. Chicken and beef carcasses now pass by inspectors twice as fast as they did before Reagan took office. Much regulation is simply done less frequently.

Part of the argument for deregulation and disinvolvement in the private sector is that it helps stimulate the economy. The measures to revitalize the economy have not been noticeably better than the efforts of other administrations. His administration has had the largest deficits in our history. He has doubled and almost tripled the national debt in the course of his years in office. We simply cannot compare the waste of government mismanagement with the trillions of dollars of debt, and interest on that debt, we must somehow pay for.

Another part of Reagan's policy of smaller government is called *pri-*

vatization. In its simplest form, it means letting the private sector do the job. In some cases that means selling or leasing government functions or facilities to people in business. For example, we the people are willing to sell our railroads to private enterprise because we see no reason we should be in the train business. Some states are even contracting with private businesses to run prisons.[11]

Perhaps the extreme case of privatization has gone on in foreign affairs, where the administration appeared to have bypassed Congress by organizing and supporting "private" forces, negotiators, and donors. This is perhaps part of a larger attitude many Americans share. Certainly Reagan revitalized Americans' sense of themselves and their country, but the uglier side of capitalism also seems to be tolerated. One example of this is the widespread scandal on Wall Street involving "insider" trading, some of it by high-ranking government officials.

This kind of privatizing of public roles raises key issues. Should we encourage a profit-making corporation to enter into the business of running prisons? Won't we still be paying for it? Is efficiency the bottom line of our prison system? Are people in private organizations really better at running organizations than those in government? What of the spirit of service that draws many people into public careers? Can we honestly say that the national defense is the only place where public spirit is appropriate?

Finally, one of the lasting effects of Reagan will be on the judicial branch. He has been able to appoint more than half of all sitting federal judges, including important seats on the Supreme Court. The people he has selected seem to agree on these issues: less government intervention in the economy; stronger state powers in dealing with crime; less government intervention in dealing with individual cases of discrimination; stronger government powers over individuals in the areas of mandatory drug testing, and searches and seizure of evidence.

What is interesting about the Reagan shift is that while there has been a serious attempt to decentralize, cut back, or privatize some governmental power, there has been a corresponding increase of governmental powers over individuals. These developments should leave citizens uneasy. What began with disillusionment with the role of government turned into a shift of public objectives, and the public in administration fell before other, seemingly more important problems.

Liberalism

Liberalism, historically, has been a global event. It was a mind-set well suited to exploring and exploiting different parts of the world. It began to bloom when Europeans came to the Americas. The institutions that were invented placed a remarkable emphasis on the individual. For 400 years, the people in those institutions produced a great deal of wealth.

But, the frontier and the new countries are now closed. By the twentieth century, capitalism and liberalism reached about as far as they could go. Competing systems — the socialist countries — closed off part of it, and the newly independent countries, the old colonial possessions, began to look for their own answers. The global community that we now speak about — a community with extreme inequalities — really means that the raw resources that capitalist countries need are no longer as cheap or as easily available.

BOX 15.1 Drug Testing — The New Loyalty Oaths

During the 1940s and 1950s, it was a fairly common practice to screen employees for subversives — people who were disloyal to the United States. It made sense to people, during the "cold war," to make sure that communists had not infiltrated our public administration.

The trouble was that loyalty was a difficult idea to define. Some organizations defined subversive in a very broad fashion, and it included many moral and political ideas that had nothing to do with disloyalty toward the government.* Many people were intimidated, and many lost their jobs, because of the practice. In an overzealous attempt to solve what seemed at the time an important problem, the government ran roughshod over people's rights.

The new concerns with drug testing are remarkably similar. Our normal standards of justice are turned on their head, as everyone is suspected until their innocence is proved. In the words of one newspaper editor who supported the move to drug testing, "What decent American — especially one working in a sensitive or defense related industry — would object to being certified drug-free and fit for such responsibilities?" What decent American, indeed. Here are some examples of decent Americans who objected:

> A woman was fired from her job for refusing to give a urine sample to her supervisor. Her reasons: She was three months pregnant, which the test would have revealed, and she did not trust her employer's reaction to such information.
>
> Epileptics have an unemployment rate twice that of the population, and the reason is simple: employers fear the disease and what might happen in the workplace. Most employed epileptics do not let their supervisors know about the disease, and they perform their jobs as well as anyone. The tests would reveal their condition because of the drugs they take to control the disease.

> A large number of Americans take diet pills, allergy pills, cold medicines, and similar over-the-counter drugs, many of which trigger a "false positive" on the drug tests. Remember the tests are unannounced, and mandatory.
>
> It is important to note that when President Reagan offered to start the program with a drug test of his own, he delayed the test for two weeks. Drugs he was taking for an upcoming urology examination would have registered a false positive on the test. What decent American, indeed.
>
> *See the discussion in Jay Shafritz et al., *Personnel Management in Government*, 3d ed. (New York: Marcel Dekker, 1986), Chapter 8.

The global village is also going electronic. Capitalists (or communists, for that matter) can no longer have an empire without the world knowing about it at once. We are plugged into the world, and the shape of the world we are to become is far from clear. What seems reasonable to assume is that our traditional values cannot stay unchanged.

It is possible that capitalism and our sense of individualism are artifacts of the 400-year boom. Increasing prosperity seems to be the cement that holds liberal societies together. Many of the values from the older ages — community, family, religion — are eroded by the emphasis on individual achievement and consumption. Even with the reintroduction of these themes into our politics, we understand that they are more a wish for the past than a plan for the future. It is quite possible that liberalism itself is now poised to be part of our past.

Our public administration is in the middle of this problem. It is through our public organizations that we will work out how much freedom an individual will continue to have, and how much say the government will have. Even capitalism, which the Reagan administration so wanted to encourage, is being saved at a high cost. To rejuvenate capitalism, there has been an increase in state and corporate power, and a seeming loss of individualism.

This is not to say we are heading for a centrally planned economy. Far from it. But government management of different sectors of the economy increases in spite of the trend toward deregulation. The micromanagement of industries is slowing dramatically, as are inspections of various kinds. That is deregulation. The government presence in the overall direction of the economy is growing, however. The government still is the leader in new technologies. The "Star Wars" antimissile program is well underway in its research phase — research that will spin off into developments in computers, telecommunications, and applied high-energy physics. New industries may grow around its by-products. International trade is increasingly a matter of national policy, and more new tariffs were enacted under Reagan than under the three previous presidents. The infrastructure of the economy — the roads, the basic city services, the contract and patent laws — are in the charge of government, and although federal aid to state and local governments is rapidly declining, states have taken it upon themselves to spend more in these areas. It is seen as good business. The debate over privatization (see Box 2.7) points to the tensions in this area. We want a great many things done through public policy, but we are uncomfortable asking government to do them. What is it about our liberalism that leads to this confusion?

Politics and Administration

In the earlier chapters we saw politics and administration mixed and stirred in many ways. Whatever the answer is for one generation, at the first sign of trouble politics and administration separates again. Every new generation tries to rearrange the workings of our government.

BOX 15.2 Privatization in the National Parks

The move to "privatization" should not be confused with efficiency and productivity. The experience in the National Parks Service shows how antigovernment feelings came to prevail over the ostensible reasons for privatization.

Campers pay money to stay in most national campgrounds. The National Parks Service, an agency within the Interior Department, collects this money in most places. In California, some of the fee collecting was "privatized" so that the Interior Department would not have to pay for the service. The private people would collect the fees and keep them, except for a small contract fee.

The Interior Department had a slightly smaller budget than before. Privatization certainly helped to cut their budget. But it also increased the nation's budget deficit by a like amount. Previously the fees went into the general fund, not the Interior Department budget. So while privatization lowered part of the government budget, it deprived another part of the budget of a source of revenue.

In the search for ways to shrink government, the original objectives were lost. Privatization should not be confused with efficiency, productivity, or automatic solutions to better serve the public.

For some time (we actually saw it begin with Woodrow Wilson) there has been a great fear that politics will corrupt administration. The logic goes something like this: For our administration to run efficiently, we must have professional administrators. The less the administrators are bothered by politicians, the better off our public organizations will be. To politicize the bureaucracy is to ruin it.

A more compelling argument is this: Our politics is becoming bureaucratized. The very categories of thought used by complex organizations now dominate our public life. The problem has become the loss of politics to the imperatives of organizations.

To take one example, let us look at how the forces of the electronic age push bureaucratic business into our public and private lives. In an important way, computers have changed the conduct of administrators. The ability of government to compile information on citizens and to automate many administrative functions has been a concern for several decades. The main problem, so far, has been finding ways to safeguard citizens so that government does not know too much, and thereby too closely control, citizens. The idea of a "Fednet," allowing the national government's computers to talk to each other, arises from time to time. It makes sense to keep people who have defrauded one agency from getting loans, benefits, and contracts from others. By linking the computers such cheaters could get caught. But the rest of us would acquire national identity numbers and be subject to whole new forms of government power. To now, the idea has not gotten far in the Congress.

But computers have not yet had their real impact on government. Computer applications have only sped up what people were doing before. The next step in the information age will be to create whole new possibilities for the creation and application of knowledge — and of power. Let us take a look at just two developments, the electronic office and the electronic judge.

The electronic office is one without much paper. The people who work in it must know how to use computers, and they will have a remarkable amount of information available to them with a stroke on a keyboard. The reason such offices will be adopted by government is the promise of greater productivity. We are told, "it costs less." There are three dimensions to this productivity promise. First, it simply takes less time to register the automobiles of thousands of people if done by computer instead of by handling paper records.

Second, much of the work can be done by lower-paid people. Jobs that require answering the telephone, responding directly to the public, filing, and so on, are more varied, and classified as more responsible, than jobs limited to feeding information to a computer. Not only can many clerical duties be performed more efficiently with computers, but the human component costs less. The savings will in many cases pay for the machines.

Third, and this is where the electronic office most affects professional workers, the electronic office can be closely supervised. A decentralized organization, such as the General Accounting Office or a state welfare bureaucracy, can require that employees keep certain records in specific computer files. The files can be checked at any time to see that employees are spending their time as superiors require. We have argued throughout the book there is a politics of organization. The electronic office makes decentralized service organizations as controllable as centralized administrative agencies.

This may create an interesting dynamic. Although there may be a kind of increased access at the bottom (each of us may have a computer terminal), that does not necessarily mean more local control. Indeed, if we are all hooked up to a hierarchical, centralized power, it is easy to imagine that we will all become more dependent on that centralized source. In other words, we will have centralized power in the country to a greater degree than ever.

The electronic judge is simply the next extension beyond the electronic office. As we discussed in Box 10.4, computers with "artificial intelligence" (AI) should be here by the year 2000. They do not suffer the well-known human limits on cognitive capacity. The machines may not be as varied and creative as the human mind, but within precisely defined problem situations they can make judgments in highly complicated situations. The most likely candidates for early applications of AI are program and financial auditing, air traffic controlling, testing of employees and job applicants, and medical diagnoses and epidemiological studies. Some of the more important applications will come as government copies the private sector. Already many financial institutions use AI programs to help them make decisions on which stocks and securities to buy and sell. Fiscal and monetary policies are likely to be guided by AI programs in the future, as are policies toward international trade. It may be that such areas where politics are so important right now will come to be defined as essentially technical issues.

Technology makes its own demands. These demands follow naturally and unmistakably from human decisions. If, for example, we decide that we need nuclear energy, then there are problems we must face and solve. Where to locate? There must be a river or ocean to cool the reactors, for example. But, what about proximity to population? Although it makes sense to have it close to population centers, more would be harmed in the case of an accident. What to do with the waste? It needs to be buried for tens of thousands of years, but *where*? That cannot be a purely political question because the nature of radioactivity restricts the choices.

Nuclear energy is a dramatic example. In our everyday living, we see the needs of technology being met. The more we process information about ourselves so that it can fit the requirements of computers, the more we lose the pluralistic and individualistic nature of our society. That we must frame questions for the requirements of machinery has become an almost invisible reality of our speech and our actions. This kind of technological dynamic makes stiff and precise demands on administration, and cuts out the demands of the public.

Democracy and Public Administration

We end where we began, asking what it means to have a public administration. We will consider three ideas for dealing with the question: Enhancing citizenship, building the professionalism of public employees, and finding ways to make public organizations more democratic.

Enhancing Citizenship

If the public does not fit well into administration, why not change the public? Serious proposals are put forth recommending, for instance, that television be used as a positive educational force that will give citizens a better dose of reality.[12] Yet no neutral controller is known that will deliver "reality" instead of commercial diatribe.[13]

The well-worn path to enhancing citizenship lies in altering institutions. Among recent proposals are: More "friendly" decision support models, so citizens can use their own computers to look at the information and the comparisons available to policymakers;[14] complex voting, in which citizens are able to choose from a variety of taxing levels and program mixes; more complicated or "deep" participation, such as getting involved in analysis instead of just public hearings; more marketlike decision systems, such as educational vouchers; and increased "coproduction," using citizen volunteers working alongside government professionals.[15]

All of these proposals assume many things about citizens. Most importantly, they assume that citizens are willing to change just a little of their lives a great deal. Citizens will be content to live as they do, but learn more about how governments make decisions, and spend a great deal more time studying and acting upon issues. It is asking for a very public response from our very private politics. It is not at all being skeptical to assert that the organized groups, the Madisonian factions, will be the first and most ambitious people in line to participate. Somehow that is not what advocates of enhanced citizenship mean.

Building Professionalism of Government Workers

If we are going to ask public administrators to provide a solution to the dilemma of politics and administration, we will be relying on their virtue. And that is just where proposals for building professionalism point to.[16]

Essentially, professionalism has to be much more than competence in doing a job. It has to include a public character, a set of public virtues. The public service never is just a producer for citizen consumers. The first virtues are those shared with other citizens: A belief in the legitimacy of the American regime, a willingness to accept individual moral responsibility, and a civility, a respect, toward other people. To this, professional public servants must add a great deal. A moral heroism is required, strengthening the public servant to implement the honorable policies and rejecting the dishonorable. Public professionals must care — and be known to care — about the individual citizens they serve. The nobility of character extends to a *noblesse oblige,* a commitment to serve the public by standing for the central values of American government.

The details of enhanced professionalism are difficult to define, let alone accept. A textbook cannot offer answers here; this is a matter for discussion among citizens (and students). We do offer this: By so embracing the public, will administration not take its place?

Democratic Organizations

A middle ground between asking more of citizens and asking a great deal of public servants might be to create new organizational forms. These will ask a great deal of both citizens and public servants, but perhaps ask for something that can be given. As we have seen, a bureaucratic structure is not the only way to organize. For years, there have been alternative ways to organize. In Israel, for instance, there are *kibbutzim.* These are communities of people who have organized in a democratic self-management way. On the whole, these have been very successful communities. In Eastern Europe, there have been many attempts at self-management. Probably the most impressive have been in Yugoslavia, where worker participation is widespread. In Poland, we see outbreaks of attempts by the workers to control the workplace.[17]

Throughout the history of the United States, there have been experiments in organizing in different ways.[18] The latest attempts were started in the 1960s, when collective-democratic organizations were started. Throughout the country, there are now collective organizations of all kinds. There are restaurants, food coops, medical clinics. For just about any enterprise you can think of, there is an example of its being collectivized.

On a larger scale, there are examples of plants and big businesses being bought by the workers.[19] The way it has happened in most places is that a company on the verge of bankruptcy is sold to its workers, who then run it. These experiments have been successful, even though they started with failing businesses.

In a strange way, our public administration is behind the private sector in experimenting with more democratic and participatory forms.

Although there are still town meetings in many smaller New England villages, our public administration is still mostly the property of administrators and elected representatives. Given the particular form of change brought about by the Reagan administration, one can guess that the trend will continue.

We can, of course, only speculate about the future of public administration. We would like to suggest the following possibility: The combination of large public organizations *and* large private organizations running the business of the country may come to be resented. That kind of largeness and centralization runs counter to the basic beliefs in federalism, pluralism, and individualism. The next generation, nervous about the future and unwilling to have important decisions made in large organizations, may insist on participation in both decision making and the carrying out of policies. If that is the case, the next period in the history of public administration may well be filled with alternative ways of organizing.

NOTES

1. The categories come from Felix A. Nigro and Lloyd G. Nigro, *Modern Public Administration,* 6th ed. (New York: Harper & Row, 1984).
2. See Bernard Rosen, "Crisis in the U.S. Civil Service," *Public Administration Review* 46, no. 3 (May/June 1986), pp. 207–214.
3. The American Society for Public Administration, for instance, is sponsoring a series of workshops and publications with the theme of "III Centuries." The main idea is to have public administrators contribute to an improved understanding of the American administrative state and of their own professionalism.
4. See Paul Appleby, *Morality and Administration in Democratic Government* (Baton Rouge: Louisiana State University Press, 1952); and Herbert Finer, "Administrative Responsibility and Democratic Government," *Public Administration Review* 1 (Summer 1941), pp. 335–350.
5. See Stephen Bailey, "Ethics and the Public Service," in Roscoe Martin, *Public Administration and Democracy* (Syracuse, N.Y.: Syracuse University Press, 1965); and Carl J. Friedrich, "Public Policy and the Nature of Administrative Responsibility," *Public Policy* 1 (1940), pp. 3–24.
6. See Douglas Yates, *Bureaucratic Democracy: The Search for Democracy and Efficiency in American Government* (Cambridge, Mass.: Harvard University Press, 1982); and John A. Rohr, *To Run a Constitution: The Legitimacy of the Administrative State* (Lawrence: University Press of Kansas, 1986). For a recent discussion of the dilemmas in administrative ethics, see Dennis F. Thompson, "The Possibility of Administra-

tive Ethics," *Public Administration Review* 45 (September/October 1985), pp. 555–561.
7. Charles T. Goodsell, *The Case for Bureaucracy: A Public Administration Polemic*, 2d ed. (Chatham, N.J.: Chatham House, 1985).
8. See H. George Frederickson and Ralph Clark Chandler, eds., "Citizenship and Public Administration," a special issue of *Public Administration Review* 44 (March 1984); and Charles Wise and David O'Brian, "Law and Public Affairs," a special issue of *Public Administration Review* 45 (November 1985).
9. Peter Koehn tells the story of one attempt to make it easier for the public by putting several different agencies in one building. Indeed, the new federal building in Helena, Montana, houses nearly all the local offices of federal government agencies. It was in a rather isolated area, so they had to build a parking lot. The problem was this: they provided a total of twelve visitor parking places. Where is the citizen convenience, asks Koehn, if citizens cannot find a place to park?
10. For a clear statement of this, see Robert L. Kahn et al., "Americans Love Their Bureaucrats," in Francis E. Rourke, *Bureaucratic Power in National Policy Making*, 4th ed. (Boston: Little, Brown, 1986), pp. 281–292.
11. See the review article by Lauran A. Wollan, Jr., "Prisons: The Privatization Phenomenon," *Public Administration Review* 46, no. 6 (November/December 1986), pp. 678–681.
12. See Richard L. McDowell, "Sources and Consequences of Citizen Attitudes Toward Government," in a special issue of *Public Administration Review* 44 (March 1984), pp. 152–156.
13. There is a remarkable advertisement for a twenty-four hour cable-television station. The ad is this: "Experience life on CNN." What makes it so remarkable is that television is not life, it is an electronic method of reporting. There is not, for example, a way for an individual to have a conversation with a television set. Strictly speaking, the television broadcasts and the individual receives. It would be wrong to assume that we could become more public or more political through television. Television, while showing us many things, also isolates us in the place we are receiving it.
14. See Bruce Gates, "Knowledge, Networks, and Neighborhoods: Will Microcomputers Make Us Better Citizens?" in a special issue of *Public Administration Review* 44 (March 1984), pp. 164–169.
15. See F. Stevens Redburn and Yong Hyo Cho, "Government Responsibility for Citizenship and the Quality of Community Life," in a special issue of *Public Administration Review* 44 (March 1984), pp. 158–161.

16. This section is drawn from David K. Hart, "The Virtuous Citizen, the Honorable Bureaucrat, and 'Public' Administration," in a special issue of *Public Administration Review* 44 (March 1984), pp. 111–120.
17. For a start, see Paul Bernstein, *Workplace Democratization: Its Internal Dynamics* (Kent, Ohio: Kent State University Press, 1976); and Paul Blumberg, *Industrial Democracy: The Sociology of Participation* (New York: Schocken Books, 1976).
18. See John Humphrey Noyes, *Strange Cults and Utopias of Nineteenth-Century America* (New York: Dover, 1966); Arthur Bestor, *Backwoods Utopias* (Philadelphia: University of Pennsylvania Press, 1970); James J. Martin, *Men Against the State* (Boulder, Co.: Ralph Myles Publishing, 1952); and Ralph Borsodi, *The Distribution Age* (New York: Appleton & Company, 1927).
19. See Daniel Zwerdling, *Workplace Democracy* (New York: Harper Colophon Books, 1980); David Jenkins, *Job Power: Blue and White Collar Democracy* (New York: Doubleday, 1973); Katrina Berman, *Worker-Owned Plywood Companies: An Economic Analysis* (Pullman, Wa.: Washington State University Press, 1967); and Paul Dickson, *The Future of the Workplace* (New York: Weybright and Talley, 1975).

Index

ADEA (Age Discrimination in Employment Act) 1967, 217
Adjusted gross income, 330
Administrative agencies, 32
  congressional, 31
  differences among, 57
  executive agencies, 29
  and policy implementation decisions, 369
  rule-making by, 380
Administrative Behavior (Simon), 95
Administrative efficiency, 325, 327
Administrative Justice System model, Figure 13.2, 378
Administrative Office of the United States, 32
Administrative Organization (Pfiffner and Sherwood), 101
Administrative Procedures Act (APA), 379, 386
Administrative process, 160
  adversary relationship of hearings, 369, 379
  APA guidance, 380
  authority as limitation on, 86
Administrative State, The (Waldo), 98
Affirmative action
  and cutback management, 286
  and representative bureaucracy, 159
  See also EEO/AA
Agency shop, 275
AI. *See* artificial intelligence
Allen, Richard, 162, 417
Allison, Graham, 371
Ambiguity
  state and market, 375
  in laws, 362
American Farm Bureau Federation, 50
American Federation of Labor, 264
American Institute of Certified Public Accountants, 354
American Society for Public Administration, 7, 212

Amphibians (civil servants), 160
Analysis
  and decision making, 384–85
  elements of (Nagel), 78
  and guidance for administration, 368
  and implementation, 394
  rational, 383
  uncertainty in, 401
Appleby, Paul, 15, 18
Appointees, 160–63
Appropriations, 309
  as source of power, 50, 51
APA. *See* Administrative Procedures Act
Arbitration, 274
  case, an example, 278–85
Arendt, Hannah, 290
Argyris, Chris, 118, 124, 126, 134
Aristotle, 322
Artificial intelligence, 136, 426
Audit, 208
  GAO, 292
  personnel, 199
Audit trail and budget execution, 349–50
Authority, 8
  and communication, 85
  and law, 50
  legitimacy of, 86
  types of, 67–68
Authorization of budget, 292

Balanced Budget and Emergency Deficit Control Act of 1985, 10
Banovetz, James, 88
Bardach, Eugene, 393
Barnard, Chester, 84–87, 95, 240
Base rate, data interpretation, 369
Benefit-cost analysis, 384
  for budgeting, 297
Benefits
  as compensation, 213
  of government services, 324

Bennis, Warren, 131–33
Berne, Eric, 126
Best and the Brightest, The
　(Halberstam), 382
BIA (Bureau of Indian Affairs), 99, 214
Bias, 100
　in citizen view of public organization, 377
　ideological, and analysis, 382
　of individual pathology, 135
　inherent, 385
　toward expertise, 161
　toward bureaucracy, 69
　toward politics, 65
Bill of Rights, 26–27
Blacksburg Manifesto, 66
Blau, Peter, 395
Block grants, 338, 339
Boundary, organism and environment, 101
Brain skills and personnel assignment, 229, 232
Budget, 290–318
　analysis and evaluation, 395
　budget behavior, incremental, 306–8
　control, example, 356–57
　estimates for, 358
　execution, Figure 12.4, 352–53
　execution, financial plan for, 351
　federal, and local/state grants, 39
　functions of, 135
　national, 1965–1985, Table 12.3, 346–47
　and personnel management, 202
　as political document, 10
　a scientific method for preparing, 297
　size of (1987), 312
Budget and Accounting Act of 1921, 292
Budget and Accounting Procedures Act of 1950, 294
Bureau of the Budget (BOB), 292
Bureaucracy, 69, 70
　as a closed system, 111
　and democracy, 55
　as focus for conflict, 184
　forms and functions, Table 2.2, 34–35
　ideal, 68–69
　personnel administration techniques, 215
　politicization of, 159
　and professionalism, 157
　as stabilizing force, 112
Bureaucratic Experience, The
　(Hummel), 134
Bureau of Reclamation, 38
Burford, Anne, 162
Burns, James MacGregor, 184
Business administration, 7

Camus, Albert, 114
Capitalism, 25
Career officials, 145, 160–61
Carter, Jimmy (President), 161, 163, 299, 300, 318
　as a leader, 173
Case for Bureaucracy, The (Goodsell), 402
Categorical grants, 335–36, 339
CBO (Congressional Budget Office), 309
Centrifugal forces, 229, 257
Change, 123–27
　ideal-typical bureaucratic, 124
　impediments to, 87
　and power, 106
　response of bureaucracy to, 132
　training for, 213
　and workplace discipline, 233
Change agents, 130
Charismatic authority, 67–68
CIA (Central Intelligence Agency), 49
Civil Rights Act of 1964, 217
Civil service, 142–65
　European model, 236
　grade and pay, federal, Table 6.1, 143
　ideal, 65–66
　personnel, characteristics of, 152, 154, 155
Civil Service Commission, 148
Civil Service Reform Act of 1978, 151, 154, 198, 262, 268
Class conflict, 264
　as control over benefits of technology, 233
　and productivity, 253
Clearinghouses, regional, for federal grants, 339
Closed shop, 275
Closed system, 101, 111
Cognitive capacity, limited, 97, 374
Collective bargaining
　impasses, 273–74

legal framework for, 265–75
practice of, 275–78
and union security, 274–75
Collective-democratic organizations, 428
Communication, 242, 85–86
conditions for accepting, 85
of expectations and rewards, 246
global, and traditional values, 423
and management, 227
Community Development Act of 1974, 43
Comparable worth, 220, 269
Compensation, legal requirements for, 213
Competition in organizational structure, 106
Complexity, decentralized response to, 132
Comptroller General, 304–5
Confederated Salish and Kootenai Tribal Government (CSKT), 214
Congressional Budget and Impoundment Control Act, 309
Congressional budgeting, 308–11
Congressional Budget Office, 304
Conrail, 305
Consensus
and decision making, 370
as decision making technique, 214–15
and organizational form, 110
Consent decrees, 379
Constituency
of agencies, 50, 51
of personnel office, 200
Constituents
casework for citizens and Congressional oversight, 44
response of public organizations to, 184
Constitution, 28–40, 420–21
Constitutional authority, 379
Constitutional controllers, 184
Consumption taxes, 327, 330
Content theories, 243, 244–45
Context of public administration
academic view, 55
of administrative system, 11–12
bureaucratic, 371
circular, of public administration, 58
and decisions, Figure 13.1, 364
for legal decision making, 368

political, of administrative rule making, 381
political, of leadership, 191
for rational decision making, 366, 367
timing and program implementation, 408
sunshine laws, 26–27
Control
through budget, 305
bureaucratic and individual values, 135
and communication, 187
functionary-manager, 234
over policy by professionals, 156
relationships, 240
and web of structure, 176
over workforce, 233, 234
Cook, Thomas, 396
Cooperation
public managers and personnel office, 200
public/private as publicization, 56
Copyright Royalty Tribunal, 163
Corporate capitalism, 25–26
Corporation, 176
Creativity. See Innovation
CSRA (Civil Service Reform Act of 1978), 151, 154, 198, 262, 268
Cultural values
in conflict, 99
in public agency personnel administration, 214–15
and trained incapacity, 373
Cutback management, 202, 203, 246, 248–52, 258
in OD, 131
tactics, Figure 9.6, 250–51

Data
facts as relative information, 87
operational, 254
realiability of, 80
Davis, Sheldon, 123
Dawes Commission, 99
Death and Life of Great American Cities (Jacobs), 382
Deaver, Michael, 417
Decentralization, 57, 106–7
functional, 172
and government power, 421
Decision analysis, 384
Decision making, 362–87
compromise, 362

by consensus, 110, 214–15, 370
and communication, 85–86
complex (Simon), 95
evaluation, 401
hierarchical decision processes, 51
and leadership, 187
processes, 190
professional, 157
Decision package (ZBB), 300
Decision rules as determinants of structure, 110
Decision support models, 427
Decision tree, selecting leadership style, 179–82
Deferred income as compensation, 213
Deficits, 322
1965–1985, Table 12.3, 346–47
budgeting, 312
as indicator of political decisions, 358
Delegation of legislative authority, 377
Democratic organizations
active role of citizens, 186
collective, 428
and decentralization, 132–33
and leadership, 175–77
and organizational psychology, 137
public, 185
and public administration, 427–29
Democratizing the civil service, 145
Department of Defense, 297
Department of Labor, 218
Devine, Donald J., 263, 264–65, 417
Dialectical relationship of public administration, 24
Dickson, P., 83
Dillon's rule, 335
Dimock, Marshall E., 170
Discounting, 384
Discretion, administrative
fiscal controls on, 349–51
in implementing legislation, 49–51
and leadership, 175
Dissatisfiers, 244
Disturbed-reactive environment, 106–7
Drucker, Peter, 176, 187, 255
Dual public service, 145
Due process
in administrative processes, 380
and legal decision making, 370
Dues checkoff, 275

Dynamics
of bureaucratic growth, 70
organizational, 12
of politics, 160

Easton, David, 101
Economics
of behavior, predicting, 316
effects of taxes, 327, 329
growth and government revenue, 343
postprosperity, 365
theories of, 313–16
EEO/AA, 157, 158, 216–19
ADEA (Age Discrimination in Employment Act) 1967, 217
comparable worth, 220, 269
and cutback management, 206
in federal service, 157
Griggs v. Duke Power Company, 217
legal framework of, 223
and testing, 210, 220, 422–23
Effectiveness, 84, 186, 254
program, and budgets, 294
Efficiency, 84, 95, 108, 113, 149, 253
as administrative goal, 18, 325
and citizen satisfaction, 342
and democracy, 227
essentials of (Gulick), 80
and federalism, 40
measured in money, 315
and organizational evaluation, 186
and performance budget, 294
and privatization, 424
and public administration, 164
in public and private organizations, 138
as rationality, 69
in scientific management, 73
in taxation, 327
Ego-transcending perception, 129
Electronic judge, 426
Electronic office, 425–26
Elite
in civil service, 144
and decision conflicts in third world, 374
experts as, 89
role in organizational psychology, 137
Emery, F. E., 104
Energy trace in organizations, 103
Engen, Donald, 70
Entitlement programs, 338

Environment, 101, 104–8
  and bureaucracy, 132
  democratic, 113
  and emergence of leaders, 179–82
  and machine politics, 149
  management responses to, 228
  pollution regulations, 53
  public administration, 24
  of public managers, Figure 9.1, 230
Environmental Protection Agency (EPA), 32, 50, 52–53, 369
Epistemology, 6
  Follett's, 87
Equal employment opportunity. *See* EEO/AA
Equal Employment Opportunity Act of 1972, 218
Equal Employment Opportunity Commission, 218
Equality, in bureaucratic system, 370
Equal Pay Act (EPA) of 1964, 217
Equity in taxation, 324
Ethics, 416–19
Ethnic politics, 146
Etzioni, Amitai, 371–72
Eupsychian Management (Maslow), 129
Evaluation, 390–412
  alternative methodologies, 410–11
  budget analysis as tool, 395
  difficulty of, 412
  errors, 385, 407
  and experiments, 398
    randomization as political liability, 400
  Head Start example, 403–7
  implementing, 411
  and management, Figure 14.3, 406
  MBO, 240
  as motivator, 242
  of new ideas, 409
  politics of, 396
  and power, 393
  problems, 402–7
  as tool, 394, 408, 410–11
Evans, John V. (Governor, Idaho), 249
Excise tax, 330
Exclusive bargaining agents, 273
Executive budget, 302–3
Executive Orders
  Order 10988, 267
  Order 11246, 217
  Order 11375, 217
  Order 11491, 267
Exemptions, tax, 333
Expectancy theory (Vroom), 245
Experimental method, 397
  and bias, 398–99, 402
Expert judgments, 368–69
  as a source of power, 47, 49
Experts
  career officials as, 160–61
  in Follett's theory, 89
  in Weberian bureaucracy, 71
External norms, 135

FAA (Federal Aviation Administration), 70, 374
Fact-finding, 273
Factor comparison, 207
Factor-point job classification, 204
Factory system, 144
Failure
  as a change agent, 149
  evaluation of, 408
  of expert judgment, 369
  political, in bargaining, 274
  of PPBS, 297
  of public programs (Drucker), 177
  of rational systems, 306
  of trickle-down theory, 315
Fayol, Henry, 79
FCC. *See* Federal Communications Commission
Federal Communications Commission (FCC), 49
Federal Deposit Insurance Corporation (FDIC), 32
Federalism, 28–29, 33–40
  bureaucratic impact at local level, 41–43
  cooperative, 335
  politicians and bureaucracy professionals, 336
  structure of, Figure 12.3, 337
Federalists, 143–46
  as bureaucrats, 164
Federalists, The (White), 145
Federalist, The, 145, 414
Federal Labor Relations Authority (FLRA), 273
Federal Register, 45, 382
Federal Reserve Banks, 16
Federal Reserve Board, 16, 32, 335
  and money supply, 313

Fednet, 425
Fee-for-service, 335
Financial controls and management skills, 351
Financial plan for budget execution, 351
Finessing the personnel system, 221, 222
Fiscal administration, 324–58
  as politics/administration bond, 356
  and fiscal policy, 309, 314
Fish and Wildlife Service, 38
Fisher, Louis, 309
Fisher, Roger, 277
Flexibility, 106, 107
FLRA. *See* Federal Labor Relations Authority
Focus
  of incremental budgeting, 307
  on individuals in EEO/AA, 219
  of organizational psychology, 119
  on programs in audit, 355
  of public administration, 20–21
Follett, Mary Parker, 87, 89–90, 112, 160, 232
  and shifting leadership, 176
Food Safety and Inspection Service (FSS), 381
Ford, Gerald R. (President), 299, 409
Forecasting
  and benefit-cost analysis, 385
  economic behavior, 316
  fiscal, 358
  revenues, 338, 340–49
  revenues, political considerations, 341
Framework
  governmental, in private banking, 17
  legal, for EEO/AA, 223
  for studying leadership, 178
Freedom of Information Act, 380
Freedom of speech, 26
Free workings of the economy, 313, 316
  and drugs, 332
  and monopoly capitalism (Keynes), 314
Functional approach, leadership research, 182–83
Functions
  of budgets, 317
  of evaluation, 411

Functions of the Executive, The (Barnard), 84, 95
Funding and incremental budgeting, 307
Fund accounting, 355
Future shock, 94

Games people play, 126
  budget games, 306, 308
GAO (General Accounting Office), 31, 292, 426
Garfield, James (President), 147, 164
Generally accepted accounting principles (GAAP), 354
General revenues, 355
General Revenue Sharing (GRS), 336, 338, 339
General sales tax, 330
General Service (GS), 151
Getting to Yes (Fisher and Ury), 277
Gilder, George, 314
Global village, 423
GNP, 344–45
Goals, 8
  clarification of, 391
  conflicting goals, water policy example, 38–39
  of education, 157
  role in decision making, 362
Gompers, Samuel, 264
Goode, Wilson (Mayor, Philadelphia), 364
Good faith bargaining, 276–78
Goodsell, Charles, 402, 418–19
Government accounting and auditing, 354–57
Governmental Accounting, Auditing and Financial Reporting (GAAFR), 354
Governmental Reorganization, President's Committee on, 79
Government employees. *See also* Civil Service
  number, by level, 29
  Table 2.1, 30–31
Government growth trend, 345
Government Printing Office, 31
Government productivity, 253–55
Government, state and local, 4, 37–40
Grades in civil service, 151
Gramm-Rudman-Hollings Balanced Budget Act, 10, 302
Grant, Ulysses S. (President), 147
Great Society, 396, 403
Griggs v. Duke Power Company, 217

Index

Groups
  within organization, 120
  group pressure in OD, 131
GRS. *See* General Revenue Sharing
GS. *See* General Service
Guild principle, 233
Guiteau, Charles J., 147, 148
Gulick, Luther, 64, 79, 178

Halberstam, David, 382
Hall, Marianne Mele, 163
Hamilton, Alexander, 2, 145
Harmon, Michael, 190
Harris, James, 162
Hatch Act, 152
Hawthorne Studies, 81–84, 400
Hay and Associates, 208
Hayes, Rutherford B. (President), 147
Head Start, 403–7
Heclo, Hugh, 196
Herzberg, Frederick, 244
Hierarchy, 68, 135
  in administration, 161
  implications of Hawthorne, 83
  and management science, 81
  and motivation, 246
  of personal values, 134–35
  and professionals, 70
  as response to size and environment, 106
  selecting leaders, 187
  vertical division of labor, 232
  of workers, 75
Hierarchy of needs, 119, 121–22, 127, 243
  Figure 5.1, 128
Hobbes, Thomas, 25, 69
Hobhouse, L.T., 102
Hoover Commission Report, 226
  on budgeting, 294
House and Senate Budget Committees, 309
Household manufacture, 144
HUD (Housing and Urban Development), 41–43
Human Condition, The (Arendt), 290
Human resources plan, 202–7
Hummel, Ralph P., 134, 234, 362

Idaho, cutback example, 249
Idealism, in civil service, 155
Identity, and organization, 135

Ideology
  and ethics, 418
  bias, 382
  in context, 28
Ideological hegemony, 188
Image making and public organizations, 418–19
Impact study, components of, 397
Implementation
  of budget, 349–54
  of laws, 57–58
  MBO, 239
  program evaluation, 393–95
  of union contract, 278
Implementation (Pressman and Wildavsky), 393
Implementation Game, The (Bardach), 393
Impoundment, 309
Income and wealth, 344–49
Income taxes, 329–30
Incremental decision making, 371
  muddling through, 99, 100, 113, 371
Incrementalism
  and budget behavior, 306, 308
  and cutbacks, 248
  in the policy process, 46
  in program implementation, 363
  and spending priorities, 316
Individual
  as focus for organizational psychology, 119, 127–29
  as focus of EEO/AA, 219
  government power over, 135, 421
  and motivation, 243
  and organizational problems, example, 125
  and organizational structure, 133–34
Individualism, 25
Industrial citizenship, 123
Informal groups, 120
Information
  from accounting reports, 355
  for decision making, 385
  individual response to, 97
  in placid-clustered environment, 106
  as power, 136
  processing with computers, 426
  processing by individuals, 120
  quality, for decision making, 375
Information flows, 242, 339

Inherent bias, 385
Innovation, 132, 185, 409
  and level of government, 40
  in organizational theory, 108
In Search of Excellence (Peters and Waterman), 108
Institutionalization and turbulence, 106
Institutional memory, 160
Integrative brain, 232
Interactions
  human, categories of, 126
  local interests and elected officials, 47
  organization and environment, 85
Interchangeable labor, 68
Interdependence and turbulence, 107
Interest, budgeting of, 312
Intergovernmental relationships, 335–38
  block grants, 338, 339
  and local government, 340
  transfers as nontax revenue, 335
Interior Department, 424
Internal norms and personal value, 135
International City Management Association, 39, 47, 88, 149, 212, 340
Interstate Commerce Commission, 32
Introduction to the Study of Public Administration (White), 77
IPA (Intergovernmental Personnel Act), 214

Jackson, Andrew (President), 143–46, 164
Jacobs, Jane, 382
James, E. Pendleton, 161
Janis, Irving, 373
Jefferson, Thomas (President), 145
Jenckes, Thomas Allen, 147
Job (position)
  action, 274
  analysis, 207
  classification, 207–8, 223
    factor-point, 204
  characteristics of (Gulick), 80
  description, 207
  as focus of government personnel management, 207
  security, 286–87
Johnson, Lyndon (President), 28, 297, 375, 409
  Great Society, 396
  as a leader, 173
Judgment and scientific decision making, 369
Judicial norms and administrative decision making, 377
Justice Department, 32, 219

Kahn, Robert, 102, 103
Katz, Daniel, 102, 103
Kaufman, Herbert, 185
Keeney, Ralph L., 401
Kennedy, John (President), 161, 297
Kesterson National Wildlife Refuge, 38
Keynesians, 313–14, 318
Kibbutzim, 428

Labor Management Relations Act (Taft-Hartley), 268
Labor Railway Act of 1926, 267
Labor relations, 262–87
Laffer, Arthur, 314, 327
Laffer Curve, 314, 327
  Figure 12.1, 329
Lasswell, Harold, 391
Lavelle, Rita, 162, 417
Leadership, 170–191
  behavior continuum, Figure 7.3, 189
  components of, Figure 7.1, 174
Learning, role of in OD, 131
Left-dominant brain, 229, 232
Legal models, 386
  of decision making, 368–70
  legal-rational authority, 67, 68
Legislative administration, 31–32
Legislative oversight
  of bureaucracy, 40–44
  of public agencies, 236
  and union negotiations, 268–69
Legitimacy of the state, 67
Lenin, 72
Levels of government, cooperative roles, 37–40
Levine, Charles, 248
Liberalism, 24–28, 421–24
  and prosperity, 423
Library of Congress, 31
Life positions, 126
Limited cognitive capacity, 97
Limits on government powers, 375–82
Lindblom, Charles, 99, 371

Line workers, 80
Line-item budgeting, 292–93, 318
Links
 lawmaker/constituent, 31, 44
 personnel office and line managers, 223
Lloyd-LaFollette Act, 267
Local administration and federalism, 39–40
Locke, John, 25
Loyalty, group, 373
Lynn, Laurence E., Jr., 182, 228

McGregor, Douglas, 121, 170
Machiavelli, Niccolo, 170
Machine politics, 146
McNamara, Robert, 297
Madison, James (President), 176
Majority rule, 27
Management, 226–57. See also Public administration
 budget skills for, 351, 354
 organization theory, 96
 procedures, 183–84
 rights clauses, 272
 science, 78
Management and the Worker (Dickson and Roethlisberger), 83
Management by Objectives. See MBO
Management excellence inventory (MEI), 229
Managers, 127. See also Authority; Control; Leadership
 defined, 227
 methods used by, 228
 role in ZBB, 300
Maslow, Abraham, 119, 127, 134, 243
Mayo, Elton, 81
MBO (management by objectives), 122, 183, 237–40, 299–300
 action plan, Figure 9.3, 238–39
Measurement. See also Analysis; Evaluation
 and experimental design, 402
 of organizational work, 103
 performance, 396
Mediating structures and tension, 190
Mediation, 273
MEI (management excellence inventory), 229
Merit system, 148, 150–51, 158
Merit System Protection Board (MSPB), 151

Methodological and conceptual validity, 403
 and evaluation, 400–2
Minority rights, 27
Mintzberg, Henry, 228, 232
Mixed scanning, incrementalism, 371
Models for bargaining, state level, 268–69
Monetarism, 311, 318
Morale, 163
Mosher, Frederick, 157
Motivation, 74, 81–82, 119–20, 135, 237
 attention as motivator, 83
 and organizational psychology, 135
 reward as motivator, 242
 theory and practice, 243–46
 strokes, 126
 and supervision, 240–43
Moynihan, Daniel (Senator, New York), 407
MSPB. See Merit System Protection Board
Muddling through, 99, 100, 113, 371
Municipal Finance Officers Association, 212, 354

Nagel, Stuart, 78
NASA (National Aeronautics and Space Administration), 9
NASPAA. See National Association of Schools of Public Affairs and Administration
National Association of Letter Carriers, 267
National Association of Schools of Public Affairs and Administration (NASPAA), 256
National Civil Service Reform League, 147
National Council on Governmental Accounting, 354
National income
 1965–1985, Table 12.3, 346–47
 federal transactions, 1950–1986, 348–49
National industrial policy, 345, 350
National Labor Relations Act (Wagner Act), 268
National Labor Relations Board (NLRB), 32, 271, 272–73
National Municipal League, 292
National Parks Service, 424

National Right to Work Legal Defense Foundation, 271
Newland, Chester A., 237
Nixon, Richard (President), 161, 299, 309, 318, 336
NLRB. *See* National Labor Relations Board
Nobel Prize (Simon), 114
Norris-LaGuardia Act of 1936, 267
"Notes on the Theory of Organization" (Gulick), 79
Not-for-profit organizations, 56
 delivery of government services by, 354
NPA (new public administration), 188–89

Obedience and leadership, 173
Objectives
 and budget process, 294, 299
 of federal grant policies, 39
 for human resources plans, 206
 of OD, 130
 program, and performance budget, 294
 of public policy, 397
 in ZBB, 300
Objectivity
 in job classification, 208
 problems in, 383
Occupational Safety and Health Administration (OSHA), 381
OD. *See* Organizational Development
Office of Economic Opportunities, 403
Office of Management and Budget (OMB), 292, 304, 316, 382
 issuance of RIAs, 381–82
 local/national program planning, 339
Office of Personnel Management (OPM), 150, 214, 222, 229, 263
 and merit system, 151
Ohio University, 403
OMB. *See* Office of Management and Budget
Ombudsman, 419
On-the-job training, 257
Open Market Committees, 16–17
Openness, 8
Open system, 101, 102
Operational guidelines, 237
Operations research, 384

Organic metaphor, 102–3
Organizational Development (OD), 130–32
 position of individual, 133, 135
Organizational psychology, 118–38
 and computers, 136
 and industrial citizenship, 123
 and organizational humanists, 84
 and public administration, 118, 133
Organizational structure
 collegial, 104
 complexity, 405
 and decision making, 110, 214–15, 360–61, 370
 hierarchical, 104
 leadership positions in, 172, 175
 for public administration, 110–11
 rearranging, 129–33
 and technology, 107–8
Organization for Economic Cooperation and Development (OECD), 342
Organizations
 as focus of democracy, 186
 context and changing values (Argyris), 126
 influence of, 44–45
 instrumental role of, 185
 as technique for dealing with irrationality, 97
Organization theory, 6–9, 72, 73, 64–116
 OD, 103–32, 133, 135
 postbureaucracy, 132–33
 systems, 101–3

Pacific Gas and Electric, 38
Pareto efficiency, 383
PAR. See *Public Administration Review*
Party politics and budgeting, 309
PATCO (Professional Air Traffic Controllers Organization), 376
 strike, 270–71
Patronage, 144, 150
Payoffs, personnel training, 212
Peak experiences, 129
Pendleton Act, 147, 148–49, 151, 164
Performance
 appraisal systems, 216
 budgeting, 294, 318
 and budget execution, 350–51

evaluations, 213–16
    standards, 8
Personnel administration, 8, 196–223
    civil service personnel, 152, 154, 155
    classification system, 232
    professional guidelines, 240
    technical functions, Figure 8.3 203
    training and development, 212–13
Peters, Thomas, 108
Pfeffer, Jeffrey, 171
Pfiffner, John, 101
PFP (Program and Financial Plan), 296
Placid-clustered environment, 104, 106
Placid-randomized environment, 104
Planning, 241
    for scientific management, 73
    orientation, 296
    overselling, 408
Planning-programming-budgeting system (PPBS), 294, 296–97, 299, 318
Plato, 170
Plunkitt, George Washington, 142, 146
Pluralist theory, 99
Plural society, 316–17
PM (Program Memoranda), 296
Policy
    effectiveness as measure, 390
    evaluation, 11
    failures as change agent, 149
    formulation role of administrative agencies, 31
    implementation, 11, 49, 394
Policy process
    policy-making, administrative, 47–51
    policy process, Figure 14.1, 392
    propositions describing, 46
    study of, 391
Political environment
    activity and civil service, 152
    climate for evaluation, 404
    coalition as basis for negotiation, 276
    leadership, 174, 188
    culture
        1960s, 51
        components of, 24
    economy, 344
    functions, 20
    impact of labor settlements, 267, 274
    problems, administrative solutions to, 220
    rationality, 371
Political process, 160
    and administrative process, 65
    and administration, 163
    and budgeting, 299
    evaluation as, 404
Political relationships, 40–51
    and collective bargaining, 287
    in the national government, Figure 2.1, 44
    and revenue forecasting, 341
Political System, The (Easton), 101
Politicization, 10
    of bureaucracy, 55, 159, 425
    of senior civil service, 154
Politicos (civil servants), 160
Politics, 9–10
    of cutback management, 252
    defined, 3
    and evaluation, 411
    and public service, 159
    Weber on, 71
Politics (Aristotle), 322
"Politics as a Vocation" (Weber), 68, 71
POSDCORB, 79, 95, 178, 234
Position. *See* Job (position)
Postal Reorganization Act, 267
Postal Service, 32
Postbureaucracy era, 132–33
Postprosperity era, 4, 416–29
Power, 172–73
    access through administrative agencies, 47
    and budgeting, 316
    bureaucratic, 69–70
    and evaluation, 393
    and financing, 37
    individual, 84
    and information, 136
    and intergovernmental relationships, 336
    and knowledge, 156
    and leadership, 171
    and rule making, 380
    as a structural phenomenon, 171
    symbiotic, 240

Powers
  of central government, 37
  shared, 37
  of states, 37
PPBS. *See* Planning-programming-budgeting system
Precision and politics, 71
Pressman, Jeffrey, 393, 407
Prince, The (Machiavelli), 170
Principled negotiation, 277–78
Principles of Scientific Management, 71
Priorities
  of personnel administration, 199
  reflected in budgets, 317
Privacy Act of 1974, 380
Privatization, 56–57
  and efficiency, 424
  of foreign affairs, 421
Problem solving tasks, 391
Procedures
  budget and personnel, 240
  informed, 379
  for legal decision making, 369
  for rational decision making, 366
Process
  budget, 292
  bureaucratic, 160
  collective bargaining, Figure 10.2, 277
  Congressional budget, 310–11
  for decision making, 370
  of interaction, 84
  and MBO, 237
  and organizational theory, 109
  in organizational psychology, 129–30
  and outcome, 190
  of production, 90
Process theories, 243, 245–46
Productivity, 252–55, 258
  in civil service, 154
  and individual worker, 109
  and organizational psychology, 137
  productivity indexes, 254
Professionalism
  in civil service, 155
  in public administration, 165, 427–28
Program planning, 294
  alternatives, 296
  budget, example, 298
  cutback management, 252

decision about, 382
process of program planning and program evaluation, Figure 14.2, 399
stages, 363
Progress, as advent of machine technology, 233
Progressive tax, 325
Progress measurement, 296
Property taxes, 332–33
Proverbs of administration, 96
"Proverbs of Administration" (Simon), 95
Public administration, 7
  advocacy by, 189
  and business administration, 8–9
  characteristics of (newer definition), 18
  conflicting goals, 38–39
  defined, 3, 13–20
  goals of, 38–39, 391
  leadership in, 184–85
  management control over personnel, 199
  new public administration (NPA), 188–89
  and organizational psychology, 133–37
  and participation, 90
  police department example, 88–89
  role in United States, 112
  and science, 77
  and scientific method, 15, 18
  skills for, 173, 240, 255, 351
  Weber's views on, 67–70
Public Administration Review, (PAR) 6
"Public Administration in a Time of Revolution" (Waldo), 111
Public decision making
  expectations and organizational structure, 88
  legal foundations of, 236
  public participation, 236
Public policy, 109, 390–91
  clarifying, 385
  and meaning of activities, 98
  support for administrative agencies, 276
  public/administration split, 64
  public/private distinction, Federal Reserve Board example, 16–17
Public-sector bargaining. *See also* Collective Bargaining

model, 270, 272–73
relationships in American law, 263
public service, 9, 98
Publius, 416

Quality circles, 246
Quasi-judicial agencies, 376
Quasi-legislative agencies, 376

Raiffa, Howard, 401
Rand Corporation, 114
Random samples, 400
Rate of change, social, 1940–1970, 94
Ratification, of union contract, 278
Rational processes
    budget-making, 316
    comprehensive method, 99–100
    decision-making, 366–68
    economic decisions, 176
Rationality, 90, 372, 374
    kinds of, 100
    Simon model, 97
    models of, 386
Rayburn, Sam (Speaker of the House), 24
Reagan, Ronald (President), 28, 163, 314, 375, 416, 423
    appointees of, 161
    and budgeting, 300, 304
    as a leader, 173
    and privatization, 55
Reality and citizenship, 427
Recruiting
    in government agencies, 209–11
    as a supervisory tool, 241
Reform, 147–51
    civil service, 165
    and efficiency, 253
    and strengthening of executive administration, 292
Regional cooperation, 40
Regressive taxes, 325, 330
Regulation of money supply, 313
Regulatory agencies and public participation, 236
Regulatory impact analysis (RIA), 381–82
Rehabilitation Act of 1973, 218
Rehnquist, William (Chief Justice), 417
Representative bureaucracy, 157, 159
Republic, The (Plato), 170
Research on leadership, 177–84

Research strategy (Cook and Scioli), 396–97
Revenues, 322–54
    non-tax, 335
    tax, and total economy, 342, 344
Reverse discrimination, 217, 218
Revolution, and public administration, 111–13
RIA. *See* Regulatory impact analysis
Right-dominant brain, 232
Rights
    of management, 272
    individual, 26–27, 370
    owners' and workers', 264
Right to strike, 142, 272
    and public interest, 143
Right-to-work, 275
Ripple effect and bargaining, 286
Roethlisberger, Fritz J., 81, 94, 118
Roethlisberger, K., 83
Roles
    of administrators, 79
    in government decision making, 363
    work, 82
Romney, George, 41
Roosevelt, Franklin D. (President), 150–52
Rose, Richard, 344
Rotation in office
    and democratic ideals, 145
    and Reagan appointments, 163
Ruckleshaus, William, 53

Satisficing, 97
Satisfiers, 244
Savio, Mario, 112
Sayre, Wallace, 8
Science
    relationship to democracy, 52
    role in administration, 55
    of organizational behavior, 119–20
"Science of Muddling Through, The" (Lindblom), 99
Scientific management, 72–73
    and administration, 65
    for budgeting, 297
    hierarchy of workers in, 75
    motivation, 74
Sciolo, Frank, Jr., 396–97
Scott, W. Richard, 186
Securities and Exchange Commission, 32

Self-actualized individual, 127, 128–29
Self-management, 246
    public and private sectors, Figure 9.5, 247
Self-selection and Hawthorne effect, 400
Self-validation, 129
Sensitivity groups, 109
Separation of powers, 29–33
    impact on administrative roles, Table 2.3, 36
Service and professionalism, 156
SES (Senior Executive Service), 151, 154–55
Shafritz, Jay, 222
Sherman Anti-Trust Act, 335
Sherwood, Frank, 101
Siege mentality, 373
Simon, Herbert, 80–81, 95–98, 108, 112, 114, 374
Slowdowns, 274
Socialization as goal of education, 157
Social personality, 135
Social-psychological models, 386
    of decision making, 373
Social Psychology of Organizations, The (Katz and Kahn), 102
Social Security Administration, 32, 369, 409
Special governments, 32
Special (segregated) revenues, 355
Spending authority and budget execution, 349
Spoils system, 145
Sprecher, Gerald, 88
SS (Special Studies), 296
Stability
    of consumption tax revenues, 330
    of tax bases, 328–29, 343
    of tax base, state and local, 340–41
    of tax revenues, 327
Staff function, 79–80, 197, 223
Standards of performance (ZBB), 300
Status as compensation, 213
Stevenson, William J., 252
Stockman, David, 290, 316, 404
Strategy in incremental budgeting, 308
Structure
    bureaucratic, and red tape, 69
    county personnel department, Figure 8.1, 197
    of economy, 264
    state personnel department, Figure 8.2, 198
    of supervisory relationships, 240–41
    of work, 82
Success, organizational, and leadership, 185
Successive limited comparisons, 100
Supply-side, 314–16, 318
    view of bureaucracy, Figure 2.2, 54
Syndicalist approach to economic policy, 350
System analysis, 297
Systematic analytical techniques in personnel administration, 214
Systems theory, 72, 101, 113–14
    and leadership, 187

Taft, William Howard (President), 292
Tammany, 146
Tannenbaum, Robert, 123
Task-related groups, 120
Tasks, 107–8
    and job holder, 159
Taxes, 329–34
    ability to pay, limits on, 325
    incidence, 324
    impact
        by income, in U.S., Table 12.2, 326
        by level and type, Table 12.1, 323
    per capita, 322
Tax revolt, 333
    of the 1970s, 28
Taylor, Frederick Winslow, 71, 121, 233, 253
Technocracy, 75
    and professionalism, 156
    and professional budgeting, 305
Technology and organizational structure, 107–8
Tennessee Valley Authority, 32
Tension and administration
    in budget, 317
    in labor relations, 266
    within civil service (19th century), 147
    evaluation, 405
    impact on programs, 9
    and leadership, 190
    and organizational psychology, 137

in oversight of agencies, 33
in political decision making, 371
among regulatory agencies, 38–39
silent, 419–27
Tensions, 4
　bureaucracy and politics, 71
　competition and openness, 150
　culture and formal education, 14
　decentralization and centralization, 147
　demand for service and individualism, 52
　democracy and efficiency, 118, 147, 165, 186
　Drucker-Follett views of leadership, 176
　government/antigovernment, 27
　individualism and rule of law, 27
　majority and minority rights, 27
　organizational needs and political environment, 386
　political and administrative process, 65
　politics and professionalism, 418
　public administration and Public Administration, 6
　public administration and politics, 20, 137, 216
　public and administration, 18, 118
　public good and workers' rights, 262
　social goals and expertise for implementation, 375
　workers and management in the public sector, 265, 287
Tenure, 8
Testing personnel
　drug tests, 220, 422–23
　polygraph tests, 220
Thayer, Paul, 162, 417
Theory X, 121
Theory Y, 121, 122, 130
Third world conflicts
　and electronic communication, 423
　in representative bureaucracy, 374
Time horizon
　for evaluation, 405–6
　of programs' stages, 363
　in public administration, 8
Title VII, Civil Rights Act of 1964, 217
Tools, 240
　management, evaluation, 410

for public administration management, 229
of public managers, Figure 9.2, 231
Townsend, Robert, 196
Trade deficit and budget deficit, 34
Traditional authority (Weber), 67
Training, 241
　and productivity in government, 254–55
　public administration curriculum, 256–57
　Taylor's views, 74
Trait literature, leadership studies, 178
Transactional analysis (Berne), 126–27
Trickle-down theory, 315
Trist, E.L., 104
Turbulence in fiscal environment, 345
Turbulent fields, 107–8
Turner, Frederick Jackson, 144
Two-factor theory (Herzberg), 244–45

ULPs (unfair labor practices), 275
Uncertainty, 107
　role in organizational design, 104
Uniform Guidelines on Employee Selection Procedure, 218
Union-management relations
　bilateral, 265
　multilateral, 265
　union recognition, Figure 10.1, 267–68
Unions, 142, 244
　growth, 286
　interest groups, 264
　security, 274–75
　　breaking a union, public sector, 270
　union shop, 275
Unit determination, 273
Ury, William, 277

Value-free public administration, 79
Value-neutral bureaucracy, 69
Values
　central, in U.S., 188
　changing, 123–27
　　Figure 1.2, 12
　diversity, 32–33
　personal, 134
　and public administration, 98
VAT (value-added tax), 330

Veteran's Administration, 32
Voluntary tax (lottery), 333
Vroom, Victor, 179, 245

Waldo, Dwight, 58, 75, 77, 80, 98, 108, 111–13
War on Poverty, 409
Washington, George (President), 143–44
Waterman, Robert, 108
Watt, James, 161
Weak executive model, 149
Wealth and Poverty (Gilder), 314
Weber, Max, 67–71, 159, 370
Weik, Karl, 373
Western Electric Company study, 81
Westinghouse Learning Corporation, 403
Westlands Water District, 38
White, Leonard, 13, 15, 77, 78, 145
Wildavsky, Aaron, 306, 390, 393, 407

Willoughby, F.W., 79
Wilson, Woodrow (President), 9, 112, 434
   and administrative/politics split, 185, 64–66
Wired jobs, 158, 221
Woodward, Joan, 107
Workers, 234
   Taylor's view, Figure 3.1, 75
Work rules, 240
WS (Wage Service), 151
Wygant v. Jackson Board of Education, 286

Yetton, P.W., 179

ZBB (zero-base budget), 122, 299, 300
Zone of acceptance, 240, 241–43
Zone of indifference, 85
   Figure 3.2, 86